CLYMER®

KAWASAKI

BAYOU KLF300 • 1986-1998

The world's finest publisher of mechanical how-to manuals

INTERTEC PUBLISHING

P.O. Box 12901, Overland Park, Kansas 66282-2901

Copyright ©1999 Intertec Publishing

FIRST EDITION
First Printing December, 1995
SECOND EDITION
First Printing January, 1999
Second Printing September, 2000

Printed in U.S.A.

CLYMER and colophon are registered trademarks of Intertec Publishing.

ISBN: 0-89287-716-2

Library of Congress: 98-72836

MEMBER

Technical photography by Ron Wright.

Technical assistance by Clawsom Motorsports, Fresno, California.

Technical illustrations by Steve Amos and Robert Caldwell.

COVER: Photographed by Mark Clifford, Mark Clifford Photography, Los Angeles, California.

PRODUCTION: Dylan Goodwin

INTERTEC BOOK DIVISION

President Cameron Bishop
Executive Vice President of Operations/CFO Dan Altman
Senior Vice President, Book Division Ted Marcus

The following books and guides are published by Intertec Publishing.

CLYMER SHOP MANUALS
Boat Motors and Drives
Motorcycles and ATVs
Snowmobiles
Personal Watercraft
ABOS/INTERTEC/CLYMER BLUE BOOKS
AND TRADE-IN GUIDES
Recreational Vehicles
Outdoor Power Equipment
Agricultural Tractors
Lawn and Garden Tractors
Motorcycles and ATVs
Snowmobiles and Personal Watercraft
Boats and Motors
AIRCRAFT BLUEBOOK-PRICE DIGEST
Airplanes
Helicopters

AC-U-KWIK DIRECTORIES
The Corporate Pilot's Airport/FBO Directory
International Manager's Edition
Jet Book
I&T SHOP SERVICE MANUALS
Tractors
INTERTEC SERVICE MANUALS
Snowmobiles
Outdoor Power Equipment
Personal Watercraft
Gasoline and Diesel Engines
Recreational Vehicles
Boat Motors and Drives
Motorcycles
Lawn and Garden Tractors

CONTENTS

CHAPTER FOURTEEN

BODY **439**

QUICK REFERENCE DATA

TIRE INFLATION PRESSURE (WHEN COLD)

	kPa	psi
2-wheel drive		
Front & rear	21	3.0
4-wheel drive		
Front	35	5
Rear	28	4

MAINTENANCE TORQUE SPECIFICATIONS

Item	N·m	ft.-lb.
Valve adjusting screw locknuts	12	8.6
Engine oil drain plug	29	22
Wheel nuts	34	25
Front final drive (4-wheel drive)		
Oil fill cap	29	22
Oil drain plug	20	14.5
Rear final drive		
Oil fill cap	29	22
Oil drain plug	20	14.5
Spark plug		
2-wheel drive	27	20
4-wheel drive	14	10
Engine oil pipe banjo bolts	20	14.5

RECOMMENDED LUBRICANTS AND FUEL

Air filter	Air filter oil
Engine oil	
Grade	SF or SG
Viscosity	SAE 10W-30, 10W-40, 10W-50, 20W-40 or 20W-50
Battery refill	Distilled water
Brake fluid	DOT 3 or DOT 4
Front final gear case oil	
4-wheel drive	API GL-5 Hypoid gear oil or LSD SAE 140 or SAE 85W-140
Rear final gear case oil	
All models	
Below 5° C (41° F)	API GL-5 Hypoid gear oil SAE 80
Above 5° C (41° F)	API GL-5 Hypoid gear oil SAE 90

APPROXIMATE REFILL CAPACITIES

Engine oil	
2-wheel drive	1.7 L (1.8 U.S. qts. or 1.5 Imp. qts.)
4-wheel drive	
1989-1991	2.2 L (2.3 U.S. qts. or 1.9 Imp. qts.)
1992-on	2.4 L (2.5 U.S. qts. or 2.1 Imp. qts.)
Front final gear case	
4-wheel drive	
1989-1993	250 mL (8.45 U.S. oz. or 7.04 Imp. oz.)
1994-on	400 mL (13.53 U.S. oz. or 11.22 Imp. oz.)
Rear final gear case	
2-wheel drive	
1986-1990	300 mL (10.14 U.S. oz. or 8.4 Imp. oz.)
1991-on	350 mL (11.83 U.S. oz. or 9.86 Imp. oz.)
4-wheel drive	
1989-1992	200 mL (6.76 U.S. oz. or 5.63 Imp. oz.)
1993	
U.S. and Canada	200 mL (6.76 U.S. oz. or 5.63 Imp. oz.)
Australia, Europe and U.K.	300 mL (10.14 U.S. oz. or 8.4 Imp. oz.)
1994-on	300 mL (10.14 U.S. oz. or 8.4 Imp. oz.)

TUNE-UP SPECIFICATIONS

Engine compression	
Using recoil starter	825-1,280 kPa (119-185 psi)
Using electric starter	795-1,240 kPa (115-179 psi)
Valve clearance (engine cold)	
Intake	0.10-0.15 mm (0.004-0.006 in.)
Exhaust	0.15-0.20 mm (0.006-0.008 in.)
Ignition timing	Not adjustable, see text for inspection procedure
Spark plug gap	0.7-0.8 mm (0.028-0.031 in.)
Idle speed	See text
Pilot air screw (turns out)	
2-wheel drive	
1986-1988; 1996-on	2 1/8
1989-1995	2 1/4
4-wheel drive	
1989-1995	2 1/8
1996-on	2

SPARK PLUGS

Model	NGK spark plug
2-wheel drive	
U.S. & Australia	B8ES
Canada & UK	BR8ES
4-wheel drive	
1989-1990	
U.S.	D8EA
All other models	DR8ES-L
1991-1992	
U.S.	DR8EA
Australia and Canada	DR8ES-L
UK	DR7EA
1993-on	
U.S.	D8EA
Australia and Canada	DR8ES-L
UK and Europe	DR7EA

Table 5 REPLACEMENT BULBS

Headlight	
Type	Semi-sealed beam
Bulb	
2-wheel drive	
1986-1987	12 volt, 60 watt
1988-1994	12 volt, 65/60 watt
1995-on	12 volt, 25/25 watt
4-wheel drive	12 volt, 25/25 watt
Taillight	12 volt, 8 watt

TIRE AND WHEEL SPECIFICATIONS

Front tire	
Type	Tubeless
Size/Manufacturer	
2-wheel drive	22 × 9.00-10/Dunlop KT761
4-wheel drive	AT24 × 8-11/Dunlop KT962
Rear tire	
Type	Tubeless
Size	
2-wheel drive	24 × 11.00-10/Dunlop KT761
4-wheel drive	AT24 × 10-11/Dunlop KT962

CLYMER®

KAWASAKI

BAYOU KLF300 • 1986-1998

CHAPTER ONE

GENERAL INFORMATION

This manual contains detailed information about maintaining and repairing your 1986-on KLF300 Bayou.

Troubleshooting, tune-up, maintenance and repair are not difficult, if you know what tools and equipment to use and what to do. Step-by-step instructions guide you through jobs ranging from simple maintenance to complete engine and suspension overhaul.

This manual can be used by anyone from a first time do-it-yourselfer to a professional mechanic. Detailed drawings and clear photographs give you all the information you need to do the work right.

Some of the procedures in this manual require the use of special tools. The resourceful mechanic can, in many cases, think of acceptable substitutes for special tools—there is always another way. This can be as simple as using a few pieces of threaded rod, washers and nuts to remove or install a bearing or fabricating a tool from scrap material. However, do not substitute a special tool as it can be dangerous to and may damage the part. When designing special tools, contact a local community college or high school that has a machine shop curriculum. Some shop teachers accept outside work for advanced student projects.

Table 1 lists model coverage with engine serial numbers.

Table 2 lists general vehicle dimensions.

Table 3 lists weight specifications.
Table 4 lists decimal and metric equivalents.
Table 5 lists conversion tables.
Table 6 lists general torque specifications.
Table 7 lists technical abbreviations.
Table 8 lists metric tap drill sizes.
Table 9 lists wind-chill factors.
Tables 1-9 are at the end of the chapter.

MANUAL ORGANIZATION

This chapter provides general information and discusses equipment and tools useful for preventive maintenance and troubleshooting.

Chapter Two provides methods and suggestions for quick and accurate diagnosis and repair of problems. Troubleshooting procedures discuss typical symptoms and logical methods to pinpoint the trouble.

Chapter Three explains all periodic lubrication and routine maintenance necessary to keep your Kawasaki operating well. Chapter Three also includes recommended tune-up procedures, eliminating the need to consult other chapters constantly on the various assemblies.

Subsequent chapters describe specific systems such as the engine top end, engine bottom end, clutch, transmission, fuel, exhaust, electrical, suspension, drive train, steering and brakes. Each chapter provides disassembly, repair, and assembly procedures in simple step-by-step form. If a repair is impractical for a home mechanic, it is so indicated. It is usually faster and less expensive to take such repairs to a Kawasaki dealer or competent repair shop. Specifications concerning a particular system are included at the end of the appropriate chapter.

NOTES, CAUTIONS AND WARNINGS

The terms NOTE, CAUTION and WARNING have specific meanings in this manual. A NOTE provides additional information to make a step or procedure easier or clearer. Disregarding a NOTE could cause inconvenience, but would not cause damage or personal injury.

A CAUTION emphasizes areas where equipment damage could occur. Disregarding a CAUTION could cause permanent mechanical damage; however, personal injury is unlikely.

A WARNING emphasizes areas where personal injury or even death could result from negligence. Mechanical damage may also occur. WARNINGS are to be taken seriously. In some cases, serious injury and death has resulted from disregarding similar warnings.

SAFETY FIRST

Professional mechanics can work for years and never sustain a serious injury. If you observe a few rules of common sense and safety, you can enjoy many safe hours servicing your machine. If you ignore these rules you can hurt yourself or damage the equipment.

1. Never use gasoline as a cleaning solvent.
2. Never smoke or use a torch in the vicinity of flammable liquids, such as cleaning solvent or gasoline.
3. If welding or brazing is required on the machine, remove the fuel tank and shocks and move them to a safe distance, at least 50 feet (15 m) away.
4. Use the proper sized wrenches to avoid damage to fasteners and injury to yourself.
5. When loosening a tight or stuck nut, be guided by what would happen if the wrench should slip. Protect yourself accordingly and be careful.
6. When replacing a fastener, make sure to use one with the same measurements and strength as the old

one. Incorrect or mismatched fasteners can result in damage to the vehicle and possible personal injury. Beware of fastener kits filled with cheap and poorly made nuts, bolts, washers and cotter pins. Refer to *Fasteners* in this chapter for additional information.
7. Keep all hand and power tools in good condition. Wipe greasy and oily tools after using them. They are difficult to hold and can cause injury. Replace or repair worn or damaged tools.
8. Keep your work area clean and uncluttered.
9. Wear safety goggles (**Figure 1**) during all operations involving drilling, grinding, the use of a cold chisel or anytime you feel unsure about the safety of your eyes. Safety goggles should also be worn when using solvent and compressed air to clean parts.
10. Keep an approved fire extinguisher (**Figure 2**) nearby. It must be rated for gasoline (Class B) and electrical (Class C) fires.
11. When drying bearings or other rotating parts with compressed air, never allow the air jet to rotate the bearing or part. The air jet is capable of rotating

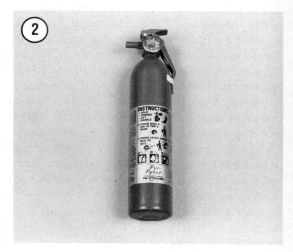

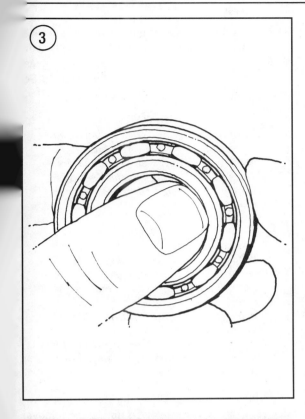

them at speeds far in excess for which they were designed. The bearing or rotating part is very likely to disintegrate and cause serious injury and damage. To prevent bearing damage when using compressed air, hold the inner bearing race by hand (**Figure 3**).

SERVICE HINTS

Most of the service procedures covered are straightforward and can be performed by anyone reasonably handy with tools. However, consider your capabilities carefully before attempting any operation involving major disassembly of the engine assembly.

Take your time and do the job right. Do not forget that a newly rebuilt engine must be broken-in the same way as a new one. Refer to *Engine Break-In* in Chapter Five.

1. Front, as used in this manual, refers to the front of the vehicle; the front of any component is the end closest to the front of the vehicle. The left- and right-hand sides refer to the position of the parts as viewed by a rider sitting on the seat facing forward. For example, the throttle control is on the right-hand side. These rules are simple, but confusion can cause major inconvenience during service.

2. Whenever servicing the engine or clutch, or when removing a suspension component, the vehicle should be secured in a safe manner and the parking brake applied.

> **WARNING**
> *Never disconnect the positive (+) battery cable unless the negative (–) cable has first been disconnected. Disconnecting the positive cable with the negative cable connected may cause a spark. This could ignite hydrogen gas given off by the battery, causing an explosion.*

3. Disconnect the negative battery cable (**Figure 4**) when working on or near the electrical, clutch, or starter systems and before disconnecting any electrical wires. The battery terminals are marked with "–" (negative) and "+" (positive) signs.

4. Tag all similar internal parts for location and mark all mating parts for position (A, **Figure 5**). Record shim number, thickness and alignment when removed. Identify and store small parts in plastic sandwich bags (B, **Figure 5**). Seal and label them with masking tape.

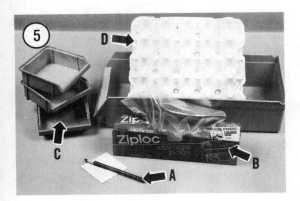

5. Place parts from a specific area of the engine (cylinder head, cylinder, clutch, shift mechanism, etc.) into plastic boxes (C, **Figure 5**) to keep them separated.

6. When disassembling transmission shaft assemblies, use an egg flat (the type that restaurants get their eggs in) to store the parts(D, **Figure 5**). Set the parts from the shaft in one of the depressions in the same order in which it was removed.

7. Label all electrical wiring and connectors before disconnecting them. Again, do not rely on memory alone.

8. Protect finished surfaces from physical damage or corrosion. Keep gasoline and brake fluid off painted surfaces.

9. Use penetrating oil on frozen or tight bolts, then strike the bolt head a few times with a hammer and punch (use a screwdriver on screws). Avoid the use of heat where possible, as it can warp, melt or affect the temper of parts. Heat also ruins finishes, especially paints and plastics.

10. Unless specified in the procedure, parts should not require unusual force during disassembly or assembly. If a part is difficult to remove or install, find out why before continuing.

11. To prevent small objects and abrasive dust from falling into the engine, cover all openings after exposing them.

12. Read each procedure completely while looking at the actual parts before starting a job. Make sure you thoroughly understand the procedural steps and then follow the procedure, step by step.

13. Recommendations are occasionally made to refer service or maintenance to a Kawasaki dealer or a specialist in a particular field. In these cases, the work will be done more quickly and economically than if you performed the job yourself.

14. In procedural steps, the term replace means to discard a defective part and replace with a new or exchange unit. Overhaul means to remove, disassemble, inspect, and replace components as required to recondition a major system or assembly.

15. Some operations require the use of a hydraulic press. It would be wiser to have these operations performed by a shop equipped for such work, rather than to try to do the job yourself with makeshift equipment that may damage your machine.

16. Repairs go much faster and easier if your machine is clean before you begin work. There are many special cleaners on the market, like Bel-Ray

Degreaser, for washing the engine and related part Follow the manufacturer's directions on the cor tainer for the best results. Clean all oily or greas parts with cleaning solvent as you remove them. Se *Washing the Vehicle* in this chapter.

> *WARNING*
> *Never use gasoline as a cleaning agent. It presents an extreme fire hazard. Be sure to work in a well-ventilated area when using cleaning solvent. Keep a fire extinguisher, rated for gasoline fires, handy in any case.*

> *CAUTION*
> *If you use a car wash to clean your vehicle, do not direct the high pressure water hose at steering bearings, carburetor hoses, suspension components, wheel bearings or electrical components. High pressure water will flush grease out of the bearings and damage the seals. The water can also enter the electrical components, causing failure of the part or system.*

17. Much of the labor charge for repairs made by a dealer is for the time involved during the removal, disassembly, assembly, and reinstallation of other parts to reach the defective part. It is frequently possible to perform the preliminary operations yourself and then take the defective unit to the dealer for repair at considerable savings.

18. When special tools are required, arrange to get them before you start. It is frustrating and time consuming to get partly into a job and then be unable to complete it.

19. Make diagrams (or take a Polaroid picture) wherever similar-appearing parts are found. For instance, crankcase bolts are often not the same length. You may think you can remember where everything came from, but mistakes are costly. There is also the possibility that you may be sidetracked and not return to work for days or even weeks during which time carefully laid out parts may have become disturbed.

20. When assembling parts, be sure all shims and washers are replaced exactly as they came out.

21. Whenever a rotating part butts against a stationary part, look for a shim or washer. Use new gaskets if there is any doubt about the condition of the old ones. A thin coat of oil on non-pressure type gaskets may help them seal more effectively.

1

22. Use heavy grease to hold small parts in place if they tend to fall out during assembly. However, keep grease and oil away from electrical and brake components.

WASHING THE VEHICLE

Regular cleaning of your KLF300 is an important part of its overall maintenance. After riding your ATV in extremely dirty areas, clean it thoroughly. More important, proper cleaning will prevent dirt from falling into critical areas undetected. Failing to clean the vehicle or cleaning it incorrectly will add to your maintenance costs and shop time because dirty parts wear out prematurely. It's unthinkable that your vehicle could break because of improper cleaning, but it can happen. When cleaning your Kawasaki, you will need a few tools, shop rags, scrub brush, bucket, liquid cleaner and access to water. Many riders use a coin-operated car wash. Coin-operated car washes are convenient and quick, but with improper use the high water pressure can do more damage than good to your vehicle.

NOTE
A safe biodegradable, nontoxic and nonflammable liquid cleaner that works well for washing your vehicle is Simple Green. Simple Green can be bought through some supermarkets, hardware, garden and discount supply houses. Follow the directions on the container for recommended dilution ratios.

When cleaning your vehicle, and especially when using a spray type degreaser, remember that what goes on the vehicle will rinse off and drip onto your driveway or into your yard. If you can, use a degreaser at a coin-operated car wash. If you are cleaning your vehicle at home, place thick cardboard or newspapers underneath the vehicle to catch the oil and grease deposits as they are rinsed off.

1. Place the vehicle on level ground and set the parking brake.
2. Check the following before washing the vehicle:
   a. Make sure the gas filler cap is screwed on tightly.
   b. Make sure the engine oil cap is on tight.
   c. Plug the muffler opening.
   d. Remove the seat and cover the air box with plastic.

3. Wash the vehicle from top to bottom with soapy water. Use the scrub brush to get excess dirt out of the wheel rims and engine crannies. Concentrate on the upper controls, engine, side panels and gas tank during this wash cycle. Do not forget to wash dirt and mud from underneath the fenders, suspension and engine crankcase.
4. Next, concentrate on the frame tube members, outer air box areas and suspension.
5. Direct the hose underneath the engine and swing arm. Wash this area thoroughly.
6. Finally, use cold water without soap and rinse the entire vehicle thoroughly. Use as much time and care when rinsing the vehicle as when washing it. Built up soap deposits will quickly corrode electrical connections and remove the natural oils from tires, causing premature cracks and wear. Make sure you thoroughly rinse off the vehicle.
7. Tip the vehicle from side to side to allow any water that has collected on horizontal surfaces to drain off.
8. Remove the plastic cover from around the air box and the plug from the muffler opening.
9. If you are washing the vehicle at home, start the engine. Idle the engine to burn off any internal moisture.
10. Before taking the vehicle into the garage, wipe it dry with a soft cloth or chamois. As you dry it, inspect the machine for further signs of dirt and grime. Make a quick visual inspection of the frame and other painted pieces. Spray any worn-down spots with WD-40 or Bel-Ray 6-in-1 to prevent rust from building on the bare metal. When the vehicle is back at your work area you can repaint the bare areas with touch-up paint after cleaning off the WD-40. A quick shot from a can of touch-up paint each time you work on the vehicle will keep it looking sharp and stop rust from building and weakening parts.

TORQUE SPECIFICATIONS

The materials used in the manufacture of your Kawasaki may be subjected to uneven stresses if the fasteners used to hold the sub-assemblies are not installed and tightened correctly. Improper bolt tightening can cause cylinder head warpage, crankcase leaks, premature bearing and seal failure and suspension failure from loose or missing fasteners. An accurate torque wrench (described in this chapter) should be used together with the torque specifications listed at the end of most chapters.

Torque specifications throughout this manual are given in Newton-meters (N•m) and foot-pounds (ft.-lb.).

Existing torque wrenches calibrated in meter kilograms can be used by performing a simple conversion. All you have to do is move the decimal point one place to the right—for example, 3.5 mkg = 35 N•m. This conversion is accurate enough for mechanical work even though the exact mathematical conversion is 3.5 mkg = 34.3 N•m.

Refer to **Table 6** for standard torque specifications for various size screws, bolts and nuts not listed in the respective chapter tables. To use the table, first determine the size of the bolt or nut. Use a vernier caliper and measure the inside dimension of the threads of the nut (**Figure 6**) and across the threads for a bolt (**Figure 7**).

FASTENERS

The materials and designs of the various fasteners used on your Kawasaki are not arrived at by chance or accident. Fastener design determines the type of tool required to work the fastener. Fastener material is carefully selected to decrease the possibility of physical failure.

Nuts, bolts and screws are manufactured in a wide range of thread patterns. To join a nut and bolt, the diameter of the bolt and the diameter of the hole in the nut must be the same. It is just as important that the threads on both be properly matched.

The best way to tell if 2 fastener threads match is to turn the nut on the bolt (or the bolt into the threaded hole in a piece of equipment) with fingers only. Be sure both pieces are clean. If excessive force is required, check the thread condition on each fastener. If the thread condition is good but the fasteners jam, the threads are not compatible. A thread pitch gauge (**Figure 8**) can be used to determine pitch. Kawasaki ATV's and motorcycles are manufactured with ISO (International Organization for Standardization) metric fasteners. The threads are cut differently than those of American fasteners (**Figure 9**).

Most threads are cut so that the fastener must be turned clockwise to tighten it. These are called right-hand threads. Some fasteners have left-hand threads; they must be turned counterclockwise to be tightened. Left-hand threads are used in locations where normal rotation of the equipment would tend to loosen a right-hand threaded fastener.

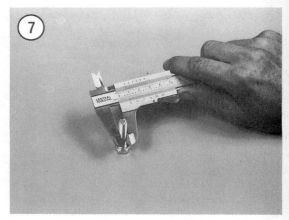

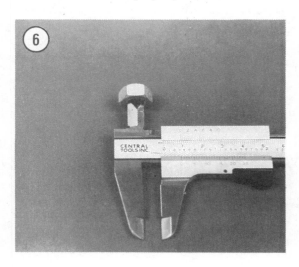

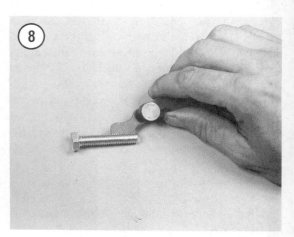

ISO Metric Screw Threads
(Bolts, Nuts and Screws)

ISO (International Organization for Standardization) metric threads come in 3 standard thread sizes: coarse, fine and constant pitch. The ISO coarse pitch is used for almost all common fastener applications. The fine pitch thread is used on certain precision tools and instruments. The constant pitch thread is used mainly on machine parts and not for fasteners. The constant pitch thread, however, is used on all metric thread spark plugs.

Metric screws and bolts are classified by length (A, **Figure 10**), diameter (B) and distance between thread crests (C). A typical bolt might be identified by the numbers 8—1.25 × 130, which would indicate that the bolt has a nominal diameter of 8 mm, the distance between thread crests is 1.25 mm and bolt length is 130 mm.

The strength of metric screws and bolts is indicated by numbers located on the top of the screw or bolt as shown in **Figure 10**. The higher the number the stronger the screw or bolt. Unnumbered screws or bolts are the weakest.

CAUTION
Do not install screws or bolts with a lower strength grade classification than installed originally by the manufacturer. Doing so may cause engine or equipment failure and possible injury.

The measurement across 2 flats on the head of the bolt indicates the proper wrench size to use. **Figure 7** shows how to determine bolt diameter.

When buying a bolt from a dealer or parts store, it is important to know how to specify bolt length. The correct way to measure bolt length is by measuring the length starting from underneath the bolt head to the end of the bolt (**Figure 11**). Always measure bolt length in this manner to avoid buying bolts that are too long.

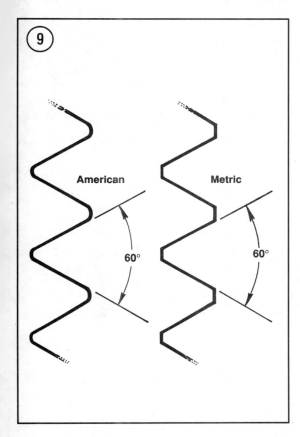

American   Metric

60°   60°

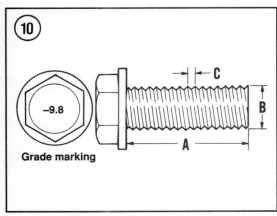

—9.8

Grade marking

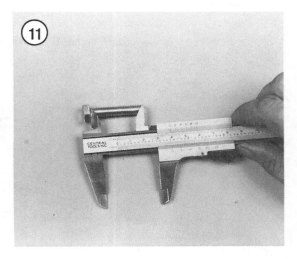

Machine Screws

There are many different types of machine screws. **Figure 12** shows a number of screw heads requiring different types of turning tools. Heads are also designed to protrude above the metal (round) or be slightly recessed in the metal (flat). See **Figure 13**.

Nuts

Nuts are manufactured in a variety of types and sizes. Most are hexagonal (6-sided) and fit on bolts, screws and studs with the same diameter and pitch. **Figure 14** shows several types of nuts. The common nut is generally used with a lockwasher. Self-locking nuts have a nylon insert which prevents the nut from loosening; no lockwasher is required. Wing nuts are designed for fast removal by hand and are used for convenience in non-critical locations.

To indicate the size of a metric nut, manufacturers specify the diameter of the opening and the thread pitch. This is similar to bolt specifications, but without the length dimension. The measurement across 2 flats on the nut indicates the proper wrench size to be used (**Figure 15**).

Self-Locking Fasteners

Several types of bolts, screws and nuts incorporate a system that develops an interference between the bolt, screw, nut or tapped hole threads. Interference is achieved in various ways: by distorting

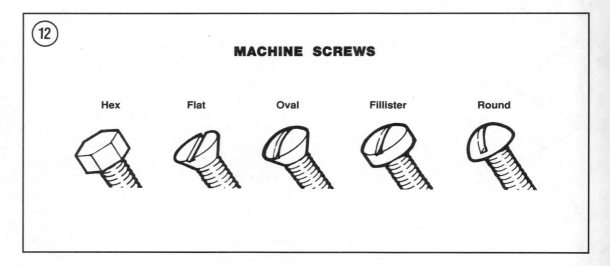

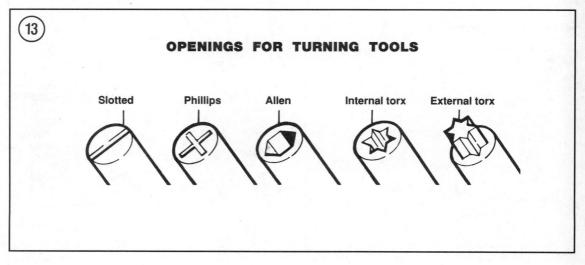

threads, coating threads with dry adhesive or nylon, distorting the top of an all-metal nut or using a nylon insert in the center or at the top of a nut, etc.

Self-locking fasteners offer greater holding strength and better vibration resistance. Some self-locking fasteners can be reused if in good condition. Others, like the nylon insert nut, form an initial locking condition when the nut is first installed; the nylon forms closely to the bolt thread pattern, thus reducing any tendency for the nut to loosen. For greatest safety, discard previously used self-locking fasteners and install new ones during reassembly.

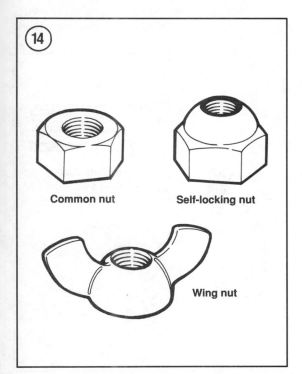

Common nut   Self-locking nut

Wing nut

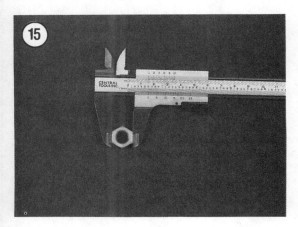

Washers

There are 2 basic types of washers: flat washers and lockwashers. Flat washers are simple discs with a hole to fit a screw or bolt. Lockwashers are designed to prevent a fastener from working loose due to vibration, expansion and contraction. **Figure 16** shows several types of washers. Washers can be used in the following functions:

a. As spacers.
b. To prevent galling or damage of the equipment by the fastener.
c. To help distribute fastener load during torquing.
d. As seals.

Note that flat washers are often used between a lockwasher and a fastener to provide a smooth bearing surface. This allows the fastener to be turned easily with a tool.

NOTE
As much care should be given to the selection and purchase of washers as that given to bolts, nuts and other fasteners. Beware of washers that are made of thin and weak materials. These will deform and crush the first time they are used in a high torque application.

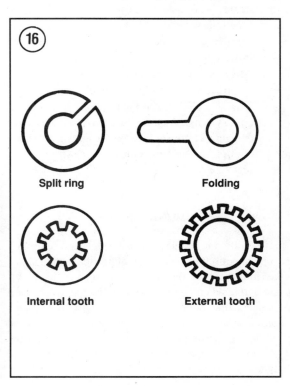

Split ring   Folding

Internal tooth   External tooth

Cotter Pins

Cotter pins (**Figure 17**) are used to secure special kinds of fasteners. The threaded stud, bolt or axle must have a hole in it; the nut or nut lock piece has castellations around which the cotter pin ends wrap. Do not reuse cotter pins.

Circlips

Circlips can be internal or external design. They are used to retain items on shafts (external type) or within tubes (internal type). In some applications, circlips of varying thicknesses are used to control the end play of assemblies. These are often called selective circlips. Circlips should be replaced during installation, as removal weakens and deforms them.

Two basic styles of circlips are available: machined and stamped circlips. Machined circlips (**Figure 18**) can be installed in either direction (shaft or housing) because both faces are machined, thus creating two sharp edges. Stamped circlips (**Figure 19**) are manufactured with one sharp edge and one rounded edge. When installing stamped circlips in a thrust situation (transmission shafts, fork tubes, etc.), the sharp edge must face away from the part producing the thrust. When installing circlips, observe the following:

a. Compress or expand circlips only enough to install them.
b. After the circlip is installed, make sure it is completely seated in its groove.
c. Selective circlips used in transmissions can become worn and cause a shaft to have excessive end play. Therefore, always closely inspect such circlips for wear or replace them with the correct size circlip.

LUBRICANTS

Periodic lubrication helps assure long life for any type of equipment. The type of lubricant used is just as important as the lubrication service itself, although in an emergency the wrong type of lubricant is better than none at all. The following paragraphs describe the types of lubricants most often used on ATV and motorcycle equipment. Be sure to follow the manufacturer's recommendations for lubricant types.

Generally all liquid lubricants are called oil. They may be mineral-based (including petroleum base), natural-based (vegetable and animal base), synthetic-based or emulsions (mixtures). Grease is an oil to which a thickening base has been added so that the end product is semi-solid. Grease is often classified by the type of thickener added; lithium soap is commonly used.

Engine Oil

Four-stroke oil for ATV, motorcycle and automotive engines is graded by the American Petroleum Institute (API) and the Society of Automotive Engi-

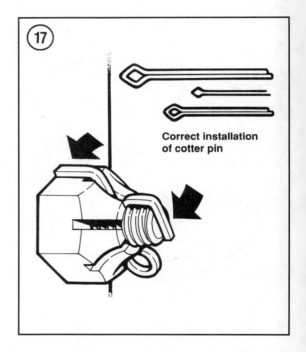

Correct installation of cotter pin

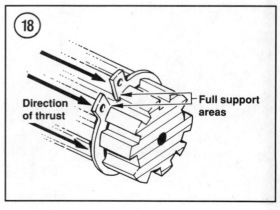

Direction of thrust

Full support areas

neers (SAE) in several categories. Oil containers display these ratings on the top or label. API oil grade is indicated by letters; oil for gasoline engines is identified by an "S." Kawasaki models described in this manual require SE or SF graded oil.

Viscosity is an indication of the oil's thickness. The SAE uses numbers to indicate viscosity; thin oils have low numbers while thick oils have high numbers. A "W" after the number indicates that the

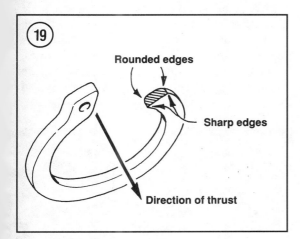

viscosity testing was done at low temperature to simulate cold-weather operation. Engine oil falls into the 5W to 50 range.

Multigrade oils (for example 10W-40) are less viscous (thinner) at low temperatures and more viscous (thicker) at high temperatures. This allows the oil to perform efficiently across a wide range of engine operating conditions. The lower the number, the better the engine will start in cold climates. Higher numbers are usually recommended when operating an engine in hot weather.

Grease

Greases are graded by the National Lubricating Grease Institute (NLGI). Greases are graded by number according to the consistency of the grease; these range from No. 000 to No. 6, with No. 6 being the most solid. A typical multipurpose grease is NLGI No. 2. For specific applications, equipment manufacturers may require grease with an additive such as molybdenum disulfide (MOS2) (**Figure 20**).

THREADLOCK

A threadlock should be used to help secure many of the fasteners used on your Kawasaki. A threadlock will lock fasteners against vibration loosening and seal against leaks. Loctite 242 (blue) and 271 (red) are recommended for many threadlock requirements described in this manual (**Figure 21**). There are other quality threadlock brands on the market.

EXPENDABLE SUPPLIES

Certain expendable supplies are required during maintenance and repair work. These include grease, oil, gasket cement, wiping rags and cleaning solvent. Ask your dealer for the special locking compounds, silicone lubricants and other products which make vehicle maintenance simpler and easier. Cleaning solvent or kerosene is available at some service stations, paint and hardware stores.

WARNING
Having a stack of clean shop rags on hand is important when performing engine and suspension service work. However, to prevent spontaneous combustion from a pile of solvent soaked rags, store them in a sealed metal con-

*tainer until they can be washed or dis-
carded.*

NOTE
*To prevent solvent and other chemicals
from being absorbed into your skin,
wear a pair of petroleum-resistance
gloves when cleaning parts. These can
be bought through industrial supply
houses or well-equipped hardware
stores.*

SERIAL NUMBERS

Kawasaki makes frequent changes during a model
year, some minor, some relatively major. When you
order parts from the dealer or other parts distributor,
always order by frame and engine numbers. The
frame serial number is stamped on the left-hand
lower frame member (**Figure 22**). The engine number is stamped on a raised pad on the right-hand side
of the crankcase (**Figure 23**).

Write the numbers down and carry them with you.
Compare new parts to old before buying them. If
they are not alike, have the parts manager explain
the difference to you. **Table 1** lists engine and frame
serial numbers for the models covered in this manual.

WARNING LABELS

A number of warning labels have been attached to
your KLF300. These labels contain information that
is important to your safety when operating, trans-
porting and storing your ATV. Refer to your Owners
Manual for a description and location of each label.
If a label is missing, order a replacement label from
a Kawasaki dealer.

BASIC HAND TOOLS

Many of the procedures in this manual can be
carried out with simple hand tools and test equipment familiar to the average home mechanic. Keep
your tools clean and in a tool box. Keep them organ-
ized with the sockets and related drives together, the
open-end and combination wrenches together, etc.
After using a tool, wipe off dirt and grease with a
clean cloth and return the tool to its correct place.

Top-quality tools are essential; they are also more
economical in the long run. If you are now starting
to build your tool collection, stay away from the
"advertised specials" featured at some parts houses,
discount stores and chain drug stores. These are
usually poor grade tools that can be sold cheaply, and
that is exactly what they are—cheap. They are usu-

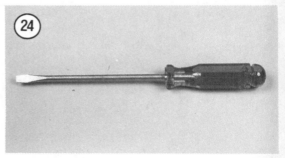

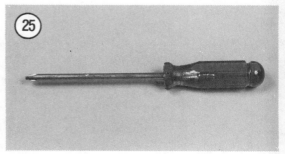

ally made of inferior material, and are thick, heavy and clumsy. Their rough finish makes them difficult to clean, and they usually do not last very long. If it is ever your misfortune to use such tools, you will probably find out that the wrenches do not fit the heads of bolts and nuts correctly and will damage the fastener.

Quality tools are made of alloy steel and are heat-treated for greater strength. They are lighter and better balanced than cheap ones. Their surface is smooth, making them a pleasure to work with and easy to clean. The initial cost of good quality tools may be more, but they are cheaper in the long run. Do not try to buy everything in all sizes in the beginning; buy a few at a time until you have the necessary tools.

Screwdrivers

The screwdriver is a very basic tool, but if used improperly it will do more damage than good. The slot on a screw has a definite dimension and shape. A screwdriver must be selected to conform with that shape. Use a small screwdriver for small screws and a large one for large screws or the screw head will be damaged.

Two basic types of screwdrivers are required: common (flat-blade) screwdrivers (**Figure 24**) and Phillips screwdrivers (**Figure 25**).

Screwdrivers are available in sets which often include an assortment of common and Phillips blades. If you buy them individually, buy at least the following:
a. Common screwdriver—5/16 × 6 in. blade.
b. Common screwdriver—3/8 × 12 in. blade.
c. Phillips screwdriver—size 2 tip, 6 in. blade.
d. Phillips screwdriver—size 3 tip, 6 and 10 in. blade.

Use screwdrivers only for driving screws. Never use a screwdriver for prying or chiseling metal. Do not try to remove a Phillips or Allen head screw with a common screwdriver (unless the screw has a combination head that will accept either type); you can damage the head so that even the proper tool will be unable to remove it. Keep screwdrivers in the proper condition and they will last longer and perform better. Always keep the tip of a common screwdriver in good condition. **Figure 26** shows how to grind the

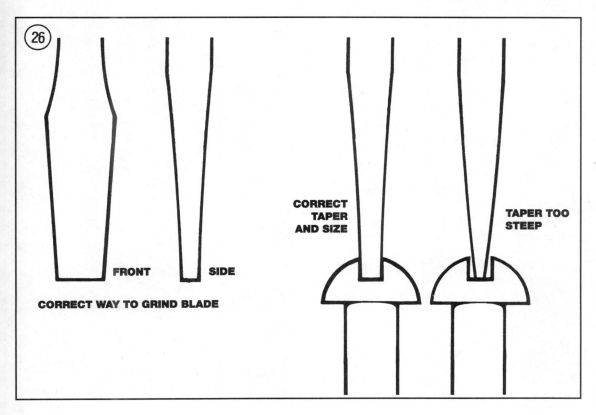

CORRECT WAY TO GRIND BLADE

FRONT SIDE

CORRECT TAPER AND SIZE

TAPER TOO STEEP

tip to the proper shape if it becomes damaged. Note the symmetrical sides of the tip.

Pliers

Pliers come in a wide range of types and sizes. Pliers are useful for cutting, bending and crimping. Do not use them to cut hardened objects or to turn bolts or nuts. **Figure 27** shows several pliers useful in ATV and motorcycle repair. Each type of pliers has a specialized function. Slip-joint pliers are general purpose pliers and are used mainly for holding things and for bending.

Needlenose pliers are used to hold or bend small objects. Adjustable pliers can be adjusted to hold various sizes of objects; the jaws remain parallel to grip around objects such as pipe or tubing. There are many more types of pliers. The ones described here are most suitable for vehicle repairs.

Locking Pliers

Locking pliers (often referred to as Vise-grips) (**Figure 28**) are used to hold objects very tightly like a vise. However, avoid using them unless necessary since their sharp jaws will permanently scar any objects which are held. Vise-grip pliers are available in many types for more specific tasks.

Circlip Pliers

Circlip pliers (**Figure 29**) are made for removing and installing circlips. External pliers (spreading) are used to remove circlips that fit on the outside of a shaft. Internal pliers (squeezing) are used to remove circlips which fit inside a gear or housing.

> *WARNING*
> *Because circlips can sometimes slip and fly off when removing and installing them, always wear safety glasses when using them.*

Box-end, Open-end and Combination Wrenches

Box-end, open-end and combination wrenches are available in sets or separately in a variety of sizes. On open and box end wrenches, the number stamped near the end refers to the distance between 2 parallel

flats on the hex head bolt or nut. On combination wrenches, the number is stamped near the center.

Box-end wrenches require clear overhead access to the fastener but can work well in situations where the fastener head is close to another part. They grip on all six edges of a fastener for a very secure grip. They are available in either 6-point or 12-point. The 6-point gives superior holding power and durability but requires a greater swinging radius during use.

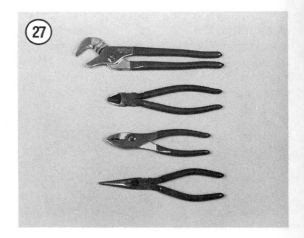

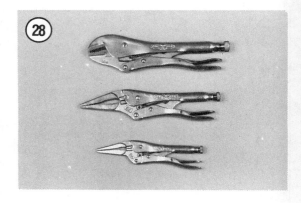

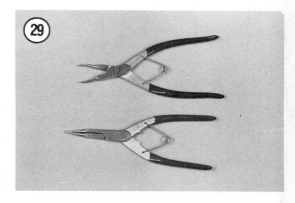

The 12-point works better in situations where the swinging radius is limited.

Open-end wrenches are speedy and work best in areas with limited overhead access. Their wide flat jaws make them unstable for situations where the bolt or nut is sunken in a well or close to the edge of a casting. These wrenches grip only two flats of a fastener so if either the fastener head or the wrench jaws are worn, the wrench may slip off.

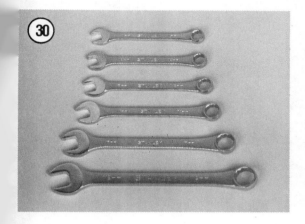

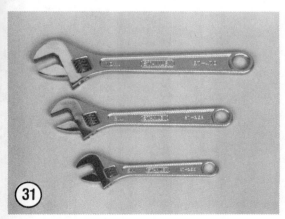

Combination wrenches (**Figure 30**) have open-end on one side and box-end on the other with both ends being the same size. Professional mechanics favor these wrenches because of their versatility.

Adjustable (Crescent) Wrenches

An adjustable wrench (sometimes called crescent wrench) can be adjusted to fit nearly any nut or bolt head which has clear access around its entire perimeter. Adjustable wrenches (**Figure 31**) are best used as a backup wrench to keep a large nut or bolt from turning while the other end is being loosened or tightened with a proper wrench.

Adjustable wrenches have only two gripping surfaces which make them more subject to slipping off the fastener and damaging the part and possibly injuring your hand. The fact that one jaw is adjustable only aggravates this shortcoming.

These wrenches are directional; the solid jaw must be the one transmitting the force. If you use the adjustable jaw to transmit the force, it will loosen and possibly slip off.

Adjustable wrenches come in all sizes but something in the 6 to 8 in. and 12 to 14 in. range is recommended.

Socket Wrenches

This type is undoubtedly the fastest, safest and most convenient to use. Sockets which attach to a ratchet handle (**Figure 32**) are available with 6-point or 12-point openings and 1/4, 3/8, 1/2 and 3/4 in. drives. The drive size indicates the size of the square hole which mates with the ratchet handle (**Figure 33**).

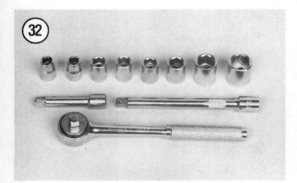

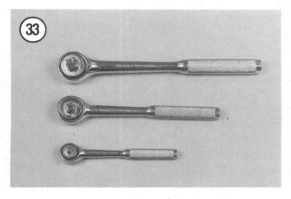

Allen Wrenches

Allen wrenches are available in sets or separately in a variety of sizes. These sets come in U.S. standard and metric size, so be sure to buy a metric set. Allen bolts are sometimes called socket bolts. Sometimes the bolts are difficult to reach and it is suggested that a variety of Allen wrenches be bought (e.g., socket driven, T-handle and extension type) as shown in **Figure 34**.

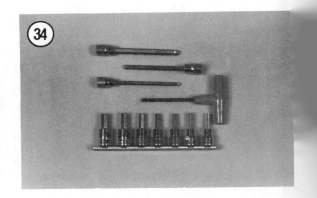

Torque Wrench

A torque wrench is used with a socket to measure how tightly a nut or bolt is installed. They come in a wide price range and with either 1/4, 3/8 or 1/2 in. square drive (**Figure 35**). The drive size indicates the size of the square drive which mates with the socket.

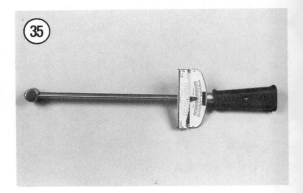

Impact Driver

This tool might have been designed with the ATV and motorcycle rider in mind. This tool makes removal of fasteners easy and eliminates damage to bolts and screw slots. Impact drivers and interchangeable bits (**Figure 36**) are available at most large hardware, motorcycle or auto parts stores. Do not buy a cheap one as it will not work as well and require more force than a moderately priced one. Sockets can also be used with a hand impact driver; however, make sure that the socket is designed for use with an impact driver or air tool. Do not use regular hand sockets, as they may shatter during use.

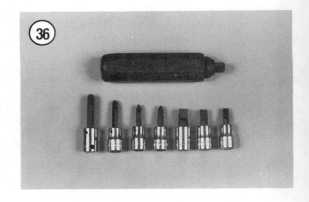

Hammers

The correct hammer (**Figure 37**) is necessary for many procedures during maintenance and repairs. A hammer with a face (or head) of rubber or plastic or a soft-faced type filled with lead shot is sometimes necessary during engine teardowns. Never use a metal-faced hammer on engine or suspension parts, as severe damage will result in most cases. You can produce the same amount of force with a soft-faced hammer. The shock of a metal-faced hammer, however, is required when using a hand impact driver.

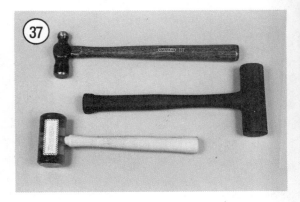

PRECISION MEASURING TOOLS

Measurement is an important part of engine and suspension service. When performing many of the service procedures in this manual, you will be required to make a number of measurements. These include basic checks such as valve clearance, engine compression and spark plug gap. As you expand your shop work into engine disassembly and service, measurements will be required to determine the size and condition of the piston and cylinder bore, valve and guide wear, camshaft wear, crankshaft runout and so on. When making these measurements, the degree of accuracy will dictate which tool is required. Precision measuring tools are expensive. If this is your first experience at engine or suspension service, it may be worthwhile to have the checks made at a Kawasaki dealer or machine shop. However, as your skills and enthusiasm for doing service work increase, you may want to buy some of these specialized tools. The following is a description of the measuring tools required during engine and suspension overhaul.

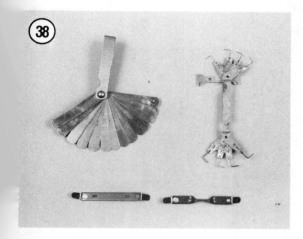

Feeler Gauge

Feeler gauges come in assorted sets and types (**Figure 38**). The feeler gauge is made of either a piece of a flat or round hardened steel of a specified thickness. Wire gauges are used to measure spark plug gap. Flat gauges are used for other measurements. Feeler gauges are also designed for specialized uses. For example, the end of a gauge is sometimes small and angled to facilitate checking valve clearances.

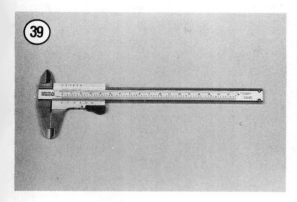

Vernier Caliper

This tool (**Figure 39**) is invaluable when reading inside, outside and depth measurements with close precision. Common uses of a vernier caliper are measuring the length of the clutch springs and the thickness of clutch plates, shims and thrust washers.

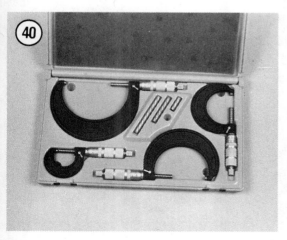

Outside Micrometers

One of the most reliable tools used for precision measurement is the outside micrometer (**Figure 40**). Outside micrometers are required to measure valve shim thickness, piston diameter and valve stem diameter. Outside micrometers are also used with other tools to measure the cylinder bore and the valve guide inside diameters. Micrometers can be bought individually or as a set.

Dial Indicator

Dial indicators (**Figure 41**) are precision tools used to check dimension variations on machined parts such as transmission shafts and axles and to check crankshaft and axle shaft end play. Dial indicators are available with various dial types and mountings for different measuring requirements.

Cylinder Bore Gauge

The cylinder bore gauge is a very specialized precision tool. The gauge set shown in **Figure 42** is comprised of a dial indicator, handle and a number of length adapters to adapt the gauge to different bore sizes. The bore gauge is used to make cylinder bore measurements such as bore size, taper and out-of-round. Depending on the bore gauge, it can sometimes be used to measure brake caliper and master cylinder bore sizes. An outside micrometer must be used together with the bore gauge to determine bore dimensions.

Small Hole Gauges

A set of small hole gauges (**Figure 43**) allows you to measure a hole, groove or slot ranging in size up to 13 mm (0.512 in.). A small hole gauge is required to measure valve guide, brake caliper and brake master cylinder bore diameters. An outside micrometer must be used together with the small hole gauge to determine bore dimensions.

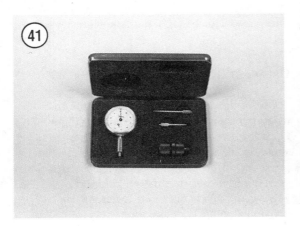

Compression Gauge

An engine with low compression cannot be properly tuned and will not develop full power. A compression gauge (**Figure 44**) measures engine compression. The one shown has a flexible stem with an extension that allows you to hold it while

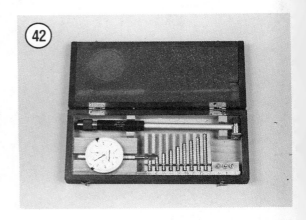

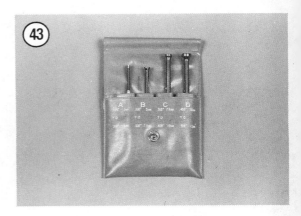

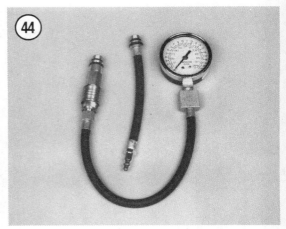

kicking the engine over. Open the throttle all the way when checking engine compression. See Chapter Three.

Cylinder Leak Down Tester

Certain engine problems (leaking valve, broken, worn or stuck piston rings) can be isolated by per-

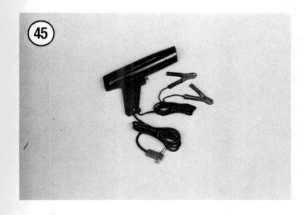

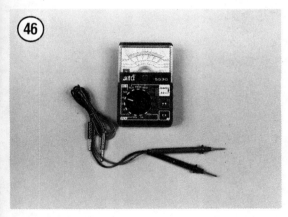

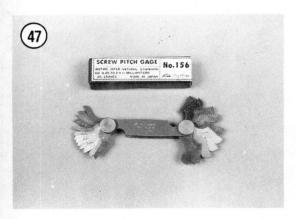

forming a cylinder leak-down test. An air compressor and a cylinder leak-down tester are required. To leak-down test a cylinder, position the piston on its compression stroke (both valves closed), then pressurize the cylinder and listen for air escaping from the exhaust system or cylinder head mating surface. This procedure is fully explained in Chapter Two. A cylinder leak-down tester can be purchased through Kawasaki dealers, tool manufacturers and automotive tool suppliers.

Strobe Timing Light

This instrument (**Figure 45**) is useful for checking ignition timing. By flashing a light at the precise instant the spark plug fires, the position of the timing mark can be seen. The flashing light makes a moving mark appear to stand still. Suitable lights range from inexpensive neon bulb types to powerful xenon strobe lights. A light with an inductive pickup is recommended to eliminate any possible damage to ignition wiring. Connect and use the timing light according to manufacturer's instructions.

Multimeter or VOM

A multimeter (**Figure 46**) is invaluable for electrical system troubleshooting and service. It combines a voltmeter, an ohmmeter and an ammeter into one unit, so it is often called a VOM.

Two types of multimeter are commonly available, analog and digital. Analog meters have a moving needle with marked bands indicating the volt, ohm and amperage scales. The digital meter (DVOM) is ideally suited for troubleshooting because it is easy to read, more accurate than analog, contains internal overload protection, is auto-ranging (analog meters must be calibrated each time the scale is changed) and has automatic polarity compensation.

Screw Pitch Gauge

A screw pitch gauge (**Figure 47**) determines the thread pitch of bolts, screws, studs, etc. The gauge is made up of a number of thin plates. Each plate has a thread shape cut on one edge to match one thread pitch. When using a screw pitch gauge to determine a thread pitch size, try to fit different blade sizes onto the bolt thread until both threads match.

Magnetic Stand

A magnetic stand (**Figure 48**) is used to hold a dial indicator securely when checking the runout of a round object or when checking the end play of a shaft.

V-Blocks

V-blocks (**Figure 49**) are precision ground blocks used to hold a round object when checking its runout or condition. In ATV and motorcycle repair, V-blocks can be used when checking the runout of such items as valve stems, camshaft, balancer shaft, crankshaft, wheel axles and other shafts and collars.

SPECIAL TOOLS

A few special tools may be required for major service. These are described in the appropriate chapters and are available either from a Kawasaki dealer or other manufacturers as indicated.

This section describes special tools unique to this type of vehicle's service and repair.

The Grabbit

The Grabbit (**Figure 50**) is a special tool used to hold various parts when loosening and tightening fasteners.

Flywheel Puller

A flywheel puller (**Figure 51**) is required to remove the flywheel from the end of the crankshaft. In addition, when disassembling the engine, the flywheel must be removed before the crankcase can be split. There is no satisfactory substitute for this tool. Because the flywheel is a tapered fit on the crankshaft, makeshift removal often results in crankshaft and flywheel damage.

MECHANIC'S TIPS

Removing Frozen Nuts and Screws

When a fastener rusts and cannot be removed, several methods may be used to loosen it. First, apply penetrating oil such as Liquid Wrench or WD-40 (available at hardware or auto supply

stores). Apply it liberally and let it penetrate for 10-15 minutes. Rap the fastener several times with a small hammer; do not hit it hard enough to cause damage. Reapply the penetrating oil if necessary.

For frozen screws, apply penetrating oil as described, then insert a screwdriver in the slot and rap the top of the screwdriver with a hammer. This loosens the rust so the screw can be removed in the normal way. If the screw head is too chewed up to

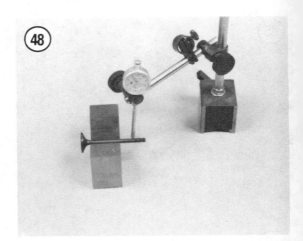

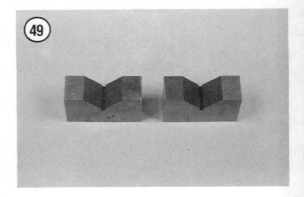

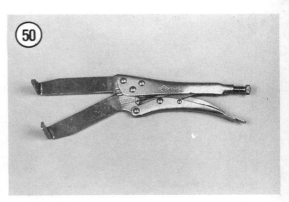

use this method, grip the head with vise-grip pliers and twist the screw out.

Avoid applying heat unless specifically instructed, as it may melt, warp or remove the temper from parts.

Removing Broken Screws or Bolts

If the head breaks off a screw or bolt, several methods are available to remove the remaining portion. If a large portion of the remainder projects out, try gripping it with vise-grip pliers. If the projecting portion is too small, file it to fit a wrench or cut a slot in it to fit a screwdriver. See **Figure 52**.

If the head breaks off flush, use a screw extractor. To do this, centerpunch the exact center of the remaining portion of the screw or bolt. Drill a small hole in the screw and tap the extractor into the hole. Back the screw out with a wrench on the extractor. See **Figure 53**.

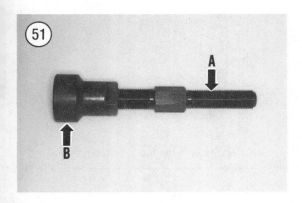

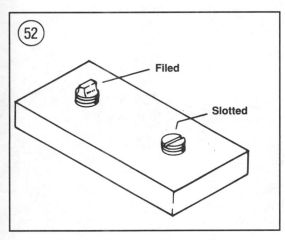

Remedying Stripped Threads

Occasionally, threads are stripped through carelessness or impact damage. Often the threads can be cleaned up by running a tap (for internal threads on nuts) or die (for external threads on bolts) through the threads. See **Figure 54**. To clean or repair spark plug threads, a spark plug tap can be used (**Figure 55**).

> *NOTE*
> *Taps and dies can be bought individually or in a set as shown in **Figure 56**.*

If an internal thread is damaged, it may be necessary to install a thread insert; see **Figure 57**, typical. Follow the manufacturer's instructions when installing their insert.

If it is necessary to drill and tap a hole, refer to **Table 8** for metric tap drill sizes.

BALL BEARING REPLACEMENT

Ball bearings (**Figure 58**) are used throughout the engine and drive assembly to reduce power loss, heat and noise resulting from friction. Because ball bearings are precision made parts, they must be maintained by proper lubrication and maintenance. If a bearing is found to be damaged, it should be replaced immediately. However, when installing a new bearing, care should be taken to prevent damage to the new bearing. While bearing replacement is described in the individual chapters where applicable, the following should be used as a guideline.

> *NOTE*
> *Unless otherwise specified, install bearings with the manufacturer's mark or number facing outward.*

Bearing Removal

While bearings are normally removed only when damaged, there may be times when it is necessary to remove a bearing that is in good condition. However, improper bearing removal will damage the bearing and maybe the shaft or case half. Note the following when removing bearings.

1. When using a puller to remove a bearing from a shaft, take care that the shaft is not damaged. Always place a piece of metal between the end of the shaft

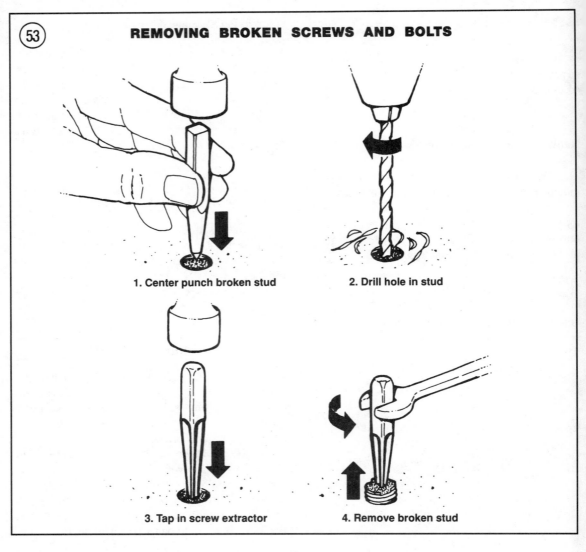

53

REMOVING BROKEN SCREWS AND BOLTS

1. Center punch broken stud

2. Drill hole in stud

3. Tap in screw extractor

4. Remove broken stud

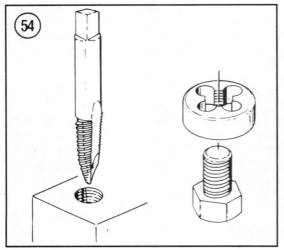

54

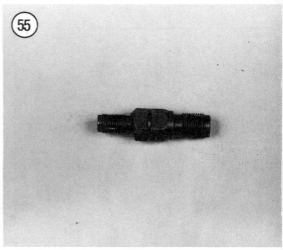

55

and the puller screw. In addition, place the puller arms next to the inner bearing race. See **Figure 59**.

2. When using a hammer to remove a bearing from a shaft, do not strike the hammer directly against the shaft. Instead, use a brass or aluminum rod between the hammer and shaft (**Figure 60**). Make sure to support both bearing races with wooden blocks as shown.

3. The ideal method of bearing removal is with a hydraulic press. However, certain procedures must

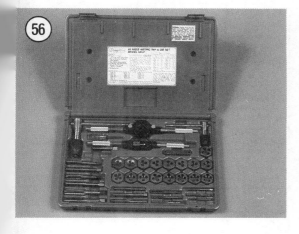

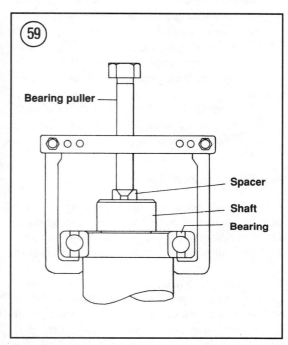

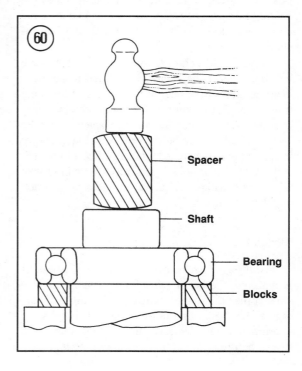

be followed or damage may occur to the bearing, shaft or bearing housing. Note the following when using a press:

    a. Always support the inner and outer bearing races with a suitable size wooden or aluminum ring (**Figure 61**). If you only support the outer race, pressure applied against the balls and/or the inner race will damage them.

    b. Always make sure the press ram (**Figure 61**) aligns with the center of the shaft. If the ram is not centered, it may damage the bearing and/or shaft.

    c. The moment the shaft is free of the bearing, it will drop to the floor. Secure or hold the shaft to prevent it from falling.

Bearing Installation

1. When installing a bearing in a housing, pressure must be applied to the outer bearing race (**Figure 62**). When installing a bearing on a shaft, pressure must be applied to the inner bearing race (**Figure 63**).

2. When installing a bearing as described in Step 1, some type of driver will be required. Never strike the bearing directly with a hammer or the bearing will be damaged. When installing a bearing, a piece of pipe or a socket with a diameter that matches the bearing race will be required. **Figure 64** shows the correct way to use a socket and hammer when installing a bearing.

3. Step 1 describes how to install a bearing in a case half and over a shaft. However, when installing a bearing over a shaft and into a housing at the same time, a snug fit is required for both outer and inner bearing races. In this situation, a spacer must be installed underneath the driver tool so that pressure is applied evenly across both races. See **Figure 65**. If the outer race is not supported as shown in **Figure 65**, the balls will push against the outer bearing track and damage it.

Shrink Fit

1. *Installing a bearing over a shaft*: When a tight fit is required, the bearing inside diameter is slightly smaller than the shaft. In this case, driving the bearing on the shaft using normal methods may cause bearing damage. Instead, the bearing should be heated before installation. Note the following:

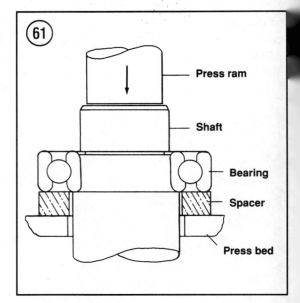

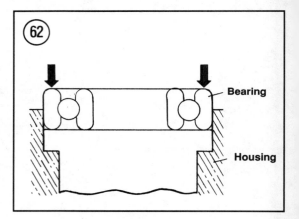

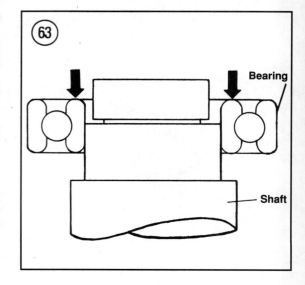

a. Secure the shaft so that it is ready for bearing installation.

b. Clean all residue from the bearing surface of the shaft. Remove burrs with a file or sandpaper.

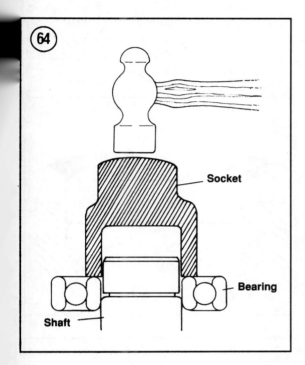

c. Fill a suitable pot or beaker with clean mineral oil. Place a thermometer (rated higher than 120° C [248° F]) in the oil. Support the thermometer so that it does not rest on the bottom or side of the pot.

d. Remove the bearing from its wrapper and secure it with a piece of heavy wire, bent to hold it in the pot. Hang the bearing in the pot so that it does not touch the bottom or sides of the pot.

e. Turn the heat on and monitor the thermometer. When the oil temperature rises to approximately 120° C (248° F), remove the bearing from the pot and quickly install it. If necessary, place a socket on the inner bearing race and tap the bearing into place. As the bearing chills, it will tighten on the shaft so you must work quickly when installing it. Make sure the bearing is installed all the way.

2. *Installing a bearing in a housing*: Bearings are generally installed in a housing with a slight interference fit. Driving the bearing into the housing using normal methods may damage the housing or cause bearing damage. Instead, the housing should be heated before the bearing is installed. Note the following:

CAUTION
Before heating the crankcases to remove the bearings, wash the cases thoroughly with detergent and water. Rinse and rewash the cases as required to remove all traces of oil and other chemical deposits.

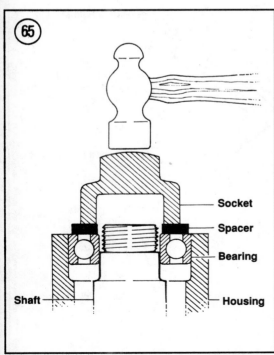

a. The housing must be heated to a temperature of about 212° F (100° C) in an oven or on a hot plate. An easy way to check that it is at the proper temperature is to drop tiny drops of water on the case; if they sizzle and evaporate immediately, the temperature is correct. Heat only one housing at a time.

CAUTION
Do not heat the housing with a torch (propane or acetylene)—never bring a flame into contact with the bearing or housing. The direct heat will destroy the case hardening of the bearing and will likely warp the housing.

b. Remove the housing from the oven or hot plate and hold it with a kitchen pot holder, heavy gloves, or heavy shop cloth—it is hot.

NOTE
A suitable size socket and extension works well for removing and installing bearings.

c. Hold the housing with the bearing side down and tap the bearing out. Repeat for all bearings in the housing.

d. Prior to heating the bearing housing to install new bearings, place the new bearings in a freezer, if possible. Chilling a bearing will slightly reduce its outside diameter while the heated bearing housing assembly is slightly larger due to heat expansion. This will make bearing installation much easier.

NOTE
Always install bearings with the manufacturer's mark or number facing outward.

e. While the housing is still hot, install the new bearing(s) into the housing. Install the bearings by hand, if possible. If necessary, lightly tap the bearing(s) into the housing with a socket placed on the outer bearing race. Do not install new bearings by driving on the inner bearing race. Install the bearing(s) until it seats completely.

OIL SEALS

Oil seals (**Figure 66**) are used to contain oil, water, grease or combustion gasses in a housing. Improper removal of a seal can damage the housing or shaft. Improper installation of the seal can damage the seal. Note the following:

a. Prying is generally the easiest and most effective method of removing a seal from a housing. However, always place a rag underneath the pry tool to prevent damage to the housing.

b. Waterproof grease should be packed in the seal lips before the seal is installed.

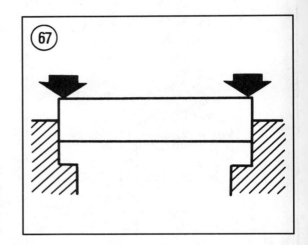

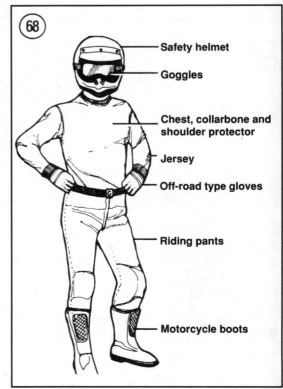

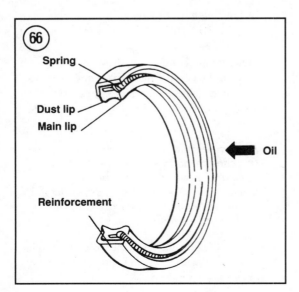

c. Unless specified otherwise, oil seals should always be installed so that the manufacturer's numbers or marks face out.

d. Oil seals should be installed with a driver placed on the outside of the seal as shown in **Figure 67**. Make sure the seal is driven squarely into the housing. Never install a seal by hitting against the top of the seal with a hammer.

RIDING SAFETY

General Tips

1. Read your owner's manual and know your machine.

2. Check the throttle and brake controls before starting the engine.

3. Know how to make an emergency stop.

WINTER PROTECTIVE CLOTHING

Inner layers   **Outer layers**

Safety helmet

Goggles

Face mask

Wool shirt

Insulated suit

Glove liners

Leather gloves

Thermal underwear

Heavy pants

Wool socks

Motorcycle or snowmobile boots

4. Never add fuel while anyone is smoking in the area or when the engine is running.

5. Never wear loose scarves, belts or boot laces that could catch on moving parts.

6. Always wear eye protection, head protection and protective clothing to protect your entire body (**Figure 68**). Today's riding apparel is very stylish, so you will be ready for action as well as being well protected.

7. Riding in the winter months requires a good set of clothes to keep your body dry and warm, otherwise your entire trip may be miserable. If you dress properly, moisture will evaporate from your body. If you become too hot and if your clothes trap the moisture, you will become cold. **Figure 69** shows some recommended inner and outer layers of cold weather clothing. Even mild temperatures can be very uncomfortable and dangerous when combined with a strong wind or while traveling at high speed. See **Table 9** for wind-chill factors. Always dress according to what the wind-chill factor is, not the ambient temperature.

8. Never allow anyone to operate the vehicle without proper instruction. This is for their bodily protection and to keep your machine from damage or destruction.

9. Use the "buddy" system for long trips, just in case you have a problem or run out of gas.

10. Never attempt to repair your machine with the engine running, except when necessary for certain tune-up procedures.

11. Check all of the machine components and hardware frequently, especially the wheels and the steering.

Operating Tips

1. Never operate the machine in crowded areas or steer toward persons.

2. Avoid dangerous terrain.

3. Cross highways (where permitted) at a 90° angle after looking in both directions. Post traffic guards if crossing in groups.

4. Do not ride the vehicle on or near railroad tracks. Engine and exhaust noise can drown out the sound of an approaching train.

5. Keep the headlight and taillight free of dirt and never ride at night without the headlight and taillight ON.

6. Do not ride your Kawasaki without the seat and fenders in place.

7. Always steer with both hands.

8. Be aware of the terrain and avoid operating the Kawasaki at excessive speed.

9. Do not panic if the throttle sticks. Turn the engine stop switch to the OFF position.

10. Do not speed through wooded areas. Hidden obstructions, hanging tree limbs, unseen ditches and even wild animals and hikers can cause injury and damage to you and your Kawasaki.

11. Do not tailgate. Rear end collisions can cause injury and machine damage.

12. Do not mix alcoholic drinks or drugs with riding—ride straight.

13. Keep both feet on the foot pegs. Do not permit your feet to hang out to stabilize the machine when making turns or in near spill situations; broken limbs could result.

14. Check your fuel supply regularly. Do not travel farther than your fuel supply will permit you to return.

15. Check to make sure that the parking brake is completely released while riding. If left on, the rear brake pads will be damaged.

Table 1 MODEL YEAR AND ENGINE SERIAL NUMBERS

Year and Model	Engine number
1986 KLF300-A1	LF300AE000001-025500
1987 KLF300-A2	LF300AE025501-on
1988 KLF300-B1	LF300AE025501-on
1989 KLF300-B2	LF300AE025501-on
1990 KLF300-B3	LF300AE025501-on
1991 KLF300-B4	LF300AE025501-503000
1992 KLF300-B5	LF300AE503001-on
1993 KLF300-B6	LF300AE503001-on
1994 KLF300-B7	LF300AE503001-on
1989 KLF300-C1 (4x4)	LF300AE025501-on
1990 KLF300-C2 (4x4)	LF300AE025501-on
1991 KLF300-C3 (4x4)	LF300AE025501-on
1992 KLF300-C4 (4x4)	LF300AE025501-503000
1993 KLF300-C5 (4x4)	LF300AE503001-on
1994 KLF300-C6 (4x4)	LF300AE503001-on
1995 KLF300-C7 (4x4)	LF300AE503001-on
1996 KLF300-C8 (4x4)	LF300AE503001-on
1997 KLF300-C9 (4x4)	LF300AE503001-on
1998 KLF300-C10 (4x4)	LF300AE503001-on

Table 2 GENERAL DIMENSIONS

Item	mm	in.
Overall length		
2-wheel drive		
1986-1988	1,910	75.2
1989-on	1,850	72.8
4-wheel drive		
1989-on	1,860	73.2
Overall width		
2-wheel drive		
1986-1988	1,100	43.3
1989-on		
Australia model	1,160	45.7
All other models	1,115	43.9
4-wheel drive		
1989-on	1,100	43.3
Overall height		
2-wheel drive		
1986-1988	1,045	41.1
1989-on	1,035	40.7
4-wheel drive		
1989-on	1,105	43.5
Seat height		
2-wheel drive	750	25.5
4-wheel drive	805	31.7
Wheelbase		
2-wheel drive		
1986-1988	1,200	47.2
1989-on	1,210	47.6
4-wheel drive		
1989-on	1,200	47.2
Ground clearance		
2-wheel drive	195	7.7
4-wheel drive	225	8.9
Minimum turning radius		
2-wheel drive		
1986-1988		
Locked axle mode	3,000	118.1
Differential mode	2,600	102.4
1989-on		
Locked axle mode	2,900	114.2
Differential mode	2,600	102.4
4-wheel drive		
1989-on	2,900	114.2

Table 3 VEHICLE WEIGHT

	kg.	lb.
2-wheel drive		
U.S.		
1986-1989	223	491.6
1990-on	226	498.2
Australia		
1989	226	498.2
1990-1992	228	502.6
1993-on	229	504.8
(continued)		

Table 3 VEHICLE WEIGHT (continued)

	kg.	lb.
Canada		
1986-1989	223	491.6
1990-1991	226	498.2
1992-on	227	500.4
Europe and UK		
1986-1991	226	498.2
1992	227	500.4
1993-on	229	504.8
4-wheel drive		
U.S.		
1989-1992	257	566.6
1993-on	260	573.2
Canada		
1989-1992	257	566.6
1993-on	261	575.4
Australia, Europe and UK		
1989-1992	260	573.2
1993-on	263	579.8

Table 4 DECIMAL AND METRIC EQUIVALENTS

Fractions	Decimal in.	Metric mm	Fractions	Decimal in.	Metric mm
1/64	0.015625	0.39688	33/64	0.515625	13.09687
1/32	0.03125	0.79375	17/32	0.53125	13.49375
3/64	0.046875	1.19062	35/64	0.546875	13.89062
1/16	0.0625	1.58750	9/16	0.5625	14.28750
5/64	0.078125	1.98437	37/64	0.578125	14.68437
3/32	0.09375	2.38125	19/32	0.59375	15.08125
7/64	0.109375	2.77812	39/64	0.609375	15.47812
1/8	0.125	3.1750	5/8	0.625	15.87500
9/64	0.140625	3.57187	41/64	0.640625	16.27187
5/32	0.15625	3.96875	21/32	0.65625	16.66875
11/64	0.171875	4.36562	43/64	0.671875	17.06562
3/16	0.1875	4.76250	11/16	0.6875	17.46250
13/64	0.203125	5.15937	45/64	0.703125	17.85937
7/32	0.21875	5.55625	23/32	0.71875	18.25625
15/64	0.234375	5.95312	47/64	0.734375	18.65312
1/4	0.250	6.35000	3/4	0.750	19.05000
17/64	0.265625	6.74687	49/64	0.765625	19.44687
9/32	0.28125	7.14375	25/32	0.78125	19.84375
19/64	0.296875	7.54062	51/64	0.796875	20.24062
5/16	0.3125	7.93750	13/16	0.8125	20.63750
21/64	0.328125	8.33437	53/64	0.828125	21.03437
11/32	0.34375	8.73125	27/32	0.84375	21.43125
23/64	0.359375	9.12812	55/64	0.859375	22.82812
3/8	0.375	9.52500	7/8	0.875	22.22500
25/64	0.390625	9.92187	57/64	0.890625	22.62187
13/32	0.40625	10.31875	29/32	0.90625	23.01875
27/64	0.421875	10.71562	59/64	0.921875	23.41562
7/16	0.4375	11.11250	15/16	0.9375	23.81250
29/64	0.453125	11.50937	61/64	0.953125	24.20937
15/32	0.46875	11.90625	31/32	0.96875	24.60625
31/64	0.484375	12.30312	63/64	0.984375	25.00312
1/2	0.500	12.70000	1	1.00	25.40000

Table 5 CONVERSION TABLES

Multiply	By	To get equivalent of
Length		
Inches	25.4	Millimeter
Inches	2.54	Centimeter
Miles	1.609	Kilometer
Feet	0.3048	Meter
Millimeter	0.03937	Inches
Centimeter	0.3937	Inches
Kilometer	0.6214	Mile
Meter	3.281	Mile
Fluid volume		
U.S. quarts	0.9463	Liters
U.S. gallons	3.785	Liters
U.S. ounces	29.573529	Milliliters
Imperial gallons	4.54609	Liters
Imperial quarts	1.1365	Liters
Liters	0.2641721	U.S. gallons
Liters	1.0566882	U.S. quarts
Liters	33.814023	U.S. ounces
Liters	0.22	Imperial gallons
Liters	0.8799	Imperial quarts
Milliliters	0.033814	U.S. ounces
Milliliters	1.0	Cubic centimeters
Milliliters	0.001	Liters
Torque		
Foot-pounds	1.3556	Newton-meters
Foot-pounds	0.138255	Meter-kilograms
Inch-pounds	0.1130	Newton-meters
Newton-meters	0.7375622	Foot-pounds
Newton-meters	8.8507	Inch-pounds
Meter-kilograms	7.2330139	Foot-pounds
Volume		
Cubic inches	16.387064	Cubic centimeters
Cubic centimeters	0.0610237	Cubic inches
Temperature		
Fahrenheit	(F − 32) 0.556	Centigrade
Centigrade	(C × 1.8) + 32	Fahrenheit
Weight		
Ounces	28.3495	Grams
Pounds	0.4535924	Kilograms
Grams	0.035274	Ounces
Kilograms	2.2046224	Pounds
Pressure		
Pounds per square inch	0.070307	Kilograms per square centimeter
Kilograms per square centimeter	14.223343	Pounds per square inch
Speed		
Miles per hour	1.609344	Kilometers per hour
Kilometers per hour	0.6213712	Miles per hour

Table 6 GENERAL TORQUE SPECIFICATIONS

Thread diameter	N•m	ft.-lb.
5 mm	3.4-4.9	30-43 in.-lb.
6 mm	5.9-7.8	52-69 in.-lb.
8 mm	14-19	10.0-13.5
	(continued)	

Table 6 GENERAL TORQUE SPECIFICATIONS (continued)

Thread diameter	N·m	ft.-lb.
10 mm	25-39	19-25
12mm	44-61	33-45
14 mm	73-98	54-72
16 mm	115-155	83-115
18 mm	165-225	125-165
20 mm	225-325	165-240

Table 7 TECHNICAL ABBREVIATIONS

ABDC	After bottom dead center
ATDC	After top dead center
BBDC	Before bottom dead center
BDC	Bottom dead center
BTDC	Before top dead center
C	Celsius (Centigrade)
cc	Cubic centimeters
CDI	Capacitor disharge ignition
cu. in.	Cubic inches
F	Fahrenheit
ft.-lb.	Foot-pounds
gal.	Gallons
hp	Horsepower
in.	Inches
kg	Kilogram
kg/cm^2	Kilograms per square centimeter
kgm	Kilogram meters
km	Kilometer
l	Liter
m	Meter
mm	Millimeter
N·m	Newton-meters
oz.	Ounce
psi	Pounds per square inch
pts.	Pints
qt.	Quarts
rpm	Revolutions per minute

Table 8 METRIC TAP DRILL SIZES

Metric tap (mm)	Drill size	Decimal equivalent	Nearest fraction
3 × 0.50	No. 39	0.0995	3/32
3 × 0.60	3/32	0.0937	3/32
4 × 0.70	No. 30	0.1285	1/8
4 × 0.75	1/8	0.125	1/8
5 × 0.80	No. 19	0.166	11/64
5 × 0.90	No. 20	0.161	5/32
6 × 1.00	No. 9	0.196	13/64
7 × 1.00	16/64	0.234	15/64
8 × 1.00	J	0.277	9/32
8 × 1.25	17/64	0.265	17/64
9 × 1.00	5/16	0.3125	5/16
9 × 1.25	5/16	0.3125	5/16

(continued)

1

Table 8 METRIC TAP DRILL SIZES (continued)

Metric tap (mm)	Drill size	Decimal equivalent	Nearest fraction
10 × 1.25	11/32	0.3437	11/32
10 × 1.50	R	0.339	11/32
11 × 1.50	3/8	0.375	3/8
12 × 1.50	13/32	0.406	13/32
12 × 1.75	13/32	0.406	13/32

Table 9 WIND-CHILL FACTORS

Estimated wind speed in mph	Actual thermometer reading (°F)											
	50	40	30	20	10	0	−10	−20	−30	−40	−50	−60
	Equivalent temperature (°F)											
Calm	50	40	30	20	10	0	−10	−20	−30	−40	−50	−60
5	48	37	27	16	6	−5	−15	−26	−36	−47	−57	−68
10	40	28	16	4	−9	−21	−33	−46	−58	−70	−83	−95
15	36	22	9	−5	−18	−36	−45	−58	−72	−85	−99	−112
20	32	18	4	−10	−25	−39	−53	−67	−82	−96	−110	−124
25	30	16	0	−15	−29	−44	−59	−74	−88	−104	−118	−133
30	28	13	−2	−18	−33	−48	−63	−79	−94	−109	−125	−140
35	27	11	−4	−20	−35	−49	−67	−82	−98	−113	−129	−145
40	26	10	−6	−21	−37	−53	−69	−85	−100	−116	−132	−148
*	Little danger (for properly clothed person)				Increasing danger			Great danger				
					• Danger from freezing of exposed flesh •							

*Wind speeds greater than 40 mph have little additional effect.

CHAPTER TWO

TROUBLESHOOTING

Diagnosing mechanical and electrical problems is relatively simple if you use orderly procedures and keep a few basic principles in mind. The first step in any troubleshooting procedure is to define the symptoms closely and then localize the problem. Subsequent steps involve testing and analyzing those areas that could cause the symptoms. A haphazard approach may eventually solve the problem, but it can be very costly in terms of wasted time and unnecessary replacement of parts.

Proper lubrication, maintenance and periodic tune-ups as described in Chapter Three will reduce the necessity for troubleshooting. Even with the best of care, however, all vehicles are prone to problems that will require troubleshooting.

Never assume anything. Do not overlook the obvious. If the engine will not start, the engine stop switch or start switch may be shorted out or damaged. When trying to start the engine, you may have flooded it.

If the engine suddenly quits, what sound did it make? Consider this and check the easiest, most accessible area first. If the engine sounded as if it ran out of fuel, check to see if there is fuel in the tank. If there is fuel in the tank, is it reaching the carburetor?

If not, the fuel tank vent hose may be plugged, preventing fuel from flowing from the fuel tank to carburetor.

If nothing obvious turns up in a quick check, look a little further. Learning to recognize and describe symptoms will make repairs easier for you or a mechanic at the shop. Describe problems accurately and fully.

Gather as many symptoms as possible to aid in diagnosis. Note whether the engine lost power gradually or all at once, what color smoke came from the exhaust and so on. Remember, the more complicated a machine is, the easier it is to troubleshoot because symptoms point to specific problems.

After defining the vehicle's symptoms, areas that could cause the problem are tested and analyzed. Guessing at the cause of a problem may provide the solution, but it can easily lead to frustration, wasted time and a series of expensive, unnecessary replacement of parts.

You do not need fancy equipment or complicated test gear to determine whether repairs can be attempted at home. A few simple checks could save a large repair bill and lost time while the ATV sits in a dealer's service department. On the other hand, be realistic and do not attempt repairs beyond your abilities. Service departments tend to charge heavily for putting together a disassembled engine that may have been abused. Some will not even take on such a job. Use common sense so that you do not get in over your head.

OPERATING REQUIREMENTS

An engine needs 3 basics to run properly: correct fuel/air mixture, compression and a spark at the right time (**Figure 1**). If one basic requirement is missing, the engine will not run. Four-stroke engine operating principles are described in Chapter Four under *Engine Principles*.

If the ATV has been sitting for a period of time and refuses to start, check and clean the spark plug. If the plug is not fouled, look to the fuel delivery system. This includes the fuel tank, fuel shutoff valve, in-line fuel filter (if used) and fuel line. If the ATV sat for a while with fuel in the carburetor, fuel deposits may have gummed up carburetor jets and air passages. Gasoline tends to lose its potency after standing for long periods. Condensation may contaminate it with water. Drain the old gas and try starting with a fresh tankful.

TROUBLESHOOTING INSTRUMENTS

Chapter One lists the instruments needed and instruction on their use.

STARTING THE ENGINE

When your engine refuses to start, frustration can cause you to forget basic starting principles and procedures. The following outline will guide you through basic starting procedures. In all cases, make sure that there is an adequate supply of fuel in the tank.

Starting a Cold Engine

1. Shift the transmission into NEUTRAL.
2. Turn on the fuel valve (**Figure 2**).

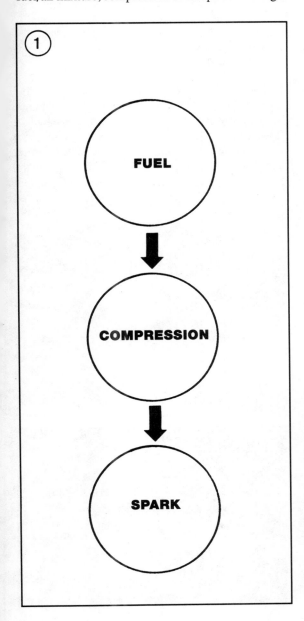

3. Move the choke knob (A, **Figure 3**) to its fully on position.

4. With the throttle completely closed, operate the starter button or pull on the starter rope.

5. When the engine starts, work the throttle slightly to keep it running.

6. Idle the engine for approximately 1 minute or until the throttle responds cleanly, then close the choke. The engine should be sufficiently warmed to prevent stalling.

Starting a Warm or Hot Engine

1. Shift the transmission into NEUTRAL.

2. Turn on the fuel valve (**Figure 2**).

3. Make sure the choke lever (A, **Figure 3**) is in the off position.

4. Open the throttle slightly and operate the starter button or pull on the starter rope.

Starting a Flooded Engine

If the engine will not start and there is a strong gasoline smell, the engine may be flooded. If so, open the throttle all the way and operate the starter button or pull the starter rope. Do not open the choke. Holding the throttle open allows more air to reach the combustion chamber.

> *NOTE*
> *If the engine refuses to start, check the carburetor overflow hose attached to the fitting at the bottom of the float bowl (**Figure 4**). If fuel runs out the end of the hose, the float is stuck open, allowing the carburetor to overfill.*

STARTING DIFFICULTIES

If the engine cranks over but is difficult to start, or will not start at all, it does not help to drain the battery or wear your arm out with the pull starter. Check for obvious problems even before getting out your tools. Go down the following list step-by-step. Do each one while remembering the 3 engine operating requirements described under *Operating Requirements* earlier in this chapter.

If the engine still will not start, refer to the appropriate troubleshooting procedures that follow in this chapter.

1. Is the choke lever in the right position? Move the choke lever to its fully on position for a cold engine and turn it off for a warm or hot engine (A, **Figure 3**).

2. Is there fuel in the tank? Fill the tank if necessary. Has it been a while since the engine was run? If in doubt, drain the fuel and fill with a fresh tank full. Check for a clogged fuel tank vent tube (**Figure 5**). Remove the tube from the filler cap, then wipe off one end and blow through it. Remove the filler cap and check for a plugged hose nozzle.

> *WARNING*
> *Do not use an open flame to check in the tank. A serious explosion is certain to result.*

3. Pull off the fuel line from the carburetor and insert the end of the hose into a clear, glass container. Turn the fuel valve on (**Figure 2**) and see if fuel flows freely. If fuel does not flow out and there is a fuel filter installed in the fuel line, remove the filter and turn the fuel valve on again. If fuel flows, the filter is clogged and must be replaced. If no fuel comes out, the fuel valve may be shut off, blocked

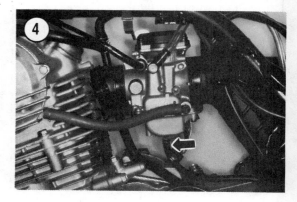

by foreign matter, or the fuel cap vent may be plugged.

4. If you suspect that the cylinder is flooded, or there is a strong smell of gasoline, open the throttle all the way and operate the starter button or pull the starter rope. If the cylinder is severely flooded (fouled or wet spark plug), remove the spark plug and dry the base and electrode (**Figure 6**) thoroughly with a soft cloth. Reinstall the plug and attempt to start the engine.

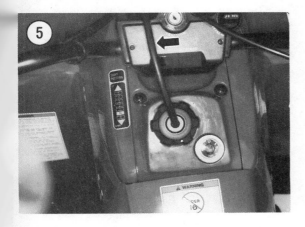

5. Check the carburetor overflow hose on the bottom of the float bowl (**Figure 4**). If fuel is running out of the hose, the float is stuck open. Turn the fuel valve off and tap the carburetor a few times. Then turn on the fuel valve. If fuel continues to run out of the hose, remove and repair the carburetor as described in Chapter Eight. Check the carburetor vent hoses to make sure they are clear. Check the end of the hoses for contamination.

> *NOTE*
> *Now that you have determined that fuel is reaching the carburetor, the fuel system could still be the problem. The jets (pilot and main) could be clogged or the air filter could be severely restricted. However, before removing the carburetor, continue with Step 6 to make sure that the ignition provides an adequate spark.*

6. Make sure the engine stop switch is not stuck or working improperly or that the wire is broken and shorting out. If necessary, test the engine stop switch as described under *Switches* in Chapter Nine.

> *NOTE*
> *If you have installed an aftermarket kill switch, check the switch for proper operation. This switch may be faulty.*

7. Is the spark plug wire (**Figure 7**) on tight? Push it on and slightly rotate it to clean the electrical connection between the plug and the connector. Push or screw the plug cap into the high-tension lead.

> *NOTE*
> *If the engine will still not start, continue with the following.*

8. Perform a spark test as described under *Engine Fails to Start (Spark Test)* in this chapter. If there is a strong spark, perform Step 9. If there is no spark or if the spark is very weak, test the ignition system as described under *Ignition System* in this chapter.

> *NOTE*
> *Now that you have established that the fuel and ignition system are working properly, the one remaining area to check is the mechanical system. Unless the engine seized, mechanical problems affecting the top end generally occur over time, depending on maintenance*

and vehicle use. What you want to do is to isolate the mechanical problem to one of these areas: top end, bottom end, clutch or transmission. Engine top and bottom end components are covered in Step 9. Clutch and transmission problems are covered elsewhere in this chapter.

9. Check cylinder compression as follows:
   a. Turn off the fuel valve.
   b. Remove and ground the spark plug shell against the cylinder head as shown in **Figure 8**.

> *CAUTION*
> *To prevent damage to the ignition system, ground the spark plug when performing the following steps.*

   c. Put your finger tightly over the spark plug hole.
   d. If equipped with a pull starter, have an assistant pull the starter rope. If not equipped with a pull starter, operate the electric starter. When the piston comes up on the compression stroke, pressure in the cylinder should force your finger from the spark plug hole. If your finger pops off, the cylinder probably has sufficient compression to start the engine.

> *NOTE*
> *You may still have a compression problem even though it seems okay with the previous test. Check engine compression with a compression gauge as described under **Tune-up** in Chapter Three.*

ENGINE STARTING TROUBLES

An engine that refuses to start or is difficult to start is very frustrating. More often than not, the problem is very minor and can be found with a simple and logical troubleshooting approach.

The following items show a beginning point from which to isolate engine starting problems.

Engine Fails to Start (Spark Test)

Perform the following spark test to determine if the ignition system is operating properly.

> *CAUTION*
> *Before removing the spark plug in Step 1, clean all dirt and debris away from the plug base. Dirt that falls into the cylinder will cause rapid engine wear.*

1. Disconnect the plug wire and remove the spark plug (**Figure 7**).
2. Insert the spark plug into its cap and touch the spark plug base against the cylinder head to ground it (**Figure 8**). Position the spark plug so you can see the electrode.

> *WARNING*
> *If the engine is flooded, do not perform this test. Fuel that is ejected through the spark plug hole can be ignited by the firing of the spark plug.*

3. Crank the engine with the starter button or pull the starter rope. A fat blue spark should be evident across the spark plug electrode. If there is strong sunlight on the plug, shade the plug with your hand so that you can see the plug better.

> *WARNING*
> *Do not hold the spark plug, wire or connector or a serious electrical shock may result.*

4. If the spark is good, check for one or more of the following possible malfunctions:
   a. Obstructed fuel line or fuel filter.
   b. Low compression or engine damage.
   c. Flooded engine.
5. If the spark is weak or if there is no spark, refer to *Engine is Difficult to Start* in this chapter.

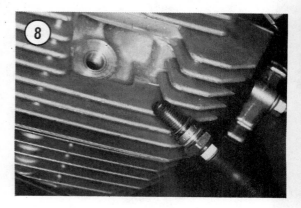

NOTE

*If the engine backfires when you are attempting to start it, the ignition timing may be incorrect. A loose flywheel, loose stator coil mounting screws or a defective ignition component will change the ignition timing. Refer to **Ignition System** in this chapter for more information.*

ENGINE IS DIFFICULT TO START

The following section groups engine starting problems to the 3 main engine operating systems (**Figure 1**) with probable causes.

Electrical System

On off-road vehicles, the electrical system is a common source of engine starting problems. Trouble usually occurs in the wiring harness and connectors.

1. *Spark plug*—check for:
   a. Fouled spark plug.
   b. Incorrect spark plug gap.

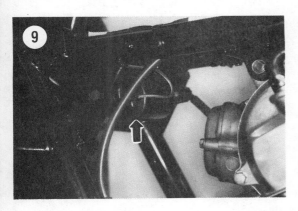

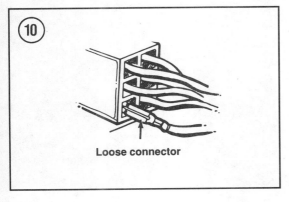

Loose connector

c. Incorrect heat range; see Chapter Three.
   d. Worn or damaged spark plug electrodes.
   e. Damaged spark plug.
   f. Damaged spark plug cap or secondary wire.

NOTE

*Refer to **Reading Spark Plugs** in Chapter Three for additional information.*

2. *Ignition coil*—check for:
   a. Loose or damaged secondary or primary wire leads.
   b. Cracked ignition coil body (**Figure 9**).
   c. Loose or corroded ground wire.
3. *Switches and wiring*—check for:
   a. Dirty or loose fitting terminals.
   b. Damaged wires or connectors (**Figure 10**).
   c. Damaged start switch.
   d. Damaged engine stop switch.
   e. Damaged main switch.
   f. Damaged neutral/reverse switch.
4. *Starter motor*—check for:
   a. Damaged starter motor.
   b. Damaged starter relay.
   c. Damaged starter circuit cut-off relay.
5. *Electrical components*—check for:
   a. Damaged pickup coil.
   b. Damaged IC ignition unit.
   c. Damaged crankshaft Woodruff key.
6. Discharged or damaged battery.

Fuel System

A contaminated fuel system will cause engine starting and performance related problems. It only takes a small amount of dirt in the fuel valve, fuel line or carburetor to cause problems.

1. *Air filter*—check for:
   a. Clogged air filter.
   b. Clogged air filter housing.
   c. Leaking or damaged air filter housing-to-carburetor air boot.
2. *Fuel valve*—check for:
   a. Clogged fuel hose.
   b. Clogged fuel valve.
   c. Damaged fuel valve pickup tubes (installed in fuel tank).
3. *Fuel tank*—check for:
   a. No fuel.
   b. Clogged fuel filter.
   c. Clogged fuel tank breather hose (**Figure 5**).

d. Contaminated fuel.
4. *Carburetor*—check for:
   a. Clogged or damaged choke system.
   b. Clogged starter jet.
   c. Clogged pilot jet.
   d. Loose pilot jet or main jet.
   e. Clogged pilot air passage.
   f. Incorrect float level.
   g. Leaking or otherwise damaged float.
   h. Severely worn or damaged needle valve.

Engine Compression

Check engine compression with a compression gauge as described in Chapter Three. To obtain a more accurate gauge of engine wear, perform an engine leak down test; refer to *Engine Leak Down Test* in this chapter.

1. *Cylinder and cylinder head*—check for:
   a. Loose spark plug.
   b. Missing spark plug gasket.
   c. Leaking cylinder head gasket.
   d. Leaking cylinder base gasket.
   e. Severely worn or seized piston, piston rings and/or cylinder.
   f. Incorrectly sealed valve(s).
   g. Worn or damaged valve and valve seat surfaces.
   h. Weak or broken valve spring(s).
   i. Incorrect valve timing.
2. *Valve train*—check for:
   a. Incorrect valve clearance (too tight).
   b. Incorrect valve timing.
   c. Weak or broken valve spring(s).
3. *Piston and piston rings*—check for:
   a. Worn piston rings.
   b. Damaged piston rings.
   c. Piston seizure or piston damage.
4. *Crankcase and crankshaft*—check for:
   a. Seized connecting rod.
   b. Damaged crankcase.
5. *Recoil starter*—check for:
   a. Broken recoil starter springs.
   b. Recoil starter pawl not engaging.

POOR IDLE SPEED PERFORMANCE

If the engine starts but off-idle performance is poor (engine hesitation, cutting out, etc.), check the following:
1. Clogged or damaged air filter.

2. *Carburetor*—check for:
   a. Clogged pilot jet.
   b. Loose pilot jet.
   c. Damaged choke system.
   d. Incorrect throttle cable adjustment.
   e. Incorrect carburetor adjustment.
   f. Flooded carburetor (visually check carburetor overflow hose for fuel). See **Figure 4**.
   g. Vacuum piston does not slide smoothly in carburetor bore.
3. *Fuel*—check for:
   a. Water or alcohol in fuel.
   b. Old fuel.
4. *Engine*—check for:
   a. Low engine compression.
   b. Incorrect valve clearance.
   c. Engine oil viscosity too high.
5. *Electrical system*—check for:
   a. Damaged battery.
   b. Damaged spark plug.
   c. Damaged ignition coil.
   d. Damaged pickup coil.
   e. Damaged IC igniter unit.

POOR MEDIUM TO HIGH SPEED PERFORMANCE

Refer to *Engine is Difficult to Start*, then check the following:
1. *Carburetor*— check for:
   a. Incorrect fuel level.
   b. Incorrect jet needle clip position (if adjustable).
   c. Clogged or loose main jet.
2. Clogged air filter.
3. *Other considerations*—check for:

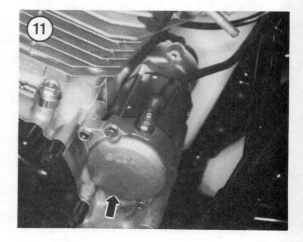

a. Overheating.

b. Clutch slippage.

c. Brake drag.

d. Engine oil level too high.

e. Final gear case oil level too high.

f. Engine oil viscosity too high.

ENGINE STARTING SYSTEM

This section describes troubleshooting procedures for the electric starting system. A fully charged battery, ohmmeter and jumper cables are required to troubleshoot the starting system.

Description

An electric starter motor is installed on all KLF300 models. The starter motor is mounted horizontally (**Figure 11**) to the front of the engine. **Figure 12** shows a schematic of the starting system and its components.

The electric starting system requires a fully charged battery to provide the large amount of current required to operate the starter motor. A charge coil (mounted on the stator plate) and a voltage regulator, connected in circuit with the battery, keeps the battery charged while the engine is running. The battery can also be charged externally.

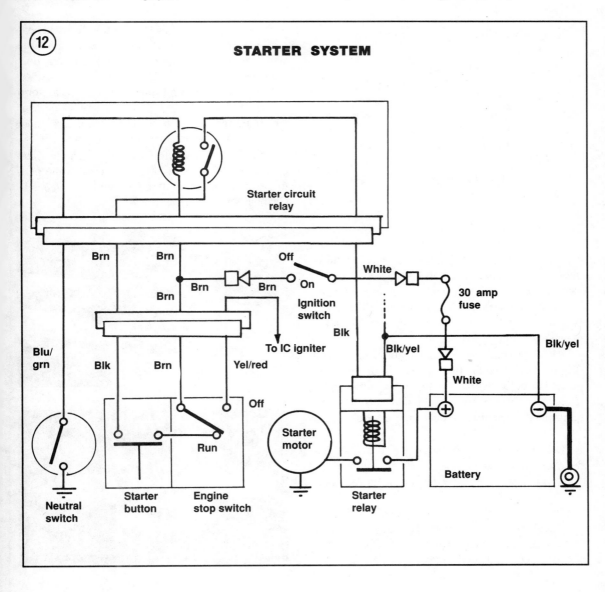

(12) STARTER SYSTEM

The starter relay carries the heavy electrical current to the motor (**Figure 11**). Depressing the starter switch (**Figure 13**) allows current to flow through the relay coil. This causes the relay contacts to close and allow current to flow from the battery through the relay to the starter motor.

> *CAUTION*
> *Do not operate the electric starter motor continuously for more than 5 seconds. Allow the motor to cool for at least 15 seconds between attempts to start the engine.*

Troubleshooting

Before troubleshooting the starting circuit, make sure that:

a. The battery is fully charged.
b. Battery cables are the proper size and length. Replace cables that are undersized or damaged.
c. All electrical connections are clean and tight.
d. The wiring harness is in good condition, with no worn or frayed insulation or loose harness sockets.
e. The fuel system is filled with an adequate supply of fresh gasoline.

Starter Troubleshooting

If the starter does not operate, perform the following tests. After completing each test, reconnect any electrical connector that was disconnected, before beginning the next test. When operating the starter switch, turn the engine stop switch to RUN and the main switch to ON.

1. Check the main fuse mounted above the battery (**Figure 14**). Open the fuse holder and pull the fuse out and visually inspect it. If the fuse is blown, refer to *Fuse* in Chapter Nine. If the main fuse is okay, reinstall it, or install a new one, then go on to the next step.

2. Test the battery specific gravity as described under *Battery* in Chapter Three. Note the following:

a. If the specific gravity reading is correct, perform Step 3.
b. If the specific gravity reading is not within the specified range, clean and recharge the battery as described under *Battery* in Chapter Three. Replace a damaged battery.

3. Disconnect the ignition switch electrical connector. Test the ignition switch as described under *Switches* in Chapter Nine. Note the following:

a. If the ignition switch tested good, perform Step 4.
b. If the ignition switch did not test good, replace the switch and retest.

4. Disconnect the starter switch electrical connectors from the wiring harness. Test the starter switch as described under *Switches* in Chapter Nine. Note the following:

a. If the starter switch tested good, perform Step 5.
b. If the starter switch did not test good, replace the switch and retest.

5. Disconnect the engine stop switch electrical connectors from the wiring harness. Test the engine stop switch as described under *Switches* in Chapter Nine. Note the following:

a. If the engine stop switch tested good, perform Step 6.
b. If the engine stop switch did not test good, replace the switch and retest.

6. Disconnect the neutral/reverse switch electrical connectors from the wiring harness. Test the neutral/reverse switch as described under *Switches* in Chapter Nine. Note the following:

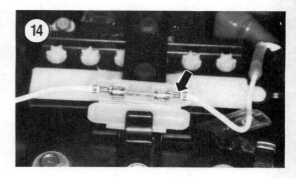

a. If the switch tested good, perform Step 7.

b. If the neutral/reverse switch did not test good, replace the switch and retest.

7. Disconnect the starter circuit relay from the wiring harness. Test the starter circuit relay as described under *Starter Relay* in Chapter Nine. Note the following:

a. If the starter circuit relay tested good, perform Step 8.

b. If the starter circuit relay did not test good, replace the relay and retest.

8. Test the starter solenoid as described under *Starter Solenoid* in Chapter Nine. Note the following:

a. If the starter solenoid tested good, perform Step 9.

b. If the starter solenoid did not test good, replace the starter solenoid and retest.

9. If you have not found the starting system problem, recheck the wiring system for dirty or loose-fitting terminals or damaged wires; clean and repair as required. If all the connectors and wires are in good condition, the starter motor is probably faulty. Remove and overhaul the starter motor as described under *Starter* in Chapter Nine.

10. Make sure all connectors disassembled during this procedure are free of corrosion and are reconnected properly.

CHARGING SYSTEM

A malfunction in the charging system generally causes the battery to remain undercharged. **Figure 15** shows a schematic of the charging system and its components.

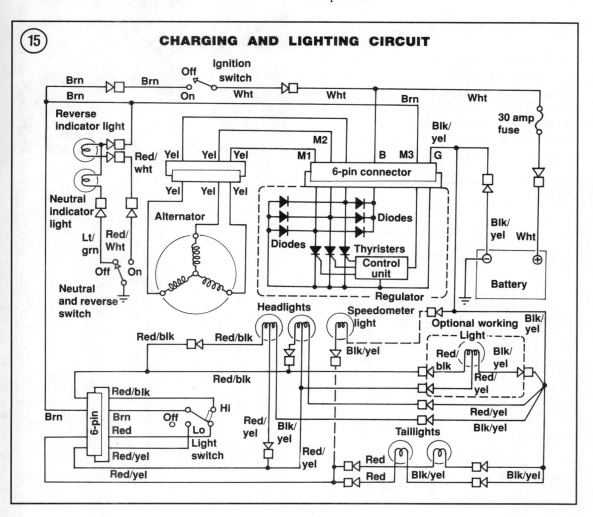

(15) CHARGING AND LIGHTING CIRCUIT

Troubleshooting

Before testing the charging system, visually check the following.

1. Check the battery connections at the battery. If polarity is reversed, check for a damaged regulator/rectifier.

2. Check for loose or dirty connectors (**Figure 16**).

3. Inspect all wiring between the battery and stator charge coils for worn or cracked insulation or loose connections. Replace wiring or clean and tighten connections as required.

4. Check battery condition. Clean and recharge as required. See *Battery* in Chapter Three.

5. Perform the *Charging System Output Test* listed under *Charging System* in Chapter Nine.

6. Test the regulator/rectifier as described under *Regulator/Rectifier* in Chapter Nine.

IGNITION SYSTEM

All models are equipped with a capacitor discharge ignition (IC Ignitor) system. This solid state system uses no contact breaker points or other moving parts. **Figure 17** shows a schematic of the ignition system and its components.

Because of the solid state design, problems with the capacitor discharge system are relatively few.

However, when problems arise, they cause one of the following symptoms:

a. Weak spark.

b. No spark.

It is possible to check an IC Ignitor system that:

a. Does not spark.

b. Has broken or damaged wires.

c. Has a weak spark.

It is difficult to check an IC Ignitor system that malfunctions due to:

a. Vibration problems.

b. Components that malfunction only when the engine is hot or under a load.

The troubleshooting procedures in **Figure 18** will help you isolate the ignition problem fast.

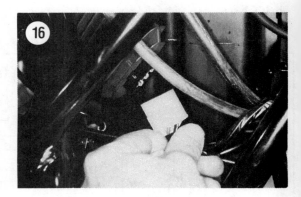

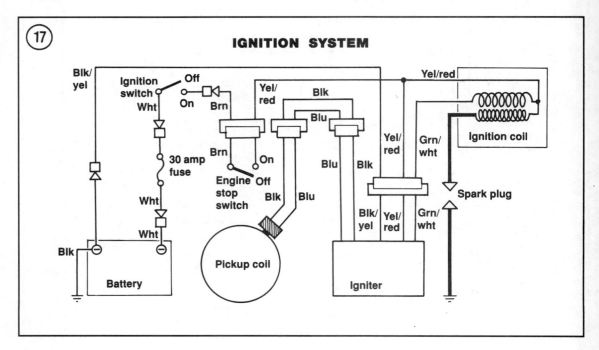

IGNITION SYSTEM

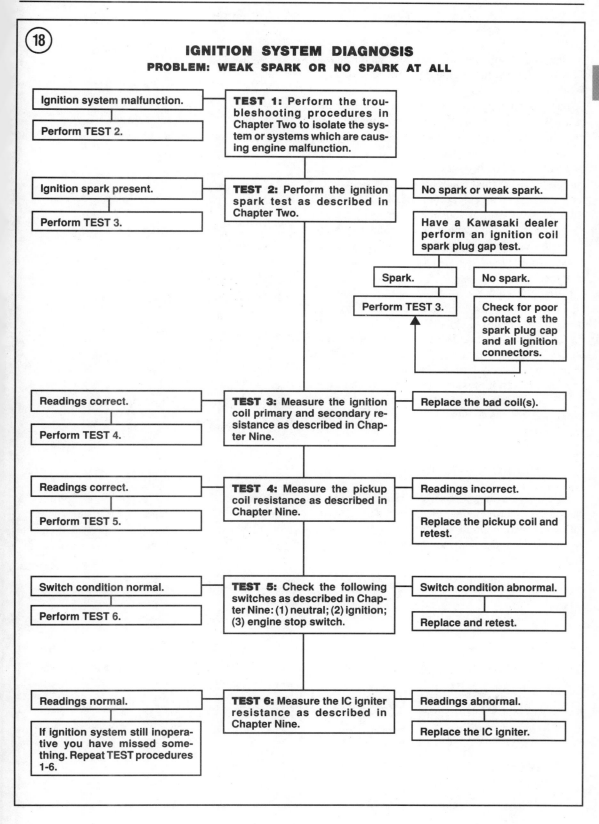

(18)

IGNITION SYSTEM DIAGNOSIS
PROBLEM: WEAK SPARK OR NO SPARK AT ALL

| Ignition system malfunction. | **TEST 1:** Perform the troubleshooting procedures in Chapter Two to isolate the system or systems which are causing engine malfunction. | |
| Perform TEST 2. | | |

| Ignition spark present. | **TEST 2:** Perform the ignition spark test as described in Chapter Two. | No spark or weak spark. |
| Perform TEST 3. | | Have a Kawasaki dealer perform an ignition coil spark plug gap test. |

Spark. | No spark.

Perform TEST 3. | Check for poor contact at the spark plug cap and all ignition connectors.

| Readings correct. | **TEST 3:** Measure the ignition coil primary and secondary resistance as described in Chapter Nine. | Replace the bad coil(s). |
| Perform TEST 4. | | |

| Readings correct. | **TEST 4:** Measure the pickup coil resistance as described in Chapter Nine. | Readings incorrect. |
| Perform TEST 5. | | Replace the pickup coil and retest. |

| Switch condition normal. | **TEST 5:** Check the following switches as described in Chapter Nine: (1) neutral; (2) ignition; (3) engine stop switch. | Switch condition abnormal. |
| Perform TEST 6. | | Replace and retest. |

| Readings normal. | **TEST 6:** Measure the IC igniter resistance as described in Chapter Nine. | Readings abnormal. |
| If ignition system still inoperative you have missed something. Repeat TEST procedures 1-6. | | Replace the IC igniter. |

2

FUEL SYSTEM

Many riders automatically assume that the carburetor is at fault if the engine does not run properly. While fuel system problems are not uncommon, carburetor adjustment is seldom the answer. In many cases, adjusting the carburetor only compounds the problem by making the engine run worse.

Fuel system troubleshooting should start at the fuel tank and work through the system, reserving the carburetor as the final point. Most fuel system problems result from an empty fuel tank, a plugged fuel filter or fuel valve, or sour fuel. Fuel system troubleshooting is covered thoroughly under *Engine Is Difficult To Start, Poor Idle Speed Performance and Poor Medium and High Speed Performance* in this chapter.

Carburetor chokes can also present problems. A choke stuck open will show up as a hard starting problem; one that sticks closed will result in a flooding condition. Check choke operation by moving the choke lever (A, **Figure 3**) by hand.. The choke should move freely without binding or sticking in one position. If necessary, remove the choke as described under *Carburetor Disassembly* in Chapter Eight and inspect its plunger and spring for severe wear or damage.

ENGINE OVERHEATING

Engine overheating is a serious problem in that it can quickly cause engine seizure and damage. The following section groups 5 main systems with probable causes that can lead to engine overheating.

1. *Ignition system*—check for:

a. Incorrect spark plug gap.

b. Incorrect spark plug heat range; see Chapter Three.

c. Faulty IC ignitor unit/incorrect ignition timing.

2. *Engine compression system*—check for:

a. Cylinder head gasket leakage.

b. Heavy carbon buildup in combustion chamber.

3. *Engine lubrication system*—check for:

a. Incorrect oil level.

b. Incorrect oil viscosity.

c. Faulty oil pump.

d. Plugged oil line.

4. *Fuel system*—check for:

a. Clogged air filter element.

b. Carburetor fuel level too low.

c. Incorrect carburetor adjustment or jetting.

d. Loose carburetor hose clamps.

e. Leaking or damaged carburetor-to-air filter housing air boot.

5. *Engine load*—check for:

a. Dragging brake(s).

b. Damaged drive train components.

c. Slipping clutch.

ENGINE

Engine problems are generally symptoms of something wrong in another system, such as ignition, fuel or starting systems. If properly maintained and serviced, the engine should experience no problems other than those caused by age and wear.

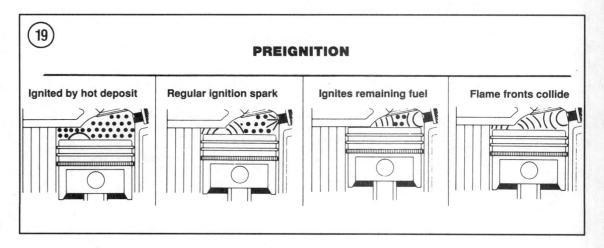

(19)

PREIGNITION

| Ignited by hot deposit | Regular ignition spark | Ignites remaining fuel | Flame fronts collide |

Preignition

Preignition is the premature burning of fuel and is caused by hot spots in the combustion chamber (**Figure 19**). The fuel ignites before it is supposed to. Glowing deposits in the combustion chamber, inadequate cooling or an overheated spark plug can all cause preignition. This is first noticed as a power loss but will eventually result in extensive damage to the internal parts of the engine because of excessive combustion chamber temperatures.

Detonation

Commonly called spark knock or fuel knock, detonation is the violent explosion of fuel in the combustion chamber instead of the controlled burn that takes place during normal combustion (**Figure 20**). Severe damage can result. Use of low octane gasoline is a common cause of detonation.

Even if using a high-octane gasoline, detonation can still occur. Other causes are over-advanced ignition timing, lean fuel mixture at or near full throttle, inadequate engine cooling, or the excessive accumulation of carbon deposits in the combustion chamber (causing higher than normal cylinder compression).

Power Loss

Several factors can cause a lack of power and speed. Look for a clogged air filter or a fouled or damaged spark plug. A piston or cylinder that is galled, incorrect piston clearance or worn or sticky piston rings may be responsible. Look for loose bolts, defective gaskets or leaking machined mating

surfaces on the cylinder head, cylinder or crankcase. On 1988 and later models, check for a stuck or damaged compression release lever.

Piston Seizure

This is caused by incorrect bore clearance, piston rings with an improper end gap, compression leak, incorrect engine oil, spark plug of the wrong heat range, incorrect ignition timing or lubrication system failure. Overheating from any cause can result in piston seizure.

Piston Slap

Piston slap is an audible slapping or rattling noise resulting from excessive piston-to-cylinder clearance. When allowed to continue, piston slap will eventually cause the piston skirt to shatter.

To prevent piston slap, clean the air filter on a regular schedule. If you hear piston slap, disassemble the engine top end and measure the cylinder bore and piston diameter. Replace parts that exceed their wear limit or show damage.

ENGINE NOISES

1. *Knocking or pinging during acceleration*—Can be caused by using a lower octane fuel than recommended or a poor grade of fuel. Incorrect carburetor jetting and a too hot spark plug can cause pinging. Refer to *Correct Spark Plug Heat Range* in Chapter Three. Check also for excessive carbon buildup in the combustion chamber or a faulty IC Igniter unit.

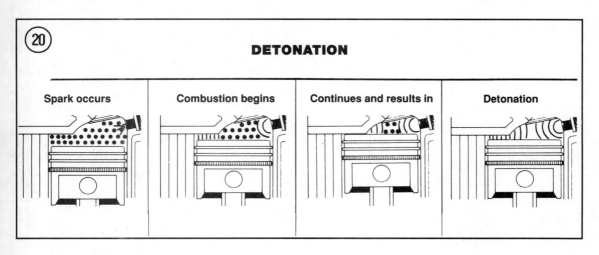

(20) **DETONATION**

| Spark occurs | Combustion begins | Continues and results in | Detonation |

2. *Slapping or rattling noises at low speed or during acceleration*—Can be caused by piston slap from excessive piston-cylinder wall clearance. Check also for a bent connecting rod or worn piston pin and/or piston pin bore in the piston.

3. *Knocking or rapping while decelerating*—Usually caused by excessive rod bearing clearance.

4. *Persistent knocking and vibration or other noise*—Usually caused by worn main bearings. If the main bearings are okay, consider the following:

   a. Loose engine mounts.
   b. Cracked frame.
   c. Leaking cylinder head gasket.
   d. Exhaust pipe leakage at cylinder head.
   e. Stuck piston ring.
   f. Broken piston ring.
   g. Partial engine seizure.
   h. Excessive small end connecting rod bearing clearance.
   i. Excessive connecting rod big end side clearance.
   j. Excessive crankshaft runout.
   k. Worn or damaged primary drive gear.

5. *Rapid on-off squeal*—Compression leak around cylinder head gasket or spark plug.

ENGINE LEAK DOWN TEST

Certain engine problems (leaking valve, broken, worn or stuck piston rings) can be isolated by performing a cylinder leak down test. A cylinder leakage test is performed by applying compressed air to the cylinder and then measuring the percent of leakage. A cylinder leakage tester and an air compressor are required to perform this test (**Figure 21**).

Follow the tester manufacturer's directions along with the following information when performing a cylinder leak down test.

1. Start and run the engine until it reaches normal operating temperature. Then turn off the engine.

2. Remove the air filter assembly. Open and secure the throttle so that it is at its wide-open position.

3. Set the piston for the cylinder being tested to TDC on its compression stroke. See *Valve Clearance Check and Adjustment* in Chapter Three.

4. Remove the spark plug.

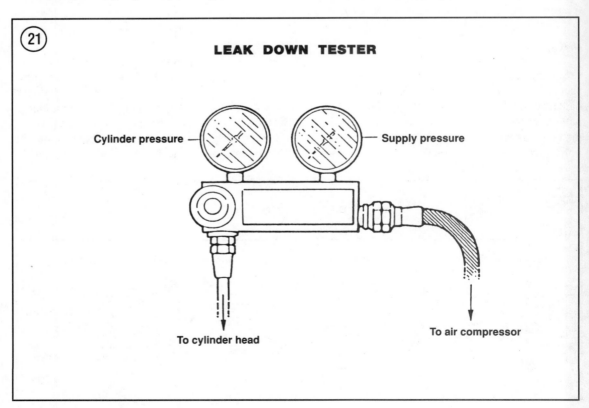

(21)

LEAK DOWN TESTER

Cylinder pressure

Supply pressure

To cylinder head

To air compressor

NOTE
The engine may turn over when air pressure is applied to the cylinder. To prevent this from happening, shift the transmission into fifth gear and set the parking brake.

5. Install the leak down tester into the cylinder spark plug hole.

6. Make a cylinder leak down test following the tester manufacturer's instructions. Listen for air leaking while noting the following:

   a. Air leaking through the exhaust pipe points to a leaking exhaust valve.

   b. Air leaking through the carburetor points to a leaking intake valve.

   c. Air leaking through the crankcase breather tube indicates worn piston rings.

7. Any cylinder with 10 percent (or more) cylinder leakage requires further service.

CLUTCH

The 2 basic clutch troubles are:

a. Clutch slipping.

b. Clutch dragging.

All clutch troubles, except adjustments, require partial engine disassembly to identify and cure the problem. Refer to Chapter Six for procedures.

Clutch Slipping

1. *Clutch wear or damage*—check the following:

   a. Loose, weak or damaged clutch springs (secondary clutch).

   b. Worn friction plates (secondary clutch).

   c. Warped steel plates (secondary clutch).

   d. Severely worn clutch hub and/or clutch housing (secondary clutch).

   e. Incorrectly assembled clutch.

   f. Incorrect clutch adjustment.

   g. Severely worn shoe linings or clutch housing (primary clutch).

2. *Engine oil*—check for the following:

   a. Low oil level.

   b. Oil additives.

   c. Low viscosity oil.

Clutch Dragging

1. *Clutch wear or damage*—check the following:

   a. Warped steel plates (secondary clutch).

   b. Swollen friction plates (secondary clutch).

   c. Warped pressure plate (secondary clutch).

   d. Incorrect clutch spring tension (secondary clutch).

   e. Weak or damaged clutch shoe spring (primary clutch).

   f. Incorrectly assembled clutch.

   g. Loose clutch nut.

   h. Burnt primary driven gear bushing.

   i. Damaged clutch boss.

   j. Incorrect clutch adjustment.

2. *Engine oil*—check for the following:

   a. Oil level too high.

   b. High viscosity oil.

TRANSMISSION

The basic transmission troubles are:

a. Difficult shifting.

b. Gears pop out of mesh.

Transmission symptoms can be hard to distinguish from clutch symptoms. Be sure that the clutch is not causing the trouble before working on the transmission.

Difficult Shifting

If the shift shaft does not move smoothly from one gear to the next, check the following.

1. *Shift shaft*—check the following:

   a. Incorrectly installed shift lever.

   b. Stripped shift lever-to-shift shaft splines.

   c. Bent shift shaft.

   d. Damaged shift shaft return spring.

   e. Shift shaft damaged where it engages the shift drum.

   f. Loose shift return spring pin.

   g. Shift drum positioning lever binding on pivot bolt.

2. *Stopper lever*—check the following:

   a. Seized or damaged stopper lever roller.

   b. Broken stopper lever spring.

   c. Loose stopper lever mounting bolt.

3. *Shift drum and shift forks*—check the following:

   a. Bent shift fork(s).

   b. Damaged shift fork guide pin(s).

c. Seized shift fork (on shaft).

d. Broken shift fork or shift fork shaft.

e. Damaged shift drum groove(s).

f. Damaged shift drum bearing.

Gears Pop Out Of Mesh

If the transmission shifts into gear but then slips or pops out, check the following:
1. *Shift shaft*—check the following:
   a. Incorrect shift lever position/adjustment.
   b. Stopper lever fails to move or set properly.
2. *Shift drum*—check the following:
   a. Incorrect thrust play.
   b. Severely worn or damaged shift drum groove(s).
3. Bent shift fork(s).
4. *Transmission*—check the following:
   a. Worn or damaged gear dogs.
   b. Excessive gear thrust play.
   c. Worn or damaged shaft circlips or thrust washers.

Transmission Overshifts

If the transmission overshifts when shifting up or down, check the following:
1. Check for a weak or broken shift mechanism arm spring.
2. Check for a weak or broken shift drum positioning lever.

Inoperative Reverse

If the transmission fails to go into or operate in reverse, check the following:
1. *Reverse lever*—check the following:
   a. Incorrect reverse lever adjustment. See *Reverse Cable Adjustment* in Chapter Seven.
   b. Stripped reverse lever-to-reverse shift drum splines.
2. *Reverse axle*—check the following:
   a. Damaged reverse axle pinion gear thrust play.
   b. Excessive reverse axle pinion gear play.
3. *Counter axle*—check for damaged counter axle gear bearings or shaft.
4. *Reverse shift drum and fork*—check the following:
   a. Damaged reverse shift drum groove.
   b. Bent reverse shift fork.

DRIVE TRAIN NOISE

This section deals with noises restricted to the final drive assembly, clutch and transmission. While some drive train noises have little meaning, abnormal noises are a good indicator of a developing problem. The problem is recognizing the difference between a normal and abnormal noise. One thing that is in your favor, however, is that by maintaining and riding your Kawasaki, you become accustomed to the normal noises that occur during engine starting and when riding. A new noise, no matter how minor, should be investigated.

1A. *Drive train noise on 2-wheel drive models*—Any noise that develops in the rear final drive unit should be investigated. First drain the drive unit oil, checking for bits of metal or other material. Check for the following conditions:
   a. Incorrect bevel gear adjustment.
   b. Worn or chipped bevel gears.
   c. Worn or damaged bevel gear bearings.
   d. Worn or damaged propeller shaft bearing.

1B. *Drive train noise on 4-wheel drive models*—Investigate any noise that develops in the front or rear final drive units. First, drain the drive unit oil, checking for bits of metal or other material. Check for the following conditions:
   a. Worn or damaged bevel gear bearings.
   b. Incorrect bevel gear adjustment.
   c. Worn or chipped bevel gears.
   d. Worn clutch friction plate(s) (front final drive).
   e. Worn clutch spring (front final drive).
   f. Damaged side gears or pinions in differential unit (front final drive).
   g. Incorrect type of oil (front final drive).
   h. Incorrect thrust plug adjustment (rear final drive).

NOTE
If there is excessive noise coming from the front axle(s) or propeller shaft, check the constant velocity joint for severe wear or damage.

2. *Clutch noise*—Investigate any noise that develops in the clutch. First, drain the clutch/transmission oil, checking for bits of metal or clutch plate material. If the oil looks and smells okay, remove the clutch cover and clutch (Chapter Six) and check for the following:
   a. Worn or damaged clutch housing gear teeth.
   b. Excessive clutch housing axial play.

c. Excessive clutch housing-to-friction plate clearance.

d. Excessive clutch housing gear-to-primary drive gear backlash.

3. *Transmission noise*—The transmission will exhibit more normal noises than the clutch, but like the clutch, a new noise in the transmission should be investigated. Drain the clutch/transmission oil into a clean container. Wipe a small amount of oil on a finger and rub the finger and thumb together. Check for the presence of metallic particles. Inspect the drain container for signs of water separation from the oil. Transmission associated noises can be caused by:

a. Insufficient transmission oil level.

b. Contaminated transmission oil.

c. Transmission oil viscosity too thin. A too thin oil viscosity will raise the transmission operating temperature.

d. Worn transmission gear(s).

e. Chipped or broken transmission gear(s).

f. Excessive transmission gear side play.

g. Worn or damaged crankshaft-to-transmission bearing(s).

HANDLING

Poor handling will reduce overall performance and may cause you to crash. If you are experiencing poor handling, check the following items:

1. If the handlebars are hard to turn, check for the following:

a. Low tire pressure.

b. Damaged tie rod end.

c. Damaged steering knuckle joint.

d. Bent steering shaft.

e. Damaged steering shaft bearings.

f. Incorrect clutch adjustment in front final gear case (4-wheel drive).

2. If there is excessive handlebar shake or vibration, check for the following:

a. Worn tires.

b. Damaged wheel rim(s).

c. Loose steering shaft.

d. Excessive rear axle(s) runout.

e. Worn wheel bearing(s).

3. If the handlebar pulls to one side, check for the following:

a. Bent tie rod.

b. Bent steering shaft.

c. Bent suspension arm.

d. Damaged rim(s).

e. Bent frame.

f. Incorrect tire air pressure.

g. Damaged shock absorber.

h. Incorrect toe-in adjustment.

4. If there is excessive noise when turning a 4-wheel model, check for the following in the front final drive housing:

a. Worn clutch friction plates.

b. Worn clutch spring.

c. Damaged side gear or pinion.

5. Shock absorbers—check the following:

a. Damaged damper rod.

b. Leaking damper housing.

c. Sagging shock spring(s).

d. Incorrect shock adjustment.

e. Loose or damaged shock mount bolts.

6. Frame—check the following:

a. Damaged frame.

b. Cracked or broken engine mount brackets.

FRAME NOISE

Noises traced to the frame or suspension are usually caused by loose, worn or damaged parts. Various noises that are related to the frame are listed below:

1. *Disc brake noise*—A screeching sound during braking is the most common disc brake noise. Some other disc brake associated noises can be caused by:

a. Glazed brake pad surface.

b. Severely worn brake pads.

c. Warped brake disc.

d. Loose brake disc mounting bolts.

e. Loose or missing caliper mounting bolts.

f. Damaged caliper.

2. *Drum brake noise*—Check for the following:

a. Overheated brakes.

b. Grease or oil on drum and lining.

c. Uneven or scored drum surface.

3. *Rear shock absorber noise*—Check for the following:

a. Loose shock absorber mounting bolts.

b. Cracked or broken shock spring.

c. Damaged shock absorber.

4. Some other frame associated noises can be caused by:

a. Broken frame.

b. Broken suspension arms.

c. Loose engine mounting bolts.
d. Damaged steering bearings.
e. Loose mounting bracket(s).

BRAKES

The front and rear brake units are critical to riding performance and safety. Inspect the brake frequently and repair any problem immediately. When replacing or refilling the brake fluid, use only DOT 3 brake fluid from a closed and sealed container. See Chapter Thirteen for additional information on brake fluid selection and disc brake service. The troubleshooting procedures in **Figure 22** (drum) and **Figure 23** (disc) will help you isolate the majority of disc brake troubles.

When checking brake pad wear, check that the brake pads in each caliper contact the disc squarely. If one of the brake pads is wearing unevenly, suspect a warped or bent brake disc or damaged caliper.

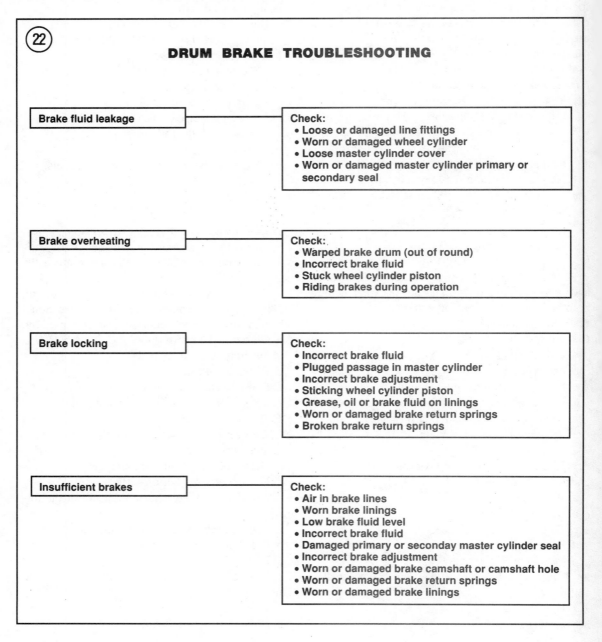

22

DRUM BRAKE TROUBLESHOOTING

Brake fluid leakage

Check:
- Loose or damaged line fittings
- Worn or damaged wheel cylinder
- Loose master cylinder cover
- Worn or damaged master cylinder primary or secondary seal

Brake overheating

Check:
- Warped brake drum (out of round)
- Incorrect brake fluid
- Stuck wheel cylinder piston
- Riding brakes during operation

Brake locking

Check:
- Incorrect brake fluid
- Plugged passage in master cylinder
- Incorrect brake adjustment
- Sticking wheel cylinder piston
- Grease, oil or brake fluid on linings
- Worn or damaged brake return springs
- Broken brake return springs

Insufficient brakes

Check:
- Air in brake lines
- Worn brake linings
- Low brake fluid level
- Incorrect brake fluid
- Damaged primary or seconday master cylinder seal
- Incorrect brake adjustment
- Worn or damaged brake camshaft or camshaft hole
- Worn or damaged brake return springs
- Worn or damaged brake linings

(23)

DISC BRAKE TROUBLESHOOTING

Disc brake fluid leakage

Check:
- Loose or damaged line fittings
- Worn caliper piston seals
- Scored caliper piston and/or bore
- Loose banjo bolts
- Damaged washers
- Leaking master cylinder diaphragm
- Leaking master cylinder secondary seal
- Cracked master cylinder housing
- Too high brake fluid level
- Loose master cylinder cover

Brake overheating

Check:
- Warped brake disc
- Incorrect brake fluid
- Caliper piston and/or brake pads hanging up
- Riding brakes during operation

Brake chatter

Check:
- Warped brake disc
- Loose brake disc
- Incorrect caliper alignment
- Loose caliper mounting bolts
- Loose front axle nut and/or clamps
- Worn wheel bearings
- Damaged front hub
- Restricted brake hydraulic line
- Contaminated brake pads

Brake locking

Check:
- Incorrect brake fluid
- Plugged passages in master cylinder
- Incorrect front brake adjustment
- Caliper piston and/or brake pads hanging up
- Warped brake disc

Insufficient brakes

Check:
- Air in brake lines
- Worn brake pads
- Low brake fluid level
- Incorrect brake fluid
- Worn brake disc
- Worn caliper piston seals
- Glazed brake pads
- Leaking primary cup seal in master cylinder
- Contaminated brake pads and/or disc

Brake squeal

Check:
- Contaminated brake pads and/or disc
- Dust or dirt collected behind brake pads
- Loose parts

2

LUBRICATION, MAINTENANCE AND TUNE-UP

Your Kawasaki requires periodic maintenance so it can operate efficiently without breaking down. This chapter covers all of the regular maintenance required to keep your Kawasaki in top shape. Regular maintenance is something you cannot afford to ignore. Neglecting regular maintenance will reduce the engine life and performance of your Kawasaki.

This chapter explains lubrication, maintenance and tune-up procedures required for the models covered in this manual. **Table 1** is a suggested maintenance schedule. **Tables 1-8** are at the end of the chapter.

> *NOTE*
> *Due to the number of models and years covered in this book, be sure to follow the correct procedure and specifications for your specific model and year. Also use the correct quantity and type of fluid as indicated in the tables.*

PRE-RIDE CHECKLIST

The following checks should be performed prior to the first ride of the day.

1. Inspect all fuel lines and fittings for leakage.
2. Make sure the fuel tank is full of fresh gasoline.
3. Make sure the engine oil level is correct; add oil if necessary.
4. Make sure the air filter is clean.
5. Check the throttle and the brake levers. Make sure they operate properly with no binding.
6. Check the brake fluid level in the front master cylinder reservoir; add DOT 3 brake fluid if necessary.
7. Check parking brake operation.
8. Check rear brake free play as described in this chapter.
9. Inspect the front and rear suspension; make sure it has a good solid feel with no looseness.
10. Check front (4-wheel drive) and rear final drive units for oil leakage.
11. Check tire pressure; refer to **Table 2** .
12. Check the exhaust system for looseness or damage.
13. Check the tightness of all fasteners, especially engine mounting hardware.
14. Make sure the headlight(s) and taillight work.
15. Turn handlebar from side-to-side to check steering play. Service steering assembly if excessive play is noted. Check also that handlebar control cables do not bind.
16. Start the engine, then stop it with the engine stop switch. If engine stop switch does not work properly,

test switch as described under *Switches* in Chapter Nine.

SERVICE INTERVALS

The services and intervals shown in **Table 1** are recommended by the factory. Strict adherence to these recommendations will ensure long service from your Kawasaki. However, if the vehicle is run in an area of high humidity, the lubrication and services must be done more frequently to prevent possible rust and corrosion damage. This is especially true if running the vehicle through water (especially saltwater) and sand. For convenience when maintaining your vehicle, most of the services shown in **Table 1** are described in this chapter. However, some procedures which require more than minor disassembly or adjustment are covered elsewhere in the appropriate chapter.

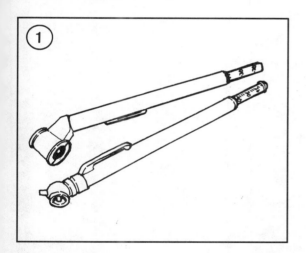

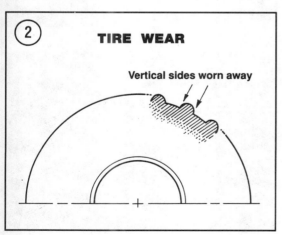

TIRES AND WHEELS

Tire Pressure

Tire pressure should be checked and adjusted to maintain the smoothness of the tire, to ensure good traction and handling and to get the maximum life out of the tire. A simple, accurate gauge (**Figure 1**) can be purchased for a few dollars and should be carried in your tool box. The appropriate tire pressures are listed in **Table 2**. Check tire pressure when the tires are cold.

> *NOTE*
> *The tire pressure specifications listed in **Table 2** are for the stock tires that originally come equipped on your Kawasaki. If you have installed different tires, follow the tire pressure recommendations specified by the tire manufacturer.*

> *WARNING*
> *Always inflate both tire sets (front and rear) to the correct air pressure. If the vehicle is run with unequal air pressures, the vehicle will run toward one side, causing poor handling.*

> *CAUTION*
> *Do not overinflate the stock tires as they will be permanently distorted and damaged. Overinflated tires will bulge out along the rim. If this happens, the tire will not return to its original contour.*

Tire Inspection

The tires take a lot of punishment due to the variety of terrain they are subject to. Inspect them periodically for excessive wear, cuts, abrasions, etc. If you find a nail or other object in the tire, mark its location with a light crayon prior to removing it. This will help locate the hole for repair. Refer to Chapter Ten for tire changing and repair information.

To gauge tire wear, inspect the shape of the tread knobs. If the drive knob vertical sides (**Figure 2**) are worn away, replace the tire as described in Chapter Ten. Kawasaki does not list minimum tire tread depth measurements.

> *WARNING*
> *Do not ride your vehicle with damaged or severely worn tires. Tires in these conditions can cause you to lose con-*

trol. Replace damaged or severely worn tires immediately.

Rim Inspection

Frequently inspect the condition of the wheel rims, especially the outer side (**Figure 3**). If the wheel has hit a tree or large rock, rim damage may be sufficient to cause an air leak or knock it out of alignment. Improper wheel alignment can cause severe vibration and result in an unsafe riding condition.

Make sure the wheel nuts (**Figure 3**) are securely in place on all wheels. If they are loose, the wheel could damage the hub studs or fall off. Tighten wheel nuts to the torque specification listed in **Table 3**.

BATTERY

The battery is an important component in the ATV electrical system, yet most electrical system troubles can be traced to battery neglect. In addition to checking and correcting the battery electrolyte level on a weekly basis, the battery should be cleaned and inspected at periodic intervals. Battery capacity is listed in **Table 4**.

> *NOTE*
> *Recycle your old battery. When you replace the old battery, be sure to turn it in at that time. The lead plates and the plastic case can be recycled. Most ATV dealers will accept your old battery in trade when you purchase a new one. Never place an old battery in your household trash since it is illegal, in most states, to place any acid or lead (heavy metal) contents in landfills. There is also the danger of the battery being crushed in the trash truck and spraying acid on the truck or landfill operator.*

Safety Precautions

When working with batteries, use extreme care to avoid spilling or splashing the electrolyte. This solution contains sulfuric acid, which can ruin clothing and cause serious chemical burns. If any electrolyte is spilled or splashed on clothing or skin, immedi-

ately neutralize it with a solution of baking soda and water, then flush with an abundance of clean water.

> *WARNING*
> *Electrolyte splashed into the eyes is extremely harmful. Safety glasses should always be worn while working with batteries. If you get electrolyte in your eyes, call a physician immediately. Then, force your eyes open and flood them with cool, clean water for approximately 15 minutes or until medical help arrives.*

If electrolyte is spilled or splashed onto any surface, it should be immediately neutralized with a baking soda and water solution and then rinsed with clean water.

While batteries are being charged, highly explosive hydrogen gas forms in each cell. Some of this gas escapes through filler cap openings and may form an explosive atmosphere in and around the battery. This condition can persist for several hours. Sparks, an open flame or a lit cigarette can ignite the gas, causing an explosion and possible serious personal injury.

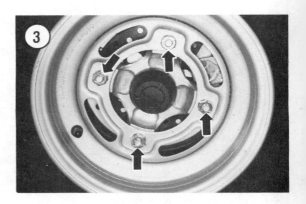

Note the following precautions to prevent an explosion:

1. Do not smoke or permit any open flame near a battery being charged or which has been recently charged.

2. Do not disconnect live circuits at battery terminals since a spark usually occurs when a live circuit is broken.

3. Take care when connecting or disconnecting any battery charger. Be sure its power switch is off before making or breaking connections. Poor connections are a common cause of electrical arcs which cause explosions.

4. Keep children and pets away from charging equipment and batteries. For maximum battery life, it should be checked periodically for electrolyte level, state of charge and corrosion. During hot weather periods, frequent checks are recommended. If the electrolyte level is below the bottom of the vent well in one or more cells, add distilled water as required. To assure proper mixing of the water and acid, operate the engine immediately after adding water. Never add battery acid instead of water as this will shorten the battery's life.

On all models covered in this manual, the negative side is grounded. When removing the battery, disconnect the negative (–) cable first, then the positive (+) cable. This minimizes the chance of a tool shorting to ground when disconnecting the battery positive cable.

WARNING
When performing the following procedures, protect your eyes, skin and clothing. If electrolyte gets into your eyes,

flush your eyes thoroughly with clean water and get prompt medical attention.

Battery Removal

The battery is mounted underneath the seat. A hold-down strap, placed across the battery, and a rubber pad mounted inside the battery box, hold the battery in place.

1. Remove the seat.
2. Disconnect the negative battery cable from the battery (A, **Figure 4**).
3. Disconnect the positive battery cable from the battery (B, **Figure 4**).
4. Disconnect the battery hold down strap. Then lift the battery slightly and disconnect the battery vent hose from the battery and remove the battery.

CAUTION
Be careful not to spill battery electrolyte on painted or polished surfaces. The liquid is highly corrosive and will damage the finish. If it is spilled, wash it off immediately with soapy water and thoroughly rinse with clean water.

Cleaning and Inspection

1. Inspect the battery pads in the battery box for contamination or damage. Clean with a solution of baking soda and water.
2. Check the entire battery case (**Figure 5**) for cracks or other damage. If the battery case is warped, discolored or has a raised top, the battery has overcharged or overheated.
3. Check the battery hold-down strap for acid damage, cracks or other damage. Replace if damaged.
4. Check the battery terminal bolts, spacers and nuts for corrosion or damage. Clean parts thoroughly with a solution of baking soda and water. Replace severely corroded or damaged parts.

NOTE
Keep cleaning solution out of the battery cells or the electrolyte level will be seriously weakened.

5. Clean the top of the battery with a stiff bristle brush using the baking soda and water solution.
6. Check the battery cable clamps for corrosion and damage. If corrosion is minor, clean the battery cable

clamps with a stiff wire brush. Replace severely worn or damaged cables.

NOTE
Do not overfill the battery cells in Step 7. The electrolyte expands due to heat from charging and will overflow if the level is above the upper level line.

7. Remove the caps (**Figure 6**) from the battery cells and check the electrolyte level. Add distilled water, if necessary, to bring the level within the upper and lower level lines on the battery case (**Figure 5**).

Battery Installation

1. Reinstall the battery into the battery compartment with the terminals facing as shown in **Figure 4**. Make sure the rubber pad is installed in the battery box prior to installing the battery.
2. Reconnect the battery vent hose to the battery while sliding the battery into position.

NOTE
*For further information on vent hose routing, refer to the Battery Vent Hose Routing decal mounted on the rear fender (**Figure 7**).*

WARNING
After installing the battery, make sure the vent hose is not pinched. A pinched

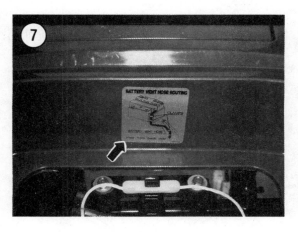

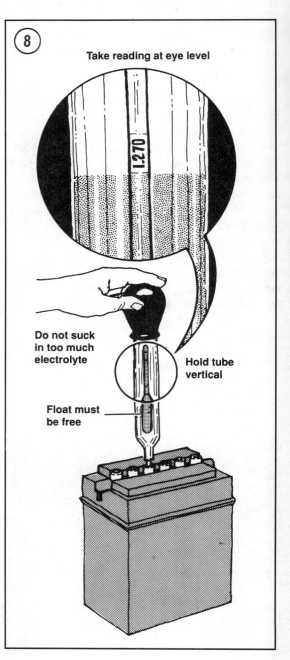

*or kinked hose would allow high pres-
sure to accumulate in the battery and
cause electrolyte to overflow. If the vent
hose is damaged, replace it.*

3. Install and tighten the positive battery cable (B,
Figure 4).

4. Install and tighten the negative battery cable (A,
Figure 4).

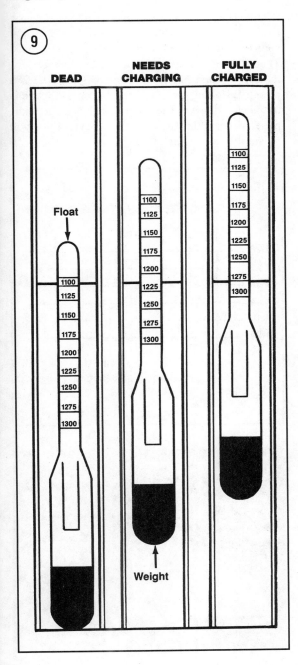

*CAUTION
Be sure the battery cables are connected
to their proper terminals. Connecting
the battery backward will reverse the
polarity and damage the rectifier.*

5. Coat the battery connections with dielectric
grease or petroleum jelly.

6. Secure the battery hold-down strap across the top
of the battery.

7. Install the seat.

Battery Testing

Hydrometer testing is the best way to check battery condition. Use a hydrometer with numbered
graduations from 1.100 to 1.300 rather than one with
just color-coded bands. To use the hydrometer,
squeeze the rubber ball, insert the tip into the cell
and release the ball (**Figure 8**).

*NOTE
Do not attempt to test a battery with a
hydrometer immediately after adding
water to the cells. Charge the battery for
15-20 minutes at a rate high enough to
cause vigorous gassing and allow the
water and electrolyte to mix thoroughly.*

Draw enough electrolyte to float the weighted
float inside the hydrometer. When using a temperature-compensated hydrometer, release the electrolyte and repeat this process several times to make
sure the thermometer has adjusted to the electrolyte
temperature before taking the reading.

Hold the hydrometer vertically and note the number aligned with the surface of the electrolyte (**Figure 9**). This is the specific gravity for this cell.
Return the electrolyte to the cell from which it came
The specific gravity of the electrolyte in each battery
cell is an excellent indication of that cell's condition
(**Table 5**). A fully charged cell will read 1.260-1.280
while a cell in acceptable condition reads from
1.230-1.250 and anything below 1.220 is weak.
Charging is also necessary if the specific gravity
varies more than 0.050 from cell to cell.

*NOTE
If a temperature-compensated hydrometer is not used, add 0.004 to the
specific gravity reading for every 10°
above 80° F (25° C). For every 10°
below 80° F (25° C), subtract 0.004.*

Charging

A good state of charge should be maintained in batteries used for starting. When charging the battery, note the following:

   a. During charging, the cells will show signs of gas bubbling. If one cell has no gas bubbles or if its specific gravity is low, the cell is probably shorted.

   b. If a battery not in use loses its charge within a week after charging or if the specific gravity drops quickly, the battery is defective. A good battery should only self-discharge approximately 1% each day.

> *CAUTION*
> *Always remove the battery from the vehicle before connecting charging equipment.*

> *WARNING*
> *During charging, highly explosive hydrogen gas is released from the battery. The battery should be charged only in a well-ventilated area, and open flames and cigarettes should be kept away. Never check the charge of the battery by arcing across the terminals; the resulting spark can ignite the hydrogen gas.*

1. Remove the battery from the vehicle as described in this chapter.

2. Connect the positive (+) charger lead to the positive battery terminal and the negative (–) charger lead to the negative battery terminal.

3. Remove all vent caps (**Figure 6**) from the battery, set the charger at 12 volts, and switch it on. Normally, a battery should be charged at a slow charge rate of 1/10 its given capacity. Refer to **Table 4** for battery capacity specifications.

> *CAUTION*
> *The electrolyte level must be maintained at the upper level during the charging cycle; check and refill with distilled water as necessary.*

4. The charging time depends on the discharged condition of the battery. The chart in **Figure 10** can be used to determine approximate charging times at different specific gravity readings. For example, if the specific gravity of your battery is 1.180, the approximate charging time would be 6 hours.

5. After the battery has charged for the predetermined time, turn the charger off, disconnect the leads and check the specific gravity. It should be within 1.275 and 1.280. If it is, and remains stable for one hour, the battery is charged.

New Battery Installation

A new battery must be charged before installation in a new vehicle. New battery electrolyte is only at approximately 80% of its potential specific gravity. Therefore, after adding electrolyte to a new battery, it must be charged to specific gravity of 1.260-1.280 prior to installing it. Using a new battery without this initial charging will cause permanent damage to the battery, after which time, no amount of charging will regain its lost potential.

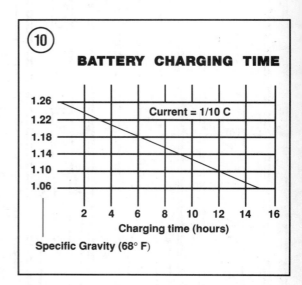

(10) BATTERY CHARGING TIME

Current = 1/10 C

Specific Gravity (68° F) — Charging time (hours)

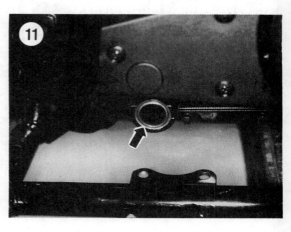

LUBRICANTS

Engine Oil

Oil is graded according to its viscosity, which is an indication of how thick it is. The Society of Automotive Engineers (SAE) distinguishes oil viscosity by numbers, called weights. Thick (heavy) oils have higher viscosity numbers than thin (light) oils. For example, a 5 weight (SAE 5) oil is a light oil while a 90 weight (SAE 90) oil is relatively heavy. The viscosity of the oil has nothing to do with its lubricating properties.

Grease

Waterproof grease should be used when grease is called for. Water does not wash grease off parts as easily as it washes off oil. In addition, grease maintains its lubricating qualities better than oil on long and strenuous events.

CLEANING SOLVENT

A number of solvents can be used to remove old dirt, grease, and oil. See your dealer or an auto parts store.

WARNING
Never use gasoline as a cleaning solvent. Gasoline is extremely volatile and contains tremendously destructive potential energy. The slightest spark from metal parts hitting each other, or a tool slipping, could cause a fatal explosion.

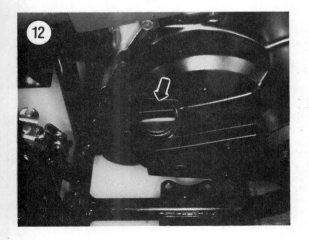

PERIODIC LUBRICATION

The services listed in this section should be performed at the maintenance intervals listed in **Table 1**. If the vehicle is exposed to harder than normal use with constant exposure to mud, water, sand, and high humidity, the services should be performed more frequently.

Engine Oil Level Check

Engine oil level is checked through the oil level gauge mounted in the lower right side of the clutch cover.

1. Start the engine and let it warm up approximately 2-3 minutes.

2. Park the vehicle on level ground and apply the parking brake.

3. Shut off the engine and let the oil settle.

4. View the oil level through the oil level gauge. The oil level should be between the upper and lower lines next to the gauge; see **Figure 11**.

5. If the oil level is low, remove the oil fill cap (**Figure 12**) and add the recommended grade and viscosity oil listed in **Table 5** to correct the level. Install the oil fill cap.

NOTE
Refer to Engine Oil and Filter Change in this chapter for additional information on oil selection.

6. If the oil level is too high, remove the oil fill cap (**Figure 12**) and suck out the excess oil with a syringe or suitable pump.

7. Recheck the oil level.

Engine Oil and Filter Change

Regular oil changes will contribute more to engine longevity than any other maintenance performed. The factory recommended oil and filter change is listed in **Table 1**. This assumes that the vehicle is operated in moderate climates. If it is operated under dusty conditions, the oil will get dirty more quickly and should be changed more frequently than recommended.

Use only a high quality detergent motor oil with an API rating of SF or SG. The quality rating is stamped or printed on top of the can or label on plastic bottles (**Figure 13**). Try to use the same brand of oil at each oil change. Refer to **Figure 14** for correct oil weight to use under anticipated ambient temperatures (not engine oil temperature).

To change the engine oil and filter you need the following:

   a. Drain pan.

   b. Funnel.

   c. Can opener or pour spout.

   d. Wrench and sockets

   e. 2-3 quarts of oil (see **Table 7**).

   f. New oil filter.

There are a number of ways to discard the old oil safely. Some service stations and oil retailers will accept your used oil for recycling; some may even give you money for it. Never drain the oil onto the ground.

NOTE
Never dispose of motor oil in the trash, on the ground, or down a storm drain. Many service stations accept used motor oil and

waste haulers provide curbside used motor oil collection. Do not combine other fluids with motor oil to be recycled. To locate a recycler, contact the American Petroleum Institute (API) at ***www.recycleoil.org***.

NOTE
Warming the engine allows the oil to heat up; thus it flows freely and carries

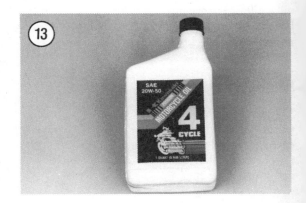

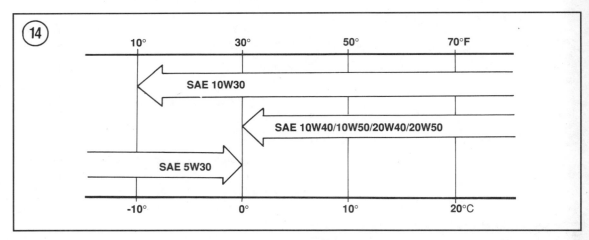

contamination and any sludge buildup out with it.

1. Start the engine and let it warm up approximately 2-3 minutes.
2. Place the vehicle on level ground and apply the parking brake.
3. Shut the engine off and place a drain pan under the engine.
4. If necessary, remove the skid plate.
5. Loosen the drain plug (**Figure 15**) mounted in the bottom of the engine. Then remove the drain plug and gasket.

6. Loosen the oil fill cap. This will speed up the flow of oil.
7. Allow the oil to drain completely.
8. To replace the oil filter, perform the following:
   a. Remove the oil filter cover (**Figure 16**) and its O-ring.
   b. Remove the oil filter and guide pin (**Figure 17**) from the filter cavity. Discard the oil filter.
   c. Thoroughly clean out the guide pin (**Figure 18**) and filter cavity. If necessary, scrape out any oil sludge.

NOTE
*The guide pin (**Figure 18**) is equipped with a bypass valve. To service the bypass valve, refer to **Bypass Valve Inspection** in this chapter.*

   d. Inspect the filter cover O-ring (**Figure 19**). Replace the O-ring if it has become hard or is starting to deteriorate.
   e. Lightly wipe both oil filter grommets (**Figure 20**) with clean engine oil.
   f. Insert the guide pin through the oil filter (**Figure 21**) and center it.

NOTE
*The guide pin is directional—one end is larger than the other (**Figure 18**). The*

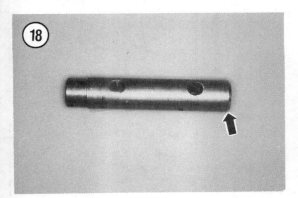

larger end seats in the crankcase filter cavity. The small end seats in the oil filter cover bore.

g. Insert the oil filter/guide pin into the crankcase so the larger guide pin O.D. seats into the crankcase filter cavity (**Figure 17**).

h. Apply a lithium soap base grease to the O-ring and install the O-ring into the oil filter cover groove.

i. Install the filter cover and O-ring—engage the end of the guide pin into the center of the filter cover.

NOTE
If you cannot install the oil filter cover, the guide pin is installed backward. Remove the oil filter and turn it around.

j. Install and tighten the filter cover mounting screws.

9. Replace the drain plug gasket if damaged or missing.

10. Install the drain plug (**Figure 15**) and its gasket. Tighten to the torque specification in **Table 3**.

11. If the engine oil was contaminated and/or the engine experienced overheating or other damage, remove and clean the oil screen (mounted behind the clutch cover) as described under *Oil Screen* in Chapter Five.

12. Insert a funnel into the oil fill hole and fill the engine with the correct weight (**Figure 14** and **Table 5**) and quantity oil. Refer to **Table 6** for refill capacity.

13. Remove the funnel and screw in the oil fill cap (**Figure 12**) securely.

NOTE
*If you are servicing a rebuilt engine, inspecting the lubrication system or replacing the external oil pipe assembly, check engine oil flow as described under **Engine Oil Flow Inspection** in this chapter.*

14. Start the engine and allow to idle.

15. Check the oil filter cover and drain plug for leaks.

16. Turn off the engine and allow the oil to settle. Then check the engine oil level as described in this chapter.

WARNING
Prolonged contact with oil may cause skin cancer. It is advisable to wash your hands thoroughly with soap and water as soon as possible after handling or coming in contact with motor oil.

Bypass Valve Inspection

A bypass valve, consisting of a spring and plunger, is installed in the guide pin (**Figure 22**). If the oil filter becomes clogged or damaged to where oil

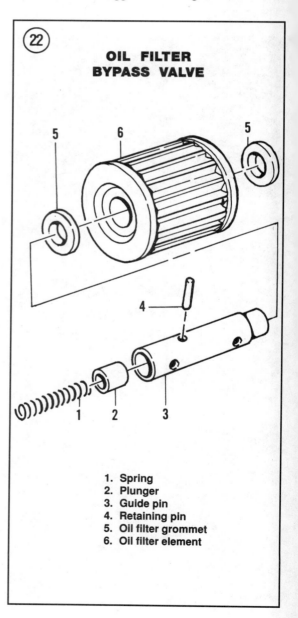

OIL FILTER BYPASS VALVE

1. Spring
2. Plunger
3. Guide pin
4. Retaining pin
5. Oil filter grommet
6. Oil filter element

oil cannot pass through it, pressure buildup in the filter will cause the bypass valve to open. This will allow engine oil to bypass the oil filter and go directly to the engine. While the bypass valve is designed to prevent engine damage, the unfiltered oil will cause rapid wear of all moving parts.

> *NOTE*
> *If you are only servicing the bypass valve, you do not have to drain the engine oil.*

1. Remove the oil filter and guide pin as described in this chapter.

2. Drive the retaining pin out of the guide pin.

3. Remove the spring and bypass valve plunger.

4. Clean all parts in solvent and dry thoroughly.

5. Check the plunger for severe wear or damage. If the plunger is worn, replace the bypass valve assembly.

6. Replace the spring if bent or distorted.

7. Install the bypass valve plunger, closed end first, into the guide pin (**Figure 22**).

8. Install the spring into the guide pin. Then compress the spring so it is beyond the retaining pin hole.

9. Drive the retaining pin into the small hole. The pin should be flush on both sides.

10. Install the oil filter and guide pin as described in this chapter.

Engine Oil Flow Inspection

Use this procedure to check engine oil flow. This procedure should be performed after reassembling the engine, when troubleshooting the lubrication system or if the external oil pipe is removed or replaced.

1. Check the engine oil level as described in this chapter.

2. Start the engine and allow to idle.

> *WARNING*
> *Oil passages deliver engine oil from the oil pump to engine components. Because the oil flowing through these passages is under pressure, do not increase engine speed above idle when checking oil flow in the following step; otherwise, the oil may squirt out and burn you.*

3. Loosen, but do not remove, the engine oil pipe banjo bolt mounted on the left-hand crankcase; see **Figure 23** (2-wheel drive) or **Figure 24** (4-wheel drive). Oil should seep out from around the bolt, indicating that the engine oil pressure is present.

4. Turn the engine off .

5. Tighten the banjo bolt to the torque specification in **Table 3**.

6. Wipe up the oil that seeped from the banjo bolt.

7. If there is no oil visible at the banjo bolt, remove and inspect the oil filter (this chapter) and the oil screen (Chapter Five). If these components are not at fault, inspect the oil pump and oil pipe as described in Chapter Five.

> *WARNING*
> *Prolonged contact with oil may cause skin cancer. It is advisable to wash your hands thoroughly with soap and water as soon as possible after handling or coming in contact with motor oil.*

Front Final Gear Case
(4-Wheel Drive)

When checking or changing the front final drive oil, do not allow any dirt or foreign matter to enter the case opening.

Oil level check

1. Park the vehicle on a level surface and set the parking brake. The vehicle must be level for a correct reading.
2. Wipe the area around the oil fill cap and unscrew the oil fill plug (**Figure 25**).
3. The oil level is correct if the oil is up to the bottom thread of the fill plug hole. If the oil level is low, add hypoid gear oil (**Table 5**) until the level is correct.
4. Inspect the oil fill plug O-ring. Replace the O-ring if it has become hard or is starting to deteriorate.
5. Screw on the oil fill plug and tighten to the torque specification in **Table 3**.

Oil change

The factory recommended oil change interval is listed in **Table 1**. Change the oil earlier if it becomes contaminated.

To drain the oil you need the following:
a. Drain pan.
b. Funnel.
c. Hypoid gear oil; see **Table 5** (oil type) and **Table 6** (oil quantity).

Discard old oil in the same manner as outlined under *Engine Oil Change* in this chapter.

> *NOTE*
> *A short ride allows the front final gear case oil to heat up; thus it flows freely and carries contamination and any sludge out with it.*

1. Ride the vehicle until normal operating temperature is reached.
2. Park the vehicle on a level surface and set the parking brake.
3. Remove the skid plate (**Figure 26**).
4. Place a drain pan underneath the drain bolt.
5. Remove the oil fill plug (**Figure 25**).
6. Remove the drain plug (**Figure 27**) and allow the oil to drain out.

7. Inspect the sealing gasket on the drain plug Replace if damaged or missing.
8. Install the drain plug (and gasket) and tighten to the torque specification in **Table 3**.
9. Insert a funnel into the fill plug hole and add the recommended type (**Table 5**) and quantity (**Table 6**) of gear oil.
10. Remove the funnel and check the oil level. It should come up to the bottom thread of the fill plug hole. Add additional oil if necessary.
11. Inspect the O-ring on the oil fill plug for wear or deterioration. Replace if necessary.

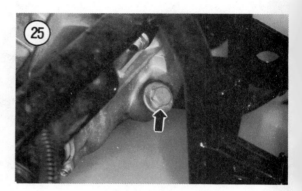

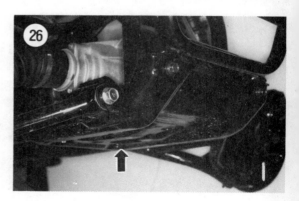

12. Screw on the oil fill plug (and O-ring) and tighten to the torque specification in **Table 3**.

13. Install the skid plate (**Figure 26**).

14. Test ride the vehicle and check for leaks. After the test ride recheck the oil level and adjust if necessary.

Rear Final Gear Case

When checking or changing the rear final drive oil, do not allow any dirt or foreign matter to enter the case opening.

Oil level check

1. Park the vehicle on a level surface and set the parking brake. The vehicle must be level for a correct reading.

2. Wipe the area around the oil fill plug and unscrew the plug. See A, **Figure 28** (2WD) or A, **Figure 29** (4-wheel drive).

3. The oil level is correct if the oil is up to the bottom thread of the fill plug hole. If the oil level is low, add hypoid gear oil (**Table 5**) until the level is correct.

4. Inspect the oil fill plug O-ring. Replace the O-ring if it has become hard or is starting to deteriorate.

5. Screw on the oil fill plug and tighten to the torque specification in **Table 3**.

Oil change

The factory recommended oil change interval is listed in **Table 1**. Change the oil earlier if it becomes contaminated.

To drain the oil you need the following:

a. Drain pan.

b. Funnel.

c. Hypoid gear oil; see **Table 5** (oil type) and **Table 6** (oil quantity).

Discard old oil in the same manner as outlined under *Engine Oil Change* in this chapter.

> *NOTE*
> *A short ride allows the rear final gear case oil to heat up; thus it flows freely and carries contamination and any sludge out with it.*

1. Ride the vehicle until normal operating temperature is reached.

2. Park the vehicle on a level surface and set the parking brake.

3. Remove the skid plate. See B, **Figure 28** (2-wheel drive) or B, **Figure 29** (4-wheel drive).

4. Place a drain pan underneath the drain plug. See **Figure 30** (2-wheel drive) or **Figure 31** (4-wheel drive).

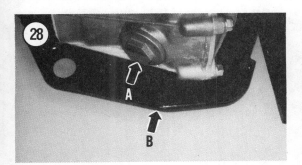

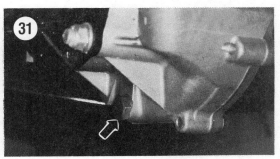

5. Wipe the area around the oil fill plug then unscrew the plug. See A, **Figure 28** (2-wheel drive) or A, **Figure 29** (4-wheel drive).

6. Remove the drain plug and allow the oil to drain out.

7. Inspect the sealing gasket on the drain plug. Replace if damaged or missing.

8. Screw on the drain plug (and gasket) and tighten to the torque specification in **Table 3**.

9. Insert a funnel into the oil fill plug hole and add the recommended type (**Table 5**) and quantity (**Table 6**) of gear oil.

10. Remove the funnel and check the oil level. It should come up to the bottom thread of the fill plug hole. Add additional oil if necessary.

11. Inspect the O-ring on the oil fill plug for wear or deterioration. Replace if necessary.

12. Screw on the oil fill plug (and O-ring) and tighten to the torque specification in **Table 3**.

13. If removed, install the skid plate.

14. Test ride the vehicle and check for leaks. After the test ride, recheck the oil level and adjust if necessary.

General Lubrication

At the service intervals listed in **Table 1**, lubricate the following items with engine oil:
   a. Brake cable joint.
   b. Brake cam levers.
   c. Brake pedal.
   d. Brake lever.

At the service intervals listed in **Table 1**, lubricate the inner throttle cable upper end with grease.

Control Cable Lubrication

The throttle, rear brake and parking brake cables should be cleaned and lubricated at the intervals indicated in **Table 1**. In addition, the cables should be checked for kinks, excessive wear, damage or fraying that could cause the cables to fail or stick. Cables are expendable items and will not last forever under the best of conditions.

The most positive method of control cable lubrication involves the use of a cable lubricator like the one shown in **Figure 32**. A can of cable lube or a general lubricant is required. Do not use chain lube as a cable lubricant.

1. Disconnect the cable to be lubricated.

2. Attach a cable lubricator to the end of the cable following its manufacturer's instructions (**Figure 33**).

3. Insert the lubricant can nozzle into the lubricator, press the button on the can and hold down until the lubricant begins to flow out of the other end of the cable. If you cannot get the cable lube to flow through the cable at one end, remove the lubricator and try at the opposite end of the cable.

> *NOTE*
> *Place a shop cloth at the end of the cable to catch the oil as it runs out.*

4. Disconnect the lubricator.

5. Apply a light coat of grease to the cable ends before reconnecting them. Reconnect the cable and adjust as described in this chapter.

6. After lubricating the throttle cable, operate the throttle lever at the handlebar. It should open and close smoothly with no binding.

7. After lubricating the brake cable(s), check brake operation.

NON-SCHEDULED LUBRICATION

The services listed in this section are not included in **Table 1** (maintenance and lubrication schedule). However, these items should be lubricated throughout the service year. Lubrication and service intervals depend on vehicle use.

Steering Shaft Lubrication

Remove the steering shaft (Chapter Ten) and lubricate the upper bearing blocks and the lower ball bearing oil seal with grease.

Front Upper and Lower Arm Lubrication

Remove the front upper and lower arms (Chapter Ten or Chapter Eleven) and lubricate the pivot bolts with grease.

Front Hub Wheel Bearings and Oil Seals

The front hub wheel bearing oil seal lips should be lubricated with a lithium base grease. Refer to Chapter Ten or Chapter Eleven for service.

Rear Suspension Arms

Remove the rear suspension arms (Chapter Twelve) and lubricate the pivot bolts with grease.

Rear Shock Absorber
Pivot Bolt Lubrication

Remove the front (Chapter Ten or Chapter Eleven) and rear (Chapter Twelve) shock absorbers and lubricate the pivot bolts with grease.

PERIODIC MAINTENANCE

Periodic maintenance intervals are listed in **Table 1**.

Air Filter

A clogged air filter will decrease the efficiency and life of the engine. Never run the ATV without

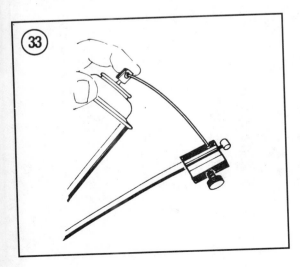

an air filter properly installed. Even minute particles of dust can cause severe internal engine wear and clogging of carburetor passages. Refer to **Figure 34** (1986-1987), **Figure 35** (1988) or **Figure 36** (1989-on).

Removal and installation

1. Remove the seat.
2A. On 1986-1987 models, remove the air filter as follows:
    a. Remove the wingscrews and remove the air filter cover (**Figure 34**). The baffle cover will come off with the filter cover.
    b. Lift the air filter out of the air box. The filter holder will come out with the filter. See **Figure 34**.
2B. On 1988-on models, remove the air filter as follows:
    a. Pry the cover snaps away from the air filter cover and remove the cover (**Figure 37**).
    b. Remove the filter holder screw (A, **Figure 38**).
    c. Loosen the filter clamp screw (B, **Figure 38**).
    d. Lift the air filter (C, **Figure 38**) out of the air box.
3. Disassemble, clean and oil the air filter as described in the following procedure.
4. Use a flashlight and check the air box-to-carburetor boot inside diameter for dirt or other contamination that may have passed through the air filter.
5. Wipe the inside of the air box with a clean rag. If you cannot clean the air box with it bolted to the frame, remove and clean the air box thoroughly with solvent. Then clean with hot soapy water and rinse with water from a garden hose. Remove and install the air box as described in Chapter Eight.
6. Cover the air box opening with a clean shop rag.
7. Inspect all fittings, hoses and connections from the air box to the carburetor. Check each hose clamp for tightness.
8A. On 1986-1987 models, install the air filter as follows:
    a. Assemble the air filter as described under *Air Filter Cleaning and Reoiling* in this chapter.
    b. Coat the foam gasket (**Figure 39**) on the front of the air filter with wheel bearing grease.
    c. Install the filter holder into the air box—insert the filter holder into the slot in the bottom of the air box.

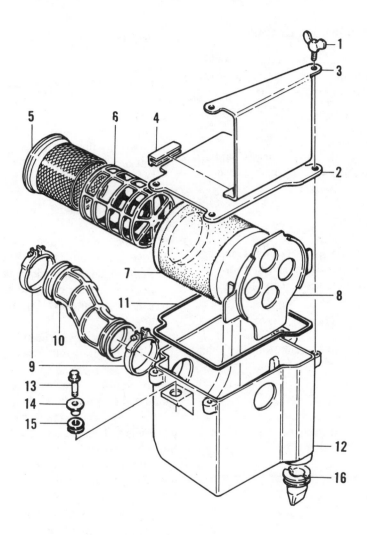

AIR BOX
(1986-1987)

1. Wing screw
2. Baffle cover
3. Cover
4. Grommet
5. Screen
6. Frame
7. Air filter element
8. Filter holder
9. Clamps
10. Boot
11. Gasket
12. Air box
13. Bolt
14. Collar
15. Grommet
16. Drain hose

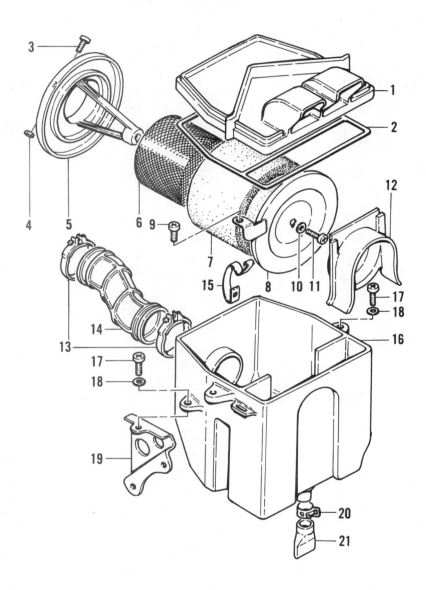

AIR BOX
(1988)

1. Cover	8. Filter holder	15. Cover snap
2. Gasket	9. Screw	16. Air box
3. Screw	10. Washer	17. Screw
4. Nut	11. Screw	18. Washer
5. Filter holder	12. Front holder	19. Bracket
6. Screen	13. Clamps	20. Clamp
7. Air filter element	14. Boot	21. Drain hose

AIR BOX
(1989-ON)

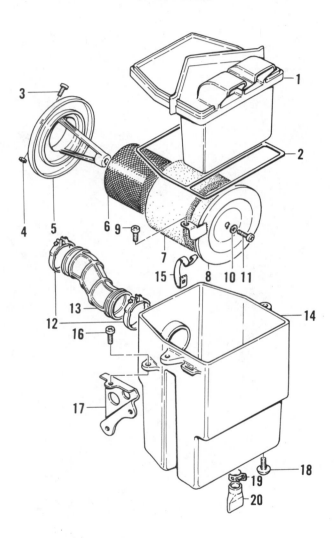

1. Cover	11. Screw
2. Gasket	12. Clamps
3. Screw	13. Boot
4. Nut	14. Air box
5. Filter holder	15. Cover snap
6. Screen	16. Screw
7. Air filter element	17. Bracket
8. Filter holder	18. Screw
9. Screw	19. Clamp
10. Washer	20. Drain hose

d. Slide the air filter into the air box. Then check that the air filter is centered between the air box and filter holder.

e. Install the air filter cover and baffle and secure with the wing screws.

8B. On 1988-on models, install the air filter as follows:

a. Assemble the air filter as described under *Air Filter Cleaning and Reoiling* in this chapter.

b. Install the air filter into the air box. Align the bracket on the filter holder with the bracket in the air box, then install the holder screw (A, **Figure 38**) and tighten securely.

c. Tighten the filter clamp screw (B, **Figure 38**) securely.

d. Install the air filter cover (**Figure 37**) and secure it with the cover snaps.

9. Install the seat.

Air filter cleaning and reoiling

Service the air filter element in a well-ventilated area, away from all sparks and flames.

1A. On 1986-1987 models, remove the screen and frame from the air filter element (**Figure 40**).

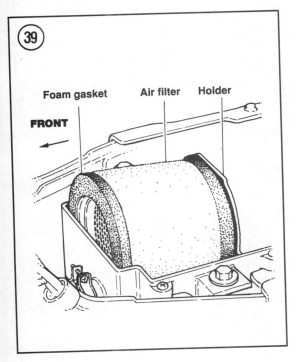

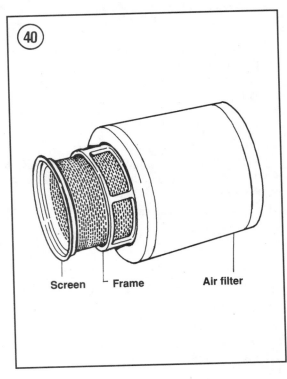

1B. On 1988-on models, remove filter mounting screw and washer (**Figure 41**) and remove the filter holder. Then separate the air filter element from the front holder and remove the screen from inside the element. See **Figure 42**.

> *WARNING*
> *Do not clean the air filter element with a low-flash point solvent or gasoline. A fire or explosion could occur.*

2. Clean the filter element with the manufacturers filter solvent or a general high-flash point solvent. Allow the element to air dry.

3. Inspect the element carefully. If it is torn or broken in any area, replace the air filter element. If the element is okay, continue with Step 4.

4. Fill a clean pan with liquid detergent cleaner and warm water.

5. Submerge the filter into the cleaning solution and gently work the cleaner into the filter pores. Soak and squeeze (gently) the filter to clean it.

> *CAUTION*
> *Do not wring or twist the filter when cleaning it. This harsh action could damage the filter pores or tear the filter loose at a seam. This will allow unfiltered air to enter the engine and cause severe and rapid wear.*

6. Rinse the filter under warm water while soaking and gently squeezing it.

7. Repeat Step 5 and Step 6 two or three times or until there are no signs of dirt being rinsed from the filter.

8. After cleaning the element, inspect it carefully. If it is torn or broken in any area, replace it. Do not run the engine with a damaged element as it may allow dirt to enter the engine and cause severe engine wear.

9. Set the filter aside and allow it to dry thoroughly.

10. Clean the filter screen and holder(s) in solvent and dry thoroughly.

> *CAUTION*
> *Make sure the filter is completely dry before oiling it.*

11. Properly oiling an air filter element is a messy job. You may want to wear a pair of disposable rubber gloves when performing this procedure. Oil the filter as follows:

a. Purchase a box of gallon size storage bags. The bags can be used when cleaning the filter as well as for storing engine and carburetor parts during disassembly.

b. Place the air filter into a storage bag.

c. Pour foam air filter oil onto the filter to soak it.

d. Gently squeeze and release the filter to soak filter oil into the filter's pores. Repeat until all of the filter's pores are saturated with the oil.

e. Remove the filter from the bag and check the pores for uneven oiling. This is indicated by

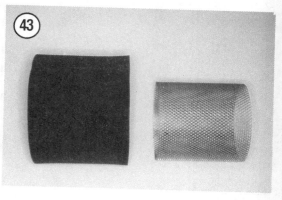

light or dark areas. If necessary, soak the filter and squeeze it again.

f. When the filter oiling is even, squeeze the filter a final time.

12A. On 1986-1987 models, assemble the air filter element as follows:

a. Slide the screen into the frame (**Figure 40**).

b. Slide the element over the frame (**Figure 40**).

12B. On 1988-on models, assemble the air filter element as follows:

a. Slide the element over the screen (**Figure 43**).

b. Apply wheel bearing grease to the front and rear element contact surfaces (**Figure 44**).

c. Place the element onto the front filter holder.

d. Install the rear filter holder onto the filter assembly. Align the marks on both filter holders (**Figure 45**).

e. Screw on the rear filter guide mounting screw (**Figure 41**) and washer and tighten securely.

13. Pour the leftover filter oil from the bag back into the bottle for reuse.

14. Dispose of the plastic bag.

15. Install the air filter as described in this chapter.

Air Box Drain

Squeeze the drain hose (**Figure 46**) on the bottom of the air box to drain out water and other debris collected in the air box.

Fuel Line Inspection

> *WARNING*
> *Some fuel may spill when performing the procedures in this section. Because gasoline is extremely flammable and explosive, perform the following procedure away from all open flames (including pilot lights) and sparks. Do not smoke or allow someone who is smoking into the work area. Always work in a well ventilated area. Wipe up any spills immediately.*

Inspect the fuel line (**Figure 47**) from the fuel tank to the carburetor. Replace the fuel line if it is cracked or starting to deteriorate. Make sure the small hose

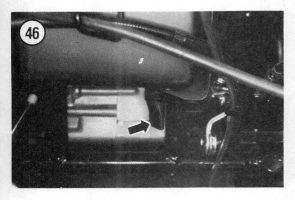

clamps are in place and holding securely. Check that the overflow and vent hoses are in place.

> *WARNING*
> *A damaged or deteriorated fuel line presents a very dangerous fire hazard to both the rider and machine. A serious problem can occur if fuel should spill onto a hot engine or exhaust pipe.*

Fuel Tank Vent Hose

Check the fuel tank vent hose (**Figure 48**) for proper routing. Check the end of the hose for contamination.

Front Brake Lever Free Play Inspection (Drum Brake)

1. Support the vehicle with the front wheels off the ground. Set the parking brake and block the rear wheels.
2. Pull the front brake lever until resistance is felt. Then measure the lever's travel, between the at-rest and applied positions, as shown in **Figure 49**. This measurement is brake lever free play. The correct free play is 25-30 mm (0.98-1.18 in.). Note the following:
   a. If the front brake lever free play is correct, continue with Step 3.
   b. If the front brake lever free play is incorrect, adjust the front brakes as described under *Front and Rear Brake Shoe Adjustment* in this chapter. Then recheck front brake lever free play.
   c. If the free play cannot be corrected after adjusting the front brake shoes, check for air in the front brake lines. See *Brake Bleeding* in Chapter Thirteen.

3. Squeeze and release the front brake lever (**Figure 49**). The brake lever should return to its rest position after releasing it.
4. Rotate the front wheels and check for brake drag. If drag seems excessive, adjust the front brakes as described under *Front and Rear Brake Shoe Adjustment* in this chapter.
5. Lower the front wheels to the ground.

Front and Rear Brake Shoe Adjustment (1986-1987 Drum Brake)

1. Support the vehicle with the front or rear wheels off the ground. Block the other wheels so the vehicle cannot roll in either direction.
2. Pull the wheel cap off the wheel.
3. Rotate the wheel until the inspection hole aligns with one of the brake shoes.
4. Looking through the inspection hole (**Figure 50**), measure the brake shoe lining thickness. Repeat for each brake shoe (2 per wheel). Measure thickness at several points on each shoe. The standard brake shoe lining thickness is 4.0 mm (0.157 in.). The service limit is 2.0 mm (0.078 in.). Note the following:

> *NOTE*
> *If you cannot accurately determine the brake shoe lining thickness, remove the wheel and hub as described in Chapter Ten.*

   a. If the brake shoe lining thickness is within specification, continue with Step 5.
   b. If the brake shoe lining is less than the service limit, replace the brake shoes (both sides) as described in Chapter Thirteen.

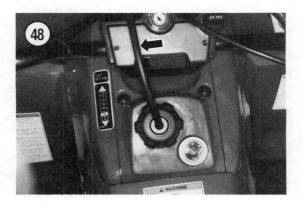

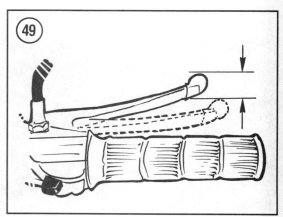

5. Rotate the wheel until the wheel hole marked SHOE ADJUST (**Figure 50**) aligns with the brake adjuster. Then apply the front brake several times.

6. Insert a flat bladed screwdriver through the SHOE ADJUST hole in the wheel and onto the notches of the adjuster (**Figure 51**). Move the screwdriver handle *down* and rotate the adjuster *up*, expanding the brake shoes.

7. Continue to rotate the adjuster up while rotating the wheel. Rotate the adjuster until the wheel is locked in place.

8. Now move the screwdriver handle in the opposite direction and rotate the adjusters down until the wheel just turns free. Then rotate the adjusters down 3 clicks. At this time the wheel should rotate freely without any brake shoe drag.

9. Perform Steps 2-8 for the other wheel.

CAUTION
When rotating the wheels and applying the brakes, if there is a metal-to-metal sound, the brake linings may be worn down to the metal backing plate.

10. Rotate both wheels and apply the brake lever or pedal several times. Both wheels should stop at the same time.

11. Rotate each wheel and make sure the brakes are not dragging. Readjust if necessary.

12. Insert the wheel cap into the wheel.

Front Brake Lever Adjustment (Disc Brake)

Adjustment of the front disc brake is not necessary. Front brake pad wear is automatically compensated for as the caliper piston(s) move outward in their bore(s). However, if the front brake lever feels spongy or soft when pulling it, check the brake fluid level in the front master cylinder. If air enters the brake system, bleed the front brakes as described under *Brake Bleeding* in Chapter Thirteen.

Rear Brake Pedal Free Play Inspection (2-Wheel Drive)

The rear brake pedal adjustment should be inspected at the interval indicated in **Table 1** and adjusted if necessary to maintain the proper amount of free play. Free play is the distance the pedal travels from the at-rest position to the applied position as the pedal is pushed down.

1. Press the rear brake pedal (**Figure 52**) until resistance is felt. The brake pedal should travel about

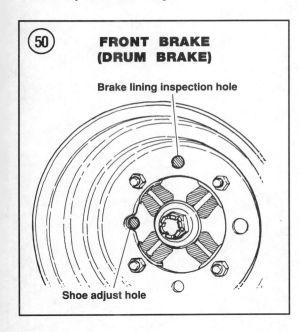

50 FRONT BRAKE (DRUM BRAKE)

Brake lining inspection hole

Shoe adjust hole

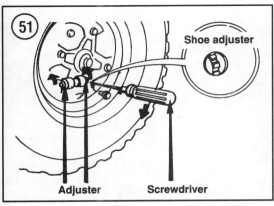

51 Shoe adjuster

Adjuster   Screwdriver

52

20-30 mm (0.78-1.18 in.) before the brake shoes contact the brake drum. The brake shoes must not contact the brake drum with the pedal at rest.

2. Apply the brake fully and check the brake wear indicator on each rear wheel; see A, **Figure 53**. The wear indicator should be within the USABLE RANGE (B, **Figure 53**) indicated on the brake panel. If the indicator falls outside the USABLE RANGE, replace the rear brake shoes as described in Chapter Thirteen. Replace both sides (left and right) at the same time.

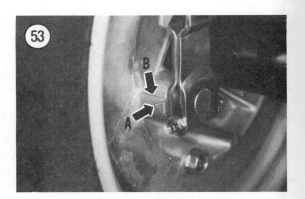

NOTE
*The USABLE RANGE is the raised part on the brake panel; see B, **Figure 53**.*

3. If the brake shoes are usable and the rear brake pedal free play is incorrect, perform the *Rear Brake Pedal Free Play Adjustment (2-Wheel Drive)* procedure in this chapter. If the brake shoes are usable and the rear brake pedal free play is correct, continue with Step 4.

4. Operate the rear brake pedal a few times. The brake pedal should return to its rest position after releasing it.

5. Raise the vehicle so that both rear wheels clear the ground. Block the front wheels so that the vehicle cannot roll in either direction.

6. Release the parking brake.

7. Rotate the rear wheels and check for brake drag. If drag seems excessive, perform the *Rear Brake Pedal Free Play Adjustment (2-Wheel Drive)* procedure in this chapter.

8. Lower the rear wheels to the ground.

Rear Brake Pedal Free Play Adjustment (2-Wheel Drive)

1. Raise the vehicle so that both rear wheels clear the ground. Block the front wheels so that the vehicle cannot roll in either direction. Release the parking brake.

2. Loosen the brake pedal adjust bolt locknut (A, **Figure 54**).

3. Loosen the adjust bolt (B, **Figure 54**) until the brake cable equalizer (A, **Figure 55**) contacts the frame bracket (B, **Figure 55**).

4. Shift the rear axle to the unlocked axle mode.

5. Turn the rear cable adjuster (**Figure 56**) until a slight drag is felt when rotating the rear wheel.

6. Repeat Step 5 for the other wheel.

NOTE
If there is not enough cable adjustment at the rear cable adjuster (Figure 56), use the cable adjusters (Figure 57) at the equalizer. Loosen the locknuts and turn the adjusters (Figure 57) as required. Then tighten the locknuts.

7. Turn the brake pedal adjust bolt (B, **Figure 54**) to set the rear brake pedal height to your personal preference. Tighten the locknut (A, **Figure 54**).

8. Turn both rear cable adjusters (**Figure 56**) until the brake pedal has the correct amount of free play—

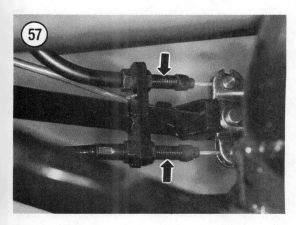

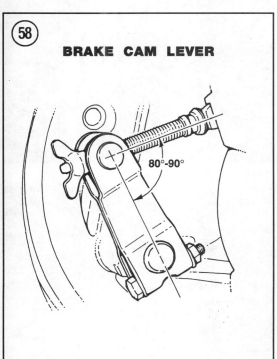

BRAKE CAM LEVER

80°-90°

turn both rear cable adjusters the same number of turns. This will keep the equalizer (A, **Figure 55**) facing straight ahead. If the equalizer is turned to one side, it is adjusted incorrectly.

9. Apply the rear brake and check the cam lever angle as shown in **Figure 58**. When the brake is fully applied the cam angle position should be at 80-90°. If the cam lever angle is incorrect, perform the *Brake Cam Lever Removal/Installation* procedure in Chapter Thirteen.

10. Repeat Step 9 for the other side.

Rear Brake Pedal Position Adjustment (4-Wheel Drive)

1. Park the vehicle on a level surface.

2. Measure the distance from the top of the right-hand footpeg to the top of the rear brake pedal. The correct distance is 0-5 mm (0-0.19 in.).

3. If the height distance is incorrect, loosen the brake pedal adjust bolt locknut (A, **Figure 59**) and turn the adjust bolt (B, **Figure 59**) until the proper height distance is achieved. Hold the adjust bolt and tighten the locknut securely.

4. Perform the *Rear Brake Free Play Adjustment (4-Wheel Drive)* procedure in this chapter.

Rear Brake Free Play Adjustment (4-Wheel Drive)

The rear brake pedal should travel about 15-25 mm (0.59-0.98 in.) before the brake shoes contact the brake drum. If adjustment is necessary, turn the

brake pedal adjuster (A, **Figure 60**) in or out to achieve the correct amount of pedal travel.

After adjusting the rear brake free play, perform the *Parking Brake Lever Free Play Adjustment (4-Wheel Drive)* procedure in this chapter.

Parking Brake Lever Free Play Adjustment (4-Wheel Drive)

1. Perform the *Rear Brake Free Play Adjustment (4-Wheel Drive)* procedure in this chapter, then continue with Step 2.
2. Loosen the parking brake cable adjuster locknut (A, **Figure 61**) and turn the adjuster (B, **Figure 61**) in as far as it will go. Tighten the locknut (A, **Figure 61**).
3. Turn the parking brake adjuster (B, **Figure 60**) in or out to achieve 1-2 mm (1/16 in.) free play at the parking brake lever (**Figure 62**).

Brake Fluid Level Check

The front brake fluid level should always be kept at its maximum level (**Figure 63**). If the brake fluid drops below half-full, correct by adding fresh DOT 3 brake fluid.

> *NOTE*
> *If the brake fluid level lowers rapidly, check the brake hose and fittings for leakage.*

1. Park the vehicle on level ground.
2. Clean any dirt from the cover prior to removing the cover.
3. Turn the handlebar so that the master cylinder reservoir is level.
4. Remove the 2 top cover screws and remove the cover and diaphragm.
5. Add fresh DOT 3 brake fluid from a sealed container.

> *WARNING*
> *Use brake fluid clearly marked DOT 3 and specified for disc brakes. Others may vaporize and cause brake failure. Do not intermix different brands or types of brake fluid as they may not be compatible. Do not intermix a silicone based (DOT 5) brake fluid as it can cause brake component damage leading to brake system failure.*

> *CAUTION*
> *Be careful when handling brake fluid. Do not spill it on painted or plastic surfaces as it will destroy the surface. Wash the area immediately with soap and water and thoroughly rinse it off.*

6. Reinstall the diaphragm and top cover. Install the screws and tighten securely.

Disc Brake Hoses

Inspect the brake hoses for cracks, cuts, bulges, deterioration and leaks. Check the metal brake lines for cracks and leaks. Replace the brake hoses at the intervals specified in **Table 1**. Refer to Chapter Thirteen.

Disc Brake Pad Wear

Replace the brake pads when the lining thickness is worn to the wear limit specified in Chapter Thirteen, when a pad shows uneven wear and scoring, or if there is grease or oil on the friction surface. Refer to Chapter Thirteen.

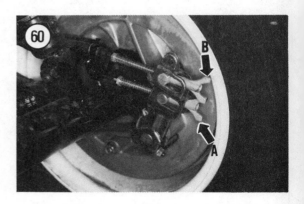

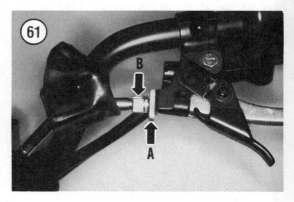

If the front brake seems to grab and release (pulsate) when using it, check the brake discs for warpage or other damage.

Disc Brake Fluid Change

Every time the reservoir cap is removed, a small amount of dirt and moisture enters the brake fluid. The same thing happens if a leak occurs or any part of the hydraulic system is loosened or disconnected. Dirt can clog the system and cause unnecessary wear. Water in the brake fluid vaporizes at high temperature, impairing the hydraulic action and reducing the brake's stopping ability.

To maintain peak performance, change the brake fluid every year or when rebuilding a caliper or master cylinder. To change brake fluid, follow the brake bleeding procedure in Chapter Thirteen.

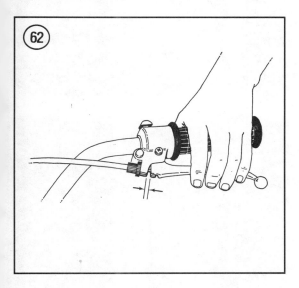

WARNING
Use brake fluid clearly marked DOT 3 only. Others may vaporize and cause brake failure. Dispose of any unused fluid according to local EPA regulations—never reuse brake fluid. Contaminated brake fluid can cause brake failure.

Brake Master Cylinder

The master cylinder piston assembly should be replaced at the intervals specified in **Table 1**. Refer to Chapter Thirteen for the service procedure.

Brake Caliper

The brake caliper piston seals (dust and piston) should be replaced at the intervals specified in **Table 1**. Refer to Chapter Thirteen for service procedures.

Clutch Adjustment

The clutch should be adjusted at the intervals specified in **Table 1**.

This adjustment pertains only to the manual clutch as the centrifugal clutch requires no adjustment. Since there is no clutch cable, the mechanism is the only component requiring adjustment. This adjustment takes up slack due to clutch component wear.

2-wheel drive

1. Remove the clutch adjust cover (**Figure 64**).

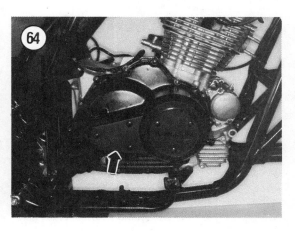

2. Loosen the clutch adjust screw locknut (**Figure 65**).

3. Turn the adjust screw (**Figure 65**) clockwise until resistance is felt, then stop.

4. From this point, turn the adjust screw (**Figure 65**) counterclockwise until resistance is felt, then stop.

Hold the adjust screw and tighten the locknut securely.

> *NOTE*
> *Make sure the adjust screw does not move when tightening the locknut.*

5. Install the clutch adjust cover.

6. Test ride the vehicle and make sure the clutch is operating correctly. Readjust if necessary.

4-wheel drive

1. Remove the clutch adjust cover (**Figure 66**).

2. Loosen the clutch adjust screw locknut (**Figure 67**).

3. Turn the adjust screw (**Figure 67**) clockwise until resistance is felt, then stop.

4. From this point, turn the adjust screw (**Figure 67**) counterclockwise until resistance is felt, then stop.

Hold the adjust screw and tighten the locknut securely.

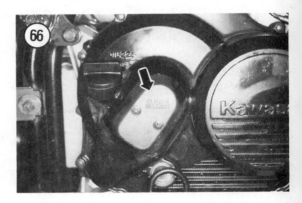

> *NOTE*
> *Make sure the adjust screw does not move when tightening the locknut.*

5. Install the clutch adjust cover.

6. Test ride the vehicle and make sure the clutch is operating correctly. Readjust if necessary.

Throttle Cable Adjustment and Operation

Check the throttle cable free play at the interval indicated in **Table 1**. The throttle cable should have 2-3 mm (3/32 in.) free play measured at the tip of the throttle lever (**Figure 68**).

In time, the throttle cable free play will become excessive from cable stretch. This will delay throttle response and affect low speed operation. On the other hand, if there is no throttle cable free play, an excessively high idle can result.

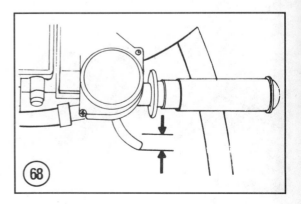

Minor adjustments can be made at the throttle lever adjuster. Major adjustments can be made at the throttle cable adjuster at the carburetor.

1. At the throttle lever, slide back the throttle cable rubber boot.

2. Loosen the locknut (A, **Figure 69**) and turn the adjuster (B, **Figure 69**) in either direction until the correct amount of free play is achieved.

3. Hold the adjuster and tighten the locknut securely.

4. If the proper amount of free play cannot be achieved, make fine adjustments at the throttle cable

locknuts at the carburetor (**Figure 70**). Tighten the locknuts securely.

5. If the throttle cable cannot be adjusted properly, the cable has stretched excessively and must be replaced.

6. Make sure the throttle lever rotates freely from a fully closed to fully open position.

7. Start the engine and allow it to idle in NEUTRAL. Turn the handlebar from side to side. If the idle increases, the throttle cable is routed incorrectly or there is not enough cable free play.

NOTE
A damaged throttle cable will prevent the engine from idling properly.

Speed Limiter Screw Adjustment

The throttle housing is equipped with a speed limiter screw (**Figure 71**) that can be set to prevent the rider from opening the throttle all the way. The speed limiter screw can be set for beginning riders or to control engine rpm when breaking in a new engine.

The speed limiter adjustment is set by varying the length of the speed limiter screw. Turning the screw out increases engine speed and turning the screw in decreases engine speed.

WARNING
Do not operate the vehicle with the speed limiter screw removed from the housing. If you are adjusting the speed limiter for a beginning rider, start and ride the vehicle yourself, making sure it is positioned where you want it.

Reverse and Differential Cable Adjustment

For the cable adjustments not listed in this chapter, refer to the following:

    a. Reverse cable; see Chapter Seven.

    b. Differential cable; see Chapter Twelve.

Steering System and Front Suspension Inspection

Check the steering system and front suspension at the interval indicated in **Table 1**.

1. Park the vehicle on level ground and set the parking brake.

2. Visually inspect all components of the steering system. Pay close attention to the tie rods and steering shaft, especially after a hard spill or collision. If damage is apparent, the steering components must be repaired. Refer to service procedures described in Chapter Ten.

3. Check the tightness of the handlebar holder bolts.

4. Make sure the front axle nuts are tight and that the cotter pins are in place.

5. Check that the cotter pins are in place on all steering components. If any cotter pin is missing, check the nut(s) for looseness. Torque the nut(s) and install new cotter pins.

CAUTION
If any of the previously mentioned bolts and nuts are loose, refer to Chapter Ten for correct procedures and torque specifications.

6. Check steering shaft play as follows:
  a. To check steering shaft radial play, move the handlebar from side to side (without attempting to move the wheels). If radial play is excessive, the upper steering bearings are probably worn and should be replaced.
  b. To check steering shaft thrust play, lift up and then push down on the handlebar. If excessive thrust play is noted, check the lower steering shaft nut for looseness. If the nut is torqued properly, then the lower steering shaft bearing is worn and should be replaced.
  c. Replace worn or damaged steering shaft parts as described in Chapter Ten.

7. Check steering knuckle and tie rod ball joints as follows:
  a. Turn the handlebar quickly from side to side. If there is appreciable looseness between the handlebar and tires, check the ball joints for severe wear or damage. See **Figure 72** and **Figure 73**, typical.
  b. Replace worn or damaged steering knuckle and tie rod components as described in Chapter Ten.

NOTE
When removing cotter pins to check fastener tightness, new cotter pins must be installed.

Front Axle Joint Boot Inspection (4-Wheel Drive)

At the interval specified in **Table 1**, inspect the front axle joint boots (**Figure 74**) for tearing or other damage. Replace damaged boots as described in Chapter Eleven.

Exhaust Pipe Baffle and Muffler Cleaning

Clean the exhaust pipe baffle and muffler at the intervals indicated in **Table 1**, or sooner if a considerable amount of slow riding is done.

3

WARNING
To avoid burning your hands, heavy gloves should be worn if the exhaust system is hot. Work in a well ventilated area (outside your garage) that is free of any fire hazards. Be sure to protect your eyes with safety glasses or goggles.

. Remove the drain bolt and washer at the bottom of the muffler (**Figure 75**).

. Start the engine.

. Raise and lower the engine RPM while tapping on the muffler with a plastic mallet. Continue until carbon stops coming out of the opening.

. Turn the engine off.

. Remove the baffle (**Figure 76**) and pull the baffle out of the muffler. See **Figure 77**.

. Remove all carbon residue from the baffle.

. Reinstall the baffle and its mounting bolt. Tighten the bolt securely.

Nuts, Bolts, and Other Fasteners

Constant vibration can loosen many of the fasteners on the vehicle. Check the tightness of all fasteners, especially those on:

a. Engine mounting hardware.
b. Cylinder head bracket bolts.
c. Engine crankcase covers.
d. Handlebar.
e. Gearshift lever.
f. Brake pedal and lever.
g. Exhaust system.

NON-SCHEDULED MAINTENANCE

Fuel Valve Cleaning

Periodically remove and clean the fuel valve as described in Chapter Eight.

Carburetor Cleaning

Remove, disassemble and clean the carburetor as described in Chapter Eight.

Exhaust System

1. Inspect the exhaust pipe for cracks or dents which could alter performance.
2. Check all of the exhaust pipe fasteners and mounting points for loose or damaged parts.

Front Hub Bearings (2-Wheel Drive)

The front hub bearings are sealed and do not require periodic lubrication. However, the front hubs

should be removed and the bearings and oil seals in-spected for excessive wear or damage. Replace the oil seals if there is excessive grease on the outside of the seal or if there is a deposit of reddish-brown res-idue around the seal. Refer to Chapter Ten.

Steering Knuckle Bearings (4-Wheel Drive)

The steering knuckle bearings are sealed and do not require periodic lubrication. However, the steer-ing knuckles should be removed and the bearings and seal inspected for excessive wear or damage. Refer to Chapter Ten.

Handlebar

Inspect the handlebar weekly for any sign of damage. A bent or damaged handlebar should be re-placed. The knurled section of the bar should be very rough. Keep the clamps clean with a wire brush. Anytime the bars slip in the clamps they should be removed and wire brushed clean to pre-vent small balls of aluminum from gathering in the clamps and reducing gripping abilities.

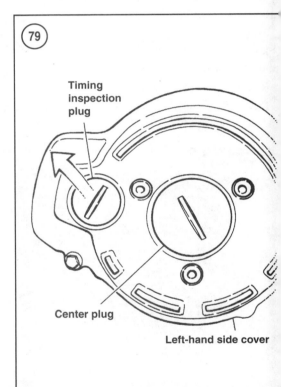

Timing inspection plug

Center plug

Left-hand side cover

NOTE
If you have installed aluminum bars, make sure you follow their manufac-turer's directions for installing the bars and clamps.

Handlebar Grips

Inspect the handlebar grips (**Figure 78**) for tear-ing, looseness or severe wear. Install new grips when required. Follow manufacturer's instructions when installing grips.

Frame Inspection

Routinely inspect the frame and brackets for cracks or other damage.

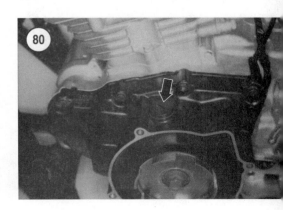

ENGINE TUNE-UP

The number of definitions of the term "tune-up" is probably equal to the number of people defining it. For the purposes of this book, a tune-up is general adjustment and maintenance to insure peak engine performance.

The following paragraphs discuss each facet of a proper tune-up which should be performed in the order given. Unless otherwise specified, the engine should be thoroughly cool before starting any tune-up procedure.

Have the new parts on hand before you begin.

To perform a tune-up on your Kawasaki, you need the following tools and equipment:

a. Spark plug wrench.
b. Socket wrench, assorted sockets and wrenches.
c. Phillips head screwdriver.
d. Spark plug feeler gauge (wire type) and gap adjusting tool.
e. Feeler gauge set.
f. Timing light.

Cam Chain Adjustment

An automatic cam chain tensioner assembly is used. No adjustment is required.

Valve Clearance
Check and Adjustment

Valve clearance should be checked and adjusted with the engine cold. The exhaust valve is located at the front of the engine and the intake valve is at the rear of the engine.

1. Park the vehicle on level ground and set the parking brake.
2. Remove the fuel tank as described in Chapter Eight.
3. If necessary, remove the front fender as described in Chapter Fourteen.
4A. On 1986-1987 models, perform the following:
    a. Remove the left-hand side cover guard.
    b. Remove the timing inspection plug and the center plug (**Figure 79**) from the left-hand side cover.
4B. On 1988-on models, perform the following:
    a. Remove the recoil starter assembly as described in Chapter Five.
    b. Remove the timing inspection plug (**Figure 80**) from the left-hand side cover.
5. Remove the exhaust and intake valve covers and the cylinder head side cover (**Figure 81**).
6. Remove the spark plug. This will make it easier to turn the engine by hand.
7. The piston must be set to top dead center (TDC) on its compression stroke before checking and adjusting the valve clearance. Perform the following:
    a. With a socket on the flywheel bolt or the starter pulley (**Figure 82**), turn the crankshaft counterclockwise and align the "LF300" mark on the cam sprocket (A, **Figure 83**) with the cylinder head "TOP" mark (B, **Figure 83**).
    b. Check the position of the "T" mark on the rotor. It should be aligned with the left-hand side cover

index groove mark as shown in **Figure 84** (1986-1987) or **Figure 85** (1988-on). If these marks are not aligned, turn the crankshaft to align them.

   c. When the cam sprocket and rotor marks are properly aligned, both rocker arms will have a valve clearance, indicating that both the intake and exhaust valves are closed. Move each rocker arm (**Figure 86**, typical) by hand. There should be some side movement.

8. Check the clearance of both the intake valve and exhaust valve by inserting a flat feeler gauge between the end of the valve stem and the valve adjuster (screw) as shown in **Figure 87**. The correct valve clearances for the intake and exhaust valves are listed in **Table 8**. If the clearance is correct, there will be a slight resistance on the feeler gauge when it is inserted and withdrawn.

9. To correct the clearance, perform the following:

   a. Use a wrench and back off the valve adjuster locknut.

   b. Use a screwdriver and turn the adjuster in or out so there is a slight resistance felt on the feeler gauge (**Figure 87**).

   c. Hold the adjuster to prevent it from turning and tighten the locknut to the torque specification listed in **Table 3**.

   d. Then recheck the clearance to make sure the adjuster did not slip when the locknut was tightened. Readjust the valve clearance if necessary.

10. Inspect the rubber O-rings used in the valve covers, cylinder head side cover and timing hole plug. Replace any O-ring that has become hard or is starting to deteriorate.

NOTE
Apply a lithium soap base grease to the valve cover and cylinder head side cover O-rings prior to installation.

11. Install the valve covers so the "UP" mark on each cover faces up (**Figure 88**).

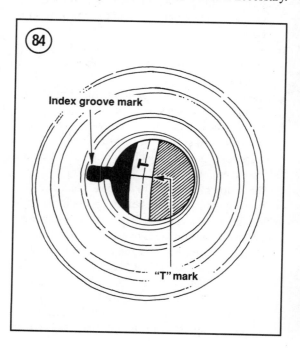

3

12. Install the cylinder head side cover and O-ring. Tighten the mounting bolts securely.

13A. On 1986-1987 models, perform the following:

   a. Install the timing inspection plug and the center plug.

   b. Install the left-hand side cover guard.

13B. On 1988-on models, perform the following:

   a. Install the timing inspection plug into the left-hand side cover.

   b. Install the recoil starter assembly as described in Chapter Five.

14. Install the spark plug and reconnect the spark plug cap.

15. If removed, install the front fender as described in Chapter Fourteen.

16. Install the fuel tank as described in Chapter Eight.

Cylinder Compression

A cylinder cranking compression check is one of the quickest ways to check the internal condition of the engine: rings, piston, head gasket, etc. It's a good

idea to check compression at each tune-up, write it down, and compare it with the reading you get at the next tune-up. This will help you spot any developing problems.

1. Warm the engine to normal operating temperature. Turn the engine off.

2. Make sure the compression release lever (**Figure 89**) is in its OFF or down position.

3. Remove the spark plug. Then insert the plug into the plug cap and ground the plug against the cylinder head (**Figure 90**).

4. Thread or insert the tip of a compression gauge into the cylinder head spark plug hole. Make sure the gauge is seated properly.

> *NOTE*
> *Make sure the engine stop switch is in the OFF position when performing Step 5.*

5. Hold the throttle wide open and turn the engine over with the starter motor or recoil starter for several revolutions until the gauge gives its highest reading. Record the pressure reading and compare it to the compression specifications listed in **Table 7**.

> *NOTE*
> *Kawasaki lists different compression readings when using the electric starter and recoil starter to crank the engine; see Table 7.*

6. If the reading is higher than normal, there may be a buildup of carbon deposits in the combustion chamber or on the piston crown.

7. If a low reading is obtained, it indicates a leaking cylinder head gasket, valve(s) or piston ring trouble. To determine which, pour about a teaspoon of engine oil through the spark plug hole onto the top of the

piston. Crank the engine over one revolution to distribute the excess oil, then make another compression test and record the reading. If the compression increases significantly, the valves are good but the rings are worn or damaged. If compression does not increase, the valves require servicing. A valve could be hanging open, but not burned, or a piece of carbon could be on the valve seat.

> *NOTE*
> *If the compression is low, the engine cannot be tuned to maximum performance; the engine must be repaired.*

8. Remove the compression gauge and install the spark plug and plug cap.

Correct Spark Plug Heat Range

Spark plugs are available in various heat ranges, both hotter and colder than the plugs originally installed at the factory.

Select a plug of the heat range designed for the loads and conditions under which your Kawasaki will be operating. Use of incorrect heat range can cause the plug to foul or engine to overheat, resulting in piston damage.

In general, use a hot plug for low speeds and low temperatures. Use a cold plug for high speeds, high engine loads and high temperatures. The plug should operate hot enough to burn off unwanted deposits, but not so hot that they burn themselves or cause preignition. A spark plug of the correct heat range will show a light tan color on the portion of the

insulator within the cylinder after the plug has been in service.

The reach (length) of a plug is also important. A spark plug that is too short will cause excessive carbon build-up, hard starting and plug fouling. A plug that is too long will cause overheating or may contact the top of the piston. Both conditions will cause engine damage. See **Figure 91**. If the spark plug is too long, the exposed threads will be coated with carbon and removal of the spark plug will probably damage the threads in the cylinder head.

The standard heat range spark plug for the various models is listed in **Table 9**.

Spark Plug Removal

> *CAUTION*
> *Whenever the spark plug is removed, dirt around it can fall into the plug hole. This can cause expensive engine damage.*

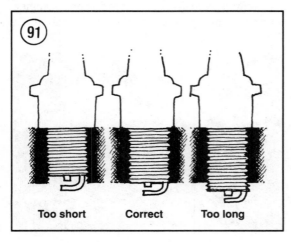

Too short   Correct   Too long

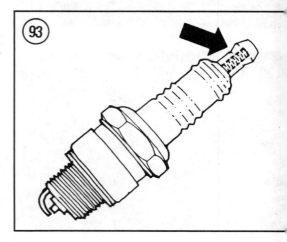

1. Grasp the spark plug lead as near the plug as possible and pull it off the plug. If it is stuck to the plug, twist it slightly to break it loose.

2. Blow away any dirt that has collected around the spark plug.

3. Remove the spark plug with a spark plug socket.

NOTE
If the plug is difficult to remove, apply penetrating oil, like WD-40 or Liquid Wrench, around the base of the plug and let it soak in about 10-20 minutes.

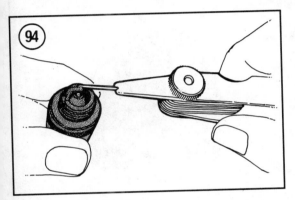

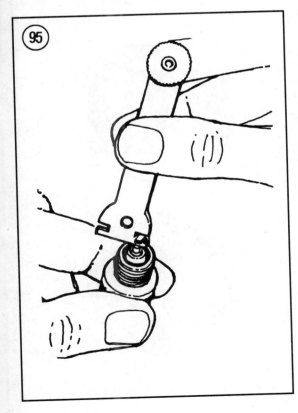

4. Inspect the plug carefully. Look for a broken center porcelain, excessively eroded electrodes, and excessive carbon or oil fouling (**Figure 92**).

Gapping and Installing the Plug

A new spark plug should be carefully gapped to ensure a reliable, consistent spark. You must use a special spark plug gapping tool and a wire-type feeler gauge.

1. If necessary, screw the small terminal onto the end of the plug (**Figure 93**).

2. Insert a wire feeler gauge between the center and side electrode (**Figure 94**). The correct gap is listed in **Table 8**. If the gap is correct, you will feel a slight drag as you pull the wire through. If there is no drag, or the gauge won't pass through, bend the side electrode with a gapping tool (**Figure 95**) to set the proper gap.

3. Apply antiseize compound to the plug threads before installing the spark plug. Do not use engine oil on the plug threads.

NOTE
Antiseize compound can be purchased at most automotive parts stores.

4. Screw the spark plug in by hand until it seats. Very little effort should be required. If force is necessary, you have the plug cross-threaded or there is carbon on the cylinder head threads. Unscrew it and try again.

5. Use a spark plug wrench and tighten the spark plug to the torque specification in **Table 3**. If you do not have a torque wrench, tighten the plug an additional 1/4 to 1/2 turn after the gasket has made contact with the head. If you are installing an old, regapped plug and reusing the old gasket, only tighten an additional 1/4 turn.

NOTE
Do not overtighten. This will only squash the gasket and destroy its sealing ability.

6. Install the spark plug wire. Make sure it is on tight.

CAUTION
Make sure the spark plug wire is located away from the exhaust pipe.

SPARK PLUG CONDITIONS

NORMAL USE

OIL FOULED

CARBON FOULED

OVERHEATED

GAP BRIDGED

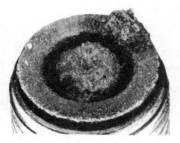

SUSTAINED PREIGNITION

WORN OUT

Reading Spark Plugs

Much information about engine and spark plug performance can be determined by careful examination of the spark plug. This information is only valid after performing the following steps.

1. Ride the ATV a short distance at full throttle in any gear.
2. Push the engine stop switch to OFF before closing the throttle and shift into NEUTRAL; coast and brake to a stop.
3. Remove the spark plug and examine it (**Figure 92**). Compare it to **Figure 96** and note the following:

Normal condition

If the plug has a light tan- or gray-colored deposit and no abnormal gap wear or erosion, good engine, carburetion and ignition condition are indicated. The plug in use is of the proper heat range and may be serviced and returned to use.

Carbon fouled

Soft, dry, sooty deposits covering the entire firing end of the plug are evidence of incomplete combustion. Even though the firing end of the plug is dry, the plug's insulation decreases. An electrical path is formed that lowers the voltage from the ignition system. Engine misfiring is a sign of carbon fouling. Carbon fouling can be caused by one or more of the following:

a. Too rich fuel mixture.
b. Spark plug heat range too cold.
c. Clogged air filter.
d. Over-retarded ignition timing.
e. Ignition component failure.
f. Low engine compression.
g. Prolonged idling.

Oil fouled

The tip of an oil fouled plug has a black insulator tip, a damp oily film over the firing end and a carbon layer over the entire nose. The electrodes will not be worn. Common causes for this condition are:

a. Incorrect carburetor jetting.
b. Low idle speed or prolonged idling.
c. Ignition component failure.
d. Spark plug heat range too cold.

e. Engine still being broken in.
f. Valve guides worn.
g. Piston rings worn or broken.

Oil fouled spark plugs may be cleaned in an emergency, but it is better to replace them. It is important to correct the cause of fouling before the engine is returned to service.

Gap bridging

Plugs with this condition exhibit gaps shorted out by combustion deposits between the electrodes. If this condition is encountered, check for an improper oil type or excessive carbon in the combustion chamber. Be sure to locate and correct the cause of this condition.

Overheating

Badly worn electrodes and premature gap wear are signs of overheating, along with a gray or white "blistered" porcelain insulator surface. The most common cause for this condition is using a spark plug of the wrong heat range (too hot). If you have not changed to a hotter spark plug and the plug is overheated, consider the following causes:

a. Lean fuel mixture.
b. Ignition timing too advanced.
c. Engine lubrication system malfunction.
d. Engine air leak.
e. Improper spark plug installation (overtightening).
f. No spark plug gasket.

Worn out

Corrosive gases formed by combustion and high voltage sparks have eroded the electrodes. A spark plug in this condition requires more voltage to fire under hard acceleration. Replace with a new spark plug.

Preignition

If the electrodes are melted, preignition is almost certainly the cause. Check for carburetor mounting or intake manifold leaks and over-advanced ignition timing. It is also possible that a plug of the wrong heat range (too hot) is being used. Find the cause of the preignition before returning the engine into service. For additional information on preignition, refer to *Preignition* in Chapter Two.

Ignition Timing

All models are equipped with a capacitor discharge ignition system (CDI). This system uses no breaker points, but timing does have to be checked to make sure all components of the ignition system are functioning properly.

Incorrect ignition timing can cause a drastic loss of engine performance and efficiency. It may also cause overheating.

Before starting on this procedure, check all electrical connections related to the ignition system. Make sure all connections are tight and free of corrosion and that all ground connections are clean and tight.

1. Start the engine and let it warm up approximately 2-3 minutes.

2. Park the vehicle on level ground and set the parking brake. Shut off the engine.

3A. On 1986-1987 models, perform the following:
   a. Remove the left-hand side cover guard.
   b. Remove the timing inspection plug (**Figure 79**).

3B. On 1988-on models, remove the timing inspection plug (**Figure 80**) from the left-hand side cover.

4. Connect a portable tachometer following its manufacturer's instructions.

5. Connect a timing light following its manufacturer's instructions.

6. Restart the engine and allow to idle.

7. Aim the timing light at the timing window and pull the trigger while checking ignition timing at the following engine speeds:
   a. Below 2,100 rpm: The timing is correct if the "F" mark on the flywheel aligns with the fixed index mark on the crankcase. See **Figure 97** (1986-1987) or **Figure 98** (1988-on).
   b. Above 4,200 rpm: The timing is correct if the advanced timing marks on the flywheel align with the fixed index mark on the crankcase. See **Figure 97** (1986-1987) or **Figure 98** (1988-on).

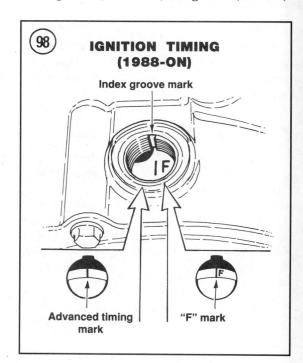

(98)
IGNITION TIMING (1988-ON)
Index groove mark
Advanced timing mark
"F" mark

(97)
IGNITION TIMING (1986-1987)
Index groove mark
"F" mark
Advanced timing marks

. If the timing is incorrect, troubleshoot the ignition system as described under *Ignition System* in Chapter Two.

. Disconnect the timing light and portable tachometer.

0A. On 1986-1987 models, perform the following:

a. Install the timing inspection plug.

b. Install the left-hand side cover guard.

0B. On 1988-on models, install the timing inspection plug in the left-hand side cover.

Pilot Air Screw Adjustment

Using a short flat-tipped screwdriver, carefully turn the pilot air screw (**Figure 99**) in (clockwise) until it *lightly* seats, then back it out (counterclockwise) the number of turns listed in **Table 7**.

NOTE
Figure 100 shows the pilot air screw with the carburetor removed for clarity.

Idle Speed Adjustment

Before making this adjustment, the air filter must be clean.

1. Start the engine and let it warm up approximately 2-3 minutes.

2. Park the vehicle on level ground and set the parking brake.

3. Turn the idle speed adjust screw (**Figure 101**) in or out to obtain the slowest smooth idle speed. If it is difficult to obtain a smooth idle speed, make fine adjustments with the pilot air screw (**Figure 99**). To do this, turn the pilot air screw to the point where the idle goes up one way and then drops off when turned the other way. Find the best idle position between these 2 points, readjusting the idle speed screw if necessary.

4. Open and close the throttle a couple of times; check for variation in idle speed. Readjust if necessary.

> *WARNING*
> *With the engine idling, move the handlebar from side to side. If idle speed increases during this movement, the throttle cable needs adjusting or may be incorrectly routed through the frame. Correct this problem immediately. Do not ride the vehicle in this unsafe condition.*

5. Turn the engine off.

STORAGE

Several months of inactivity can cause serious problems and a general deterioration of the ATV's condition. This is especially true in areas of weather extremes. During the winter months it is advisable to prepare the ATV specially for lay-up.

Selecting a Storage Area

Most riders store their ATV's in their home garages. If you do not have a home garage, facilities suitable for long-term ATV storage are readily available for rent or lease in most areas. When selecting a building, consider the following points.

1. The storage area must be as dry as possible. Heating is not necessary, but the building should be

well insulated to minimize extreme temperature variations.

2. Buildings with large window areas should be avoided, or such windows should be masked (also a good security measure) if direct sunlight can fall on the ATV.

Preparing Vehicle for Storage

Careful preparation will minimize deterioration and make it easier to return the ATV to service later. Use the following procedure.

1. Wash the vehicle completely. Make certain to remove all dirt in all the hard to reach parts like the cooling fins on the head and cylinder. Completely dry all parts of the ATV to remove all moisture.

2. Run the engine for about 20-30 minutes to warm up the oil. Drain the oil, regardless of the time since the last oil change. Refill with the normal quantity and type of oil as described in this chapter.

3. Change the final drive gear oil as described in this chapter.

4. Drain all gasoline from the fuel tank, fuel hose, and the carburetor.

5. Remove the spark plug and add about one teaspoon of engine oil into the cylinder. Reinstall the spark plug and turn the engine over to distribute the oil to the cylinder walls and piston.

6. Tape or tie a plastic bag over the end of the muffler to prevent the entry of moisture.

7. Check the tire pressure. If necessary, inflate to the correct pressure and move the vehicle to the storage area. Place it securely on a stand with all 4 wheels off the ground.

8. Cover the ATV with a tarp, blanket or heavy plastic drop cloth. Place this cover over the ATV mainly as a dust cover—do not wrap it tightly especially any plastic material, as it may trap moisture. Leave room for air to circulate around the ATV.

Inspection During Storage

Try to inspect the vehicle weekly while in storage. Any deterioration should be corrected as soon as possible. For example, if corrosion is observed cover it with a light coat of grease or silicone spray.

Crank the engine over a couple of times. Do not start it.

Restoring Vehicle to Service

A vehicle that has been properly prepared and stored in a suitable area requires only light maintenance to restore to service. It is advisable, however, to perform a spring tune-up.

1. Before removing the vehicle from the storage area, inflate the tires to the correct pressures. Air loss during storage may have nearly flattened the tires.

2. Remove the plug from the end of the muffler.

3. When the vehicle is brought to the work area refill the fuel tank with fresh gasoline.

4. Install a fresh spark plug and start the engine.

5. Perform the standard tune-up as described earlier in this chapter.

6. Check the operation of the engine stop switch. Oxidation of the switch contacts during storage may make it inoperative.

7. Clean and test ride the vehicle.

Table 1 MAINTENANCE AND LUBRICATION SCHEDULE

After first 10 hours of service or after break-in	Clean air filter Check clutch adjustment; adjust if necessary Check valve adjustment; adjust if necessary Change engine oil and replace oil filter Clean and regap spark plug; replace if necessary Inspect fuel system for contamination or leakage Check battery condition Check fasteners for tightness Change final gear case oil on 2-wheel drive Change front and rear final gear case oil on 4-wheel drive Check all cable adjustments; adjust if necessary Check steering operation; adjust if necessary Check condition of joint boots on 4-wheel drive Check brake fluid level Check front brake pads Check rear brake linings Check rear brake adjustment; adjust if necessary
Every 10 days of service	Clean air filter Check clutch adjustment; adjust if necessary Check all cable adjustments; adjust if necessary Check fasteners for tightness Check rear brake linings Check rear brake adjustment; adjust if necessary Check condition of joint boots on 4-wheel drive
Every 30 days of service	Check front brake pads Check brake fluid level Check battery condition Perform general lubrication
Every 90 days of service	Check valve adjustment; adjust if necessary Inspect fuel system for contamination or leakage Change engine oil and replace oil filter Clean and regap spark plug; replace if necessary Check steering operation; adjust if necessary
After one year service	Clean spark arrestor Change brake fluid Change final gear case oil on 2-wheel drive Change front and rear final gear case oil on 4-wheel drive

Every 2 years of service	Replace brake hoses
	Replace master cylinder piston assembly
	  and dust seal
	Replace brake caliper piston seal and dust seal
	Replace wheel cylinder piston seal
	  and dust seal on 1986-1987 models

Table 2 TIRE INFLATION PRESSURE (WHEN COLD)

	kPa	psi
2-wheel drive Front & rear	21	3.0

4-wheel drive
  Front
  Rear
	35
	28
		5
		4

Table 3 MAINTENANCE TORQUE SPECIFICATIONS

Item	N·m	ft.-lb.
Valve adjusting screw locknuts	12	8.6
Engine oil drain plug	29	22
Wheel nuts	34	25
Front final drive (4-wheel drive)		
Oil fill cap	29	22
Oil drain plug	20	14.5
Rear final drive		
Oil fill cap	29	22
Oil drain plug	20	14.5
Spark plug		
2-wheel drive	27	20
4-wheel drive	14	10
Engine oil pipe banjo bolts	20	14.5

Table 4 BATTERY CAPACITY

Model	Capacity
2-wheel drive	
1986-1987	12 volts, 19 amp hours
1988-1991	12 volts, 14 amp hours
1992	
U.S. and Australia	12 volts, 14 amp hours
All other models	12 volts, 19 amp hours
1993-on	
U.S.	12 volts, 14 amp hours
All other models	12 volts, 19 amp hours
4-wheel drive	
1989	12 volts, 14 amp hours
1990-on	
U.S.	12 volts, 14 amp hours
All other models	12 volts, 19 amp hours

Table 5 RECOMMENDED LUBRICANTS AND FUEL

Air filter	Air filter oil
Engine oil	
Grade	SF or SG
Viscosity	SAE 10W-30, 10W-40, 10W-50, 20W-40 or 20W-50
Battery refill	Distilled water
Brake fluid	DOT 3 or DOT 4
Front final gear case oil	
4-wheel drive	API GL-5 Hypoid gear oil or LSD SAE 140 or SAE 85W-140
Rear final gear case oil	
All models	
Below 5° C (41° F)	API GL-5 Hypoid gear oil SAE 80
Above 5° C (41° F)	API GL-5 Hypoid gear oil SAE 90

Table 6 APPROXIMATE REFILL CAPACITIES

Engine oil	
2-wheel drive	1.7 L (1.8 U.S. qts. or 1.5 Imp. qts.)
4-wheel drive	
1989-1991	2.2 L (2.3 U.S. qts. or 1.9 Imp. qts.)
1992-on	2.4 L (2.5 U.S. qts. or 2.1 Imp. qts.)
Front final gear case	
4-wheel drive	
1989-1993	250 mL (8.45 U.S. oz. or 7.04 Imp. oz.)
1994-on	400 mL (13.53 U.S. oz. or 11.22 Imp. oz.)
Rear final gear case	
2-wheel drive	
1986-1990	300 mL (10.14 U.S. oz. or 8.4 Imp. oz.)
1991-on	350 mL (11.83 U.S. oz. or 9.86 Imp. oz.)
4-wheel drive	
1989-1992	200 mL (6.76 U.S. oz. or 5.63 Imp. oz.)
1993	
U.S. and Canada	200 mL (6.76 U.S. oz. or 5.63 Imp. oz.)
Australia, Europe and U.K.	300 mL (10.14 U.S. oz. or 8.4 Imp. oz.)
1994-on	300 mL (10.14 U.S. oz. or 8.4 Imp. oz.)

Table 7 TUNE-UP SPECIFICATIONS

Engine compression	
Using recoil starter	825-1,280 kPa (119-185 psi)
Using electric starter	795-1,240 kPa (115-179 psi)
Valve clearance (engine cold)	
Intake	0.10-0.15 mm (0.004-0.006 in.)
Exhaust	0.15-0.20 mm (0.006-0.008 in.)
Ignition timing	Not adjustable, see text for inspection procedure
Spark plug gap	0.7-0.8 mm (0.028-0.031 in.)
Idle speed	See text
Pilot air screw (turns out)	
2-wheel drive	
1986-1988; 1996-on	2 1/8
1989-1995	2 1/4
4-wheel drive	
1989-1995	2 1/8
1996-on	2

Table 8 SPARK PLUGS

Model	NGK spark plug
2-wheel drive	
U.S. & Australia	B8ES
Canada & UK	BR8ES
4-wheel drive	
1989-1990	
U.S.	D8EA
All other models	DR8ES-L
1991-1992	
U.S.	DR8EA
Australia and Canada	DR8ES-L
UK	DR7EA
1993-on	
U.S.	D8EA
Australia and Canada	DR8ES-L
UK and Europe	DR7EA

ENGINE TOP END

The engine is an air-cooled, single cam, two-valve single. Valves are operated by a single chain-driven camshaft.

This chapter provides complete service and overhaul procedures, including information for disassembly, removal, inspection, service and reassembly of the engine top end components. These include the camshaft, valves, cylinder head, piston, piston rings and cylinder block.

Before starting any work, read the service hints in Chapter One. You will do a better job with this information fresh in your mind.

Table 1 lists general engine specifications and **Table 2** lists engine service specifications. **Tables 1-4** are at the end of the chapter.

ENGINE PRINCIPLES

Figure 1 explains basic 4-stroke engine operation. This will be helpful when troubleshooting or repairing your engine.

CYLINDER HEAD

The cylinder head can be removed with the engine mounted in the frame. Refer to **Figure 2** (1986-1987), **Figure 3** (1988-on) and **Figure 4** when servicing the cylinder head.

① **4-STROKE PRINCIPLES**

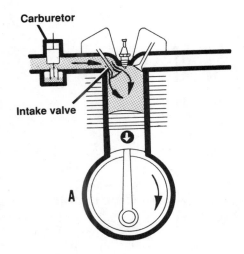

A

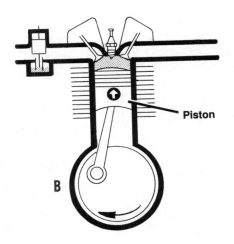

B

As the piston travels downward, the exhaust valve is closed and the intake valve opens, allowing the new air-fuel mixture from the carburetor to be drawn into the cylinder. When the piston reaches the bottom of its travel (BDC), the intake valve closes and remains closed for the next 1 1/2 revolutions of the crankshaft.

While the crankshaft continues to rotate, the piston moves upward, compressing the air-fuel mixture.

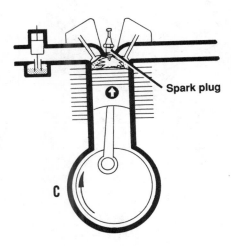

C

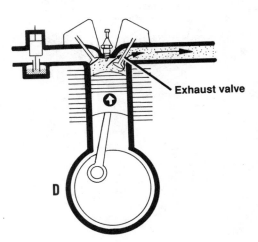

D

As the piston almost reaches the top of its travel, the spark plug fires, igniting the compressed air-fuel mixture. The piston continues to top dead center (TDC) and is pushed downward by the expanding gases.

When the piston almost reaches BDC, the exhaust valve opens and remains open until the piston is near TDC. The upward travel of the piston forces the exhaust gases out of the cylinder. After the piston has reached TDC, the exhaust valve closes and the cycle starts all over again.

4

CYLINDER HEAD
(1986-1987)

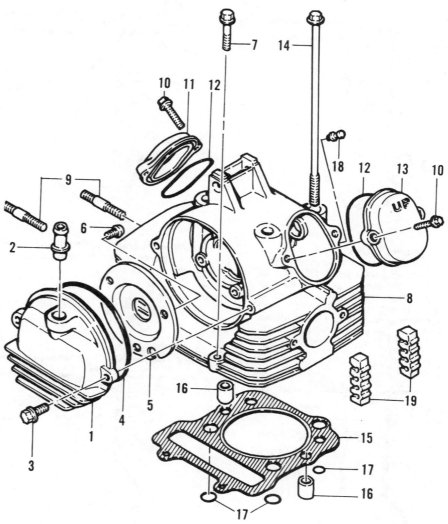

1. Cylinder head
   side cover
2. Hose nozzle
3. Bolt
4. O-ring
5. Plate
6. Screw
7. Bolt

8. Cylinder head
9. Stud
10. Bolt
11. Exhaust valve
    cover
12. O-ring
13. Intake valve
    cover

14. Cylinder head
    mounting bolt
15. Cylinder
    head gasket
16. Dowel pins
17. O-rings
18. Plug
19. Sound dampers

③

CYLINDER HEAD
(1988-ON)

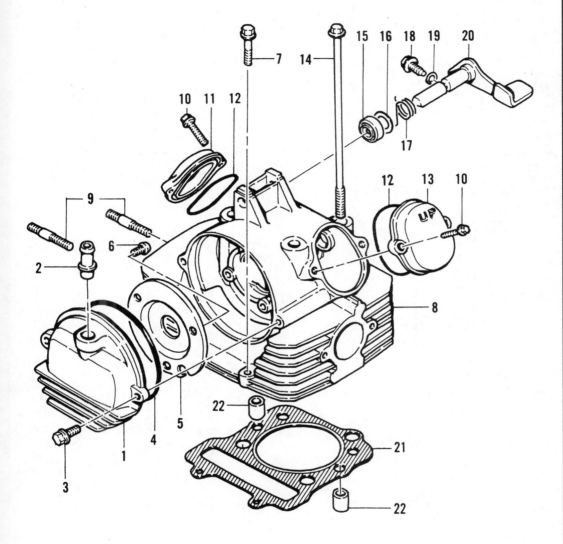

1. Cylinder head
   side cover
2. Hose nozzle
3. Bolt
4. O-ring
5. Plate
6. Screw
7. Bolt
8. Cylinder head
9. Studs

10. Bolt
11. Exhaust valve
    cover
12. O-ring
13. Intake valve
    cover
14. Cylinder head
    mounting bolt
15. Oil seal

16. Washer
17. Spring
18. Bolt
19. Washer
20. Compression
    release lever
21. Cylinder head
    gasket
22. Dowel pins

4

CAMSHAFT AND ROCKER ARMS

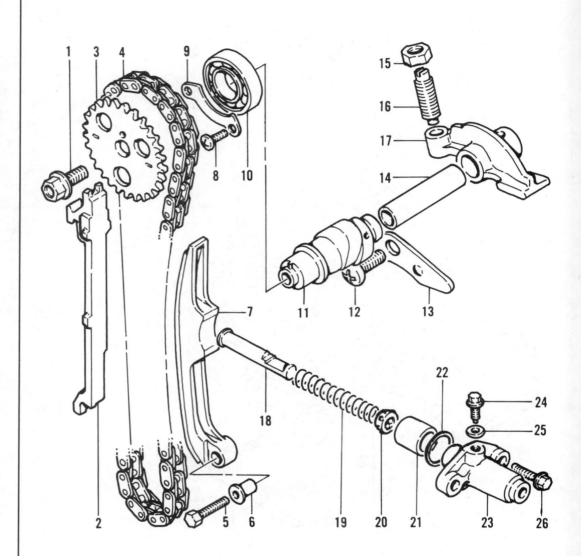

1. Bolt
2. Front chain guide
3. Cam sprocket
4. Cam chain
5. Bolt
6. Collar
7. Rear chain guide
8. Screw

9. Plate
10. Bearing
11. Camshaft
12. Screw
13. Plate
14. Rocker arm shaft
15. Locknut
16. Valve adjuster
17. Rocker arm

18. Pushrod
19. Spring
20. Ball and retainer
21. Collar
22. O-ring
23. Cam chain tensioner housing
24. Bolt
25. Washer
26. Bolt

Cylinder Head Removal

1. Remove the following components as described in Chapter Fourteen:
   a. Seat.
   b. Front fender.
2. Disconnect the negative battery cable (**Figure 5**).
3. Disconnect the breather hose from the cylinder head cover (**Figure 6**).
4. Remove the following components as described in Chapter Eight:
   a. Fuel tank.
   b. Carburetor.
   c. Exhaust system.
5. Remove the cylinder head bracket mounting bolts. Then remove the cylinder head mounting bolts and remove the bracket(s). See **Figure 7** (1986-1987) or **Figure 8** (1988-on).
6A. On 1986-1987 models, perform the following:
   a. Remove the left-hand side cover guard.

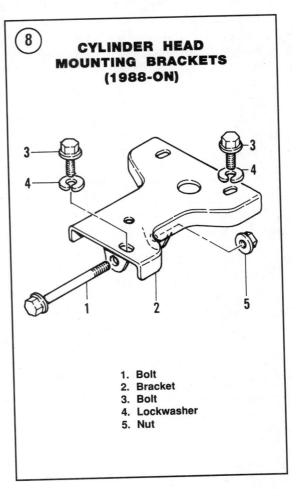

CYLINDER HEAD
MOUNTING BRACKETS
(1988-ON)

1. Bolt
2. Bracket
3. Bolt
4. Lockwasher
5. Nut

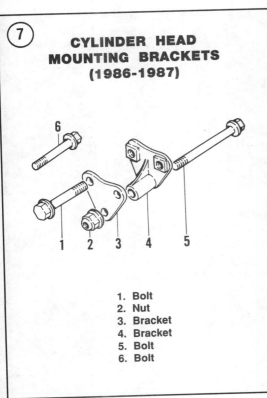

CYLINDER HEAD
MOUNTING BRACKETS
(1986-1987)

1. Bolt
2. Nut
3. Bracket
4. Bracket
5. Bolt
6. Bolt

b. Remove the timing inspection plug and the center plug (**Figure 9**).

6B. On 1988-on models, perform the following:

a. Remove the recoil starter assembly as described in Chapter Five.

b. Remove the timing inspection plug (**Figure 10**) from the left-hand side cover.

7. Remove the cylinder head side cover and O-ring (A, **Figure 11**).

8. Remove the exhaust (B, **Figure 11**) and intake (C, **Figure 11**) valve covers.

9. Remove the spark plug. This will make it easier to turn the engine by hand.

10. The engine must be set to top dead center (TDC) on its compression stroke before removing the upper cam sprocket bolt and sprocket in the following procedure. Perform the following:

a. With a socket on the flywheel bolt (**Figure 12**) or starter sprocket, turn the crankshaft counter-clockwise and align the "LF300" mark on the cam sprocket (A, **Figure 13**) with the cylinder head "TOP" mark (B, **Figure 13**).

b. Check the position of the "T" mark on the flywheel. It should be aligned with the left-hand

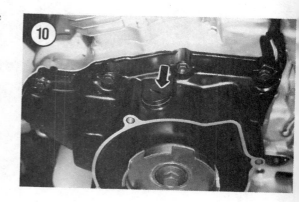

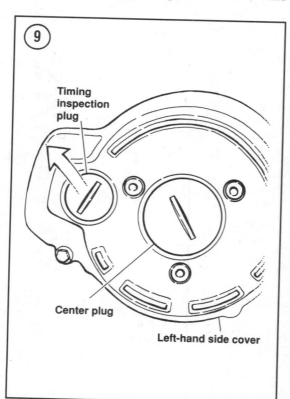

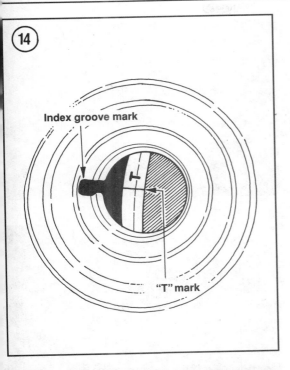

Index groove mark

"T" mark

side cover index groove mark as shown in **Figure 14** (1986-1987) or **Figure 15** (1988-on). If these marks are not aligned, turn the crankshaft to align them.

c. When the cam sprocket and flywheel marks are properly aligned, both rocker arms will have a valve clearance, indicating that both the intake and exhaust valves are closed. Move each rocker arm (**Figure 16**, typical) by hand. There should be some side movement.

11. Remove the cam chain tensioner as follows:

a. Loosen, but do not remove, the lockbolt (A, **Figure 17**) on top of the tensioner housing.

b. Remove the cam chain tensioner mounting bolts (B, **Figure 17**) and remove the cam chain tensioner assembly from the cylinder block.

12. Secure the cam chain with safety wire. This will prevent the chain from falling down into the cylinder chain tunnel.

13. Hold the flywheel bolt (**Figure 12**) or starter sprocket with a wrench and loosen the cam sprocket bolt (**Figure 18**).

CAUTION
Do not remove the cam sprocket bolt until the engine has been set at top dead

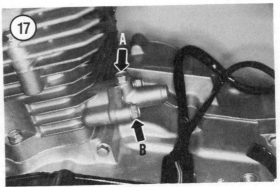

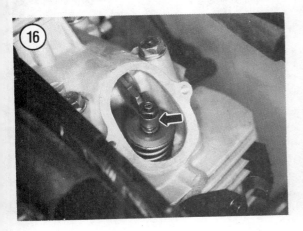

center (TDC) on its compression stroke; otherwise one or both valves may bend when the sprocket and chain are removed from the camshaft.

14. Remove the cam sprocket bolt (**Figure 18**) then slide the cam sprocket (**Figure 19**) off of the camshaft and remove it.

NOTE
*The camshaft and both rocker arms can be removed with the cylinder head mounted on the engine and the engine installed in the frame. Refer to **Camshaft and Rocker Arm Removal** in this chapter.*

15. Loosen and remove the 2 cylinder head mounting bolts (6 mm) shown in **Figure 20**.

16. Using the crisscross pattern shown in **Figure 21**, loosen the 8 mm cylinder head mounting bolts (bolts 1, 2, 3 and 4) in equal amounts until all of the bolts are loose. Remove the bolts.

17. Tap the cylinder head with a rubber mallet to break it free from the head gasket.

18. Remove the cylinder head (**Figure 22**).

19A. On 1986-1987 models, remove the head gasket, 2 dowel pins and 3 O-rings (**Figure 23**) from the top of the cylinder block.

19B. On 1988-on models, remove the head gasket and 2 dowel pins (**Figure 24**) from the top of the cylinder block.

20. If necessary, remove the exhaust side cam chain guide.

21. Cover the cylinder block with a clean shop rag or paper towels.

22. If necessary, remove the camshaft and rocker arms as described in this chapter.

Cylinder Head Inspection

1. Remove all traces of gasket material from the cylinder head and cylinder mating surfaces. Do not scratch the gasket surfaces.

2. Without removing the valves, remove all carbon deposits from the combustion chamber (**Figure 25**). Use a fine wire brush dipped in solvent or make a scraper from hardwood. Take care not to damage the head, valves or spark plug threads.

CAUTION
Cleaning the combustion chamber with the valves removed can damage the valve seat surfaces. A damaged or even slightly scratched valve seat will cause poor valve seating.

3. Examine the spark plug threads in the cylinder head for damage. If damage is minor or if the threads are dirty or clogged with carbon, use a spark plug thread tap to clean the threads following its manufacturer's instructions. If thread damage is severe, the threads can be restored by installing a steel thread insert. Thread insert kits can be purchased at automotive supply stores or you can have the inserts installed by a Kawasaki dealer or machine shop.

NOTE
When using a tap to clean spark plug threads, coat the tap with an aluminum tap cutting fluid or kerosene.

NOTE
Aluminum spark plug threads are commonly damaged due to galling, cross-threading and overtightening. To prevent galling, apply an antiseize compound to the plug threads before installation and do not overtighten.

4. After all carbon is removed from combustion chambers and valve ports, and the spark plug thread hole is repaired, clean the entire head in solvent.

NOTE
If the cylinder head is bead-blasted, make sure to clean the head thoroughly with solvent and then with hot soapy water. After bead blasting, gritty residue can seat in small crevices and other areas and can be hard to get out. Also, chase each exposed thread with a tap to remove grit between the threads or you may damage a thread later. Residue grit left in the engine will contaminate the oil and cause premature piston, ring and bearing wear.

5. Examine the piston crown. The crown should show no signs of wear or damage. If the crown appears pecked or spongy-looking, also check the spark plug, valves and combustion chamber for aluminum deposits. If these deposits are found, the cylinder is suffering from excessive heat caused by a lean fuel mixture or preignition.

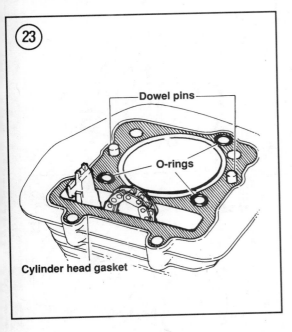

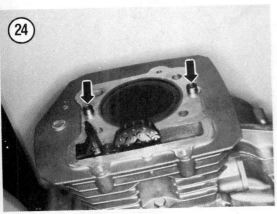

6. Inspect the intake manifold (**Figure 26**) for cracks or other damage that would allow unfiltered air to enter the engine. If necessary, remove the intake manifold and replace the O-ring(s); see **Figure 27**.

When installing the insulator, install it with its projection tab (**Figure 26**) facing up.

7. Check for cracks in the combustion chamber and exhaust port (**Figure 28**). A cracked head must be replaced if it cannot be repaired by welding.

8. After the head has been thoroughly cleaned, place a straightedge across the gasket surface at several points (**Figure 29**). Measure warp by attempting to insert a feeler gauge between the straightedge and cylinder head at each location. Maximum allowable warpage is listed in **Table 2** . Warpage or nicks in the cylinder head surface (**Figure 30**) could cause an air leak and result in overheating. If warpage exceeds the specified limit, the cylinder head must be resurfaced or replaced. Consult a Kawasaki dealer or machine shop experienced in this type of work.

9. Check the cylinder head bolts (**Figure 31**) for thread damage, cracks and twisting.

Cam Chain Tensioner Inspection

The automatic cam chain tensioner should be checked for damaged parts prior to reassembly.

1. Remove the lockbolt and washer (**Figure 32**) and disassemble the cam chain tensioner assembly.

2. Replace the tensioner housing O-ring if it has become hard or is starting to deteriorate.

3. Clean all parts (**Figure 33**) in solvent and dry thoroughly.

4. Replace the ball and retainer assembly if damaged.

5. Replace the pushrod if scored or damaged.

6. Check the spring for bending, unequally spaced coils or other damage.

7. Replace any component as required.

8. Reassemble and install the cam chain tensioner as described under *Cylinder Head Installation* in this chapter.

Cylinder Head Installation

1. Clean the cylinder head and cylinder mating surfaces of all gasket residue.

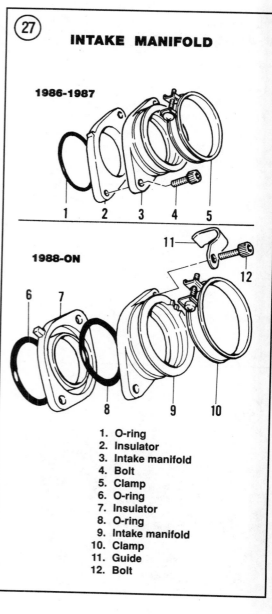

INTAKE MANIFOLD

1986-1987

1 2 3 4 5

1988-ON

6 7 8 9 10 11 12

1. O-ring
2. Insulator
3. Intake manifold
4. Bolt
5. Clamp
6. O-ring
7. Insulator
8. O-ring
9. Intake manifold
10. Clamp
11. Guide
12. Bolt

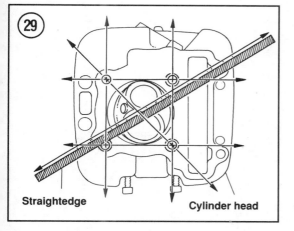

Straightedge   Cylinder head

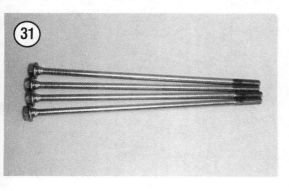

2. If removed, install the following components as described in this chapter:
   a. Valves.
   b. Camshaft.
   c. Rocker arms and shafts.

3. Install the exhaust side cam chain guide into the cylinder head chain guide slot (**Figure 34**). Make sure the chain guide's sliding surface faces toward

the cam chain and that the cam chain is positioned between both chain guides (**Figure 35**).

4A. On 1986-1987 models, install the head gasket, 2 dowel pins and 3 O-rings onto the cylinder (**Figure 23**).

4B. On 1988-on models, install the head gasket and 2 dowel pins onto the cylinder (**Figure 24**).

5. If the crankshaft is rotated away from TDC, perform the following:

a. Lift the cam chain and make sure it is engaged with the crankshaft cam chain sprocket. Hold the chain in this position when turning the crankshaft.

CAUTION
The cam chain must be kept tight against its sprocket when turning the crankshaft; otherwise, the chain can roll off the sprocket and bind in the lower end, causing chain damage.

b. Turn the crankshaft counterclockwise and align the "T" mark on the flywheel with the left-hand side cover index groove as shown in **Figure 36** (1986-1987) or **Figure 37** (1988-on).

6. Position the cylinder head between the frame and cylinder block and run the cam chain and its safety wire through the cylinder head chain tunnel (**Figure 38**). Tie the safety wire to the frame.

7. Seat the cylinder head on the cylinder block (**Figure 38**). Make sure the dowel pins engage the cylinder.

8. Pull up on the chain and make sure it is properly engaged with the crankshaft sprocket before continuing.

9. Install the 4 long cylinder head mounting bolts (**Figure 39**). Tighten the bolts finger-tight.

10. Install the 2 cylinder head mounting bolts (6 mm) and tighten finger-tight (**Figure 40**).

NOTE
Table 4 *lists a "new" and "used" bolt torque specification for the 8 mm cylinder head bolts. Make sure to use the correct torque specification for the bolts being used.*

11. Tighten the cylinder mounting bolts in 2-3 stages in the crisscross pattern shown in **Figure 41**.

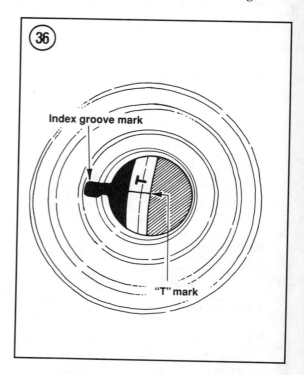

Index groove mark

"T" mark

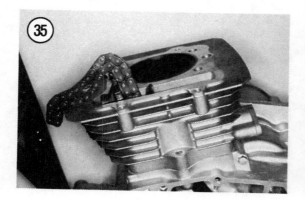

Tighten to the final torque specification listed in **Table 4**.

12. Install the camshaft and rocker arms, if previously removed, as described in this chapter.

NOTE
Steps 13-20 set camshaft timing. The crankshaft was set at TDC in Step 5.

13. Confirm that the flywheel "T" mark is aligned with the left-hand side cover index groove mark as shown in **Figure 36** (1986-1987) or **Figure 37** (1988-on). If not, repeat Step 5.

14. Remove the safety wire from the top of the cam chain and reconnect it at a lower part on the chain so that you can remove it after installing the cam sprocket.

15. Align the cam sprocket so that its "LF300" timing mark faces out and is positioned at the top (12 o'clock). Then install the cam chain onto the cam sprocket (**Figure 42**).

16. Slide the cam sprocket onto the camshaft, engaging the round tab on the back of the sprocket (A,

CYLINDER HEAD BOLT TORQUE

Figure 43) with the small hole in the camshaft (B, **Figure 43**). See A, **Figure 44**.

17. Check that the cam sprocket timing mark "LF300" (B, **Figure 44**) aligns with the cylinder head "TOP" timing mark (C, **Figure 44**). If not, remove the sprocket and reposition it in the cam chain.

18. When the timing marks align, install the cam sprocket mounting bolt and washer and tighten finger-tight (**Figure 45**).

> **CAUTION**
> *When performing Step 19, do not rotate the crankshaft more than 1/2 turn (180°) or piston and valve damage may occur.*

19. Turn the crankshaft clockwise and then counterclockwise (less than 1/4 turn both ways) and then realign the timing marks (**Figure 44**). This step removes slack from the cam chain.

20. Insert your finger through the cam chain tensioner hole in the cylinder block and push hard against the cam chain. Now check that the cam sprocket timing mark aligns with the cylinder head timing mark (**Figure 44**). If the timing marks align, perform Step 21. If not, remove the cam sprocket and reinstall it so that the timing marks align.

21. Hold the flywheel bolt or starter pulley with a wrench and tighten the cam sprocket bolt to the torque specification in **Table 4**.

22. Assemble and install the cam chain tensioner as follows:

   a. Install the spring onto the pushrod, compress it, then secure it with a piece of wire as shown in **Figure 46**.

   b. Slide the ball and retainer assembly (A, **Figure 47**) onto the pushrod.

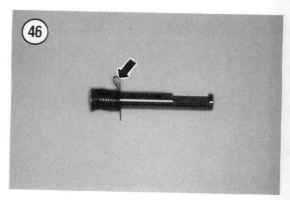

c. Slide the pushrod (**Figure 48**) into the tensioner housing so that the flat section on the pushrod (B, **Figure 47**) faces toward the lockbolt hole (**Figure 48**). Then push the pushrod into the tensioner housing until it bottoms out. Hold it in this position.

d. Install the lockbolt and washer and tighten the lockbolt to lock the pushrod in position; see **Figure 49**. The lockbolt should tighten against the upper flat section on the pushrod.

e. Remove the piece of wire from the pushrod to release the spring (**Figure 50**).

f. Insert the cam chain tensioner into the cylinder block with the lockbolt (B, **Figure 51**) facing up.

g. Install the tensioner body 6 mm mounting bolts (A, **Figure 51**) and tighten securely.

h. Loosen the lockbolt (B, **Figure 51**), then retighten it. The cam chain tensioner is now set.

23. Check valve adjustment as described in Chapter Three.

24. Apply a lithium soap base grease to the valve cover and cylinder head side cover O-rings (**Figure 52**) prior to installation.

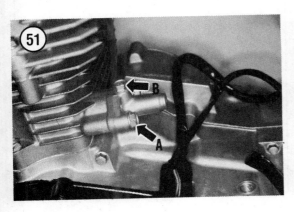

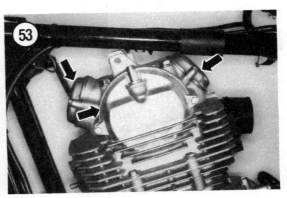

25. Install the valve covers (UP mark facing up) and the cylinder head side cover (**Figure 53**). Tighten the bolts securely.

26A. On 1986-1987 models, perform the following:

   a. Install the timing inspection plug and the center plug.

   b. Install the left-hand side guard.

26B. On 1988-on models, perform the following:

   a. Install the timing inspection plug into the left-hand side cover.

   b. Install the recoil starter assembly as described in Chapter Five.

27. Install the spark plug and reconnect the spark plug cap.

28. Install the cylinder head mounting brackets, bolts and nuts. Tighten the nuts and bolts to the torque specification in **Table 4**. See **Figure 54** (1986-1987) or **Figure 55** (1988-on).

29. Reconnect the breather hose to the cylinder head cover (**Figure 6**).

30. Install the following components as described in Chapter Eight:

   a. Exhaust system.

   b. Carburetor.

   c. Fuel tank.

31. Reconnect the negative battery cable (**Figure 5**) to the battery.

32. Install the following components as described in Chapter Fourteen:

   a. Front fender.

   b. Seat.

33. If new parts were installed, the engine should be broken-in just as though it were new. Refer to *Engine Break-In* in Chapter Five.

COMPRESSION RELEASE LEVER (1988-ON)

The compression release lever (**Figure 56**) is installed on the right-hand side of the cylinder head.

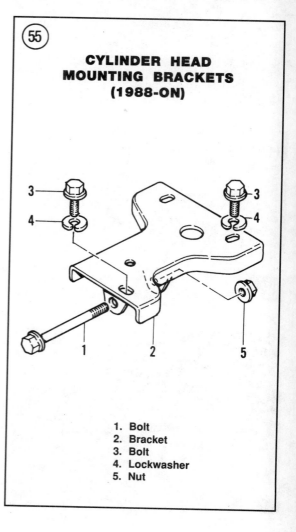

55

CYLINDER HEAD MOUNTING BRACKETS (1988-ON)

1. Bolt
2. Bracket
3. Bolt
4. Lockwasher
5. Nut

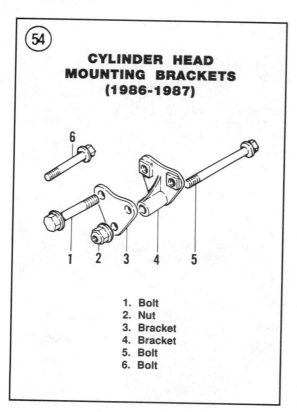

54

CYLINDER HEAD MOUNTING BRACKETS (1986-1987)

1. Bolt
2. Nut
3. Bracket
4. Bracket
5. Bolt
6. Bolt

When starting the engine with the recoil starter, first pull the compression release lever up until it locks in place. Then pull the recoil starter. When the engine starts, push the compression release lever down.

Compression Release Lever Removal/Inspection/Reassembly

The following procedure is shown with the cylinder head removed for clarity.

1. If the cylinder head is mounted in the frame, remove the front fender as described in Chapter Fourteen.
2. Push the compression release lever down.

> *CAUTION*
> *Do not remove the compression release lever while it is holding the exhaust rocker arm down; otherwise damage to the rocker arm and compression release lever may occur.*

3. Remove the compression release lever bolt and washer (A, **Figure 57**) and pull the lever assembly (B) out of the cylinder head.
4. Inspect the compression release lever assembly for worn, missing or damaged parts. The compression release lever assembly is shown in **Figure 58**.
5. Replace the compression release lever oil seal (**Figure 59**) if leaking or damaged. To replace the oil seal:

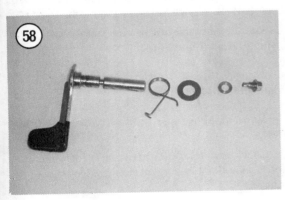

  a. Pry the oil seal out of the cylinder head with a small, wide-blade screwdriver. Pad the screwdriver to prevent it from damaging the seal bore.
  b. Pack the oil seal lip with a waterproof, bearing grease.
  c. Press in the oil seal until its outer surface is flush with the oil seal bore as shown in **Figure 59**.

6. Install and hook the spring onto the compression release lever as shown in A, **Figure 60**.

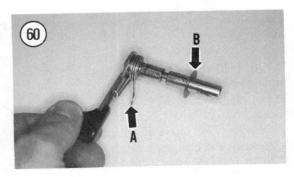

7. Slide the washer (B, **Figure 60**) onto the compression release lever.

8. Apply a light film of grease onto the compression release lever shaft.

> *CAUTION*
> *Do not force the compression release lever shaft into the oil seal when installing it in Step 9; doing so will damage the oil seal resulting in oil leakage.*

9. Install the compression release lever shaft by slowly turning it into the oil seal (**Figure 61**). Hook the free end of the spring on the cylinder head post.

10. Install the bolt and washer (A, **Figure 57**)—insert the end of the bolt into the groove in the compression release lever shaft. Tighten the bolt securely.

11. Operate the compression release lever by hand. It should move smoothly and lock in its up and down positions.

12. If removed, install the front fender.

CAMSHAFT AND ROCKER ARMS

A single camshaft is mounted in the cylinder head. The camshaft is held in place with a ball bearing and retainer. The camshaft is driven by a chain off of the sprocket mounted on the crankshaft. The cam and both rocker arms can be removed with the engine in the frame, or you can remove the cylinder head as previously described.

Refer to **Figure 62** when performing this procedure.

> *NOTE*
> *Many of the following steps are shown with the engine removed from the frame. As previously mentioned, the camshaft can be removed with the engine in or out of the frame.*

Removal

1. Park the vehicle on level ground and set the parking brake.

2. On 1988-on models, remove the compression release lever as described under *Compression Release Lever (1988-on)* in this chapter.

3. Remove the cam sprocket as described under *Cylinder Head Removal* in this chapter.

> *NOTE*
> *If the engine is mounted in the frame, it is unnecessary to remove the upper engine mount bracket, carburetor and exhaust pipe when removing the camshaft and rocker arms.*

4. Remove the rocker arm shaft retainer (A, **Figure 63**).

5. Remove the camshaft retainer (B, **Figure 63**).

> *NOTE*
> *Both rocker arms and shafts are identical (same part numbers). However, because these parts have taken a set wear pattern, the rocker arms and shafts should labeled to avoid intermixing the parts. When removing the rocker arm assemblies in the following steps, mark them in sets: "E" (exhaust) or "I" (intake).*

6. Using a magnet, remove the exhaust side rocker arm shaft (A, **Figure 64**) and rocker arm (**Figure 65**) from the cylinder head.

7. Repeat Step 6 to remove the intake side rocker arm shaft (B, **Figure 64**) and rocker arm.

8. Pull the camshaft and bearing straight out of the cylinder head (**Figure 66**).

Camshaft Inspection

Camshaft service specifications are listed in **Table 2**.

1. Check cam lobes (A, **Figure 67**) for wear. The lobes should not be scored and the edges should be square.

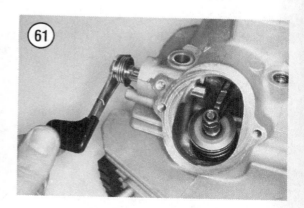

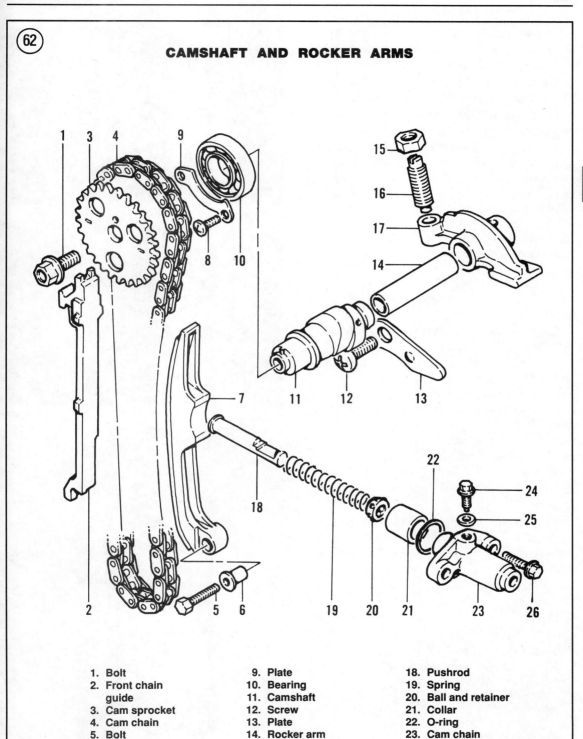

CAMSHAFT AND ROCKER ARMS

1. Bolt
2. Front chain guide
3. Cam sprocket
4. Cam chain
5. Bolt
6. Collar
7. Rear chain guide
8. Screw
9. Plate
10. Bearing
11. Camshaft
12. Screw
13. Plate
14. Rocker arm shaft
15. Locknut
16. Valve adjuster
17. Rocker arm
18. Pushrod
19. Spring
20. Ball and retainer
21. Collar
22. O-ring
23. Cam chain tensioner housing
24. Bolt
25. Washer
26. Bolt

2. Measure cam lobe height for both lobes (**Figure 68**). Replace the camshaft if the cam lobe height is less than the service limit.

3. Check the camshaft bearing journal (B, **Figure 67**) for wear and scoring. If the journal is severely worn or damaged, check the journal bore in the cylinder head for damage.

4. The left-hand camshaft bearing (C, **Figure 67**) is pressed on the camshaft. Do not remove the bearing for routine inspection. Refer to *Camshaft Bearing Inspection/Replacement* in this chapter.

Camshaft Bearing Inspection/Replacement

The left-hand camshaft bearing is a single-row ball bearing (**Figure 69**) and is a press-fit on the camshaft.

1. Clean the camshaft/bearing assembly in solvent. Blow dry with compressed air.

2. Hold the camshaft and rotate the outer bearing race by hand. The bearing should turn smoothly with no roughness, binding or excessive play. The bearing should show no signs of overheating. If the bearing does not show visual damage, but turns roughly, reclean the bearing and recheck. If this condition persists, replace the bearing as described in Step 3.

3. To replace the ball bearing, refer to *Ball Bearing Replacement* in Chapter One while noting the following:

  a. Support the bearing in a press and press the camshaft off the bearing. Discard the bearing.

  b. Reclean the camshaft in solvent. Dry with compressed air.

  c. Align the new bearing with the camshaft (manufacturers marks facing out) and press the bear-

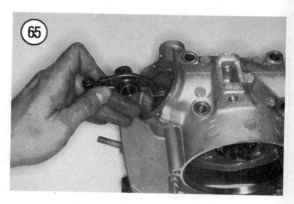

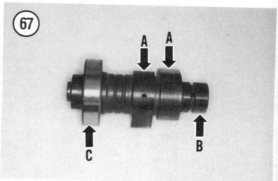

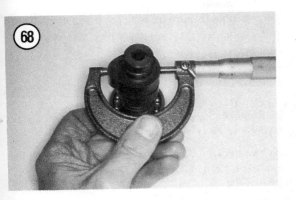

ing onto the camshaft until it bottoms out on the camshaft shoulder.

d. Lubricate the bearing with new engine oil.

Cam Sprocket
Inspection

Inspect the upper cam sprocket (**Figure 70**) for broken or chipped teeth. Also check the teeth for cracking or rounding. If the upper sprocket is damaged or severely worn, inspect the drive (lower) sprocket mounted on the crankshaft. See *Crankshaft Sprocket and Main Bearing Replacement* in Chapter Five.

> *NOTE*
> *If the cam and crankshaft sprockets are worn, check the camshaft chain, chain guides and chain tensioner for damage.*

Rocker Arms and Shafts
Inspection

1. Clean all parts in solvent. Blow dry with compressed air.

2. Inspect the rocker arm pad (A, **Figure 71**) where it rides on the cam lobe and where the adjuster (B, **Figure 71**) rides on the valve stem. Check for scratches, flat spots, uneven wear and scoring.

3. Replace the valve adjuster (B, **Figure 71**) if it has stretched or is damaged in any way.

4. Inspect the rocker arm shaft (A, **Figure 72**) for severe wear, scoring or seizure marks.

5. Measure the rocker arm shaft O.D. with a micrometer and check against the specification in **Table 2**. Replace if worn beyond the service limit.

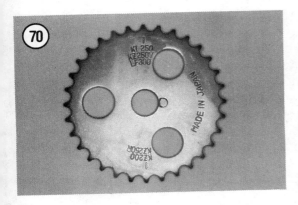

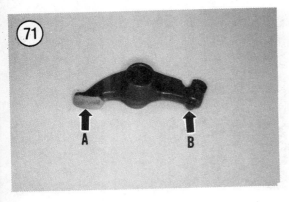

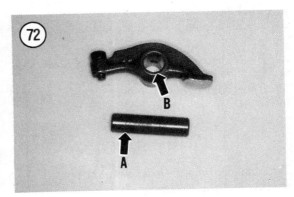

6. Measure the rocker arm bore I.D. with a gauge. Measure the gauge with a micrometer and check against the dimension in **Table 2**. Replace if worn beyond the service limit.

NOTE
Kawasaki does not list rocker arm-to-shaft clearance specifications.

7. Repeat for the other rocker arm assembly.

Installation

Figure 73 shows the camshaft, rocker arm and shaft assembly.
1. Coat the camshaft journal, lobes and bearing with new engine oil.
2. Install the cam through the cylinder head opening (**Figure 66**) and seat it in the cylinder head.
3. Turn the cam so that the cam sprocket index hole is set at the 2-3 o'clock position as shown in **Figure 74**. This positions the cam with both cam lobes facing down.
4. Install the camshaft retainer (B, **Figure 63**) and the 2 mounting screws. Tighten the screws securely.
5. Coat the rocker arm shaft and rocker arm bore with engine oil.

NOTE
Install the rocker arms and shafts in their original positions.

6. Install the exhaust rocker arm, pad end first, into the cylinder head (**Figure 65**).
7. Install the rocker arm shaft (A, **Figure 64**) through the cylinder head and exhaust rocker arm until it bottoms out.
8. Repeat Step 6 and Step 7 for the intake rocker arm and shaft.
9. Install the rocker arm shaft retainer (A, **Figure 63**) and its mounting screw. Tighten the screw securely.
10. Install the compression release lever as described in this chapter.
11. If the cylinder head is mounted on the engine, install the cam sprocket as described in this chapter.

CAM CHAIN

A continuous cam chain is used on all models. Do not cut the chain; replacement link components are not available. **Figure 62** is an exploded view of the cam chain, cam sprocket and both chain guides.

Removal/Installation

1. Remove the cam sprocket as described under *Cylinder Head Removal* in this chapter.
2. Remove the starter clutch as described under *Starter Clutch, Chain and Sprockets* in Chapter Five.

3. Remove the cam guide plate screw and remove the guide plate (A, **Figure 75**).

4. Slip the cam chain (B, **Figure 75**) off the lower sprocket and remove it from around the crankshaft.

5. Inspect the cam chain as described under *Inspection* in this section.

6. Install the cam chain over the crankshaft and pull it up through the chain tunnel with a piece of wire. Secure the chain with a piece of safety wire.

7. Engage the chain with the drive (lower) sprocket on the crankshaft.

8. Install the cam chain guide plate (A, **Figure 75**) and screw—fit the guard plate holes into the crankcase pins. Tighten the screw securely.

9. Reverse Steps 1 and 2.

Inspection

If the following procedure shows that the cam chain is severely worn or damaged, the automatic

chain tensioner may not be tensioning the chain properly; refer to *Cam Chain Tensioner Inspection* in this chapter. Likewise, the chain guides should be checked for excessive wear and damage; refer to *Chain Guides* in this chapter.

1. Clean cam chain in solvent. Blow dry with compressed air.

2. Check cam chain (**Figure 76**) for:

   a. Worn or damaged pins and rollers.

   b. Cracked or damaged side plates.

3. Place the chain on a flat surface and pull the chain tight (no slack between pins). Then measure the length of any 20 links (21 pins) with a vernier caliper (**Figure 77**) and check against the specification in **Table 2**. Replace chain if stretched to the service limit or greater. Do not attempt to repair the chain.

4. If the cam chain is severely worn or damaged, inspect the cam sprocket and the crankshaft drive sprocket for the same wear conditions. If the sprockets show wear or damage, replace them at the same time.

> *CAUTION*
> *Do not run a new chain over worn or damaged sprockets. Doing so will cause rapid and excessive chain wear.*

CHAIN GUIDES

Front and rear chain guides are used (**Figure 62**).

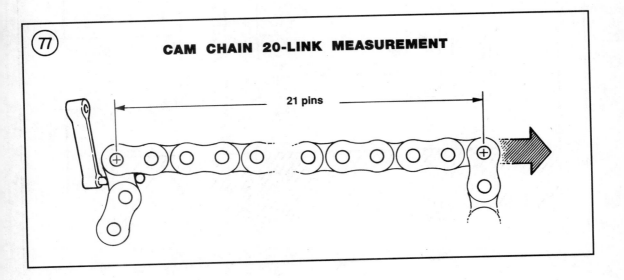

CAM CHAIN 20-LINK MEASUREMENT

21 pins

Removal/Installation

1. To remove the front chain guide (**Figure 78**), remove the cylinder head as described in this chapter. Then remove the front chain guide.

2. To remove the rear chain guide, perform the following:

   a. Remove the cylinder as described in this chapter.

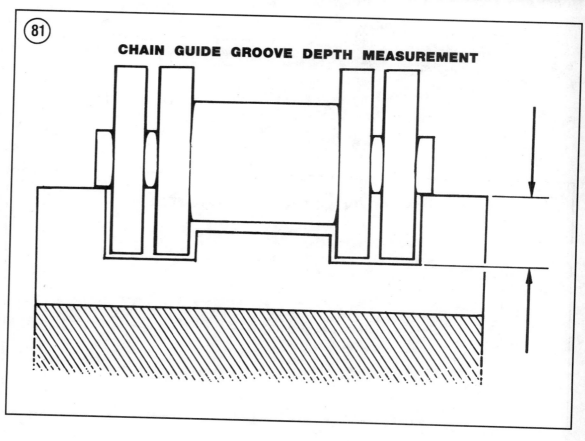

CHAIN GUIDE GROOVE DEPTH MEASUREMENT

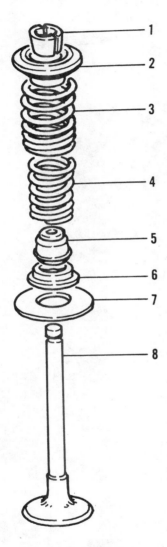

**VALVE
(1986-1987)**

1. Valve keepers
2. Upper spring seat
3. Outer spring
4. Inner spring
5. Oil seal
6. Inner spring seat
7. Outer spring seat
8. Valve

b. Remove the starter clutch as described in Chapter Five.

c. Remove the rear chain guide pivot bolt (A, **Figure 79**) and remove the rear chain guide (B, **Figure 79**) and its collar.

3. Inspect the chain guides as described under *Inspection* in this section.

4. Install by reversing these steps while noting the following.

5. The front chain guide upper end is marked "UP." Install the front chain guide so that its bottom end fits into the crankcase notch as shown in **Figure 80**.

6. When installing the rear cam chain guide, oil the collar (**Figure 62**) before installing it into the guide. Apply Loctite 242 (blue) to the rear chain guide pivot bolt. Tighten the rear chain guide pivot bolt to the torque specification in **Table 4**.

Inspection

1. Visually inspect the chain guides for severe wear, cuts or other damage. On high use engines, the chain guides may feel very brittle.

2. Measure the depth of the chain groove in each chain guide (**Figure 81**) and check against the dimension in **Table 2**. Replace if worn to the service limit or greater.

NOTE
New chain guides do not have chain grooves. The grooves are caused from normal wear.

VALVES AND VALVE COMPONENTS

Complete valve service requires a number of special tools. The following procedures describe how to check for valve component wear and to determine what type of service is required. In most cases, valve troubles are caused by poor valve seating, worn valve guides and burned valves. A valve spring compressor is required to remove and install the valves.

Refer to **Figure 82** (1986-1987) or **Figure 83** (1988-on) for this procedure.

1. Remove the cylinder head as described in this chapter.

2. On 1988-on models, remove the compression release lever as described under *Compression Release Lever* in this chapter.

4

**VALVE
(1988-ON)**

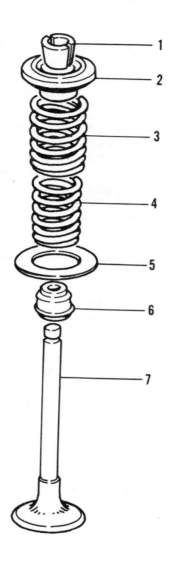

1. Valve keepers
2. Spring seat
3. Outer spring
4. Inner spring
5. Lower spring seat
6. Oil seal
7. Valve

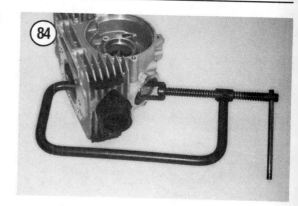

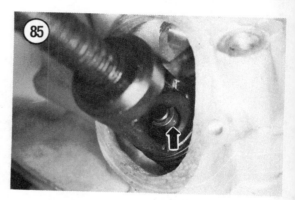

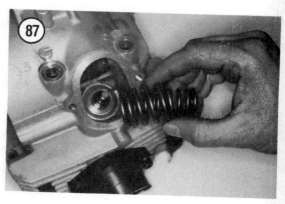

3. Install a valve spring compressor squarely over the valve spring seat with the other end of tool placed against the valve head (**Figure 84**).

4. Tighten valve spring compressor until the valve keepers (**Figure 85**) separate. Lift the valve keepers out through the valve spring compressor with a magnet or needlenose pliers.

5. Gradually loosen the valve spring compressor and remove it from the head.

6. Remove the upper spring seat (**Figure 86**) and both valve springs (**Figure 87**).

7. On 1988-on models, remove the lower spring seat (**Figure 88**).

CAUTION
*Remove any burrs from the valve stem groove before removing the valve (**Figure 89**); otherwise the valve guide will be damaged as the valve stem passes through it.*

8. Remove the valve.

9. Pull the oil seal (**Figure 90**) off of the valve guide. Discard the oil seal.

10. On 1986-1987 models, remove the inner and outer spring seats (**Figure 82**).

CAUTION
All component parts of each valve assembly must be kept together. Do not intermix components from the 2 valves or excessive wear may result.

11. Repeat Steps 3-10 and remove the remaining valve.

Inspection

Refer to the troubleshooting chart in **Figure 91** when performing valve inspection procedures in this section. Valve service specifications are listed in **Table 3**.

1. Clean valves in solvent. Do not gouge or damage the valve seating surface.

2. Inspect the valve face (**Figure 92**). Minor roughness and pitting can be removed by lapping the valve as described in this chapter. Excessive unevenness to the contact surface is an indication that the valve is not serviceable.

3. Inspect the valve stem for wear and roughness. Then measure the valve stem outside diameter with a micrometer (**Figure 93**) and check against the dimension in **Table 3**. Replace if excessively worn.

4. Remove all carbon and varnish from the valve guides with a stiff spiral wire brush before measuring wear.

NOTE
If you do not have the required measuring tools, proceed to Step 6.

5. Measure the valve guide I.D. with a small hole gauge. Measure at the top, center and bottom positions. Then measure the small hole gauge and check

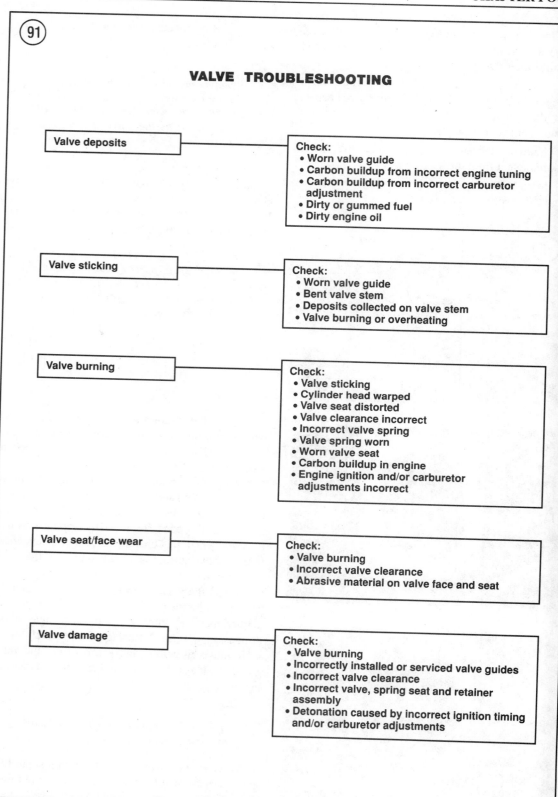

91

VALVE TROUBLESHOOTING

Valve deposits

Check:
- Worn valve guide
- Carbon buildup from incorrect engine tuning
- Carbon buildup from incorrect carburetor adjustment
- Dirty or gummed fuel
- Dirty engine oil

Valve sticking

Check:
- Worn valve guide
- Bent valve stem
- Deposits collected on valve stem
- Valve burning or overheating

Valve burning

Check:
- Valve sticking
- Cylinder head warped
- Valve seat distorted
- Valve clearance incorrect
- Incorrect valve spring
- Valve spring worn
- Worn valve seat
- Carbon buildup in engine
- Engine ignition and/or carburetor adjustments incorrect

Valve seat/face wear

Check:
- Valve burning
- Incorrect valve clearance
- Abrasive material on valve face and seat

Valve damage

Check:
- Valve burning
- Incorrectly installed or serviced valve guides
- Incorrect valve clearance
- Incorrect valve, spring seat and retainer assembly
- Detonation caused by incorrect ignition timing and/or carburetor adjustments

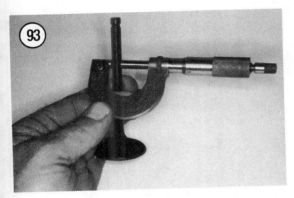

against the specification in **Table 3**. Replace if worn to the service limit.

6. If a small hole gauge is not available, insert each valve in its guide. Hold the valve just slightly off its seat and rock it sideways. If the valve rocks more than slightly, the guide is probably worn. However, as a final check, take the cylinder head to a dealer or machine shop and have the valve guides measured.

7. Check the inner and outer valve springs as follows:

    a. Check each of the valve springs for visual damage.

    b. Use a square and visually check each spring for distortion or tilt (**Figure 94**).

    c. Measure the valve spring free length with a vernier caliper (**Figure 95**) and check against the specification in **Table 3**. Replace the spring if free length is less than the service limit.

    d. Repeat for each valve spring.

    e. Replace defective springs as a set (inner and outer).

8. Check the valve spring seats and valve keepers for cracks or other damage.

9. Inspect the valve seats (**Figure 96**) in the cylinder head. If worn or burned, they may be reconditioned as described in this chapter. Seats and valves in near-perfect condition can be reconditioned by lapping with fine carborundum paste. Check as follows:

    a. Clean the valve seat and corresponding valve mating areas with contact cleaner.

    b. Coat the valve seat with layout fluid.

    c. Install the valve into its guide and rotate it against its seat with a valve lapping tool. See *Valve Lapping* in this chapter.

    d. Lift the valve out of the guide and measure the seat width with a vernier caliper.

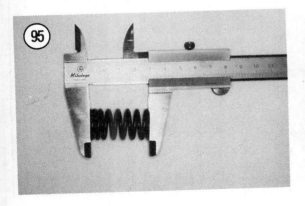

e. The seat width for intake and exhaust valves should be within the specifications listed in **Table 3** all the way around the seat. If the seat width exceeds the service limit (**Table 3**), regrind the seats as described in this chapter.

f. Remove all layout fluid residue from the seats and valves.

10. Check the valve stem runout with a V-block and dial indicator as shown in **Figure 97**. Runout should not exceed the service limit listed in **Table 3**.

11. Measure the valve head thickness with a vernier caliper (**Figure 98**) and check against the dimension in **Table 3**. Replace if worn to less than the service limit.

Valve Guide Replacement

Two different types of valve guides (**Figure 99**) are used on the engines covered in this manual. The differences are:

a. Shoulderless valve guides with a removable clip are used on 1986-1987 models. The clip, installed on the valve guide prior to installation, sets the guides height position in the cylinder head.

b. Shoulder type valve guides are installed on 1988 and later models. On 1988-1991 2-wheel drive and 1989-1992 4-wheel drive models, an O-ring is installed on the bottom of the valve guide. The O-ring is not used on models manufactured after these dates.

The valve guides must be removed and installed with special tools that can be ordered from a Kawasaki dealer. The required special tools are listed as follows:

a. Valve guide remover/installer, Kawasaki part No. 57001-163.

b. Valve guide reamer, Kawasaki part No. 57001-162.

1. When ordering new valve guides, make sure to order new clips and O-rings, if applicable to your model. See **Figure 99**.

2. On 1986-1987 models, install a new clip into the valve guide clip groove (**Figure 99**).

3. Place the new valve guides in a freezer.

NOTE
The freezing temperature will shrink the new guides slightly and ease installation.

4. The valve guides are installed with a slight interference fit. Heat the cylinder head to approximately 250-300° F (120-150° C) in a shop oven or on a hot plate.

CAUTION
Do not heat the cylinder head with a torch (propane or acetylene)—never bring a flame into contact with the cylinder head. The direct heat may cause warpage of the cylinder head.

WARNING
Heavy gloves must be worn when performing this procedure—the cylinder head will be very hot.

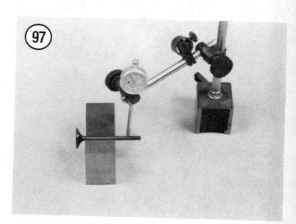

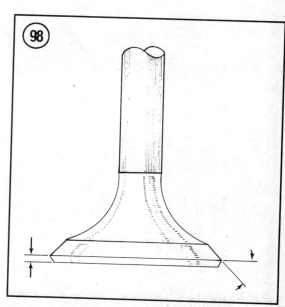

5. Remove the cylinder head from the oven or hot plate and place onto wooden blocks with the combustion chamber facing up.

6. Drive the old valve guide out from the combustion chamber side of the cylinder head with the valve guide remover (**Figure 100**). Note the position of the O-ring on the valve guide, if used, for reassembly reference.

7. After the cylinder head cools, check the guide bore for carbon or other contamination. Clean the bore thoroughly.

8. Reheat the cylinder head to approximately 250-300° F (120-150° C).

9. Remove the cylinder head from the oven or hot plate and place it on wooden blocks with the combustion chamber facing down.

10. Remove one valve guide from the freezer.

11. On 1988-1991 2-wheel drive and 1989-1992 4-wheel drive models, install a new O-ring onto the valve guide (**Figure 99**).

NOTE
Use the Kawasaki valve guide remover/installer tool to install the valve guides.

12A. On 1986-1987 models, drive the new valve guide into the cylinder head until the clip on the guide bottoms out in the clip recess.

12B. On 1988-on models, drive the new valve guide into the cylinder until the shoulder on the guide bottoms out in the guide recess.

13. If necessary, repeat Steps 2-12 to replace the other valve guide.

14. After the cylinder head has cooled to room temperature, ream the new valve guides as follows:

  a. Coat the valve guide and valve guide reamer with cutting oil.

CAUTION
Always rotate the valve guide reamer in the same direction when installing and removing it from the guide. If the reamer is rotated in the opposite direction, the guide will be damaged and will require replacement.

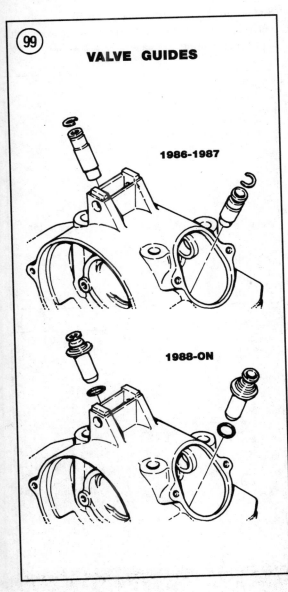

VALVE GUIDES

1986-1987

1988-ON

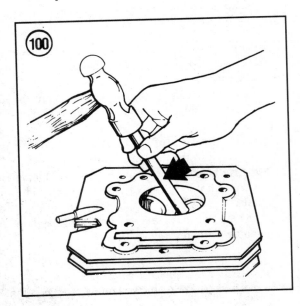

b. Insert the reamer from the top side and rotate the reamer (**Figure 101**). Continue to rotate the reamer and work it down through the entire length of the new valve guide. Apply additional cutting oil during this procedure.

c. While rotating the reamer in the same direction, withdraw the reamer from the valve guide.

d. Measure the valve guide I.D. with a small hole gauge. Then measure the small hole gauge with a micrometer and check against the dimension in **Table 3**.

15. Repeat for the other valve guide.

16. Thoroughly clean the cylinder head and valve guides with solvent to wash out all metal particles. Dry with compressed air.

17. Lightly oil the valve guides to prevent rust.

18. Reface the valve seats as described under *Valve Seat Reconditioning* in this chapter.

Valve Seat Inspection

The most accurate method for checking the valve seal is to use a layout fluid, available from auto parts and tool stores. Layout fluids are used for locating high or irregular spots when checking or making close fits and when scraping bearing surfaces. Follow the manufacturers directions.

> *NOTE*
> *Because of the close operating toler-*
> *ances within the valve assembly, the*
> *valve stem and guide must be in good*
> *condition (within tolerance); otherwise*
> *the inspection results will be inaccurate.*

1. Remove the valves as described in this chapter.

2. Clean the valve seat and valve mating areas with contact cleaner.

3. Thoroughly clean all carbon deposits from the valve face with solvent or detergent, then dry thoroughly.

4. Spread a thin layer of layout fluid evenly on the valve face. Allow the fluid to air dry.

5. Moisten the end of a suction cup valve lapping tool and attach it to the valve. Insert the valve into the guide.

6. Turn the valve in the seat by spinning the lapping tool in both directions.

> *NOTE*
> *Instead of turning the valve in Step 6,*
> *some mechanics tap the valve up and*

down in the cylinder head and then check the contact area. They feel that spinning the valve can cause incorrect results. Kawasaki recommends to spin the valve when checking the seat.

7. Remove the valve and examine the impression left by the layout fluid. If the impression left in the fluid (on the valve or in the cylinder head) is not even and continuous and the valve seat width (**Figure 102**) is not within the specified tolerance listed in **Table 3**, the cylinder head valve seat must be reconditioned.

8. Closely examine the valve seat in the cylinder head (**Figure 96**). It should be smooth and even, with a polished seating surface.

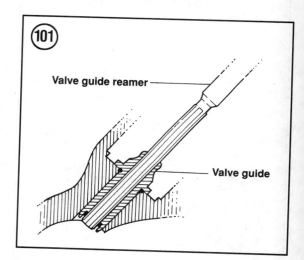

Valve guide reamer

Valve guide

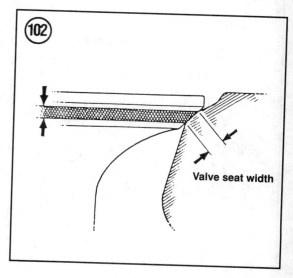

Valve seat width

9. If the valve seat is okay, install the valve as described in this chapter.

10. If the valve seat is not correct, recondition the valve seat as described in this chapter.

11. Repeat for the opposite valve.

Valve Seat Reconditioning

Special valve cutter tools and considerable experience are required to recondition the valve seats in the cylinder head properly. If you are not equipped with these tools, you can save considerable expense by removing the cylinder head and taking just the cylinder head and valves to a dealer to have the valve seats ground.

The following procedure is provided if you choose to perform this task yourself.

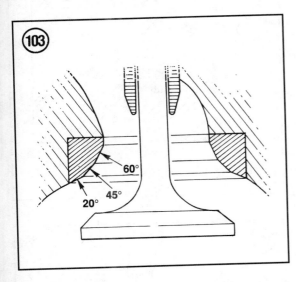

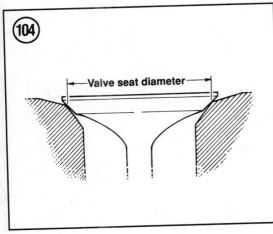

The valve seats must be cut with special tools that are available from a Kawasaki dealer. The following tools are required:

   a. Valve seat cutters (see Kawasaki dealer for part numbers).

> *NOTE*
> *The valve seat cutters listed in **Figure** 103 are required for this procedure.*

   b. Vernier caliper.
   c. Layout fluid.
   d. Valve lapping tool.

> *NOTE*
> *When using valve facing equipment, follow the manufacturer's instructions.*

> *CAUTION*
> *When grinding valve seats, work slowly to avoid overgrinding the seats. Overgrinding the valve seats will sink the valves too far into the cylinder head. Sinking the valves too far may reduce valve clearance and make it impossible to obtain the correct clearance. In this condition, it may be possible to grind the end of the valve stem to gain additional clearance. Because there is a maximum amount that can be ground from the end of the valve stem, refer this procedure to a dealer. If the valve clearance cannot be increased sufficiently by grinding the valve stems, the cylinder head will have to be replaced as replacement valve seats are not available.*

> *NOTE*
> *Steps 1-3 cut the valve seat to its proper diameter. Steps 4 and 5 cut the valve seat to its proper width.*

1. Install a 45° cutter onto the valve tool and lightly cut the seat to remove roughness.

2. Measure the valve seat diameter (**Figure 104**) with a vernier caliper and compare to the specification listed in **Table 3**. If the diameter is too small, cut the seat once again with the 45° cutter. If the diameter is too large, cut the seat with the 32° cutter as described in Step 3.

> *CAUTION*
> *The 32° cutter removes material quickly. Work carefully and check your progress often.*

3. Install a 32° cutter (**Figure 105**) onto the valve tool. Press down very lightly and turn the 32° cutter one turn. Measure the seat diameter. Repeat until the seat diameter is within the specification listed in **Table 3**.

NOTE
When the valve seat diameter is correct,
proceed with Step 4.

4. Measure the valve seat width (**Figure 102**) with a vernier caliper and compare to the dimension listed in **Table 3**. Measure at several places around the seat. Note the following:

   a. If the seat width is too narrow, cut the seat with the 45° cutter. Then remeasure the seat width and, if necessary, recut it to its proper width (see Steps 1-3).

   b. If the seat width is too wide, cut the seat with the 60° cutter as described in Step 5.

   c. If the seat width is correct, lap the valve to the seat as described in this chapter.

5. Install a 60° cutter (**Figure 105**) onto the valve tool. Press down very lightly and turn the 60° cutter one turn. Measure the seat width (Step 4). Repeat until the seat width is within the specification listed in **Table 3**.

6. After the desired valve seat diameter and width is obtained, use the 45° cutter and very lightly clean off any burrs that may have been caused by the previous cuts.

7. Lap the valve to the seat as described under *Valve Lapping* in this chapter.

8. Repeat Steps 1-7 for the other valve.

9. Clean the cylinder head and all valve components in solvent or detergent and hot water. Dry all parts thoroughly.

10. If the cylinder head and valve components are cleaned in detergent and hot water, apply a light coat of engine oil to all bare metal surfaces to prevent any rust formations.

Valve Lapping

This procedure must only be performed after cutting the valve seats.

1. Smear a light coating of coarse grade valve lapping compound on seating surface of valve.

2. Insert the valve into the head.

3. Wet the suction cup of the lapping tool and stick it onto the head of the valve. Lap the valve to the seat by spinning the lapping stick in both directions (**Figure 106**). Every 5 to 10 seconds, rotate the valve 180° in the valve seat. Continue this action until the mating surfaces on the valve and seat are smooth and equal in size.

4. Repeat Step 3 with a fine grade lapping compound.

5. Closely examine the valve seat in the cylinder head. It should be smooth and even with a smooth, polished seating ring. The seating ring mark should be approximately in the middle of the valve face.

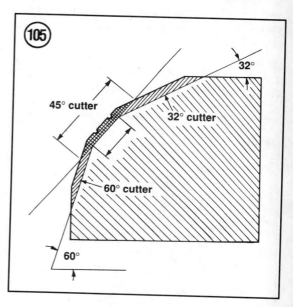

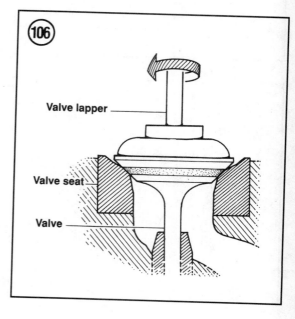

6. Thoroughly clean the valves and cylinder head in solvent to remove all grinding compound. Any compound left on the valves or the cylinder head will cause excessive engine wear and damage.

7. After the lapping has been completed and the valves have been reinstalled into the head, the valve seal should be tested. Check the seal of each valve by pouring solvent into the intake and exhaust ports. There should be no leakage past the seat in the combustion chamber. If leakage occurs, the combustion chamber will appear wet. If fluid leaks past any of the seats, disassemble that valve assembly and repeat the lapping procedure until there is no leakage.

Installation

1. Clean the end of the valve guide.

2A. On 1986-1987 models, perform the following:

   a. Install the outer valve spring seat.

   b. Install the inner valve spring seat.

   c. Oil the inside of the new oil seal and install it over the end of the valve guide.

   d. Push the new seal clip down and over the seal so that it seats in the oil seal groove.

2B. On 1988-on models, oil the inside of the new oil seal and install it over the end of the valve guide (**Figure 107**).

3. Coat a valve stem with molybdenum disulfide paste. Install the valve partway into the guide. Then, slowly turn the valve as it enters the oil seal and continue turning it until the valve is installed all the way.

4. On 1988-on models, install the lower spring seat. Center the spring seat in the spring recess as shown in **Figure 108**.

5. Position the valve springs with their *closer* wound coils (**Figure 109**) facing the cylinder head.

6. Install the inner and outer valve springs (**Figure 110**).

7. Install the upper valve spring seat on top of the valve springs (**Figure 111**).

> *CAUTION*
> *To avoid loss of spring tension, do not compress the springs any more than necessary to install the valve keepers.*

8. Compress the valve springs with a valve spring compressor (**Figure 112**) and install the valve keepers (**Figure 113**).

9. When both valve keepers are seated around the valve stem, slowly release tension from the compressor. Remove the compressor and inspect the valve keepers (**Figure 114**). Then tap the end of the valve stem with a soft-faced hammer. This will ensure that the keepers are properly seated.

10. Repeat Steps 1-9 for opposite valve.

11. On 1988-on models, install the compression release lever as described under *Compression Release Lever* in this chapter.

12. After installing the cylinder head, set valve clearance as described in Chapter Three.

CYLINDER

The alloy cylinder block has a pressed-in cast iron cylinder liner which can be bored to 0.50 mm (0.020 in.) and 1.0 mm (0.040 in.) oversize. These oversize pistons and rings are available through Kawasaki dealers and aftermarket piston suppliers.

The cylinder can be removed with the engine mounted in the frame. Refer to **Figure 115** when servicing the cylinder.

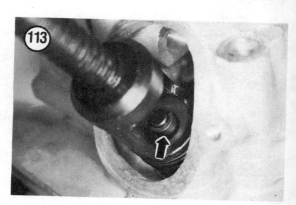

Removal

1. Remove the cylinder head as described under *Cylinder Head Removal* in this chapter.

2. Remove the cylinder Allen bolt (**Figure 116**).

3. Loosen the cylinder by tapping around its perimeter with a rubber or plastic mallet.

4. Pull the cylinder (**Figure 117**) straight up and off the crankcase. Remove and discard the base gasket.

5. If necessary, remove the piston as described under *Piston Removal/Installation* in this chapter.

6. Remove the 2 cylinder dowel pins (**Figure 118**).

7. Cover the crankcase opening to prevent objects and abrasive dust from falling into the crankcase.

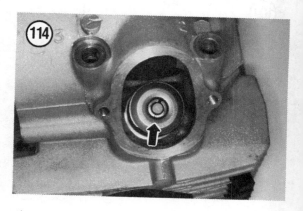

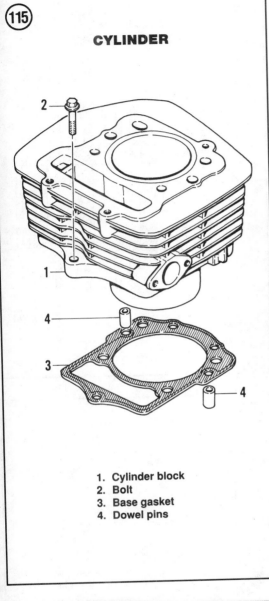

CYLINDER

1. Cylinder block
2. Bolt
3. Base gasket
4. Dowel pins

Inspection

1. Remove all gasket residue from the top and bottom cylinder block gasket surfaces.

2. Wash the cylinder block in solvent. Dry with compressed air.

3. Check the dowel pin holes for cracks or other damage.

4. Check the cylinder bore (**Figure 119**) for scoring, rust or other visible damage.

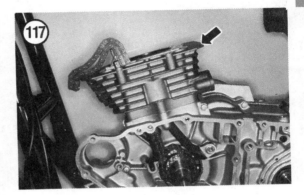

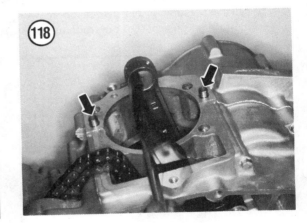

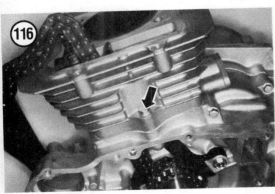

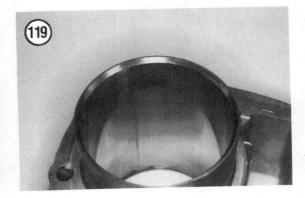

5. Measure the cylinder bore I.D., taper and out-of-round with a bore gauge or inside micrometer (**Figure 120**). Measure the cylinder bore at the 3 positions, measured from the top and bottom surfaces, shown in **Figure 121**. Measure in line with the piston pin and 90° to the pin (**Figure 121**). Check all measurements against the specifications in **Table 2**. If any measurement is greater that the service limit in **Table 2**, the cylinder must be rebored to the next oversize and oversize piston and rings installed.

6. If the cylinder is not worn past the service limit, check the bore carefully for scratches or gouges. The bore still may require reconditioning.

7. If cylinder bore is within specification, determine piston-to-cylinder clearance as described under *Piston Clearance* in this chapter.

8. After the cylinder has been serviced, wash the bore in hot soapy water. This is the only way to clean the cylinder wall of the fine grit material left from the bore or honing job. After washing the cylinder wall, run a clean white cloth through it. The cylinder wall should show no traces of grit or other debris. If the cloth is dirty, the cylinder wall is not clean and must be rewashed. When the cylinder bore is thoroughly cleaned, lubricate the cylinder bore with clean engine oil to prevent the bore from rusting.

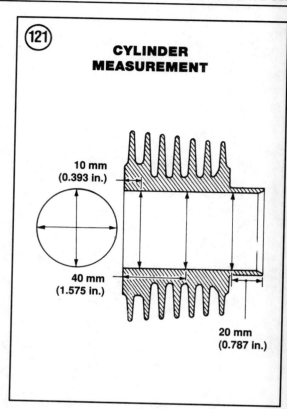

CYLINDER MEASUREMENT

10 mm (0.393 in.)

40 mm (1.575 in.)

20 mm (0.787 in.)

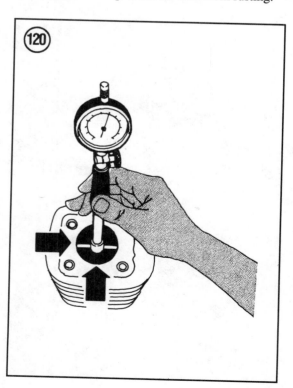

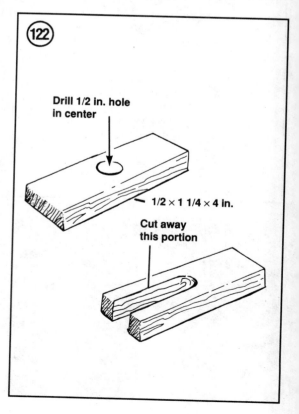

Drill 1/2 in. hole in center

1/2 × 1 1/4 × 4 in.

Cut away this portion

CAUTION
A combination of soap and water is the only solution that will completely clean the cylinder bore. Solvent and kerosene cannot wash fine grit out of cylinder crevices. Grit left in the cylinder bore will act as a grinding compound and cause premature wear to the new rings.

Installation

1. Clean the crankcase surface of all gasket residue.

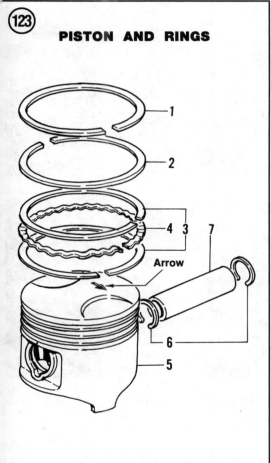

(123)

PISTON AND RINGS

1. **Top compression ring**
2. **Second compression ring**
3. **Oil rings**
4. **Oil ring expander spacer**
5. **Piston**
6. **Circlips**
7. **Piston pin**

2. Make sure the top and bottom cylinder surfaces are clean of all gasket residue.

3. Install the 2 lower cylinder block dowel pins (**Figure 118**).

4. Install a new base gasket. Make sure all holes align.

5. If removed, install the piston as described in this chapter.

6. Make sure the piston pin circlips are installed and seated correctly.

7. Install a piston holding fixture under the piston.

NOTE
*A piston holding fixture can be made out of wood as shown in **Figure 122**.*

8. Stagger the piston rings around the piston as shown in **Figure 123**.

9. Lubricate the cylinder wall, piston and rings liberally with engine oil prior to installation.

10. Carefully align the cylinder with the piston and install the cylinder. Compress each ring as it enters the cylinder with your fingers.

11. Remove the piston holding fixture and slide the cylinder all the way down.

12. While holding the cylinder down with one hand, operate the recoil starter or turn the crankshaft with a wrench. The piston should move smoothly in the bore.

13. Run the cam chain up through the cylinder block.

14. Install the cylinder Allen bolt (**Figure 116**) and tighten to the torque specification in **Table 4**.

15. Install the cylinder head as described in this chapter.

PISTON AND PISTON RINGS

The piston is made of an aluminum alloy. The piston pin is made of steel and is a precision fit in the piston. The piston pin is held in place by a clip at each end.

Refer to **Figure 123** when servicing the piston and rings in the following section.

Piston
Removal/Installation

1. Remove the cylinder as described in this chapter.

2. Block off the crankcase below the piston with clean paper towels to prevent the piston pin circlips from falling into the crankcase.

3. Before removing the piston, hold the rod tightly and rock the piston (**Figure 124**). Any rocking motion (do not confuse with the normal sliding motion) indicates wear on the piston pin, rod bushing, pin bore, or more likely, a combination of all three.

4. Remove the circlips from the piston pin bore (**Figure 125**).

> *NOTE*
> *Discard the piston circlips. New circlips must be installed during reassembly.*

5. Push the piston pin (**Figure 126**) out of the piston by hand. If the pin is tight, use a homemade tool (**Figure 127**) to remove it. Do not drive the piston pin out as this action may damage the piston pin, connecting rod or piston.

6. Lift the piston off the connecting rod.

7. Inspect the piston as described in this chapter.

Piston Inspection

1. Remove the piston rings as described in this chapter.

2. Carefully clean the carbon from the piston crown (**Figure 128**) with a soft scraper or wire wheel mounted in a drill. Large carbon accumulation re-

duces piston cooling and can result in detonation and piston damage.

> *CAUTION*
> *Be careful not to gouge or otherwise damage the piston or cylinder when removing carbon. Never use a wire brush to clean the piston skirt or ring grooves. Do not attempt to remove carbon from the sides of the piston above the top ring or from the cylinder bore near the top.*

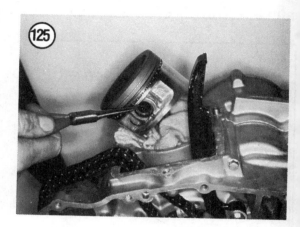

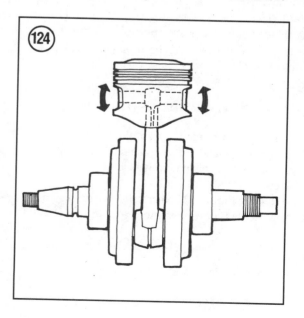

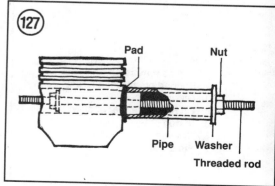

Removal of carbon from these two areas may cause increased oil consumption.

3. After cleaning the piston, examine the crown. The crown should show no sign of wear or damage. If the crown appears pecked or spongy-looking, also check the spark plug, valves and combustion chamber for aluminum deposits. If these deposits are found, the engine is overheating.

4. Examine each ring groove (**Figure 129**) for burrs, dented edges or other damage. Pay particular attention to the top compression ring groove as it usually wears more than the others. Because the oil rings are constantly bathed in oil, these rings and grooves wear little compared to compression rings and their grooves. If there is evidence of oil ring groove wear or if the oil ring assembly is tight and difficult to remove, the piston skirt may have collapsed due to excessive heat. Replace the piston.

5. Check the oil control holes in the piston (**Figure 130**) for carbon or oil sludge buildup. Clean the holes with wire.

6. Check the piston skirt for cracks or other damage. If a piston shows signs of partial seizure (bits of aluminum build-up on the piston skirt), the piston should be replaced and the cylinder bored (if necessary) to reduce the possibility of engine noise and further piston seizure.

NOTE
If the piston skirt is worn or scuffed unevenly from side-to-side, the connecting rod may be bent or twisted.

7. Check the circlip grooves in the piston for wear, cracks or other damage. If the grooves are questionable, check the circlip fit by installing a new circlip into each groove and then attempt to move the circlip from side-to-side. If the circlip has any side play, the groove is worn and the piston must be replaced.

8. Measure piston-to-cylinder clearance as described under *Piston Clearance* in this chapter.

9. If damage or wear indicates piston replacement is necessary, select a new piston as described under *Piston Clearance* in this chapter. If the piston, rings and cylinder are not damaged and are dimensionally correct, they can be reused.

Piston Pin
Inspection

1. Clean the piston pin in solvent and dry thoroughly.

2. Inspect the piston pin for flaking or cracks. Replace if necessary.

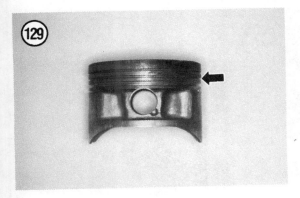

3. Oil the piston pin and install it in the connecting rod. Slowly rotate the piston pin and check for radial play (**Figure 131**).

4. Oil the piston pin and install it in the piston (**Figure 132**). Check the piston pin for excessive play.

5. Replace the piston pin and/or piston or connecting rod if necessary.

Piston Clearance

1. Make sure the piston skirt and cylinder wall are clean and dry.

2. Measure the cylinder bore I.D. with a bore gauge or inside micrometer (**Figure 120**). Measure the cylinder bore at the 3 positions, measured from the top and bottom surfaces, as shown in **Figure 121**. Measure in line with the piston pin and 90° to the pin (**Figure 121**). Write down the bore diameter.

3. Measure the piston diameter with a micrometer at a right angle to the piston pin bore (**Figure 133**). Measure up 5 mm (0.20 in.) from the bottom edge of the piston skirt (**Figure 134**).

4. Subtract the piston diameter from the largest cylinder bore diameter; the difference is piston-to-cylinder clearance. If clearance exceeds the specification in **Table 2**, the piston should be replaced and the cylinder bored oversize and then honed. Purchase the new piston first. Measure its diameter and add the specified clearance to determine the proper cylinder oversize diameter.

Piston Installation

1. Coat the connecting rod bushing, piston pin and piston with clean engine oil.

2. Slide the piston pin into the piston until its end is flush with the piston pin boss as shown in **Figure 135**.

3. Place the piston over the connecting rod so that the arrow on the piston crown (**Figure 136**) faces forward.

4. Align the piston pin with the hole in the connecting rod. Push the piston pin (**Figure 126**) through the connecting rod and into the other side of the piston until it is centered in the piston.

5. Install new piston pin clips in both ends of the pin boss (**Figure 125**). Make sure both clips are seated in the grooves in the piston. The end gap of the pin clips should be facing down toward bottom of piston.

6. Install the piston rings as described in this chapter.

(132) CHECKING PISTON PIN PLAY IN PISTON

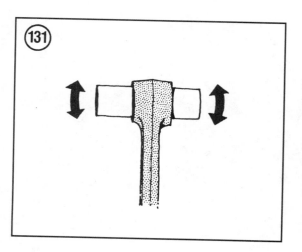

(131)

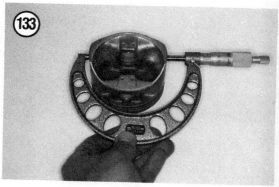

(133)

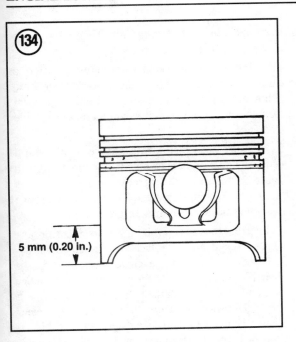

5 mm (0.20 in.)

Piston Ring
Inspection and Removal

A 3-ring type piston and ring assembly are used (**Figure 123**). The top and second rings are compression rings. The lower ring is an oil control ring assembly (consisting of 2 ring rails and an expander spacer). **Figure 137** identifies the top and second compression rings.

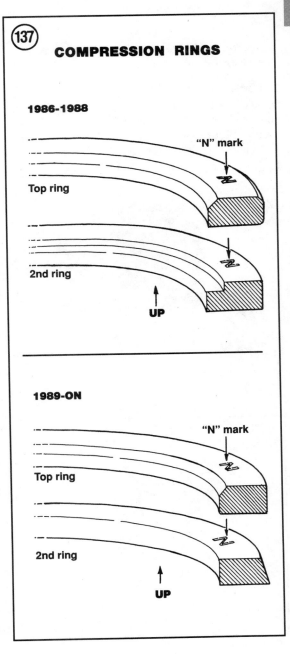

COMPRESSION RINGS

1986-1988

"N" mark

Top ring

2nd ring

UP

1989-ON

"N" mark

Top ring

2nd ring

UP

1. Measure the side clearance of each compression ring in its groove with a flat feeler gauge (**Figure 138**) and compare with the specifications in **Table 2**. If the clearance is greater than specified, the rings must be replaced. If the clearance is still excessive with the new rings, the piston must also be replaced.

WARNING
The edges of all piston rings are very sharp. Be careful when handling them to avoid cutting your fingers.

NOTE
Store the old rings in the order in which they are removed.

2. Remove the compression rings with a ring expander tool (**Figure 139**) or by spreading the ring ends with your thumbs and lifting the rings up evenly (**Figure 140**).

3. Remove the oil ring assembly (**Figure 141**) by first removing the upper (A, **Figure 142**) and the lower (B, **Figure 142**) ring rails. Then remove the expander spacer (C, **Figure 142**).

4. Using a broken piston ring, carefully remove carbon and oil residue from the piston ring grooves (**Figure 143**). Do not remove aluminum material from the ring grooves as this will increase ring side clearance.

5. Measure each piston ring groove width with a vernier caliper and check against the dimensions in **Table 2**. Measure each groove at several points around the piston. Replace the piston if any groove is worn to the service limit, or greater.

6. Inspect grooves carefully for burrs, nicks or broken or cracked lands. Replace the piston if necessary.

7. Check the end gap of each compression ring. To check, insert the ring into the bottom of the cylinder bore and square it with the cylinder wall by tapping it with the piston. Measure the end gap with a feeler gauge (**Figure 144**) and check against the specification in **Table 2** . Replace the ring if end gap is

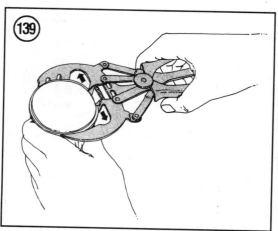

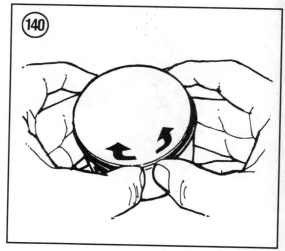

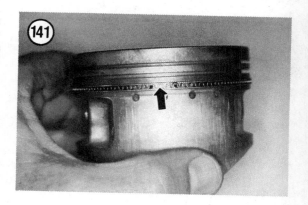

excessive. If the gap on a new compression ring is smaller than specified, hold a small file in a vise, then grip the ends of the ring with your fingers and enlarge the gap.

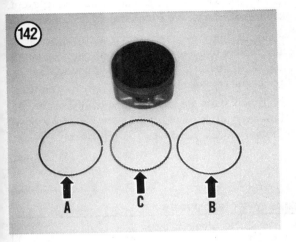

Piston Ring Installation

1. If new rings are installed, the cylinders must be deglazed or honed. This will help to seat the new rings. If necessary, refer honing service to a Kawasaki dealer or motorcycle repair shop. After honing, measure the end gap of each ring and compare to specifications in **Table 2** .

> *NOTE*
> *If the cylinders are deglazed or honed, clean the cylinders as described under* **Cylinder Block Inspection** *in this chapter.*

2. Clean the piston and rings. Dry with compressed air.

3. Install piston rings as follows:

> *NOTE*
> *Install the piston rings, first the bottom, then the middle, then the top ring, by carefully spreading the ends with your thumbs and slipping the rings over the top of the piston. Remember that the piston rings must be installed with the marks on them facing toward the top of the piston. Incorrectly installed piston rings can wear rapidly and/or allow oil to escape past them.*

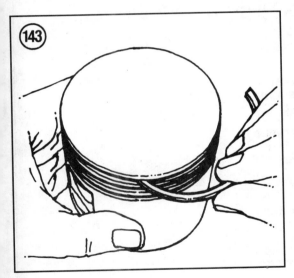

a. Install the oil ring assembly into the bottom ring groove. First install the expander spacer (C, **Figure 142**). Install the expander spacer so its ends butt together (**Figure 145**). Do not overlap the ends. Then install the top (A, **Figure 142**) and bottom (B, **Figure 142**) ring rails.

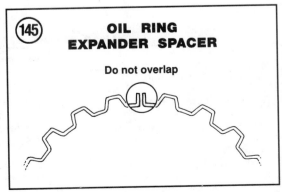

NOTE
*The 2 ring rails (A and B, **Figure 142**) are identical.*

b. Install the compression rings with the manufacturer's "N" mark facing up (**Figure 137**).

NOTE
When installing aftermarket piston rings, follow the manufacturers directions.

c. Install the 2nd or middle compression ring.
d. Install the top compression ring.

4. Make sure the rings are seated completely in their grooves all the way around the piston and that the end gaps are distributed around the piston as shown in **Figure 123**. It is important that the ring gaps are not aligned with each other when installed to prevent compression pressure from escaping past them.

5. If installing oversize compression rings, check the number to make sure the correct rings are being installed. The ring numbers should be the same as the piston oversize number.

6. If new parts are installed, the engine should be broken-in just as though it were new. Refer to *Engine Break-In* in Chapter Five.

Table 1 GENERAL ENGINE SPECIFICATIONS

Engine type	4-stroke, SOHC, single cylinder
Cooling system	Air cooled
Bore and stroke	76.0 × 64.0 mm (2.992-2.520 in.)
Displacement	290 cc (17.7 cu. in.)
Compression ratio	8.6:1
Valve timing	
2-wheel drive	
Intake	
Open	27° BTDC
Close	65° ABDC
Duration	272°
Exhaust	
Open	62° BBDC
Close	30° ATDC
Duration	272°
4-wheel drive	
Intake	
Open	21° BTDC
Close	59° ABDC
Duration	260°
Exhaust	
Open	56° BBDC
Close	24° ATDC
Duration	260°

Table 2 ENGINE SERVICE SPECIFICATIONS

	New mm (in.)	Service limit mm (in.)
Cylinder head warp limit	–	0.05 (0.002)
Rocker arm bore diameter	13.000-13.018 (0.5118-0.5125)	13.05 (0.514)
Rocker arm shaft diameter	12.976-12.99 (0.5108-0.5116)	12.95 (0.510)
Camshaft		
Lobe height	40.876-40.984 (1.6090-1.6135)	40.78 (1.606)

(continued)

Table 2 ENGINE SERVICE SPECIFICATIONS (continued)

	New mm (in.)	Service limit mm (in.)
Cam chain		
20-link measurement*	160.00-160.56 (6.299-6.321)	162.4 (6.394)
Cam chain guide depth measurement		
Front	No groove –	2.0 (0.079)
Rear	No groove –	1.5 (0.059)
Cylinder		
Inside diameter		
2-wheel drive	76.000-76.012 (2.9921-2.9925)	76.10 (2.996)
4-wheel drive	76.000-76.012 (2.9921-2.9925)	76.01 (2.992)
Taper limit	–	0.01 (0.0003)
Out-of-round limit	–	0.01 (0.0003)
Piston diameter		
2-wheel drive		
1986-1988	75.950-75.965 (2.9901-2.9907)	75.81 (2.9846)
1989-on	75.960-75.975 (2.9905-2.,9911)	75.81 (2.9846)
4-wheel drive	75.960-75.975 (2.9905-2.9911)	75.81 (2.9846)
Piston-to-cylinder clearance		
2-wheel drive		
1986-1988	0.035-0.062 (0.0010-0.0024)	–
1989-on	0.025-0.052 (0.00098-0.0020)	–
4-wheel drive	0.025-0.052 (0.00098-0.0020)	–
Piston rings		
Side clearance		
Top	0.03-0.07 (0.001-0.003)	0.17 (0.007)
Second	0.02-0.06 (0.001-0.002)	0.16 (0.006)
Groove width		
Top		
2-wheel drive		
1986-1988	1.22-1.24 (0.048-0.049)	1.32 (0.052)
1989-on	1.02-1.04 (0.040-0.041)	1.12 (0.044)
4-wheel drive	1.02-1.04 (0.040-0.041)	1.12 (0.044)
Second		
2-wheel drive		
1986-1988	1.21-1.23 (0.048-0.048)	1.32 (0.052)
1989-on	1.01-1.03 (0.039-0.040)	1.11 (0.043)
4-wheel drive	1.01-1.03 (0.039-0.040)	1.11 (0.043)
Oil	2.51-2.53 (0.099-0.100)	2.61 (0.103)

(continued)

4

Table 2 ENGINE SERVICE SPECIFICATIONS (continued)

	New mm (in.)	Service limit mm (in.)
Thickness		
Top and second rings		
2-wheel drive		
1986-1988	1.170-1.190	1.10
	(0.046-0.047)	(0.043)
1989-on	0.97-0.99	0.90
	(0.0382-0.0389)	(0.035)
4-wheel drive	0.97-0.99	0.90
	(0.0382-0.0389)	(0.035)
End gap		
Top and second compression rings	0.20-0.35	0.7
	(0.008-0.014)	(0.028)

Table 3 VALVE SERVICE SPECIFICATIONS

	New mm (in.)	Service limit mm (in.)
Valve seat angle	45°	—
Valve seat width	0.5-1.0	—
	(0.020-0.039)	
Valve seat outer diameter		
Intake	35.7-36.3	—
	(1.406-1.429)	
Exhaust	29.7-30.3	—
	(1.169-1.193)	
Valve head thickness		
Intake	0.80-1.20	0.5 (0.020)
	(0.031-0.047)	
Exhaust	0.80-1.20	0.7 (0.028)
	(0.031-0.047)	
Valve stem runout	0.02 (0.001)	0.05 (0.002)
Valve stem diameter		
Intake	6.965-6.980	6.95 (0.274)
	(0.2742-0.2748)	
Exhaust	6.950-6.970	6.94 (0.273)
	(0.2736-0.2744)	
Valve guide inside diameter	7.000-7.015	7.08 (0.279)
	(0.2756-0.2762)	
Valve spring free length		
Inner	32.4 (1.276)	31.1 (1.224)
Outer	37.3 (1.469)	35.8 (1.409)

Table 4 ENGINE TOP END TIGHTENING TORQUE

	N·m	ft.-lb.
Cylinder head bolts		
6 mm	12	9.0
8 mm		
New bolts	34	25
Used bolts	29	21
Cylinder Allen bolt	12	9.0
Cam sprocket bolt	41	30
Rear chain guide pivot bolt	9.8	7.2
Valve adjusting screw locknuts	12	9.0
Cylinder head bracket		
mounting nuts and bolts	25	18

ENGINE LOWER END

5

This chapter describes service procedures for the following lower end components:

a. Crankcase.

b. Crankshaft.

c. Connecting rod.

d. Transmission and reverse shift assembly (removal and installation).

e. Internal shift mechanism (removal and installation).

f. Recoil starter.

Before removing and disassembling the crankcase, clean the entire engine and frame with a good grade commercial degreaser, like Gunk or Bel-Ray engine degreaser. It is easier to work on a clean engine and you will do a better job.

Make certain that you have all the necessary hand and special tools that you will need. Also make sure you have a clean place to work.

One of the more important aspects of engine overhaul is preparation. Improper preparation and failure to identify and store parts during removal will make it difficult to reassemble the engine. Before removing the first bolt, get a number of boxes, plastic bags and containers to store the parts when removed (**Figure 1**). Also, have on hand a roll of masking tape and a permanent, waterproof marking pen to label parts as required.

The text makes frequent references to the left- and right-hand side of the engine. This refers to the engine as it sits in the vehicle's frame, not as it sits on your workbench.

Table 1 and **Table 2** lists engine service specifications. **Table 3** lists engine tightening torques. **Tables 1-3** are at the end of the chapter.

SERVICING ENGINE IN FRAME

Many components can be serviced with the engine mounted in the frame—(the vehicle's frame is a

great holding fixture, especially for breaking loose stubborn bolts and nuts):

    a. Cylinder head.

    b. Cylinder and piston.

    c. Gearshift mechanism.

    d. Clutch.

    e. Recoil starter.

    f. Oil pump

    g. Carburetor.

    h. Flywheel.

    i. Starter.

    j. Front gear case (2-wheel drive).

    k. Sub-transmission (4-wheel drive).

ENGINE REMOVAL

This procedure describes engine removal. If service work requires only the removal of a top end component, leave the engine in the frame and service the top end as required to remove the desired sub-assembly. If the engine requires crankcase disassembly, it is easier to remove as many sub-assemblies as possible before removing the engine from the frame. By following this method, the frame can be used as a holding fixture when servicing the engine. Attempting to disassemble the complete engine while placed on a workbench is more time consuming. You may need an assistant to help hold the engine while you loosen many of the larger nuts and bolts.

1. Park the vehicle on a level surface. Set the parking brake.

2. Remove the following components as described in Chapter Fourteen:

    a. Seat.

    b. Front fender.

    c. Rear fender.

3. Disconnect the negative battery cable (**Figure 2**).

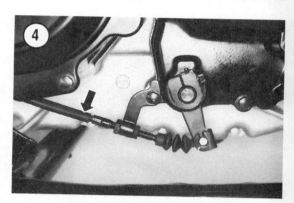

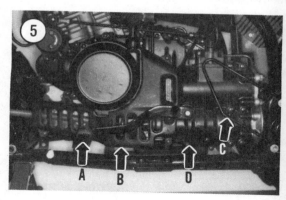

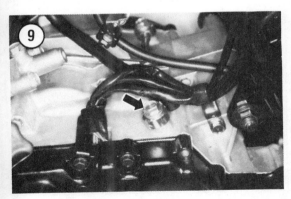

4. Remove the fuel tank as described in Chapter Eight.

5. Remove the exhaust system as described in Chapter Eight.

6. Remove the carburetor as described in Chapter Eight.

7. On 2-wheel drive models, remove the differential shift lever case (**Figure 3**).

8A. On 2-wheel drive models, loosen the 2 reverse cable adjust nuts and disconnect the cable from the reverse lever (**Figure 4**).

8B. On 4-wheel drive models, perform the following:

    a. Remove the left-hand footpeg assembly.

    b. Remove the shift lever (A, **Figure 5**) and the shift lever side cover (B, **Figure 5**).

    c. Remove the guard (C, **Figure 5**).

    d. Remove the front propeller shaft (**Figure 6**) as described in Chapter Eleven.

NOTE
*On 4-wheel drive models, the engine can be removed with the sub-transmission (D, **Figure 5**) and the rear propeller shaft left in their installed positions.*

    e. If necessary, remove the sub-transmission (D, **Figure 5**) as described in Chapter Seven.

    f. Remove the reverse cable holder mounting bolt (**Figure 7**).

    g. Remove the reverse lever mounting bolt and remove the reverse lever.

    h. Loosen the 2 reverse cable adjust nuts and disconnect the cable (**Figure 7**) from the lever.

9. Disconnect the engine ground cable from the engine.

10. Disconnect the starter motor lead from the starter motor (**Figure 8**).

11. Disconnect the alternator, pickup coil and the neutral/reverse switch electrical leads. **Figure 9** shows the wire harness leading out of the engine. Follow the harness to the connector blocks and disconnect them.

12. Disconnect the spark plug lead from the spark plug.

13. Disconnect the cylinder head vent hose (**Figure 10**).

14. If the engine requires disassembly, remove the following sub-assemblies:

    a. Cylinder head (Chapter Four).

    b. Cylinder and piston (Chapter Four).

5

c. Flywheel/starter clutch (this chapter).

d. Clutch (Chapter Six).

e. Primary drive gear and balancer driven gear assemblies (this chapter).

f. Oil pump (this chapter).

g. Front gear case (2-wheel drive). See Chapter Twelve.

15. If the engine is being removed with the top end installed, remove the cylinder head bracket mounting bolts. Then remove the cylinder head mounting bolts and remove the bracket(s). See **Figure 11** (1986-1987) or **Figure 12** (1988-on).

16. Loosen the rear propeller shaft dust cover front clamp. See **Figure 13** (2-wheel drive) or **Figure 14** (4-wheel drive).

17. Remove the engine mounting bolts as follows:

a. If you are going to use a jack to steady the engine, remove the engine skid plate from the frame tubes. See **Figure 15**, typical.

b. If necessary, place a jack underneath the engine. Raise the jack so that the pad just rests against the bottom of the engine. Place a block of wood on the jack pad to protect the engine case.

c. Remove the front engine mounting bolts and brackets. See **Figure 16** (2-wheel drive) or **Figure 17** (4-wheel drive).

d. Remove the 2 bottom mounting bolts and nuts (A, **Figure 18**).

e. Remove the upper rear mounting bolt and nut (B, **Figure 18**).

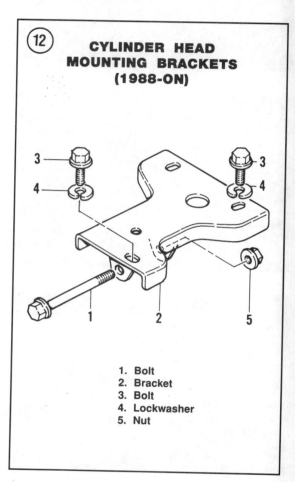

12

CYLINDER HEAD MOUNTING BRACKETS (1988-ON)

1. Bolt
2. Bracket
3. Bolt
4. Lockwasher
5. Nut

11

CYLINDER HEAD MOUNTING BRACKETS (1986-1987)

1. Bolt
2. Nut
3. Bracket
4. Bracket
5. Bolt
6. Bolt

13

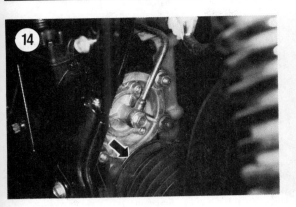

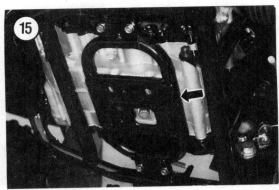

5

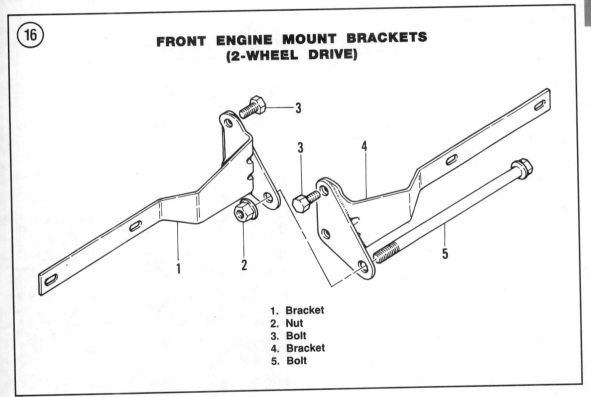

**FRONT ENGINE MOUNT BRACKETS
(2-WHEEL DRIVE)**

1. Bracket
2. Nut
3. Bolt
4. Bracket
5. Bolt

18. Move all cables, wires and harnesses out of the way.

NOTE
A minimum of 2 people are required to remove an assembled engine.

19A. *2-wheel drive*: Slide the engine forward to disconnect it from the propeller shaft. Then remove the engine from the right-hand side of the frame.

19B. *4-wheel drive with sub-transmission case removed from engine*: Lift the engine and remove it from the left-hand side of the frame.

19C. *4-wheel drive with sub-transmission case installed on engine*: Slide the engine forward to disconnect it from the propeller shaft. Then remove the engine from the left-hand side of the frame.

20. After the engine is removed, check the engine frame mounts for cracks or other damage.

ENGINE INSTALLATION

1. Clean all engine mount bolts and nuts in solvent. Dry with compressed air. Remove corrosion from bolts with a wire wheel.

2. Prior to installation, spray the engine mount bolts with a commercial type of rust inhibitor.

NOTE
A minimum of 2 people are required to install an assembled engine.

3. Apply grease to the propeller shaft splines.

4. Jack up the rear of the vehicle so that the rear wheels just clear the ground.

5. Install the engine into the frame while fitting the propeller shaft to the front splines. Have another person turn the rear wheel to help the shaft splines engage.

6. Install the upper rear mounting bolt and nut from the right-hand side (B, **Figure 18**). Tighten the nut finger-tight.

7. Install the 2 bottom mounting bolts and nuts from the right-hand side (A, **Figure 18**). Tighten the nuts finger-tight.

8. Install the front engine mounting brackets, bolts and nuts; see **Figure 16** (2-wheel drive) or **Figure 17** (4-wheel drive). Tighten the nuts finger-tight.

9. Tighten the engine mounting bolts to the torque specification in **Table 3**.

10. If the top end is installed on the engine, install the cylinder head bracket, bolts and nuts; see **Figure**

11 (1986-1987) or **Figure 12** (1988-on). Tighten the cylinder head bracket bolts and nuts to the torque specification in **Table 3**.

11. If removed, install the engine skid plate (**Figure 15**). Tighten the bolts securely.

12. Reposition the rear propeller shaft dust cover; see **Figure 13** (2-wheel drive) or **Figure 14** (4-wheel drive). Tighten the front clamp securely.

13. If the engine is partially assembled, install the following sub-assemblies:
   a. Oil pump (this chapter).
   b. Primary drive gear and balancer driven gear assemblies (this chapter).
   c. Clutch (Chapter Six).
   d. Flywheel/starter clutch (this chapter).
   e. Piston and cylinder (Chapter Four).
   f. Cylinder head (Chapter Four).
   g. Front gear case (2-wheel drive [Chapter Twelve]).

14. Reconnect the cylinder head vent hose (**Figure 10**).

15. Reconnect the spark plug lead to the spark plug.

16. Clean the electrical connectors with contact cleaner.

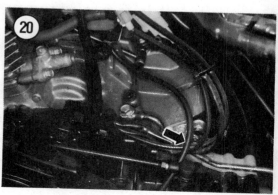

17. Reconnect the following electrical connectors:
   a. Alternator leads.
   b. Pickup coil leads.
   c. Neutral/reverse switch leads.
   d. Starter motor lead (**Figure 8**).
   e. Engine ground cable; see **Figure 19** (2-wheel drive) or **Figure 20** (4-wheel drive).
18A. On 2-wheel drive models, perform the following:
   a. Install the differential shift lever case (**Figure 3**).
   b. Reconnect the reverse cable to the reverse lever (**Figure 4**).
18B. On 4-wheel drive models, perform the following:
   a. Reconnect the reverse cable and reverse lever (**Figure 7**).
   b. Secure the reverse cable to the engine with the cable holder and mounting bolt (**Figure 7**).
   c. If removed, install the sub-transmission (D, **Figure 5**) as described in Chapter Seven.
   d. Install the front propeller shaft (**Figure 6**) as described in Chapter Eleven.
   e. Install the guard (C, **Figure 5**).

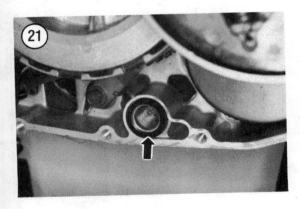

f. Install the shift lever side cover (B, **Figure 5**) and the shift lever (A, **Figure 5**).
   g. Install the left-hand footpeg assembly.
19. Install the carburetor as described in Chapter Eight.
20. Install the exhaust system as described in Chapter Eight.
21. Install the fuel tank as described in Chapter Eight.
22. Install the engine oil filter and refill the engine with new oil (if drained) as described under *Engine Oil and Filter Change* in Chapter Three.
23. Adjust the reverse cable as described in Chapter Seven.
24. Adjust the clutch as described in Chapter Three.
25. Install the following components as described in Chapter Fourteen:
   a. Rear fender.
   b. Front fender.
   c. Seat.
26. Reconnect the negative battery cable (**Figure 2**) to the battery.

OIL SCREEN

An oil screen is mounted in the crankcase behind the clutch cover; see **Figure 21**. Removal and cleaning of the oil screen is not part of the engines periodic maintenance schedule described in Chapter Three. However, the oil screen should be inspected and serviced whenever the clutch cover is removed, if troubleshooting a lubrication system problem, or if servicing the engine after it overheated or seized.

Removal/Cleaning/Installation

1. Drain the engine oil as described under *Engine Oil and Filter Change* in Chapter Three.
2. Remove the clutch cover as described under *Clutch Removal* in Chapter Five.
3. Pull the oil screen out of the crankcase (**Figure 22**).
4. Inspect the oil screen for contamination or sludge buildup.

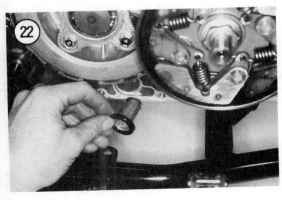

NOTE
Any metal particles detected in the screen indicates internal engine damage.

5. Clean the oil screen in solvent and dry with compressed air.

6. Check the oil screen (A, **Figure 23**) for broken wires, tears, a loose or damaged gasket (B, **Figure 23**) or other damage.

7. Replace the oil screen (A, **Figure 23**) if damaged.

8. Replace the gasket (B, **Figure 23**) if damaged.

9. Before installing the oil screen, check that the gasket (B, **Figure 23**) seats squarely around the oil screen.

10. Apply new engine oil to the oil screen gasket and install the screen into the crankcase (**Figure 21**).

11. Install the clutch as described in Chapter Five.

12. Refill the engine oil as described under *Engine Oil and Filter Change* in Chapter Three. Check the clutch cover and drain plug for leaks.

OIL PUMP

The oil pump is mounted behind the clutch on the right-hand side of the engine. The oil pump can be removed with the engine mounted in the frame.

The oil pump is a nonserviceable unit. If the rotors are scored or if the oil pump driven gear is damaged, the oil pump must be replaced as an assembly.

Refer to **Figure 24** when servicing the oil pump cover.

Removal

1. Remove the clutch as described in Chapter Six.

2. Remove the oil pump cover screws and remove the cover (**Figure 25**).

NOTE
On early models, the oil pump driven gear can be removed from the oil pump shaft. On late models, the driven gear is permanently fixed to the shaft.

3. On early models, remove the oil pump driven gear and dowel pin.

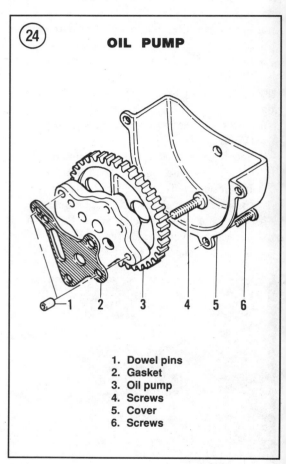

OIL PUMP

1. Dowel pins
2. Gasket
3. Oil pump
4. Screws
5. Cover
6. Screws

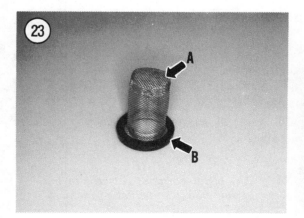

CAUTION
Use an impact driver with a No. 3 Phillips bit to loosen the oil pump mounting screws in Step 3. Loosening the screws with a Phillips screwdriver may ruin the screw heads.

4. Remove the oil pump mounting screws (A, **Figure 26**) and remove the oil pump (B, **Figure 26**) assembly.
5. Remove the oil pump gasket (A, **Figure 27**) and 2 dowel pins (B, **Figure 27**). Discard the gasket.
6. Store the oil pump in a sealed plastic bag to prevent dirt and other abrasive dust from contaminating the pump rotors.

Oil Pump
Disassembly/Inspection

Kawasaki does not list service specifications for the oil pump rotors.
1. Remove the Phillips head screw (**Figure 28**) securing the pump cover to the pump body and disassemble the oil pump assembly. See **Figure 29** .
2. Remove all gasket residue from the oil pump body and crankcase mating surfaces.
3. Clean all parts in solvent and dry with compressed air. Place parts on a clean lint-free cloth.
4. Inspect the oil pump body and cover for excessive wear, cracks or uneven wear (**Figure 30**).
5. Inspect the inner and outer rotors (**Figure 30**) for cracks, scoring or other damage.
6. Inspect the oil pump driven gear for broken or chipped teeth. Inspect the driven gear shaft for scoring, excessive wear or other damage.
7. If any part of the oil pump is severely worn or damaged, replace the oil pump assembly. Individual parts are not available.

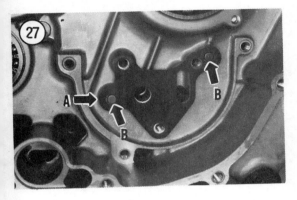

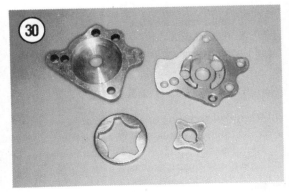

Oil Pump Assembly

1. Coat all parts with clean engine oil prior to assembly.
2. Insert the oil pump shaft (A, **Figure 31**) (and gear on late models) through the outer cover.
3. Install the pin (B, **Figure 31**) through the oil pump shaft hole.
4. Align the slot in the inner rotor with the pin and install the inner rotor (**Figure 32**).
5. Install the outer rotor around the inner rotor (**Figure 33**).
6. Install the pump cover (**Figure 34**) and secure it with the Phillips screw (**Figure 28**). Tighten the screw securely.
7. Turn the driven gear by hand, making sure it turns smoothly with no roughness or binding. Install the pin and driven gear on early models prior to checking the oil pump.

Installation

1. Install the 2 dowel pins (B, **Figure 27**) and a new oil pump gasket (A, **Figure 27**).
2. Fill the oil pump with new engine oil (**Figure 35**).
3. Install the oil pump onto the crankcase and install the 3 Phillips screws (A, **Figure 26**). Tighten the Phillips screws securely.
4. On early models, install the pin and driven gear (B, **Figure 26**).
5. Turn the driven gear by hand. The oil pump should turn smoothly with no roughness or binding.
6. Install the oil pump cover (**Figure 25**) and screws. Tighten the screws securely.
7. Install the clutch as described in Chapter Five.

OIL PIPE
(2-WHEEL DRIVE)

A single external oil pipe is used on all 2-wheel drive models. Banjo fittings, bolts and washers are used at each pipe nozzle. Refer to **Figure 36**.

Removal/Inspection/Installation

1. Record the position of each wire and hose routed over the oil pipe for reassembly reference.
2. Remove the banjo bolts and washers securing the oil pipe to the engine. Remove the oil pipe (**Figure 37**).

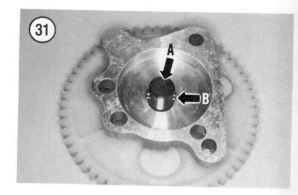

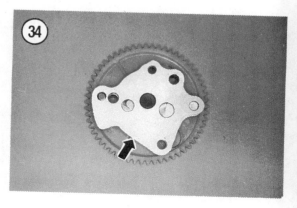

3. Clean the oil pipe, banjo bolts and washers (**Figure 36**) in solvent and dry thoroughly.

4. Replace cracked or otherwise damaged washers.

5. Check the oil pipe for cracks or other damage. Replace if necessary.

6. Install the oil pipe by reversing these steps, while noting the following.

7. Install a washer on each side of the oil pipe as shown in **Figure 36**.

8. Tighten the oil pipe banjo bolts to the torque specification in **Table 3**.

OIL PIPES
(4-WHEEL DRIVE)

Two external oil pipes are used on all 4-wheel drive models. Banjo fittings, bolts and washers are used at each pipe nozzle. Refer to **Figure 38**.

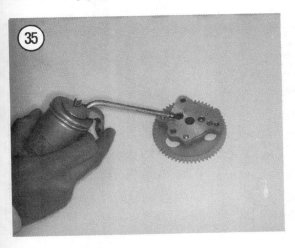

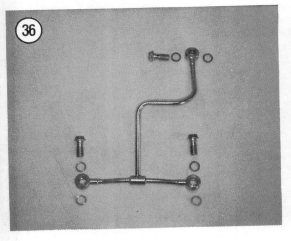

Removal/Inspection/Installation

1. Record the position of each wire and hose routed over the oil pipe for reassembly reference.

2. *Sub-transmission oil pipe*: Remove the banjo bolts and washers securing the oil pipe to the engine and sub-transmission. Remove the oil pipe (**Figure 39**).

3. *Engine oil pipe*: Remove the banjo bolts and washers securing the oil pipe to the engine. Remove the oil pipe (**Figure 40**).

4. Clean the oil pipes, banjo bolts and washers (**Figure 38**) in solvent and dry thoroughly.

5. Replace cracked or otherwise damaged washers.

6. Check the oil pipes for cracks or other damage. Replace if necessary.

7. Install the oil pipes by reversing these steps, while noting the following.

8. Install a washer on each side of the oil pipe as shown in **Figure 38**.

9. Tighten the oil pipe banjo bolts to the torque specification in **Table 3**.

OIL COOLER
(CANADA AND EUROPE)

An oil cooler is available as an optional part for 1992-on 4-wheel drive models sold in Canada and Europe. Refer to **Figure 41** when servicing the oil cooler and oil pipes. Tighten the banjo bolts to the torque specification in **Table 3**.

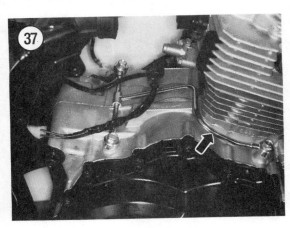

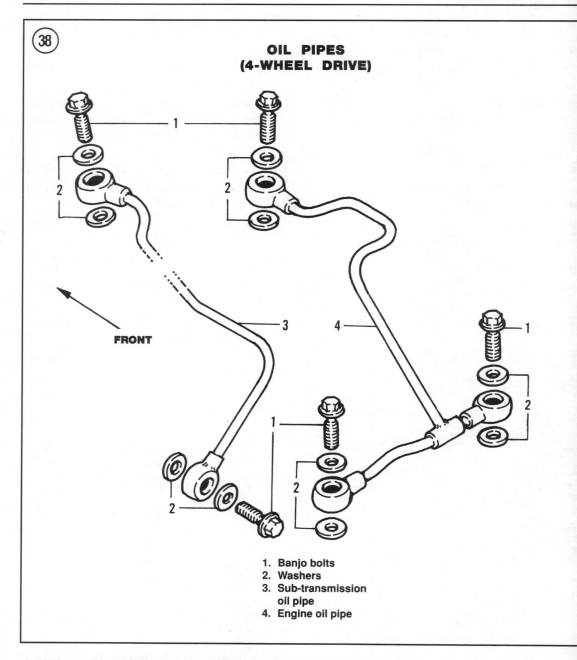

**OIL PIPES
(4-WHEEL DRIVE)**

FRONT

1. Banjo bolts
2. Washers
3. Sub-transmission
   oil pipe
4. Engine oil pipe

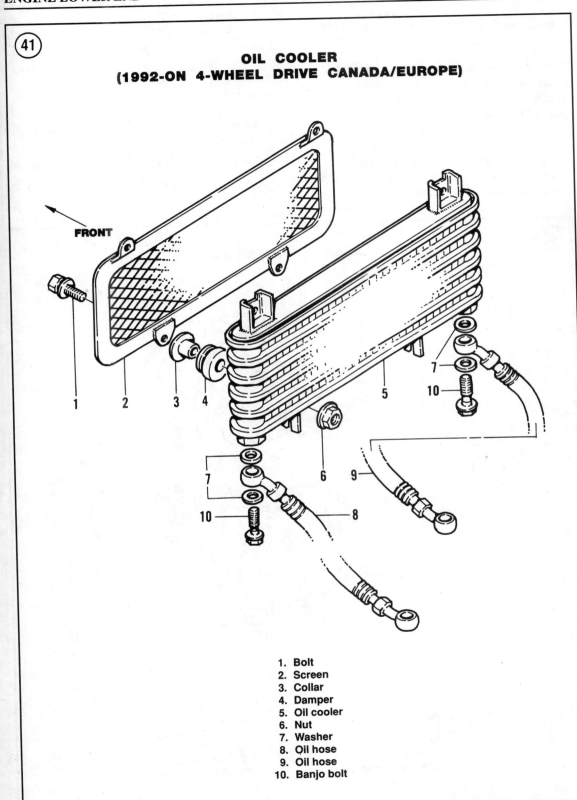

OIL COOLER
(1992-ON 4-WHEEL DRIVE CANADA/EUROPE)

FRONT

1. Bolt
2. Screen
3. Collar
4. Damper
5. Oil cooler
6. Nut
7. Washer
8. Oil hose
9. Oil hose
10. Banjo bolt

5

BALANCER GEARS AND OIL PUMP DRIVE GEAR

The balancer drive and driven gears and the oil pump drive gear (**Figure 42**) are mounted on the right-hand side of the engine. The gears are identified in **Figure 43**:

    a. Balancer driven gear (A, **Figure 43**).
    b. Balancer drive gear (B, **Figure 43**).
    c. Oil pump drive gear (C, **Figure 43**).

The Kawasaki socket wrench (part No. 57001-1214), or equivalent, is required to remove and tighten the crankshaft nut. This tool is shown in the removal and installation steps.

Removal

1. Remove the clutch as described under *Clutch Removal* in Chapter Six.

2. Remove the oil pump as described in this chapter.

3A. On 1986-1987 models, remove the left-hand side cover.

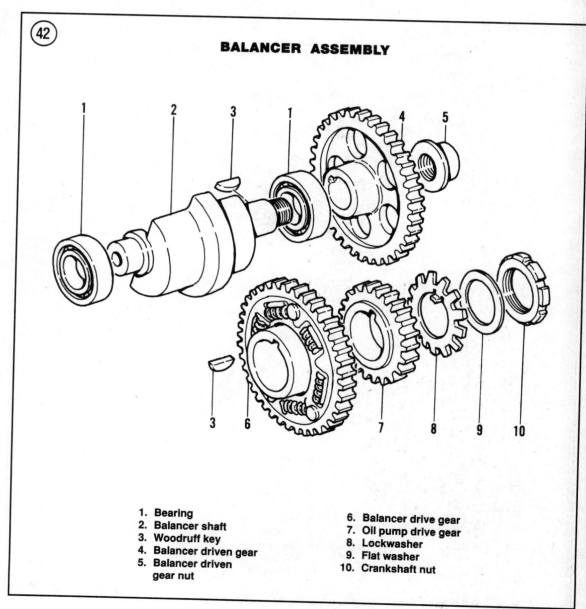

42

BALANCER ASSEMBLY

1. Bearing
2. Balancer shaft
3. Woodruff key
4. Balancer driven gear
5. Balancer driven gear nut
6. Balancer drive gear
7. Oil pump drive gear
8. Lockwasher
9. Flat washer
10. Crankshaft nut

3B. On 1988-on models, remove the pull-starter assembly as described in Chapter Five.

4. Bend the lockwasher tab (**Figure 44**) away from the crankshaft nut.

5. Slide the Kawasaki socket wrench over the crankshaft and engage it with the crankshaft nut as shown in **Figure 45**.

6. Hold the flywheel bolt or starter pulley (**Figure 46**) with a wrench (to prevent the crankshaft from turning) and loosen the crankshaft nut. Do not remove the nut.

7. Hold the flywheel bolt or starter pulley (**Figure 46**) and loosen the balancer driven gear (A, **Figure 43**) nut.

8. Remove the crankshaft nut (A, **Figure 47**).

9. Remove the flat washer (B, **Figure 47**), if used.

10. Remove the lockwasher (C, **Figure 47**).

11. Slide off the oil pump drive gear (A, **Figure 48**).

12. Slide off the balancer drive gear (B, **Figure 48**).

13. Remove the balancer driven gear nut (C, **Figure 48**) and slide off the gear (D, **Figure 48**).

14. Remove the Woodruff key from the balancer shaft.

15. Remove the Woodruff key from the crankshaft.

Inspection

1. Clean all parts in solvent. Dry with compressed air.

2. Check the balancer drive and oil pump drive gears (**Figure 49**) and the balancer driven gear (**Figure 50**) for:

    a. Broken or chipped teeth.

    b. Heat discoloration and excessive wear

    c. Worn or damaged center hole.

3. Replace severely worn or damaged washers (**Figure 49**).

Balancer Drive Gear Disassembly/Reassembly

The balancer drive gear (**Figure 51**) is a sub-assembly consisting of an outer gear, inner boss, springs and pins.

1. Push the boss (A, **Figure 51**) out of the balancer drive gear (B, **Figure 51**) and disassemble the gear assembly.

2. Separate the springs and pins.

3. Check components for severe wear or damage. Replace the balancer drive gear if damage is noted to any part; replacement parts are not available separately.

4. Reverse Steps 1 and 2 to reassemble the balancer drive gear. Install a spring in every slot and a pin assembly in every other spring.

Installation

1. Apply clean engine oil to all bearing surfaces prior to installation.

2. Rotate the crankshaft so that its keyway faces up (12 o'clock); see **Figure 52**.

NOTE
*The 2 Woodruff keys (**Figure 42**) installed in this procedure are identical (same part number).*

3. Install the Woodruff key into the crankshaft keyway (**Figure 52**).

4. Install the Woodruff key into the balancer shaft keyway (**Figure 53**).

5. Slide the balancer drive gear (**Figure 54**)—timing mark facing out—onto the crankshaft. Align the gear keyway with the Woodruff key and push the gear into position.

6. Slide the balancer driven gear (**Figure 55**)—timing mark facing out—onto the balancer shaft. Align the gear keyway with the Woodruff key. Then align the index mark on the balancer driven gear with the index mark on the balancer drive gear (**Figure 56**) and push the gear into position.

NOTE
*When tightening the nuts in the following steps, hold the crankshaft with a wrench on the starter pulley or flywheel bolt (**Figure 46**).*

7. Screw on the balancer driven gear nut (**Figure 57**) and tighten to the torque specification in **Table 3**.

8. Slide the oil pump drive gear—shoulder side (**Figure 58**) facing in—onto the crankshaft. Align the gear keyway with the Woodruff key and push the gear into position; see **Figure 48**.

9. Install the lockwasher onto the crankshaft. Install the lockwasher claw into the oil pump drive gear keyway (**Figure 59**).

10. Install the flat washer (A, **Figure 60**), if used, onto the crankshaft and seat it against the lockwasher.

11. Install the crankshaft nut—tapered side facing in (**Figure 61**)—over the crankshaft. Screw the nut onto the crankshaft threads. Tighten the crankshaft nut with the Kawasaki socket wrench (**Figure 62**) to the torque specification in **Table 3**.

12. Bend one of the lockwasher tabs into one of the nut slots (**Figure 63**). If none of the tabs or slots align, tighten the nut until an alignment is made.

13. Install the clutch as described under *Clutch Installation* in Chapter Six.

STATOR COIL AND LEFT-HAND SIDE COVER

The stator assembly is mounted inside the left-hand side cover. See **Figure 64** (1986-1987) or **Figure 65** (1988-on).

Left-Hand Side Cover
Removal

1. Place a drain pan underneath the left-hand side cover.

2. Remove the seat.

3. Disconnect the alternator and pickup coil electrical connectors.

4A. On 1986-1987 models, perform the following:
  a. Remove the differential shift lever case.
  b. Remove the left-hand side cover mounting bolts and remove the left-hand side cover.

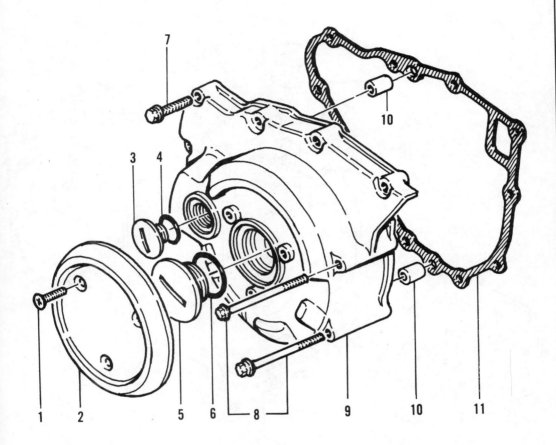

**LEFT-HAND SIDE COVER
(1986-1987)**

1. Screw
2. Left-hand side
   cover guard
3. Plug
4. O-ring
5. Plug
6. O-ring
7. Screw
8. Screw
9. Left-hand
   side cover
10. Dowel pin
11. Gasket

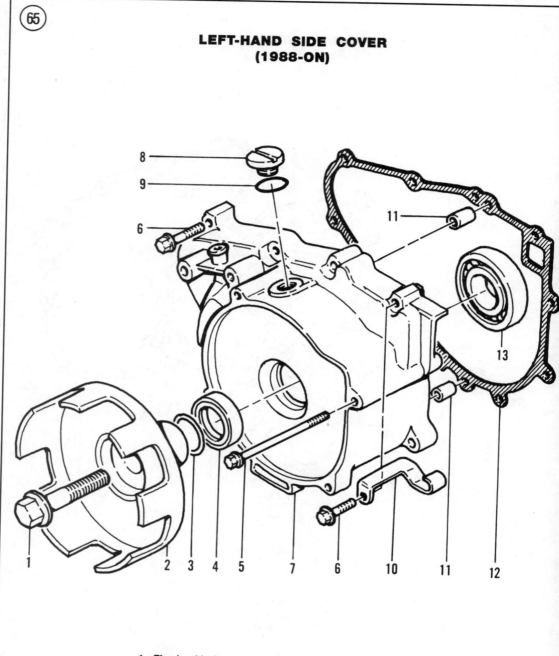

**LEFT-HAND SIDE COVER
(1988-ON)**

1. Flywheel bolt
2. Starter pulley
3. O-ring
4. Oil seal
5. Bolt
6. Bolt
7. Left-hand side cover

8. Plug
9. O-ring
10. Clip
11. Dowel pin
12. Gasket
13. Bearing

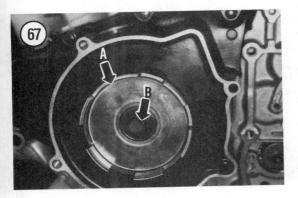

4B. On 1988-on 2-wheel drive models, perform the following:

   a. Remove the differential shift lever case (A, **Figure 66**).

   b. Remove the recoil starter assembly (B, **Figure 66**) as described in this chapter.

   c. Hold the starter pulley (A, **Figure 67**) with a wrench and loosen the flywheel mounting bolt (B, **Figure 67**).

   d. Remove the flywheel mounting bolt (B, **Figure 67**).

   e. Slide the starter pulley (A, **Figure 67**) off the crankshaft and remove it.

   f. Remove the key (**Figure 68**) from the crankshaft groove.

   g. Remove the left-hand side cover mounting bolts and remove the left-hand side cover (**Figure 69**).

4C. On 4-wheel drive models, perform the following:

   a. Remove the sub-transmission lever assembly (A, **Figure 70**).

   b. Remove the shift lever (B, **Figure 70**).

   c. Remove the propeller shaft cover (C, **Figure 70**).

   d. Remove the recoil starter assembly (D, **Figure 70**) as described in this chapter.

   e. Hold the starter pulley (A, **Figure 67**) with a wrench and loosen the flywheel mounting bolt (B, **Figure 67**).

   f. Remove the flywheel mounting bolt (B, **Figure 67**).

   g. Slide the starter pulley (A, **Figure 67**) off the crankshaft and remove it.

   h. Remove the key (**Figure 68**) from the crankshaft groove.

5

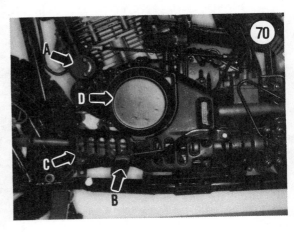

i. Remove the left-hand side cover mounting bolts and remove the left-hand side cover (**Figure 69**).

4. Remove the gasket and 2 dowel pins (**Figure 71**).

5. If necessary, remove the stator coil and pickup coil as described in this chapter.

Stator and Pickup Coil Testing

Refer to *Stator Coil Testing* and *Pickup Coil Testing* in Chapter Nine.

Stator and Pickup Coil Removal/Installation

The stator and pickup coils can be replaced separately. Do not cut any wires when removing the coil(s).

1. Remove the left-hand side cover as described in this section.

2. Remove the wire guide screw and guide (A, **Figure 72**).

3. Remove the pickup coil mounting screws (B, **Figure 72**).

4. Remove the stator coil Allen bolts (C, **Figure 72**).

5. Pull the wiring harness grommets out of the side cover grooves.

6. Remove the pickup coil and stator coil from the side cover. Remove the wire guide mounted below the pickup coil.

7. 1988-on models: If you are going to replace the left-hand side cover oil seal and/or bearing, do so now as described in the following procedure. Clean the left-hand side cover in solvent and dry thoroughly. Do not clean the left-hand side cover in solvent with the stator coils mounted inside it.

8. Install the stator coil (C, **Figure 72**) into the side cover. Install the stator coil Allen bolts and tighten securely. Route the stator coil wiring harness through the pickup coil mounting position.

9. Install the wire guide and pickup coil (**Figure 73**) into the side cover. Route the pickup coil and stator coil wiring harnesses around the cover as shown in **Figure 72**. Install the pickup coil screws (B, **Figure 72**) and tighten securely.

10. Push the rubber grommets firmly into the side cover grooves.

11. Install the wire guide and screw (A, **Figure 72**). Tighten the screw securely.

Left-Hand Side Cover Oil Seal and Bearing Replacement (1988-on)

Refer to **Figure 65** when performing this procedure.

1. To remove the bearing (**Figure 74**):
   a. The bearing is installed with a slip fit.

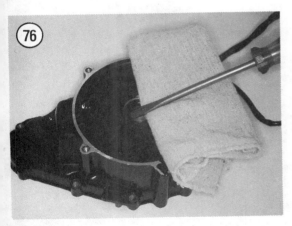

b. Working through the outside of the housing, push the bearing out of its bore (**Figure 75**).

2. Pry the oil seal out of the side cover with a large wide-blade screwdriver (**Figure 76**). Support the screwdriver with a rag to avoid damaging the side cover. Pry at different points around the seal so it does not bind in the bore.

3. Wipe out the oil seal and bearing bores with a clean rag.

4. To install a new oil seal:
   a. Pack the oil seal lips with waterproof bearing grease.
   b. Align the oil seal so its manufacturer's name and size code on the oil seal face toward the outside of the side cover.
   c. Press in the oil seal (**Figure 77**) until its outer surface is flush with or slightly below the oil seal bore inside surface as shown in **Figure 78**.

5. To install the new bearing:
   a. Align the bearing with the inside of the housing, so its manufacturer's name and size code on the bearing face toward the inside of the side cover (**Figure 75**).
   b. Push or press the bearing into the side cover until it bottoms out squarely in the bore (**Figure 74**).

6. Install the stator coil and pickup coil, if removed.

Left-Hand Side Cover Installation

1. Apply grease to the left-hand side cover oil seal lips (**Figure 78**).

2. Install the 2 dowel pins (**Figure 71**) and a new gasket.

5

3. Check that the 2 wiring harness grommets (**Figure 79**) are flush with the side cover gasket surface.

4. Install the left-hand side cover as follows:

a. Install the left-hand side cover (**Figure 69**) over the flywheel and seat it against the crankcase.

b. Check the gasket fit around the left-hand side cover.

c. On 1988-on models, install the wiring harness guide (**Figure 80**).

d. Install the left-hand side cover mounting bolts finger-tight. Then tighten the bolts securely.

5. On all 1988-on models, perform the following:

a. If removed, install the starter pulley O-ring into the pulley groove as shown in **Figure 81**. Apply a waterproof bearing grease to the O-ring.

b. Slide the starter pulley over the crankshaft and align the 2 key grooves as shown in **Figure 82**.

c. Slide the key into the key grooves (**Figure 83**).

d. Install the flywheel mounting bolt (B, **Figure 67**) and tighten to the torque specification in **Table 3**.

e. Install the recoil starter assembly as described in this chapter.

6A. On 2-wheel drive models, install the differential shift lever case (A, **Figure 66**).

6B. On 4-wheel drive models, perform the following:

a. Install the propeller shaft cover (C, **Figure 70**).

b. Install the shift lever (B, **Figure 70**).

c. Install the sub-transmission lever assembly (A, **Figure 70**).

7. Reconnect the alternator and pickup coil electrical connectors.

8. Install the seat.

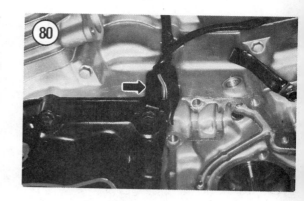

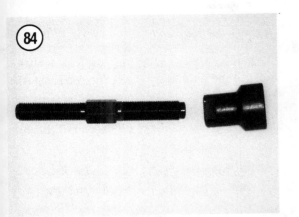

84

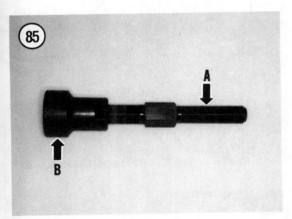

85

A

B

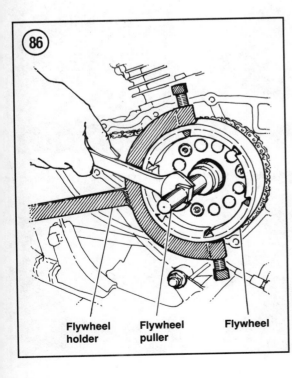

86

Flywheel holder   Flywheel puller   Flywheel

FLYWHEEL

Special Tools

A puller assembly is required to remove the flywheel from the crankshaft. When purchasing a puller, note the following:

    a. All 1986-1987 flywheels have internal threads. To remove this flywheel, the Kawasaki flywheel puller (part No. 57001-1099) is required. See **Figure 84**.

    b. All 1988 and later flywheels have external threads. To remove this flywheel, the Kawasaki flywheel puller (part No. 57001-1099 [A, **Figure 85**]) and the Kawasaki flywheel holder (part No. 57001-1191 [B, **Figure 85**]) is required.

    c. On flywheels with internal threads, a special tool is required to hold the flywheel. Use the Kawasaki flywheel holder (part No. 57001-308), or an equivalent tool. See **Figure 86**.

Removal

1. Park the vehicle on level ground and set the parking brake.
2. Remove the left-hand side cover as described in this chapter.

> *NOTE*
> *Refer to **Special Tools** in this section for special tools and part numbers.*

> *CAUTION*
> *Do not try to remove the flywheel without a puller; any attempt to do so will ultimately lead to some form of damage to the crankshaft and flywheel. If you cannot buy or borrow a puller, have a dealer remove the flywheel.*

> *CAUTION*
> *If normal flywheel removal attempts fail, do not force the puller. Excessive force will strip the flywheel threads, causing expensive damage. Take the engine to a dealer and have them remove the flywheel.*

3A. On 1986-1987 models, perform the following:
    a. Hold the flywheel with the flywheel holder (**Figure 86**) and remove the flywheel bolt.
    b. Screw the flywheel puller into the flywheel as shown in **Figure 86**.

c. Hold the flywheel with the flywheel holder and gradually tighten the flywheel puller (**Figure 86**) until the flywheel disengages from the crankshaft.

3B. On 1988 and later models, perform the following:

a. Screw the flywheel puller holder (A, **Figure 87**) onto the flywheel until it stops, then back it out 1/2 turn or less.

b. Screw the flywheel puller into the flywheel puller holder as shown in B, **Figure 87**.

c. Hold the flywheel puller holder and gradually tighten the flywheel puller (**Figure 88**) until the flywheel disengages from the crankshaft.

4. Slide the flywheel off of the crankshaft and remove it.

5. Remove the Woodruff key (**Figure 89**) from the crankshaft groove.

Inspection

1. Clean the flywheel in solvent and dry with compressed air.

2. Check the flywheel (**Figure 90**) for cracks or breaks.

> *WARNING*
> *A cracked or chipped flywheel must be replaced. A damaged flywheel can fly apart at high rpm, throwing metal fragments into the engine. Do not attempt to repair a damaged flywheel*

3. Check the flywheel tapered bore and the crankshaft taper for damage.

4. Check the crankshaft and flywheel bolt threads for damage.

5. Replace damaged parts as required.

6. To service the one-way clutch mounted on the back of the flywheel, refer to *Starter Clutch* in this chapter.

Installation

1. Install the Woodruff key (**Figure 89**) into the crankshaft keyway.

> *CAUTION*
> *Do not install the flywheel until you have checked the flywheel magnets for small bolts, washers or other metal*

trash; otherwise these parts can damage the stator coils.

2. Align the keyway in the flywheel with the Woodruff key and slide the flywheel (**Figure 91**) onto the crankshaft.

3. On 1986-1987 models, install the flywheel bolt and tighten to the torque specification in **Table 3**.

> *NOTE*
> *On 1988 and later models, the left-hand side cover is installed before the fly-*

wheel bolt. When trying to install the left-hand side cover, magnetic force usually pulls the flywheel off the crankshaft and toward the left-hand side cover. You then have to remove the left-hand side cover and reinstall the flywheel and Woodruff key. To prevent this from happening, push the flywheel onto the crankshaft as described in Step 4.

4. On 1988 and later models, perform the following:
   a. Thread the flywheel puller (A, **Figure 92**) onto the flywheel.
   b. Thread the flywheel bolt (B, **Figure 92**) into the crankshaft threads.

c. Hold the flywheel puller and tighten the flywheel bolt to push the flywheel deeper onto the crankshaft taper. Do not exceed the final torque specification in **Table 3**.
   d. Remove the flywheel bolt and flywheel puller.
5. Install the left-hand side cover as described in this chapter.

STARTER CLUTCH, CHAIN AND SPROCKETS

Pre-Inspection

If the starter clutch makes excessive noise, perform the following check:

1. Remove the left-hand side cover as described in this chapter.
2. On 1988 and later models, perform the following:
   a. Thread the flywheel puller holder (A, **Figure 92**) onto the flywheel.
   b. Thread the flywheel bolt (B, **Figure 92**) into the crankshaft threads and tighten it against the flywheel puller holder.
3. With a wrench on the flywheel bolt, turn the flywheel clockwise and then counterclockwise. Note the following:
   a. When the flywheel is turned clockwise, the starter chain and sprockets should turn with the flywheel.
   b. When the flywheel is turned counterclockwise, the flywheel should turn by itself (the chain and sprockets should not turn).
4. If the starter clutch operates as described in Step 3, it is working properly. If the starter clutch fails to operate as described in Step 3, remove and inspect it as described in the following sections.
5. On 1988 and later models, remove the flywheel bolt and the flywheel puller holder.
6. Install the left-hand side cover as described in this chapter.

Removal

1. Remove the flywheel as described in this chapter.

NOTE
Starter chain breakage occured on some early (1986) KLF300-A1 models if the engine backfired and kicked-back

while operating the starter motor. This breakage occurred mainly on new units, usually when the engine was cranked while cold. To prevent chain breakage, Kawasaki developed a redesigned starter motor sprocket which used a built-in torque limiter. This redesigned starter motor sprocket was installed on 1986 models that experienced a broken starter chain under warranty. The new starter motor sprocket was also installed on late 1986 models, in addition to all models with engine number 017644-on. *Figure 93* shows the early and new design starter motor sprockets and chain guides.

2. Remove the chain guide screw and chain guide (**Figure 94**).

3. Slide off both sprockets and chain (**Figure 95**) at the same time.

Starter Clutch Inspection

1. Wash all parts in solvent. Dry parts with compressed air.
2. Inspect the starter motor sprocket (**Figure 93**) for:

> *CAUTION*
> *Do not attempt to disassemble the starter motor sprocket equipped with a built-in torque limiter (**Figure 96**).*

a. Broken or chipped gear teeth.
b. Worn or scored shaft surface.
c. Worn or damaged splines.

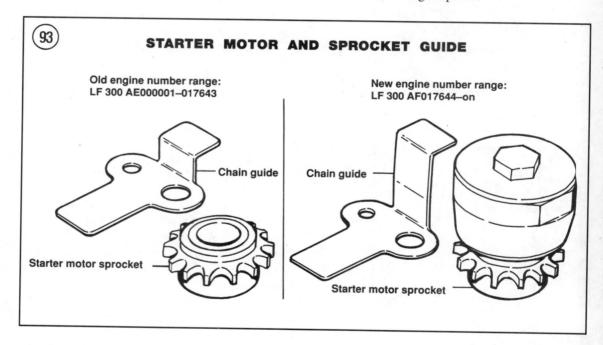

93 STARTER MOTOR AND SPROCKET GUIDE

Old engine number range:
LF 300 AE000001–017643

New engine number range:
LF 300 AF017644–on

Chain guide

Chain guide

Starter motor sprocket

Starter motor sprocket

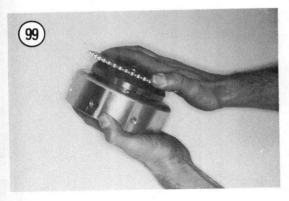

d. Blue discoloration indicating excessive heat.

3. Inspect the starter clutch sprocket (A, **Figure 97**) for:

a. Broken or chipped gear teeth.

b. Worn or scored hub surface (B, **Figure 97**).

c. Worn or scored bushing surface (C, **Figure 97**).

4. Inspect starter clutch assembly (D, **Figure 97**) for:

a. Worn or damaged starter clutch rollers.

b. Loosen mounting bolts (**Figure 90**).

5. To check starter clutch operation, perform the following:

a. Install the starter clutch sprocket (**Figure 98**) into the starter clutch.

b. Hold the flywheel (**Figure 99**) and turn the starter clutch sprocket counterclockwise. The sprocket should turn freely.

c. Now try to turn the starter clutch sprocket clockwise. The gear sprocket should engage with the starter clutch and should not turn.

d. If the starter clutch failed to operate as described in sub-step b or c, replace it as described in the following step.

6. To replace the starter clutch, perform the following:

a. Using an impact driver and socket bit, remove the bolts (**Figure 90**) securing the starter clutch housing to the flywheel.

b. Note the direction of the sprags in the starter clutch. Install sprags facing in their original direction.

c. Remove the starter clutch.

d. Remove all thread lock residue from the starter clutch bolts and the threads in the starter clutch.

e. Install the new starter clutch onto the flywheel.

f. Apply Loctite 242 (blue) to the starter clutch mounting bolt threads before installation. Install the bolts and tighten to the torque specification listed in **Table 3**.

Starter Chain Inspection

1. Clean the starter chain in solvent. Blow dry with compressed air.

2. Check the starter chain for:

a. Worn or damaged pins and rollers.

b. Cracked or damaged side plates.

c. Blue discoloration.

3. Place the chain on a flat surface and pull the chain tight (no slack between pins). Then measure the

length of any 20 links (21 pins) with a vernier caliper (**Figure 100**) and check against the dimension in **Table 2**. Because the chain may wear unevenly, repeat the measurement at several places around the chain. Replace the chain if stretched to the service limit (**Table 2**). Do not attempt to repair the chain.

4. If the starter chain is severely worn or damaged, inspect the starter motor sprocket and starter clutch sprocket for the same wear conditions. If the sprockets show wear or damage, replace them at the same time.

CAUTION
Do not run a new chain over severely worn or damaged sprockets. Doing this may cause excessive chain wear and premature failure.

Installation

1. Fit the starter chain over both sprockets. Position the small non-torque limiter sprocket (**Figure 93**) with its shoulder facing toward the engine.
2. Slide both sprockets and chain onto the engine (**Figure 95**).
3. Apply Loctite 242 (blue) to the chain guide mounting screw prior to installation.
4. Install the chain guide and screw (**Figure 94**). Tighten the screw securely.

5. Install the flywheel as described in this chapter.

CRANKCASE AND CRANKSHAFT

Disassembly of the crankcase—splitting the case halves—and removal of the crankshaft assembly requires engine removal from the frame. However, first remove the cylinder head, cylinder and all other attached assemblies with the engine mounted in the frame.

The crankcase is made in 2 halves of precision diecast aluminum alloy and is of the thin-walled type. To avoid damaging them, do not hammer or pry on any of the interior or exterior projected walls—excessive force will damage these areas. They are assembled without a gasket; only gasket sealer is used while dowel pins align the crankcase halves when they are bolted together. The crankcase halves are sold as a matched set only (**Figure 101**). If one crankcase half is damaged, both case halves must be purchased.

The crankshaft assembly consists of 2 full-circle flywheels pressed together on a crankpin. The connecting rod big end bearing on the crankpin is a needle bearing assembly (**Figure 102**). Two ball bearings support the crankshaft in the crankcase.

The procedure that follows describes a complete, step-by-step major lower end overhaul. Follow the procedure when overhauling the engine.

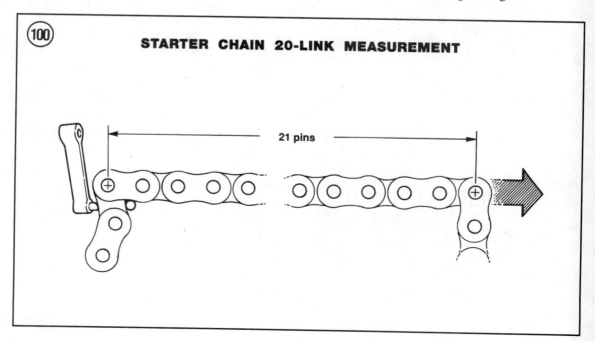

(100) STARTER CHAIN 20-LINK MEASUREMENT

21 pins

Remember that the right- and left-hand side of the engine relates to the engine as it sits in the frame, not as it sits on your workbench.

Crankcase Disassembly

This procedure describes disassembly of the crankcase halves and removal of the crankshaft, transmission, reverse assembly and internal shift mechanism. Refer to Chapter Seven for transmis-

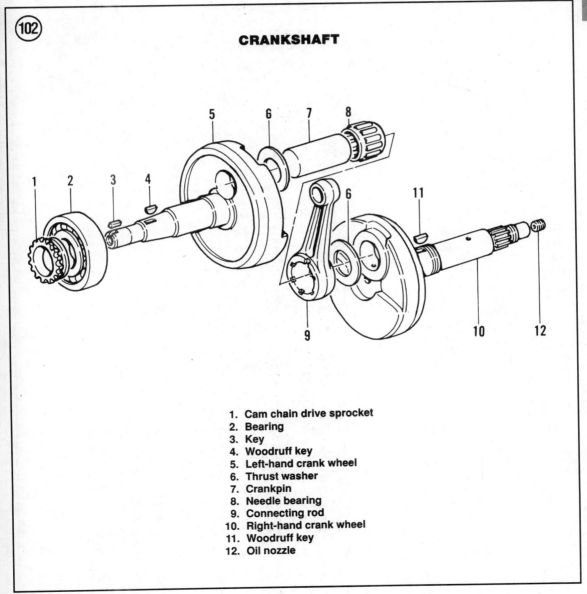

CRANKSHAFT

1. Cam chain drive sprocket
2. Bearing
3. Key
4. Woodruff key
5. Left-hand crank wheel
6. Thrust washer
7. Crankpin
8. Needle bearing
9. Connecting rod
10. Right-hand crank wheel
11. Woodruff key
12. Oil nozzle

sion, reverse assembly and internal shift mechanism service.

Refer to **Figure 103** (2-wheel drive) or **Figure 104** (4-wheel drive) when performing the following.
1. Remove all exterior engine assemblies as described in this chapter and other related chapters:

a. Front gear case (2-wheel drive).
b. Sub-transmission gear case (4-wheel drive).
c. Reverse lever.
d. Cylinder head.
e. Cylinder and piston.
f. Flywheel.

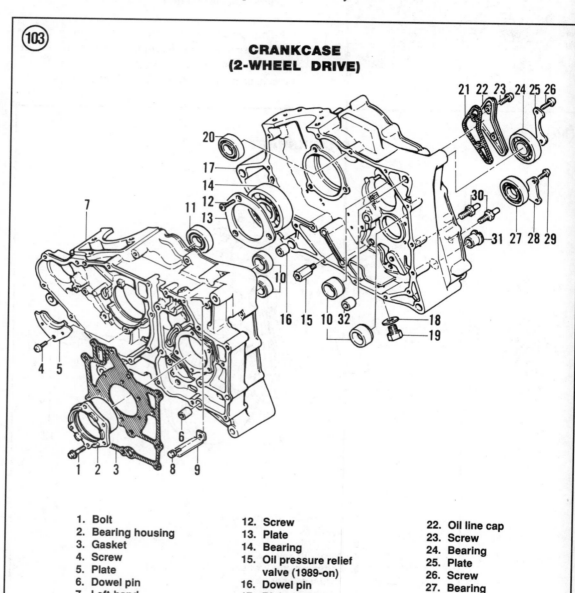

CRANKCASE (2-WHEEL DRIVE)

1. Bolt	12. Screw	22. Oil line cap
2. Bearing housing	13. Plate	23. Screw
3. Gasket	14. Bearing	24. Bearing
4. Screw	15. Oil pressure relief	25. Plate
5. Plate	valve (1989-on)	26. Screw
6. Dowel pin	16. Dowel pin	27. Bearing
7. Left-hand	17. Right-hand	28. Plate
crankcase half	crankcase half	29. Screw
8. Bolt	18. Gasket	30. Pins
9. Plate	19. Oil drain plug	31. Bushing
10. Bushings	20. Bearing	32. Dowel pin
11. Bearing	21. Oil line cap gasket	

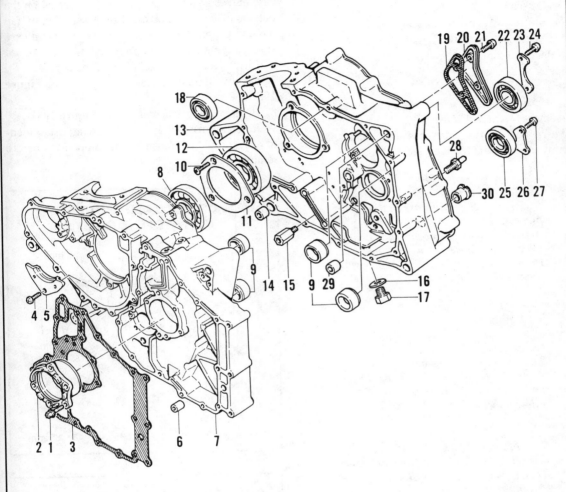

(104)

CRANKCASE
(4-WHEEL DRIVE)

1. Screw
2. Bearing housing
3. Gasket
4. Screw
5. Plate
6. Dowel pin
7. Left-hand crankcase half
8. Bearing
9. Bushing
10. Screw
11. Plate
12. Bearing
13. Right-hand crankcase half
14. Dowel pin
15. Oil pressure relief valve (1989-on)
16. Gasket
17. Oil drain plug
18. Bearing
19. Oil line cap gasket
20. Oil line cap
21. Screw
22. Bearing
23. Plate
24. Screw
25. Bearing
26. Plate
27. Screw
28. Pin
29. Dowel pin
30. Bushing

5

g. Starter clutch, chain and sprockets.

h. Starter motor.

i. Clutch.

j. External shift mechanism.

k. Oil pump.

l. Balancer and oil pump gears.

m. Neutral/reverse switch assembly.

2. Place the engine assembly on a couple of wooden blocks with the left-hand side facing up (**Figure 105**).

3. Loosen all screws securing the crankcase halves together, 1/4 turn. **Figure 106** (2-wheel drive) or **Figure 107** (4-wheel drive) shows the crankcase screws and their individual sizes.

NOTE
*To help keep track of the crankcase bolts, draw the crankcase outline on a piece of cardboard (**Figure 106** or **Figure 107**), then number and punch holes to correspond with each screw location. Insert the screws in their appropriate locations.*

4. Remove all screws loosened in Step 3. Be sure to remove all of them.

CAUTION
The crankcase halves may separate easily in the following procedure. Therefore, work over your workbench. Do not allow either half to fall to the floor.

CAUTION
Do not pry between the crankcase mating surfaces when separating the crankcase halves. Doing so will damage the mating surfaces and result in oil leaks,

requiring replacement of both case halves.

5. Using a wide-blade screwdriver, pry the crankcase halves apart at the 2 pry points located on the outside of the case halves. If necessary, lightly tap the end of the shafts to prevent the left-hand case from hanging up as you remove it.

6. Lift the left-hand crankcase off the engine.

7. Remove the 2 crankcase dowel pins (A, **Figure 108**).

8. Remove the balancer shaft (B, **Figure 108**).

9. Refer **Figure 109** and the following list to identify the individual transmission components before removing them:

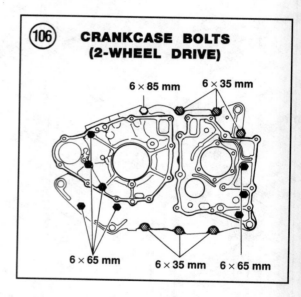

(106) CRANKCASE BOLTS (2-WHEEL DRIVE)

6 × 85 mm 6 × 35 mm

6 × 65 mm   6 × 35 mm   6 × 65 mm

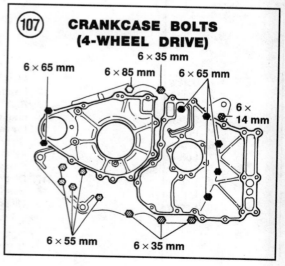

(107) CRANKCASE BOLTS (4-WHEEL DRIVE)

6 × 35 mm

6 × 65 mm   6 × 85 mm   6 × 65 mm

6 × 14 mm

6 × 55 mm   6 × 35 mm

(105)

a. Drive axle.

b. Output axle.

c. Reverse axle.

d. Shift drum.

e. Shift forks and shafts.

10A. On 2-wheel drive models, remove the shift fork shafts and shift forks as follows:

NOTE
The 2 output axle shift forks are identical. Therefore, if you are disassembling

the engine because of a shifting problem, mark the operating position of each shift fork as you remove it.

a. Remove the output axle shift fork shaft and 2 shift forks (**Figure 110**).

b. Remove the drive axle shift fork shaft and shift fork (**Figure 111**).

10B. On 4-wheel drive models, remove the shift fork shaft and shift forks as follows:

a. On these models, all 3 shift forks operate on the same shift fork shaft.

b. Remove the shift fork shaft and remove the 3 shift forks. **Figure 112** identifies the shift forks and their operating position.

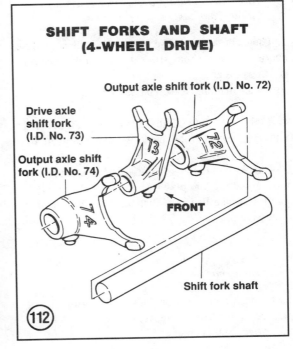

SHIFT FORKS AND SHAFT (4-WHEEL DRIVE)

Output axle shift fork (I.D. No. 72)

Drive axle shift fork (I.D. No. 73)

Output axle shift fork (I.D. No. 74)

FRONT

Shift fork shaft

11. Remove the shift drum (**Figure 113**).

12. Remove the drive axle, output axle and reverse axle (**Figure 114**) at the same time. See **Figure 115**.

13. Store the individual axles (**Figure 116**) in a plastic bag, sealed and labeled until you service them.

14. Lift the crankshaft (**Figure 117**) out of the right-hand crankcase and remove it.

15. If necessary, remove and service the oil pressure relief valve (1989-on models) as described in this chapter; see **Figure 118**.

Crankcase Inspection

1. Using a scraper, remove all sealer and gasket residue from all crankcase gasket surfaces.

> *WARNING*
> *When drying the crankcase bearings in Step 2, do not allow the inner bearing race to spin. The bearing will be dry of all lubrication and damage will result. When drying the bearings, hold the inner race with your hand. In addition, when drying bearings with compressed air, never allow the air jet to rotate the bearing. The air jet will force the bearings to turn at speeds that exceed their designed limit. The likelihood of a bearing disintegrating and causing serious injury and damage is very great.*

2. Clean both crankcase halves and all crankcase bearings with cleaning solvent. Thoroughly dry with compressed air.

3. Clean all crankcase oil passages with compressed air.

4. Lightly oil the crankcase bearings (**Figure 101**) with engine oil before checking the bearings in Step 5.

5. Check the bearings (**Figure 101**) for roughness, pitting, galling and play by rotating them slowly by hand. Replace bearings that turn roughly or show excessive play.

> *NOTE*
> *Always replace opposite bearing at the same time.*

6. Replace any worn or damaged bearings as described under *Crankcase Bearing and Bushing Replacement* in this chapter.

7. Inspect the crankcase bushings for roughness, pitting or galling. Replace any worn or damaged bushings as described under *Crankcase Bearing and Bushing Replacement* in this chapter.

8. Inspect the cases for cracks and fractures, especially in the lower areas where they are vulnerable to rock damage.

9. Check the areas around the stiffening ribs, around bearing bosses and threaded holes for damage. Repair or replaced damaged cases.

10. Check the threaded holes in both crankcase halves for thread damage, dirt or oil buildup. If necessary, clean or repair the threads with a suitable size metric tap. Coat the tap threads with kerosene or an aluminum tap fluid before use.

11. Check for loose or damaged shift shaft pin bolts (**Figure 119**); retighten or replace if necessary. Note the following:

    a. Apply Loctite 242 (blue) to the bolt threads prior to installation.

    b. Tighten the shift shaft pin bolts to the torque specification in **Table 3**.

Crankcase Bearing and Bushing Replacement

Prior to replacing the crankcase bearings and bushings, note the following:

    a. Because of the number of bearings used in the left- and right-hand crankcase (**Figure 101**), make sure to identify bearings before removing them. Identify the bearings with their size code markings.

    b. Refer to *Ball Bearing Replacement* in Chapter One for general information on bearing removal and installation.

    c. After removing bearings and bushings, clean crankcase in solvent and dry thoroughly.

    d. A pilot bearing remover is required to remove some of the blind bearings and bushings in the following procedures.

    e. When installing new bearings, press on the outer bearing race only (**Figure 120**).

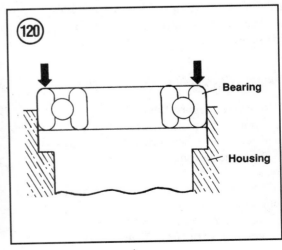

Balancer shaft bearing replacement

Refer to **Figure 121** and **Figure 122**.

1. To replace the left-hand bearing (**Figure 121**):
   a. Remove the bearing with a pilot bearing remover (**Figure 123**).
   b. Press in the new bearing until it bottoms in the crankcase.
2. To replace the right-hand bearing (**Figure 122**):
   a. Press bearing from crankcase.
   b. Press in the new bearing until it bottoms in the crankcase.

Reverse axle and drive axle bushing replacement

The bushings are identified as follows:
   a. Left-hand reverse axle bushing (A, **Figure 124**).
   b. Right-hand reverse axle bushing (A, **Figure 125**).
   c. Left-hand drive axle bushing (B, **Figure 124**).
   d. Right-hand drive axle bushing (B, **Figure 125**).

1. Remove the oil line cap and gasket from the right-hand crankcase. See **Figure 103** or **Figure 104**.

2. Remove blind bushings with a blind bearing puller set. See A and B, **Figure 124** and B, **Figure 125**.

3. Remove the right-hand reverse axle bushing (A, **Figure 125**) by pressing it out of the crankcase.

4. Align the new bushing with the crankcase and press in until its shoulder bottoms on the inside of the crankcase.

5. Install the oil line gasket and cap onto the right-hand crankcase (**Figure 103** or **Figure 104**).

6. Apply Loctite 242 (blue) to the oil line cap retaining screws. Install and tighten the screws securely.

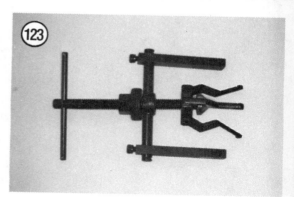

Output axle right-hand bearing replacement

Refer to A, **Figure 126**.

1. Remove the bearing retaining plate screws and remove the plate. See **Figure 103** or **Figure 104**.

2. Press the bearing (A, **Figure 126**) out of the crankcase.

3. Press the new bearing into the crankcase until it bottoms out.

4. Position the bearing retaining plate onto the crankcase (**Figure 103** or **Figure 104**).

5. Apply Loctite 242 (blue) to the bearing plate retaining screws. Then install and tighten the screws securely.

Shift drum right-hand bearing replacement

Refer to B, **Figure 126**.

1. Remove the bearing retaining plate screws and remove the plate. See **Figure 103** or **Figure 104**.
2. Press the bearing (B, **Figure 126**) out of the crankcase.

3. Press the new bearing into the crankcase until it bottoms out.
4. Position the bearing retaining plate onto the crankcase (**Figure 103** or **Figure 104**).
5. Apply Loctite 242 (blue) to the bearing plate retaining screws. Then install and tighten the screws securely.

Right-hand main bearing replacement

NOTE
*To replace left-hand main bearing, refer to **Crankshaft Sprocket and Main Bearing Replacement** in this chapter.*

1. Remove the bearing plate screws and remove the bearing plate (A, **Figure 127**).
2. Press the bearing (B, **Figure 127**) out of the crankcase.
3. Press in the new bearing until it bottoms in the crankcase.
4. Position the bearing retaining plate onto the crankcase (A, **Figure 127**).
5. Apply Loctite 242 (blue) to the bearing plate retaining screws. Then install and tighten the screws securely.

Crankshaft Inspection

Refer to **Figure 128**.

1. Clean the crankshaft thoroughly with solvent. Clean the crankshaft oil passageway with compressed air (**Figure 129**). Dry the crankshaft with compressed air. Then lubricate all bearing surfaces with a light coat of engine oil.
2. Check the oil nozzle (12, **Figure 128**) installed in the right-hand crank wheel. Make sure the nozzle is properly installed and is not plugged or damaged.
3. Check the crankshaft journals (**Figure 130** and **Figure 131**) for scratches, heat discoloration or other defects.
4. Check flywheel taper, threads, splines and keyways (**Figure 130** and **Figure 131**) for damage. Have damaged crankshaft components replaced as described under *Crankshaft Overhaul* in this chapter.
5. Check crankshaft bearing surfaces for chatter marks and excessive or uneven wear. Repair minor chatter marks with 320 grit carborundum cloth. Then, clean the crankshaft in solvent and recheck

surfaces. If they do not clean up properly, the crankshaft must be repaired or replaced.

6. Check the connecting rod big end (A, **Figure 132**) for signs of seizure, bearing or thrust washer damage or connecting rod damage.

7. Check the connecting rod small end (B, **Figure 132**) for signs of excessive heat (blue coloration) or other damage.

8. Slide the connecting rod to one side. Then measure the connecting rod big end side clearance with a flat feeler gauge as shown in **Figure 133**. Compare

to dimensions given in **Table 1**. Excessive clearance requires crankshaft overhaul.

9. Measure the connecting rod big end radial clearance as follows:

   a. Support the crankshaft journals on 2 V-blocks as shown in **Figure 134**.

   b. Support the connecting rod small end as shown in **Figure 134**.

   c. Position a dial indicator so that its stem rests against the connecting rod big end as shown in **Figure 134**. Then zero the dial gauge.

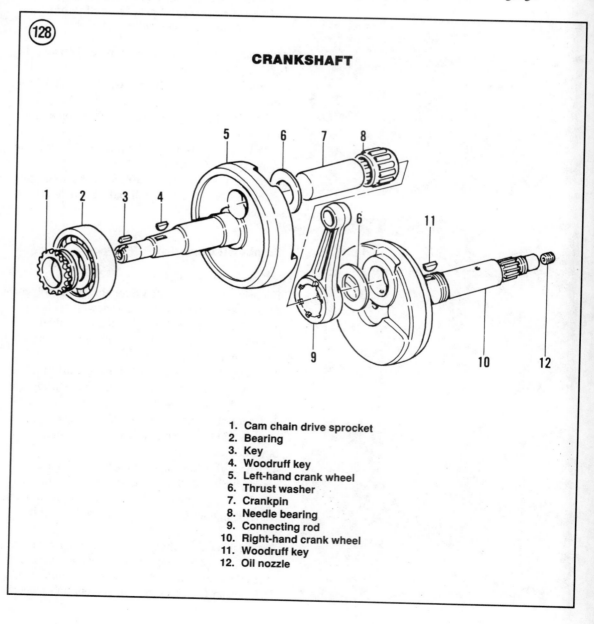

(128)

CRANKSHAFT

1. Cam chain drive sprocket
2. Bearing
3. Key
4. Woodruff key
5. Left-hand crank wheel
6. Thrust washer
7. Crankpin
8. Needle bearing
9. Connecting rod
10. Right-hand crank wheel
11. Woodruff key
12. Oil nozzle

d. Move the connecting rod toward the dial indicator and then away from it in the opposite direction.

e. The difference between the 2 gauge readings is the connecting rod big end radial clearance. Check against the specification in **Table 1**. Replace the connecting rod assembly if radial clearance exceeds the service limit (**Table 1**). See *Crankshaft Overhaul* in this chapter.

10. Measure crankshaft runout as follows:

a. Mount the crankshaft journals on 2 V-blocks as shown in **Figure 135**.

b. Position a dial indicator so that its stem rests against the left-hand crank at the position indicated in **Figure 135**. Then zero the dial gauge.

c. Slowly turn the crankshaft while reading the dial gauge. Record the runout limit.

d. Repeat with the dial indicator placed against the right-hand crank (**Figure 135**).

e. If the runout at either location exceeds the service limit in **Table 1**, the crankshaft must be retrued. See *Crankshaft Overhaul* in this chapter.

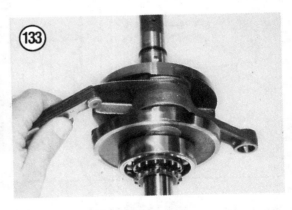

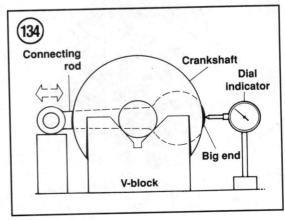

Connecting rod   Crankshaft   Dial indicator

Big end

V-block

Crankshaft Sprocket and Main Bearing Replacement

The camshaft drive sprocket (B, **Figure 136**) and the left-hand main bearing (A, **Figure 136**) are pressed on the crankshaft. A press and suitable adapters are required to replace the sprocket and/or bearing.

While the camshaft drive sprocket and left-hand main bearing are available separately, Kawasaki recommends replacing the crankshaft assembly rather than attempting to replace these parts. When replac-

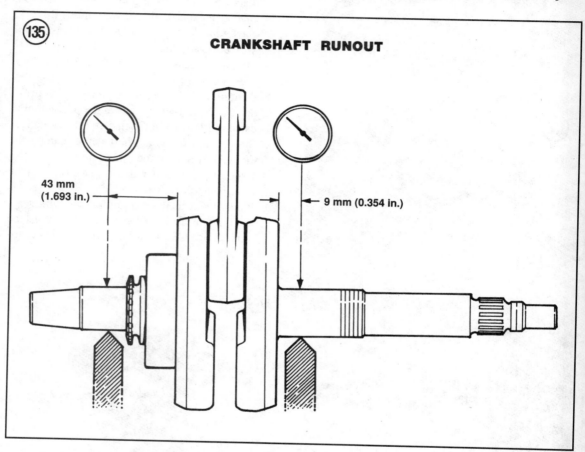

CRANKSHAFT RUNOUT

43 mm (1.693 in.)

9 mm (0.354 in.)

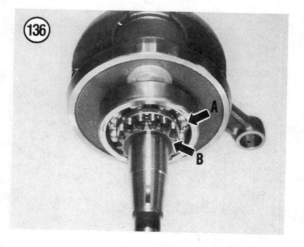

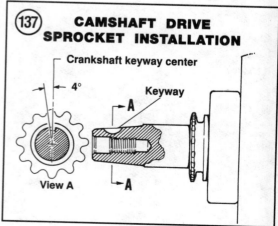

CAMSHAFT DRIVE SPROCKET INSTALLATION

Crankshaft keyway center

4°

Keyway

View A

ing these parts, special care must be given to the installation and alignment of the camshaft drive sprocket. If the camshaft drive sprocket is not installed and aligned correctly, cam timing will be incorrect.

1. Before removing the camshaft drive sprocket, note the position of the sprocket tooth in relation to the center of the crankshaft keyway as shown in **Figure 137**. This alignment must be maintained during reassembly.

2. Support the camshaft drive sprocket with a bearing remover and press the crankshaft from the sprocket.

3. Support the left-hand main bearing with a bearing remover and press the crankshaft from the sprocket.

4. Clean the crankshaft in solvent and dry with compressed air.

5. Support the crankshaft and press on the left-hand main bearing (A, **Figure 136**) until its inner race bottoms against the crankshaft.

6. Support the crankshaft. Then install the camshaft drive sprocket over the crankshaft. The drive sprocket chamfered side must face down (toward the left-hand main bearing).

7. Press the camshaft drive sprocket onto the crankshaft so that the sprocket tooth is positioned to the dimensions (from the center of the keyway) shown in **Figure 137**.

Crankshaft Overhaul

Crankshaft overhaul requires a number of special tools: a hydraulic press of 20 ton capacity (minimum), holding jigs, crankshaft alignment jig, dial indicators and a micrometer or vernier caliper. For this reason, refer crankshaft overhaul to a Kawasaki dealer or motorcycle repair shop familiar with crankshaft rebuilding. When having the crankshaft rebuilt, make sure the mechanic knows to align the crankshaft and crankpin oil passages as shown in **Figure 138**.

5

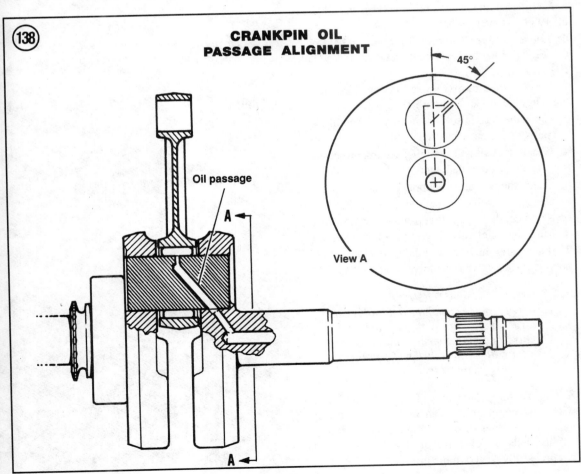

CRANKPIN OIL PASSAGE ALIGNMENT

45°

Oil passage

A

View A

A

Balancer Shaft Inspection

1. Check the balancer shaft bearing journals (**Figure 139**) for deep scoring, excessive wear, heat discoloration or cracks.
2. Check the keyway in the end of the balancer shaft for cracks or excessive wear.
3. Replace the balancer shaft if necessary.

Transmission and Reverse Assembly Inspection

Refer to Chapter Seven for all disassembly, inspection and reassembly procedures.

Oil Pressure Relief Valve Removal/Inspection/Installation (1989-on)

An internal oil pressure relief valve is installed on all 1989 and later models.

1. Loosen and remove the oil pressure relief valve (A, **Figure 140**) from the right-hand crankcase half (B).
2. Remove the circlip (**Figure 141**) and disassemble the relief valve. See **Figure 142**.
3. Clean the parts in solvent and dry thoroughly. Lay the parts on a clean, lint-free cloth.
4. Check the ball and the relief valve bore passage for scoring or other damage.
5. Check the washer for cupping or other damage.
6. Check the spring for bending, unequally spaced coils or other damage. If the spring shows any visible damage, the relief valve pressure will be altered.
7. If any parts show wear or damage, replace the oil pressure relief valve assembly.

CAUTION
Do not replace any of the internal relief valve components with "off the shelf items" that may appear similar. Doing so may alter the relief valve pressure and cause engine damage.

8. Coat the relief valve bore, ball, washer and spring with new engine oil. Then reassemble the relief valve in the order shown in **Figure 142**. Install the circlip in the relief valve groove. Make sure the circlip is fully seated in the groove.

CAUTION
Handle, clean and store the relief valve carefully to prevent dirt from entering the valve and scoring the relief valve bore and ball.

9. Hand thread the relief valve into the right-hand crankcase threads (A, **Figure 140**). Then tighten the oil pressure relief valve to the torque specification in **Table 3**.

Crankcase Assembly

This procedure describes installation of the crankshaft and transmission and crankcase assembly.

1. Refer to Chapter Seven for transmission, reverse assembly and internal shift mechanism reassembly.
2. Clean all of the components in solvent and dry thoroughly with compressed air. Oil the bearings with new engine oil.

CAUTION
Do not assemble the engine with solvent left on parts or in the oil passages;

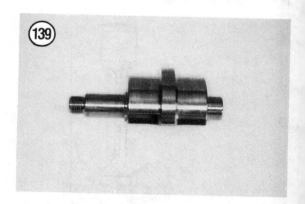

otherwise, the solvent will contaminate the new engine oil.

3. Place the right-hand crankcase assembly (B, **Figure 140**) on wooden blocks.

4. On 1988 and later models, install the oil pressure relief valve (A, **Figure 140**) as described in this section, if removed.

NOTE
Step 5 describes 2 methods of installing the crankshaft. If a press is required, the use of the Kawasaki crankshaft jig (part No. 57001-1174) is also necessary.

5A. Apply a light coat of engine oil to the right-hand crankshaft bearing journal. Then install the crankshaft into the right-hand main bearing as shown in **Figure 143**. Make sure the crankshaft bottoms out in the bearing.

NOTE
If the crankshaft cannot be installed by hand, install it with a press as described in Step 5B.

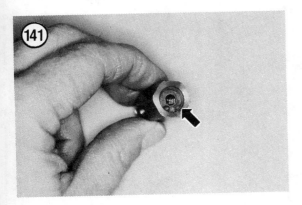

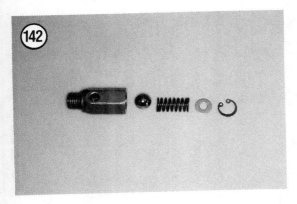

5B. Install the crankshaft with a press as follows:

CAUTION
If you do not have the crankshaft installation tools, refer this service to a dealer or machine shop. Do not drive the crankshaft and bearing into the crankcase with a hammer.

a. Position the right-hand crankcase in a press. Support the right-hand main bearing housing on a suitable press fixture and center the bearing under the press ram.

b. Apply a light coat of engine oil to the right-hand crankshaft bearing journal.

c. Install the crankshaft into the main bearing so that the crankshaft assembly is square with the crankcase mating surface.

d. Measure the distance from the left-hand crank shoulder (bottom side) to the press bed or press fixture. Adequate clearance must be maintained so the crankshaft cannot bottom out as it is being installed.

e. Position the connecting rod at bottom dead center (BDC).

f. Center the Kawasaki crankshaft jig (part No. 57001-1174) around the connecting rod. Then

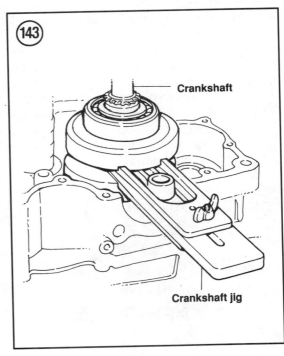

Crankshaft

Crankshaft jig

adjust the crankshaft jig so that its arms contact both crankshaft wheels as shown in **Figure 143**.

NOTE
The crankshaft jig is used to prevent crankshaft distortion when pressing the crankshaft into the bearing.

g. Press the crankshaft into the right-hand main bearing until the crankshaft shoulder bottoms out against the main bearing inner race.

h. Release pressure from the press ram.

i. Remove the crankshaft jig from the crankshaft. Then turn the crankshaft slowly by hand. It should turn freely with no sign of roughness or noise.

j. Remove the crankcase/crankshaft from the press and place onto wooden blocks.

6. Install the transmission (drive axle, output axle and reverse axle) as follows:

a. Place the drive axle, output axle and reverse axle onto the workbench as shown in **Figure 144**.

b. Mesh the 3 axles together as shown in **Figure 145**. All 3 axles are installed at the same time.

c. Install the 3 axles into the right-hand crankcase bearings. See **Figure 146** and **Figure 147**.

7. Install the shift drum into the right-hand crankcase bearing (**Figure 148**).

8A. On 2-wheel drive models, install the shift forks and shafts as follows:

a. **Figure 149** identifies the shift forks and shafts. The 2 output axle shift forks (A, **Figure 149**) are identical. The drive axle shift fork (B, **Figure 149**) rides on the shorter shift fork shaft.

b. Install the drive axle shift fork (B, **Figure 149**) into the drive axle 5th/3rd gear cluster groove; see **Figure 150**. Seat the shift fork pin into the center shift drum groove.

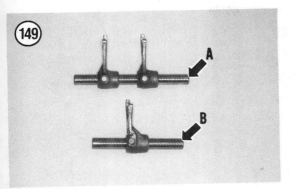

c. Insert the short shift fork shaft (B, **Figure 149**) through the drive axle shift fork; see **Figure 151**.

d. Install the first output axle shift fork (A, **Figure 149**) into the output axle 2nd gear groove; see A, **Figure 152**. Seat the shift fork pin into the right-hand (lower) shift drum groove.

e. Insert the second output axle shift fork (A, **Figure 149**) into the output axle 4th gear groove; see B, **Figure 152**. Seat the shift fork pin into the left-hand (upper) shift drum groove.

f. Insert the long shift fork shaft (**Figure 153**) through the 2 output axle shift forks.

g. Make sure both shift fork shafts bottom out in their respective bushings.

8B. On 4-wheel drive models, install the shift forks and shaft as follows:

a. On these models, all 3 shift forks operate on the same shift fork shaft. **Figure 154** identifies the shift forks with their operating position.

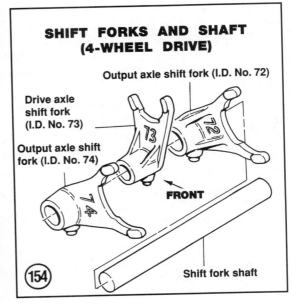

SHIFT FORKS AND SHAFT (4-WHEEL DRIVE)

Output axle shift fork (I.D. No. 72)

Drive axle shift fork (I.D. No. 73)

Output axle shift fork (I.D. No. 74)

FRONT

Shift fork shaft

b. Install the drive axle shift fork (Identification No. 73) into the drive axle 5th/3rd gear cluster groove; see **Figure 154**.

c. Install the output axle shift fork (Identification No. 72) into the output axle 4th gear groove; see **Figure 154**.

d. Install the output axle shift fork (Identification No. 74) into the output axle 2nd gear groove; see **Figure 154**.

e. Insert the shift fork shaft through the 3 shift forks.

f. Make sure the shift fork shaft bottoms out in the crankcase.

NOTE
Perform Step 9 with a helper as the assemblies do not spin easily. Have your helper spin the transmission shaft while you turn the shift drum through all the gears.

9. Spin the transmission shafts and shift through the gears using the shift drum. Make sure you can shift into all the gears, including reverse. This is the time to find a problem with the shifting—not after assembling the crankcase and installing it in the frame.

10. After making sure the transmission shifts into all the gears correctly, shift the transmission assembly into NEUTRAL.

11. Install the balancer shaft (A, **Figure 155**) into the right-hand crankcase bearing.

12. Install the 2 locating dowels (B, **Figure 155**).

13. Check the left- and right crankcase surfaces for old sealant material or other residue.

14. Apply a light coat of nonhardening liquid gasket sealer, such as Kawasaki Bond (part No. 921-4-002) or equivalent, onto the right-hand crankcase mating surface.

15. Align the left-hand crankcase with the axle shafts and crankshaft, then install it (**Figure 156**). Push it down squarely into place until it engages the dowel pins and then seats completely against the lower case half.

CAUTION
When properly lined up, the left-hand case will slide over the shafts and seat against the opposite case half. If the crankcase halves do not fit together completely, do not attempt to pull them together with the crankcase screws. Separate the crankcase halves and in-

vestigate the cause of the interference. Check the gears for proper installation. Crankcase halves are a matched set and are very expensive. Do not risk damage by trying to force them together.

16. Turn all the exposed axle shafts, crankshaft and shift drum. Each axle should turn smoothly without binding or roughness. If everything turns okay, continue with Step 17.

NOTE
Kawasaki does not list a torque sequence or tightening torque for the crankcase bolts.

17. Install all the crankcase mounting bolts finger-tight. See **Figure 157** or **Figure 158**.

18. Tighten the crankcase mounting bolts in 2-3 stages. Tighten each bolt securely.

19. Rotate the axle shafts, crankshaft and, shift drum. Each assembly should turn smoothly with no roughness or binding. If a problem is detected, re-

move the crankcase mounting bolts and the left-hand crankcase half and correct the problem.

20. Install all exterior engine assemblies as described in this chapter and other related chapters:

  a. Neutral/reverse switch assembly.

  b. Balancer and oil pump gears.

  c. Oil pump.

  d. External shift mechanism.

  e. Clutch.

  f. Starter motor.

  g. Starter clutch, chain and sprockets.

  h. Flywheel.

  i. Cylinder and piston.

  j. Cylinder head.

  k. Reverse lever.

  l. Sub-transmission gear case (4-wheel drive).

  m. Front gear case (2-wheel drive).

RECOIL STARTER

A rope-operated recoil starter assembly (**Figure 159**) is used on all 1988-on models.

The starter housing is mounted on the engine, next to the flywheel. Pulling the rope handle causes the starter sheave shaft to rotate against spring tension. Starter sheave rotation causes the drive pawl to engage the starter pulley which is affixed to the crankshaft, and therefore, cranking the engine. Releasing the rope handle allows the starter spring to reverse the sheave direction and wind the rope around the sheave.

Rewind starters are relatively trouble-free; a broken or frayed rope is the most common malfunction.

Recoil Starter Housing Removal/Installation

1. Park the vehicle on level ground. Set the parking brake.

2. On 4-wheel drive models, remove the front propeller shaft cover (**Figure 160**).

3. Remove the bolts that hold the starter housing (**Figure 161**) to the engine. Then remove the starter housing.

4. Install by reversing these steps. Tighten the recoil starter housing mounting bolts securely.

5. Check starter operation by pulling on the starter rope.

Starter Pulley Removal/Installation

The starter pulley is bolted to the left-hand end of the crankshaft.

1. Remove the recoil starter housing as described in this chapter.

2. Hold the starter pulley (A, **Figure 162**) with a wrench and loosen the flywheel mounting bolt (B, **Figure 162**).

3. Remove the flywheel mounting bolt (B, **Figure 162**).

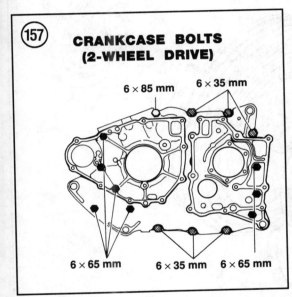

(157) CRANKCASE BOLTS (2-WHEEL DRIVE)

6 × 85 mm   6 × 35 mm

6 × 65 mm   6 × 35 mm   6 × 65 mm

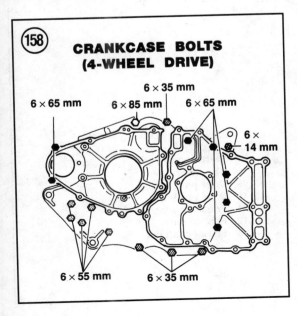

(158) CRANKCASE BOLTS (4-WHEEL DRIVE)

6 × 35 mm

6 × 65 mm   6 × 85 mm   6 × 65 mm

6 × 14 mm

6 × 55 mm   6 × 35 mm

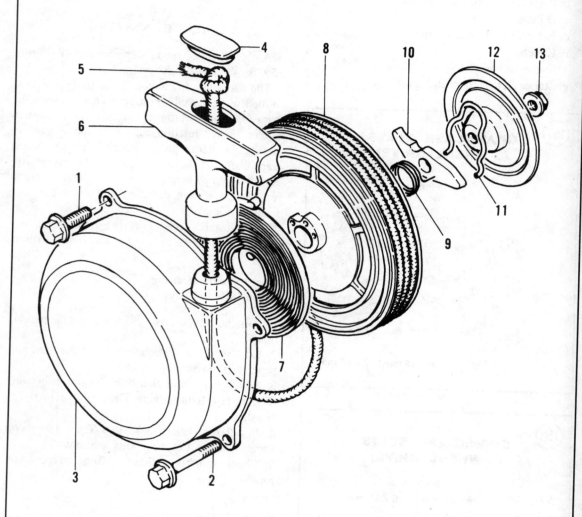

RECOIL STARTER

1. Bolt
2. Bolt
3. Recoil starter housing
4. Cap
5. Starter rope
6. Starter handle
7. Starter spring
8. Sheave drum
9. Drive pawl spring
10. Drive pawl
11. Friction spring
12. Friction plate
13. Starter shaft nut

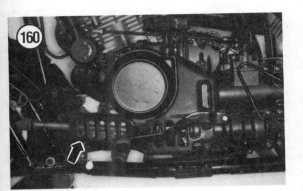

4. Slide the starter pulley (A, **Figure 162**) off the crankshaft and remove it.

5. Remove the key (**Figure 163**) from the crankshaft groove.

6. Install the starter pulley O-ring, if removed, into the pulley groove as shown in **Figure 164**. Apply a waterproof bearing grease to the O-ring.

7. Slide the starter pulley over the crankshaft and align the 2 key grooves as shown in **Figure 165**.

8. Slide the key into the key grooves (**Figure 166**).

9. Install the flywheel mounting bolt (B, **Figure 162**) and tighten to the torque specification in **Table 3**.

10. Install the recoil starter housing as described in this chapter.

Recoil Starter Housing Disassembly

WARNING
The starter spring is under pressure and may jump out when disassembling the starter housing. While the spring is not very strong, it may cut fingers and cause eye injury. Wear safety glasses when disassembling the starter housing.

1. Remove the recoil starter housing as described in this chapter.

2. Remove the starter handle as follows:
   a. Pull the handle out approximately 100-200 mm (4-8 in.).
   b. Clamp the rope with locking pliers (**Figure 167**).
   c. Pry the cap from the end of the starter handle.
   d. Slide the handle away from the rope knot and untie the knot (**Figure 168**).
   e. Remove the starter handle.

3. Hold the sheave drum with one hand and remove the locking pliers from the rope, but do not let go of the sheave drum.

4. Pull the rope through the rope hole in the housing and then catch the rope in the notch in the sheave drum (**Figure 169**)—do not let go of the sheave drum.

NOTE
When allowing the sheave to unwind in Step 5, do not let the rope catch between the sheave and starter housing. Guide the rope with your hand.

5. With your hand still controlling the sheave drum, slowly allow the sheave drum to unwind; see **Figure 170**.

6. Remove the starter shaft nut (A, **Figure 171**).

7. Remove the friction plate (B, **Figure 171**) and friction spring. The friction spring (A, **Figure 172**) is mounted on the back of the friction plate.

8. Remove the drive pawl (B, **Figure 172**) and drive pawl spring.

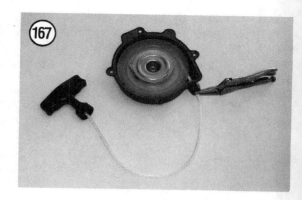

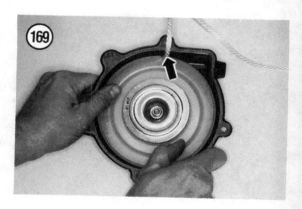

WARNING
The starter spring may jump out when removing the sheave drum in Step 9. Protect yourself accordingly.

9. Slowly lift the sheave drum (C, **Figure 172**) up and remove it from the starter housing.

10. If necessary, remove the starter spring (**Figure 173**) as follows:

    a. Place the starter housing on the floor with the spring side facing down. Tap lightly on the top of the housing while holding it tightly against

the floor. The spring should fall out of the housing and unwind inside the housing.

    b. When the spring has unwound, pick the housing up off the floor along with the spring.

Recoil Starter Housing Inspection

1. Clean all parts, except rope and sheave drum, in solvent and dry thoroughly.

2. Check the starter shaft in the starter housing. Replace the starter housing if the shaft is cracked or severely worn.

3. Check the top and bottom sheave drum surfaces for cracks or damage.

4. Inspect the drive pawl and spring (**Figure 174**) for damage.

5. Check the friction plate. Replace if severely worn or damaged.

6. Check the starter rope for fraying, splitting or breakage.

7. Check the starter spring (**Figure 173**). Replace a severely worn or damaged spring.

Recoil Starter Housing Assembly

1. If removed, install the starter spring into the starter housing as follows:

WARNING
The starter spring is put under great pressure when installing it. Safety glasses and gloves must be worn when installing the starter spring.

    a. Place the starter housing on the workbench.

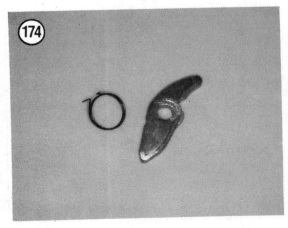

5

b. Hook the outer end of the starter spring onto the spring guide shown in **Figure 175**.

c. Wind the starter spring clockwise—working from the outside of the spring—into the starter housing. When you come to the end of the starter spring, push it down so that it contacts the starter housing shaft. Compare the installed spring ends with those in A, **Figure 176** and B, **Figure 176**.

d. Lubricate the spring with a waterproof grease.

2. Before installing the starter rope, check the rope ends for fraying. Apply heat with a heat gun (**Figure 177**) to tighten up loose or frayed rope ends. Do not overheat.

3. When installing a new rope, perform the following:

a. Tie a special knot at the end of the rope (**Figure 178**).

b. Pull the knot away from the sheave drum and lightly heat the knot to melt the nylon rope. This will help to hold the knot secure.

4. Insert the rope into the sheave drum. Pull the rope tight so that the knot seats against the sheave drum.

5. Place the sheave drum on the workbench with its top side (**Figure 179**) facing up. Then wind the rope 4 turns *clockwise* around the sheave drum (**Figure 179**).

6. Grease the bottom sheave drum surface (**Figure 180**).

7. Install the sheave drum into the starter housing as follows:

a. Align the notch in the bottom of the sheave drum (**Figure 180**) with the end of the starter

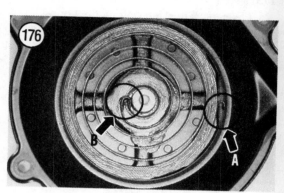

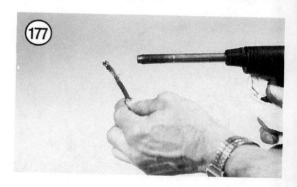

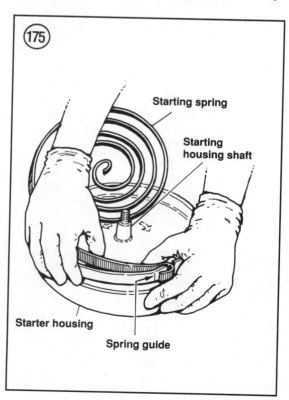

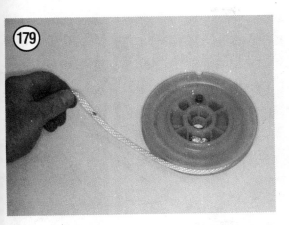

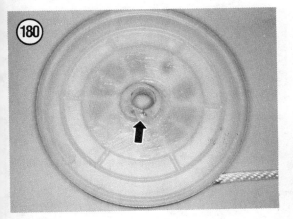

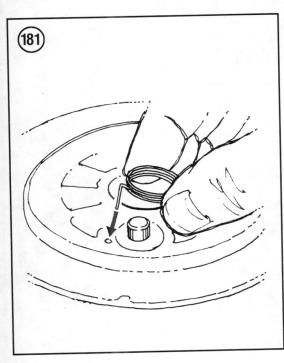

spring (B, **Figure 176**) and install the sheave drum.

b. Rotate the sheave drum slightly until it drops into place, indicating that the sheave drum notch meshed with the starter spring end.

8. Install the drive pawl spring and drive pawl as follows:

a. Insert the drive pawl spring—long end facing down—into the sheave drum hole as shown in **Figure 181**.

b. Install the drive pawl—chamfered side facing down—onto the sheave drum pin (**Figure 182**). Position the drive pawl so that the notch in the side of the pawl engages the drive pawl spring as shown in **Figure 182**.

9. Place the friction spring (**Figure 183**) onto the sheave drum. Position the friction spring so that its 2 hooks contact the drive pawl as shown in **Figure 183**.

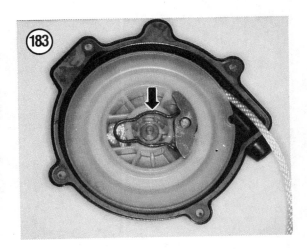

10. Grease the friction plate lower surface.

11. Place the friction plate (A, **Figure 184**) over the starter housing shaft and center it on the friction spring.

12. Install the starter shaft nut (B, **Figure 184**) and tighten to the torque specification in **Table 3**.

13. Insert the rope into the sheave drum notch (**Figure 185**).

14. Turn the sheave drum 4 turns clockwise to preload the spring (**Figure 185**). Then feed the rope through the rope hole in the starter housing (**Figure 186**).

15. Clamp the rope with locking pliers (**Figure 187**).

16. Insert the starter handle over the rope (**Figure 187**). Tie a knot in the end of the rope (**Figure 187**).

17. Install the cap (**Figure 188**) into the starter handle.

18. Remove the pliers from the rope.

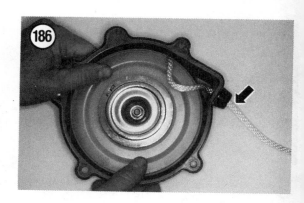

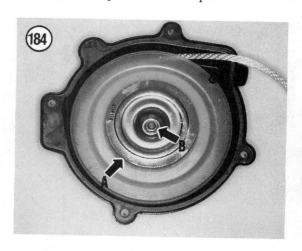

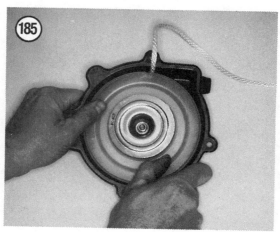

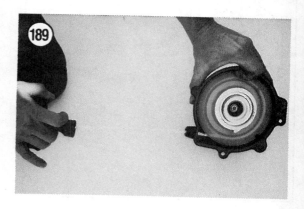

19. Pull the starter handle to check the recoil starter operation (**Figure 189**). The sheave drum should turn smoothly and return properly.

ENGINE BREAK-IN

When replacing top end components or performing major lower end work, the engine should be broken-in just as though it were new. The performance and service life of the engine depends greatly on a careful and sensible break-in.

During break-in, oil consumption will be higher than normal. It is important to check and correct the oil level frequently (Chapter Three). Never allow the oil level to drop below the minimum level. If the oil level is low, the oil will become overheated resulting in insufficient lubrication and increased wear.

Kawasaki designates the first 10 hours of vehicle operation as the break-in period. During this period, do not exceed 1/2 throttle.

After the break-in period, change the engine oil and filter as described in Chapter Three. It is essential to perform this service to remove all the particles produced during break-in, from the lubrication system. The small added expense is a smart investment that will pay off in increased engine life.

Table 1 CRANKSHAFT SERVICE SPECIFICATIONS

	New mm (in.)	Service limit mm (in.)
Crankshaft runout*		
Left-hand crank half	0-0.03 (0-0.001)	0.08 (0.003)
Right-hand crank half	0-0.04 (0-0.002)	0.10 (0.004)
Connecting rod big end side clearance	0.25-0.35 (0.010-0.014)	0.6 (0.024)
Connecting rod big end radial clearance	0.008-0.020 (0.0003-0.0008)	0.07 (0.003)

* See text for runout procedures for each crank half.

Table 2 STARTER CHAIN LENGTH

	New mm (in.)	Service limit mm (in.)
Starter chain length	155.8-156.1 (6.134-6.146)	158.00 (6.220)

* See text for chain measurement procedure.

Table 3 ENGINE TIGHTENING TORQUE

	N·m	ft.-lb.
Oil pipe banjo bolts	20	15
Balancer driven gear nut	83	61
Crankshaft nut*		
2-wheel drive	78	57
4-wheel drive	145	107
Shift drum stopper bolt	12	9.0
Shift drum pin plate bolt	12	9.0
Shift shaft return spring pin	17	12
Clutch release cam pin		
2-wheel drive	17	12
4-wheel drive	—	—
Oil pressure relief valve		
2-wheel drive	—	—
4-wheel drive	15	11
Engine mounting bolts		
8 mm	25	18
10 mm		
2-wheel drive	34	25
4-wheel drive	37	27
Cylinder head bracket mounting bolts	25	18
Flywheel mounting bolt	59	43
Starter clutch mounting bolts		
1988-on 2-wheel drive	34	25
All other models	49	36
Shift shaft pin bolts	12	9.0

* The crankshaft nut secures the balancer drive gear and the oil pump drive gear.

CHAPTER SIX

CLUTCH, PRIMARY DRIVE
AND EXTERNAL SHIFT MECHANISM

This chapter describes service procedures for the following sub-assemblies:

    a. Clutch cover.
    b. Clutch release mechanism.
    c. Clutch assembly.
    d. Primary drive.
    e. External shift mechanism.

These sub-assemblies can be removed with the engine still in the frame. Clutch service specifications are listed in **Table 1**. **Tables 1** and **2** are found at the end of the chapter.

CLUTCH COVER

The clutch release mechanism is mounted in the clutch cover.

Removal

Refer to **Figure 1** (2-wheel drive) or **Figure 2** (4-wheel drive).

1. Park the vehicle on level ground and set the parking brake.

2. Remove the right-hand footpeg.

3. Drain the engine oil as described in Chapter Three.

4. Remove the clutch cover mounting bolts and remove the clutch cover. See **Figure 3** (2-wheel drive) or **Figure 4** (4-wheel drive).

5. Remove the 2 dowel pins (**Figure 5**, typical) and gasket.

6. Service the oil screen (**Figure 6**) as described under *Oil Screen* in Chapter Five.

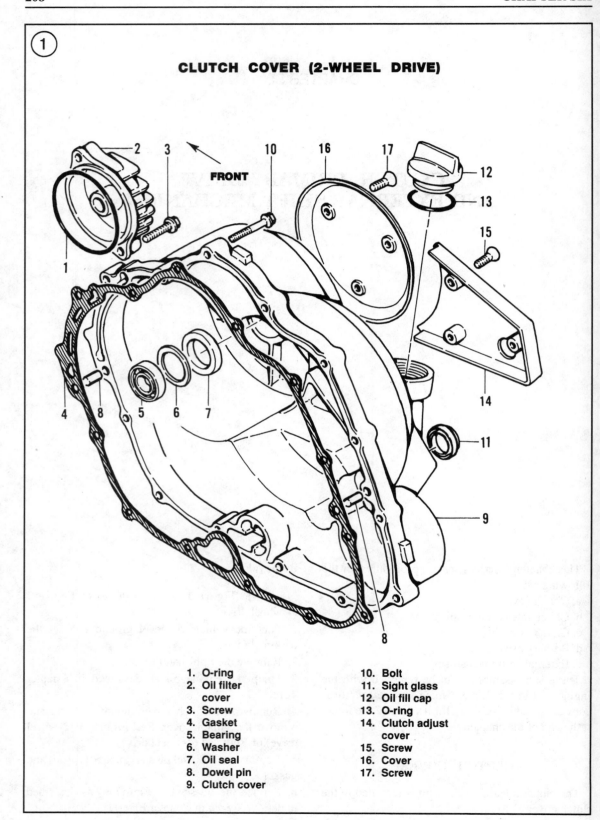

CLUTCH COVER (2-WHEEL DRIVE)

FRONT

1. O-ring
2. Oil filter cover
3. Screw
4. Gasket
5. Bearing
6. Washer
7. Oil seal
8. Dowel pin
9. Clutch cover
10. Bolt
11. Sight glass
12. Oil fill cap
13. O-ring
14. Clutch adjust cover
15. Screw
16. Cover
17. Screw

② **CLUTCH COVER (4-WHEEL DRIVE)**

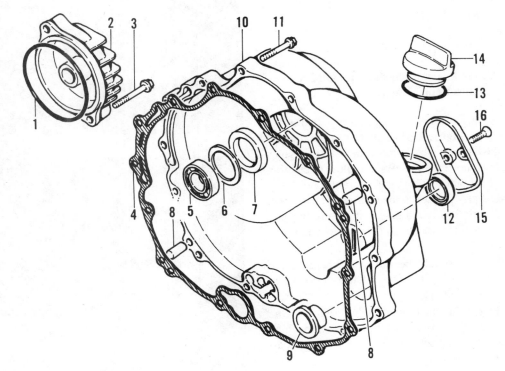

1. O-ring
2. Oil filter
   cover
3. Bolt
4. Gasket
5. Bearing
6. Washer
7. Oil seal
8. Dowel pins

9. Bushing
10. Clutch cover
11. Bolt
12. Sight glass
13. O-ring
14. Oil fill cap
15. Clutch adjust
    cover
16. Screw

6

7. Remove all gasket residue from the cover (A, **Figure 7**) and crankcase gasket surfaces.

8. If necessary, service the clutch release mechanism as described under *Clutch Release Mechanism* in this chapter.

Clutch Cover Bearing, Washer and Oil Seal Inspection and Replacement

The bearing, washer and oil seal installed in the clutch cover (**Figure 1** or **Figure 2**) are an integral part of the engines lubrication system. Oil passages in the clutch cover and crankshaft allow circulation of oil to the crankshaft big end bearing. The end of the crankshaft operates in the bearing. The oil seal, installed behind the bearing, seals the crankshaft and clutch cover oil passages so that oil does not leak out.

The oil seal should be replaced whenever the bearing is removed from the clutch cover or when rebuilding the engine.

When removing the bearing and oil seal from the clutch cover, note and record the direction in which the bearing and oil seal are facing for proper reinstallation.

1. Turn the clutch cover bearing (**Figure 8**) by hand. The bearing should turn smoothly with no roughness, catching, binding or excessive noise. If the bearing is damaged or if the oil seal requires replacement, continue with Step 2.

2. Support the clutch cover and remove the bearing with a blind bearing remover.

3. Remove the washer.

4. Carefully pry the oil seal out of the bore with a wide-blade screwdriver or oil seal removal tool. Pad the tool so that it does not damage the bearing bore.

5. Clean the clutch cover in solvent and dry thoroughly.

6. Clean the clutch cover oil passage (B, **Figure 7**) with compressed air.

7. Support the clutch cover and install the new oil seal. Install the oil seal so it faces in the direction recorded during disassembly.

8. Place the washer onto the oil seal.

9. Press the new bearing into the clutch cover bearing bore.

Installation

1. Clean the clutch cover oil passage (B, **Figure 7**) with compressed air.

2A. On 2-wheel drive models, make sure the clutch release cam and ball assembly are installed over the shift shaft as shown in A, **Figure 9**. Then make sure that the push plate (B, **Figure 9**) is installed in the secondary clutch bearing.

2B. On 4-wheel drive models, make sure the clutch release lever points toward the center of the secondary clutch as shown in **Figure 10**. Install the washer onto the shift shaft (**Figure 10**), if removed.

3. Install the 2 dowel pins (**Figure 5**, typical) and a new clutch cover gasket.

4. Install the clutch cover and its mounting bolts. Tighten the bolts securely. See **Figure 3** (2-wheel drive) or **Figure 4** (4-wheel drive).

5. Check the clutch adjustment as described in Chapter Three.

6. Refill the engine with oil as described in Chapter Three.

7. Install the right-hand footpeg.

CLUTCH RELEASE MECHANISM (2-WHEEL DRIVE)

Refer to **Figure 11** when servicing the clutch release mechanism assembly.

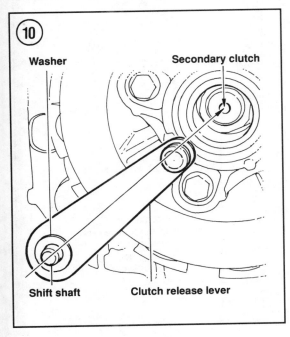

Washer
Secondary clutch
Shift shaft
Clutch release lever

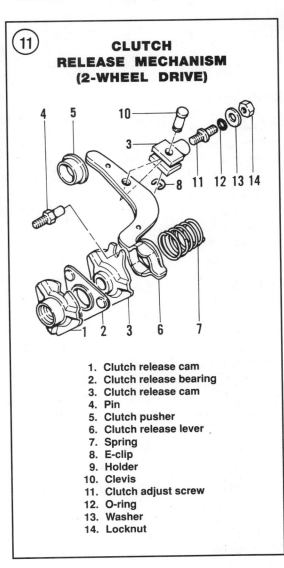

CLUTCH RELEASE MECHANISM (2-WHEEL DRIVE)

1. Clutch release cam
2. Clutch release bearing
3. Clutch release cam
4. Pin
5. Clutch pusher
6. Clutch release lever
7. Spring
8. E-clip
9. Holder
10. Clevis
11. Clutch adjust screw
12. O-ring
13. Washer
14. Locknut

Removal

1. Remove the clutch cover as described in this chapter.

2. Remove the clutch adjust cover from the outside of the clutch cover.

3. Remove the locknut, washer, O-ring and clutch adjust screw (11, **Figure 11**).

4. Remove the clutch release lever and spring (**Figure 12**) from the clutch cover.

5. Remove the E-clip and remove the clevis pin and holder (9, **Figure 11**) from the clutch release lever.

> *NOTE*
> *While the clutch release cams and release bearing (A, Figure 9) are part of the clutch release mechanism, these items are covered under External Shift Mechanism in this chapter.*

Inspection

1. Clean all parts in solvent and dry thoroughly.

2. Replace the clutch adjust screw O-ring if leaking or damaged.

3. Check the clutch release lever for severe wear or damage.

4. Check the large spring for weakness or other damage.

5. Replace worn or damaged parts.

Installation

1. Fit the holder (9, **Figure 11**) onto the clutch release shaft and secure it with the clevis and E-clip.

2. Install the clutch release lever and spring into the clutch cover (**Figure 12**).

3. Install the clutch adjust screw, O-ring, washer and locknut from the outside of the clutch cover.

4. Install the clutch cover as described in this chapter.

5. Adjust the clutch as described in Chapter Three.

CLUTCH RELEASE MECHANISM (4-WHEEL DRIVE)

Refer to **Figure 13** when servicing the clutch release mechanism assembly.

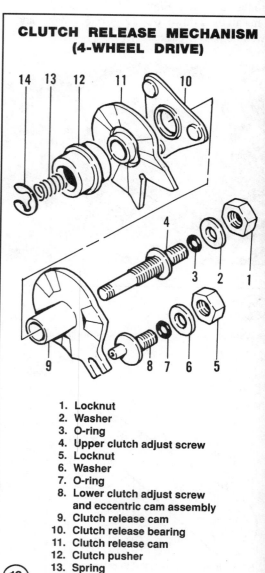

CLUTCH RELEASE MECHANISM (4-WHEEL DRIVE)

1. Locknut
2. Washer
3. O-ring
4. Upper clutch adjust screw
5. Locknut
6. Washer
7. O-ring
8. Lower clutch adjust screw and eccentric cam assembly
9. Clutch release cam
10. Clutch release bearing
11. Clutch release cam
12. Clutch pusher
13. Spring
14. E-clip

Removal

1. Remove the clutch cover as described in this chapter.

2. Remove the clutch adjust cover from the outside of the clutch cover.

3. Remove the upper clutch adjust screw locknut, washer, O-ring and the upper clutch adjust screw (4, **Figure 13**).

4. If necessary, remove the lower clutch adjust screw locknut, washer, O-ring and the lower clutch adjust screw (8, **Figure 13**).

5. Remove the E-clip and spring from inside the clutch cover.

6. Remove the clutch pusher, 2 release cams and release bearing.

7. If necessary, remove the clutch release lever (**Figure 10**) from the shift lever shaft.

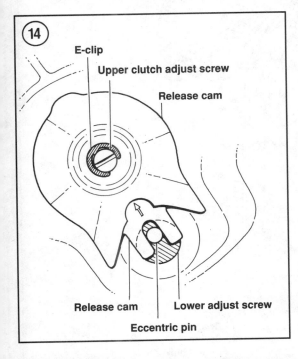

E-clip
Upper clutch adjust screw
Release cam
Release cam
Lower adjust screw
Eccentric pin

Inspection

1. Clean all parts in solvent and dry thoroughly.

2. Replace the clutch adjust screw O-rings if leaking or damaged.

3. Inspect the release cams for severe wear or damage.

4. Inspect the release bearing for severely worn or damaged balls.

5. Inspect the adjusting screws for damaged threads or adjust slots.

6. Replace all worn or damaged parts.

Installation

1. If removed, install the lower adjust screw assembly (8, **Figure 13**).

2. Screw the upper adjusting screw (4, **Figure 13**) fully into the release cam (11, **Figure 13**).

3. Install the upper adjust screw into the clutch cover. Seat the release cam groove into the lower adjust screw (**Figure 14**). Install the O-ring, washer and locknut onto the adjust screw.

4. Install the release bearing, release cam, clutch pusher, and spring over the release cam shoulder as shown in **Figure 13** and **Figure 14**. Then install the E-clip into the upper adjust screw groove (**Figure 14**).

5. Loosen the lower adjust screw locknut (5, **Figure 13**). Then turn the lower adjust screw so that its eccentric pin is as close to the upper adjust screw as possible (**Figure 14**). Tighten the lower adjust screw locknut.

6. If removed, install the clutch release lever onto the shift shaft so that the clutch release lever points toward the center of the secondary clutch as shown in **Figure 10**.

7. Install the clutch cover as described in this chapter.

8. Perform the *Clutch Release Lever Adjustment* procedure in this section.

Clutch Release Lever Adjustment

This procedure should be performed after servicing the clutch release mechanism assembly.

1. Loosen the upper clutch adjust screw locknut (A, **Figure 15**).

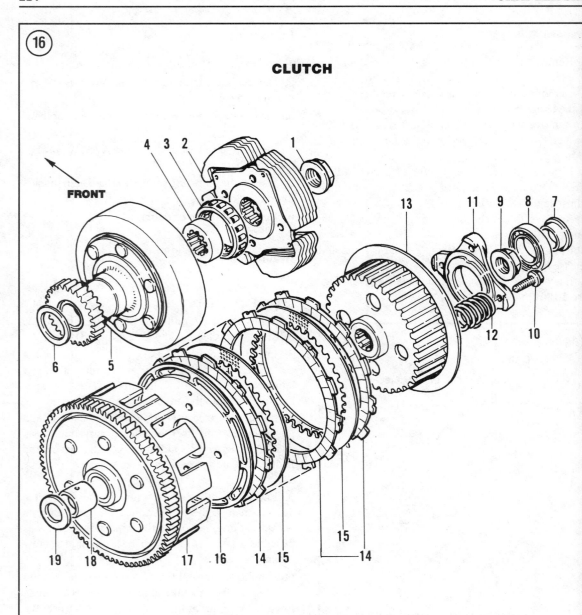

(16)

CLUTCH

FRONT

4 3 2 1

13 11 9 8 7

6 5

12 10

15

19 18 17 16 14 15 14

1. **Primary clutch housing nut**
2. **Primary clutch shoe assembly**
3. **One-way clutch**
4. **Inner race**
5. **Primary clutch housing**
6. **Spacer**
7. **Clutch pusher**
8. **Bearing**
9. **Secondary clutch nut**
10. **Bolt**
11. **Spring plate**
12. **Spring**
13. **Clutch hub**
14. **Friction plates**
15. **Clutch (steel) plates**
16. **Pressure plate**
17. **Secondary clutch housing**
18. **Spacer**
19. **Washer**

2. Turn the upper adjust screw (A, **Figure 15**) counterclockwise until it becomes hard to turn, then turn it an additional 1/2 to 1 turn counterclockwise.

3. Loosen the lower clutch adjust screw locknut (B, **Figure 15**).

4. Turn the lower adjust screw clockwise and then counterclockwise (approximately 1/2 turn total) until it becomes hard to turn in either direction. Then set the screw in the middle position (between both hard positions). Tighten the locknut without changing the screw position.

5. Turn the upper adjust screw clockwise 2-3 turns. Then stop and turn it counterclockwise until it becomes hard to turn. Tighten the locknut without changing the screw position.

6. Install the outer adjuster cover.

CLUTCH

Refer to **Figure 16** when servicing the primary (A, **Figure 17**) and secondary (B, **Figure 17**) clutch assemblies in this section.

Removal

1. Remove the clutch cover as described in this chapter.

2. Perform the *Gear Backlash Check* as described in this chapter.

3. Perform the *One-Way Clutch Check* as described in this chapter.

4. On 2-wheel drive models, remove the clutch pusher (C, **Figure 17**).

5. Remove the bearing (**Figure 18**) from the secondary clutch spring plate.

> *NOTE*
> *To prevent the crankshaft from turning when loosening the clutch nuts, hold the flywheel bolt (1986-1987) or the starter pulley (1988-on).*

6A. On 1986-1987 models, remove the left-hand side cover guard.

6B. On 1988-on models, remove the recoil starter assembly as described in Chapter Five.

7. Remove the primary clutch housing nut (**Figure 19**) with a 24 mm or 15/16 in. deep socket.

8. Remove the primary clutch shoe assembly (A, **Figure 20**).

9. Loosen, but do not remove, the secondary clutch nut (B, **Figure 20**).

10. Remove the primary clutch housing assembly as follows:

    a. Turn the secondary clutch housing (A, **Figure 21**) and align the clutch housing recess (B, **Figure 21**) with the primary drive gear (C, **Figure 21**) on the primary clutch housing.

    b. Slide the primary clutch housing (**Figure 22**) off the crankshaft.

11. Remove the spacer (**Figure 23**) from the crankshaft.

12. Loosen the clutch spring bolts (A, **Figure 24**) 2-3 turns at a time in a crisscross pattern.

13. Remove the clutch spring bolts and spring plate (B, **Figure 24**).

14. Remove the clutch springs (A, **Figure 25**).

15. Remove the secondary clutch nut (B, **Figure 25**).

16. Remove the clutch hub (C, **Figure 25**), clutch plates and pressure plate.

17. Remove the secondary clutch housing (**Figure 26**).

18. Remove the spacer and washer (**Figure 27**).

Primary Clutch Shoe Inspection

Clutch specifications are listed in **Table 1**.

1. Check the primary clutch shoe linings (**Figure 28**) for cracks, missing friction material, uneven wear or discoloration. If any of the shoe linings are damaged, replace the primary shoe lining assembly.

2. Check for weak or damaged springs.

3. Measure the groove depth of each primary clutch shoe (**Figure 29**) and check against the dimension in **Table 1**. Replace the shoes as a set if any one measurement is less than the service limit.

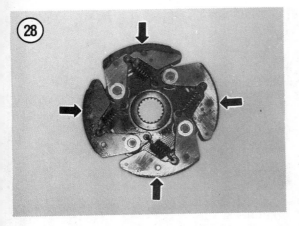

Primary Clutch Housing and One-Way Clutch Inspection

The primary clutch housing is a sub-assembly consisting of the primary clutch housing, one-way clutch and primary drive gear.

Clutch specifications are listed in **Table 1**.

1. Clean the primary clutch housing assembly in solvent and dry thoroughly.

2. Remove the one-way clutch as follows:

    a. Remove the inner race (4, **Figure 16**) from the one-way clutch.

    b. Insert a wide-blade screwdriver underneath the one-way clutch (**Figure 30**) and carefully pry the one-way clutch out of the hub bore. See **Figure 31**.

3. Inspect the inner race (A, **Figure 31**) and the one-way clutch (B, **Figure 31**) for scoring, excessive wear or damage. Replace if necessary.

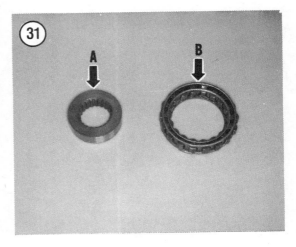

4. Inspect the one-way clutch outer race (A, **Figure 32**) for excessive wear, grooves or other damage.

5. Inspect the primary clutch housing-to-clutch shoe contact area (B, **Figure 32**) for excessive wear, grooves or other damage.

6. Measure the primary clutch housing inside diameter (**Figure 33**) and check against the specification in **Table 1**. Measure at several depth positions. Replace the primary clutch housing if any measurement exceeds the service limit.

7. Inspect the primary drive gear (A, **Figure 34**) for severely worn or chipped gear teeth.

8. Inspect the primary clutch housing bushings (C, **Figure 32** and B, **Figure 34**) for excessive wear or other damage.

9. Measure the inside diameters of the 2 primary clutch housing bushings (C, **Figure 32** and B, **Figure 34**) and check against the specification in **Table 1**. Replace the primary clutch housing if any measurement exceeds the service limit.

10. Measure the crankshaft outside diameter at the 2 primary clutch housing bushing contact areas (**Figure 35**) with a micrometer and check against the specification in **Table 1**. Replace the crankshaft if any measurement is less than the service limit.

11. Assemble the one-way clutch assembly as follows:

   a. The one-way clutch has a shoulder on one end (**Figure 36**).

   b. Install the one-way clutch so that its shoulder (**Figure 36**) seats into the groove in the bottom of the outer race (A, **Figure 32**). See **Figure 37**.

   c. Install the inner race (A, **Figure 31**) after installing the primary clutch housing onto the crankshaft.

See *Clutch Installation* in this chapter.

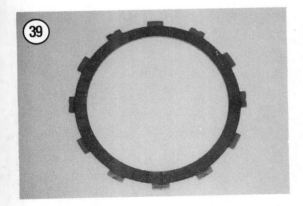

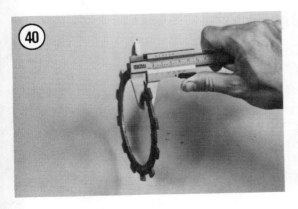

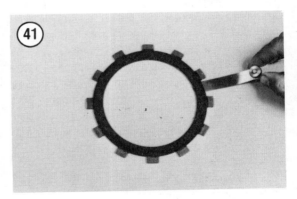

Secondary Clutch Inspection

Clutch specifications are listed in **Table 1**.

1. Clean all parts in solvent and dry with compressed air.

2. Measure the free length of each clutch spring (**Figure 38**) with a vernier caliper. Replace the springs as a set if any one spring is too short.

3. **Table 1** lists the number of friction plates (**Figure 39**) used in the stock clutch. The friction material is bonded onto an aluminum plate for warp resistance and durability. Inspect the friction plates for cracks or other obvious defects.

4. Measure the thickness of each friction plate at several places around the disc (**Figure 40**) with a vernier caliper. Replace all friction plates if any one is too thin. Do not replace only 1 or 2 plates.

5. Place each friction plate on a flat surface (surface plate or piece of plate glass) and check for warpage with a feeler gauge (**Figure 41**). If any plate is warped more than the service limit, replace all of the friction plates. Do not replace only 1 or 2 plates.

6. The friction plates have tabs that slide in the clutch housing grooves (**Figure 42**). Inspect each plate tab for cracks or galling that can cause the plate

to grab or cause groove wear. The tabs must be smooth for chatter-free clutch operation. Light damage can be repaired with an oilstone.

7. **Table 1** lists the number of clutch metal plates (**Figure 43**) used in the stock clutch. Inspect the metal plates for heat discoloration or damage.

8. Place each clutch metal plate on a surface plate or a thick piece of glass and check for warpage with a feeler gauge (**Figure 44**). If any plate is warped more than the service limit, replace the entire set of plates. Do not replace only 1 or 2 plates.

9. The clutch metal plate inner teeth mesh with the clutch hub splines (**Figure 45**). Check the splines (A, **Figure 46**) for notches, cracks or galling. They must be smooth for chatter-free clutch operation. Minor spline damage can be repaired with suitable grinding equipment. If the clutch hub splines are worn, check the clutch metal plate teeth for wear or damage.

10. Inspect the clutch hub shaft splines (B, **Figure 46**) for scoring or other damage.

11. Inspect the pressure plate (**Figure 47**) for damaged splines or for cracked or broken spring towers.

12. Inspect the secondary clutch housing tabs for notches, cracks or galling (**Figure 42** and **Figure 48**). Minor damage can be repaired with suitable grinding equipment. If the tabs are severely worn or damaged, replace the secondary clutch housing.

13. Check the secondary clutch housing gear (A, **Figure 49**) for worn or damaged gear teeth. Then check the gear for loose mounting rivets. If the gear is loose or damaged, replace the secondary clutch housing assembly.

14. Inspect the secondary clutch housing bushing (B, **Figure 49**) and spacer (C, **Figure 49**) for excessive wear or other damage.

15. Measure the inside diameter of the secondary clutch housing bushing (B, **Figure 49**) and check against the specification in **Table 1**. Replace the

secondary clutch housing if the measurement exceeds the service limit.

16. Measure the outside diameter of the secondary clutch housing spacer (C, **Figure 49**) and check against the specification in **Table 1**. Replace spacer if the measurement is less than the service limit.

17. Inspect the clutch release bearing (**Figure 50**) for damage. Hold the outer bearing race and turn the inner race by hand. The bearing should turn smoothly with no roughness or excessive noise.

18. Replace any part in questionable condition.

Installation

Refer to **Figure 16** when installing the clutch assembly.

1. Coat all clutch parts with engine oil prior to assembly.

2. Slide the washer (**Figure 51**) onto the drive axle.

3. Slide the spacer (**Figure 51**) onto the drive axle and seat it against the washer.

4. Slide the secondary clutch housing (**Figure 52**) over the drive axle and seat it onto the spacer.

5. Assemble the clutch plates onto the clutch hub as follows:

    a. Coat the clutch plates with engine oil prior to installation.

    b. Place the clutch hub (A, **Figure 53**) onto the workbench.

c. Install the clutch plates onto the clutch hub, starting with a friction plate (B, **Figure 53**) and ending with a friction plate.

d. Position the friction plates so that all of the plates tabs align as shown in **Figure 54**.

e. Install the pressure plate (**Figure 55**) onto the clutch boss—align the punch mark on both parts as shown in **Figure 56**. The pressure plate sits flush against the outer friction plate when properly installed.

f. Install a clutch spring and bolt as shown in **Figure 57**. The spring and bolt will hold the assembly together during installation.

6. Align the clutch hub assembly with the secondary clutch housing and slide the clutch hub (**Figure 58**) onto the drive axle. Seat the clutch hub against the secondary clutch housing.

7. Install the secondary clutch nut (**Figure 59**) finger-tight.

8. Remove the bolt and clutch spring (**Figure 57**).

9. Install the secondary clutch springs (**Figure 60**).

10. Install the spring plate (**Figure 61**) and the secondary clutch spring bolts. Tighten the bolts in a crisscross pattern to the torque specification in **Table 2**.

11. Slide the spacer (**Figure 62**) onto the crankshaft and seat it against the nut.

12. Turn the secondary clutch housing and align the housing recess (**Figure 63**) with the crankshaft.

13. Slide the primary clutch housing (**Figure 64**) onto the crankshaft and seat it against the spacer.

14. Slide the one-way clutch outer race over the crankshaft and seat it into the one-way clutch (**Figure 65**).

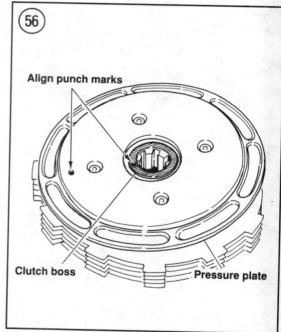

56

Align punch marks

Clutch boss

Pressure plate

54

55

57

15. Slide the primary clutch shoe assembly (A, **Figure 66**) into the primary clutch housing.

16. Install the primary clutch nut (**Figure 67**) finger-tight.

17. Secure the crankshaft with the same tool setup used to loosen the clutch nuts during disassembly.

18. Tighten the secondary clutch nut (B, **Figure 66**) to the torque specification in **Table 2**.

19. Tighten the primary clutch nut (**Figure 67**) to the torque specification in **Table 2**. Tighten the nut with a 24 mm or 15/16 in. deep socket.

20. Install the bearing (**Figure 68**) into the spring plate.

21. On 2-wheel drive models, install the clutch pusher (**Figure 69**) into the bearing.

22. Reinstall the oil screen (**Figure 70**) as described under *Oil Screen* in Chapter Five.

23. Perform the *Gear Backlash Check* as described in this chapter.

24. Perform the *One-Way Clutch Check* as described in this chapter.

25. Install the clutch cover as described in this chapter.

26A. On 1986-1987 models, install the outer left-hand side cover.

26B. On 1988-on models, install the recoil starter assembly as described in Chapter Five.

27. Refill the engine with oil as described in Chapter Three.

28. Adjust the clutch as described in Chapter Three.
29. Start the engine and allow to warm up to normal operating temperature. Shift the transmission into 1st gear and check clutch operation.

GEAR BACKLASH CHECK

This procedure checks the secondary clutch housing gear and primary clutch housing gear backlash.
1. Remove the clutch cover as described in this chapter.
2. Install a dial indicator and position its stem against the primary drive gear (**Figure 71**).
3. Hold the secondary clutch housing with one hand and move the primary clutch housing back and forth while watching the dial indicator. Gear backlash is the difference between the highest and lowest gauge readings. If the gear backlash exceeds the service limit in **Table 1**, replace the secondary clutch housing and primary clutch housing.
4. Remove the dial indicator.
5. Install the clutch cover as described in this chapter.

ONE-WAY CLUTCH CHECK

This procedure checks the one-way clutch assembly installed in the primary clutch housing.
1. Remove the clutch cover as described in this chapter.

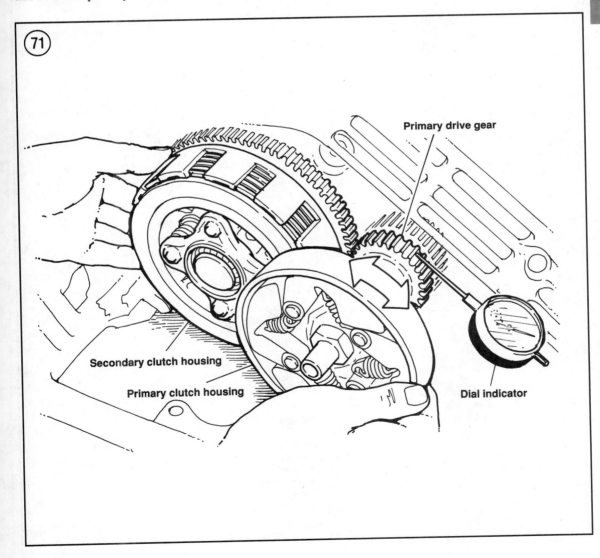

(71)

Primary drive gear

Secondary clutch housing

Primary clutch housing

Dial indicator

2. Stand on the right-hand side of the vehicle and turn the primary clutch housing (**Figure 72**) by hand. The primary housing should turn counterclockwise freely but should not turn clockwise.

3. If the one-way clutch does not operate as described in Step 2, remove the primary clutch housing and one-way clutch as described under *Clutch Removal* in this chapter. Inspect the one-way clutch components as described under *Primary Clutch Housing and One-Way Clutch Inspection* in this chapter. Replace severely worn or damaged parts.

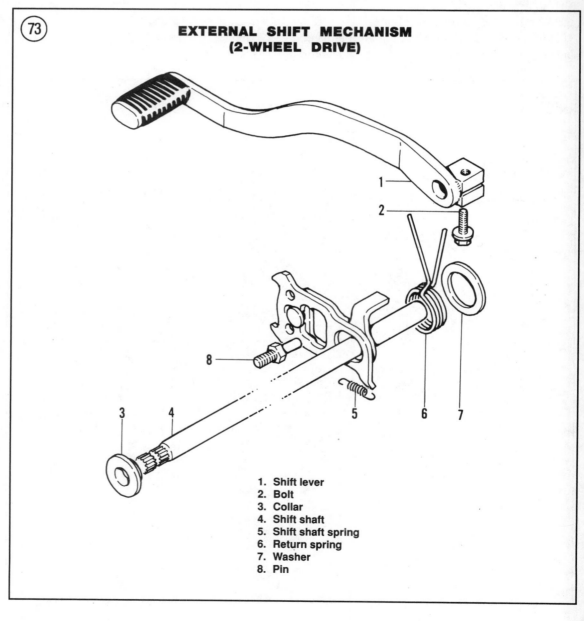

**EXTERNAL SHIFT MECHANISM
(2-WHEEL DRIVE)**

1. Shift lever
2. Bolt
3. Collar
4. Shift shaft
5. Shift shaft spring
6. Return spring
7. Washer
8. Pin

4. Reassemble the one-way clutch and install the primary clutch housing as described under *Clutch Installation* in this chapter.

5. Install the clutch cover as described in this chapter.

EXTERNAL SHIFT MECHANISM

The external shift mechanism is located on the same side of the crankcase as the clutch assembly and can be removed with the engine in the frame. To remove the shift drum and shift forks, it is necessary to remove the engine and split the crankcase (see Chapter Five).

Removal

Refer to **Figure 73** (2-wheel drive) or **Figure 74** (4-wheel drive) for this procedure.

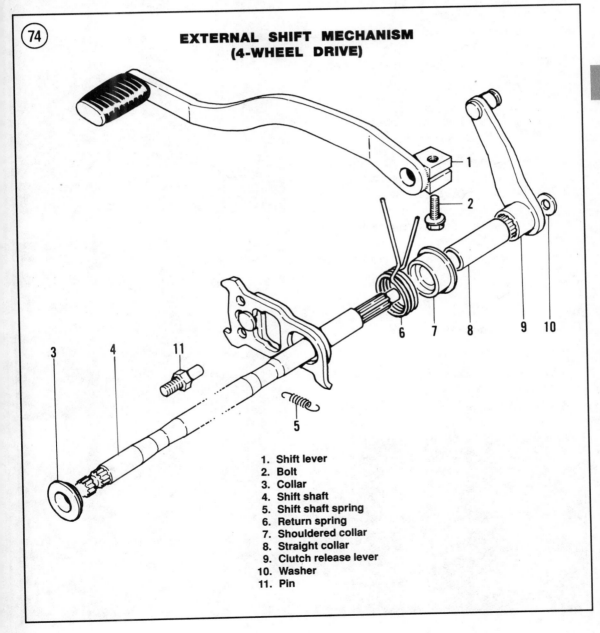

EXTERNAL SHIFT MECHANISM (4-WHEEL DRIVE)

1. Shift lever
2. Bolt
3. Collar
4. Shift shaft
5. Shift shaft spring
6. Return spring
7. Shouldered collar
8. Straight collar
9. Clutch release lever
10. Washer
11. Pin

1. Remove the clutch assembly as described in this chapter.

2. Remove the shift lever from the left-hand side of the vehicle. See **Figure 75**, typical.

3A. On 2-wheel drive models, remove the outer release cam and the release bearing.

3B. On 4-wheel drive models, remove the washer and the clutch release lever.

4. Remove the shift shaft assembly.

5. Remove the shift drum stopper lever bolt (A, **Figure 76**), then remove the stopper lever (B, **Figure 76**) and spring (**Figure 77**).

6. To remove the shift drum segment, perform the following:

   a. Remove the bolt (A, **Figure 78**) and washer (B, **Figure 78**).

NOTE
All of the pins removed in sub-steps b and c are the same size—4 × 10 mm.

   b. Remove the 6 pins (A, **Figure 79**) and remove the shift drum segment (B, **Figure 79**).

   c. Remove the pin (A, **Figure 80**) from the shift drum.

7A. On 2-wheel drive models, remove the 2 return spring bolts (B, **Figure 80**).

7B. On 4-wheel drive models, remove the return spring bolt.

Inspection
(2-Wheel Drive Models)

Refer to **Figure 73** for this procedure.

1. Clean all thread sealer residue from the return spring bolts, if removed.

2. Clean all parts in solvent and dry thoroughly.

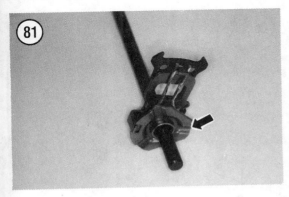

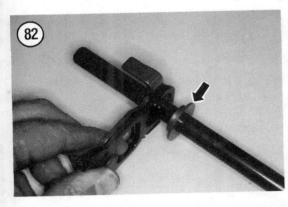

3. Remove the inner release cam and return spring (**Figure 81**) from the shift shaft.

4. Remove the collar (**Figure 82**) from the shift shaft.

5. Check the shift shaft (**Figure 83**) for cracks or bending. Check the splines on the end of the shaft for damage.

6. Inspect the 2 release cams (A and B, **Figure 84**) for scoring or other damage.

7. Inspect the return spring on the front release cam (**Figure 85**) for weakness or damage. To replace the spring:

    a. Slide the spring and washer (**Figure 86**) off the release cam shoulder.

    b. Inspect the release cam shoulder for scoring, grooves or other damage.

    c. Inspect the washer for cracks or other damage.

    d. Install the flat washer and spring onto the release cam shoulder (**Figure 85**).

8. Inspect the release bearing (B, **Figure 84**) for scoring, flat spots or other damage. Replace if necessary.

9. Check the small shift shaft spring for weakness or damage. Replace the spring if necessary.

10. Install the collar onto the shift shaft as shown in **Figure 82**.

11. Slide the inner release cam onto the shift shaft. Center the return spring arms on the shift shaft as shown in **Figure 81**.

12. Check the stopper lever assembly (**Figure 87**) for the following:

    a. Weak or damaged spring.

    b. Bent or damaged stopper lever and roller.

    c. Damaged shoulder bolt.

13. Inspect the shift drum segment for severe wear or other damage. Replace if necessary.

**Inspection
(4-Wheel Drive Models)**

Refer to **Figure 74** for this procedure.

1. Clean all thread sealer residue from the return spring bolt, if removed.

2. Clean all parts in solvent and dry thoroughly.

3. Remove the straight collar from the shift shaft.

4. Remove the shouldered collar and return spring from the shift shaft.

5. Check the shift shaft (**Figure 83**) for cracks or bending. Check the splines on the end of the shaft for damage.

6. Replace the return spring if weak or damaged.

7. Check the small shift shaft spring for weakness or damage. Replace the spring if necessary.

8. Install the return spring onto the shouldered collar and slide the collar onto the shift shaft as shown in **Figure 74**.

9. Slide the straight collar onto the shift shaft.

10. Check the stopper lever assembly (**Figure 87**) for the following:

    a. Weak or damaged spring.

    b. Bent or damaged stopper lever and roller.

    c. Damaged shoulder bolt.

11. Inspect the shift drum segment for severe wear or other damage. Replace if necessary.

Installation

1A. On 2-wheel drive models, apply Loctite 242 (blue) to the return spring bolts (B, **Figure 80**) prior to installation. Install the return spring bolts and tighten to the torque specification in **Table 2**.

1B. On 4-wheel drive models, apply Loctite 242 (blue) to the return spring bolt prior to installation. Install the return spring bolt and tighten to the torque specification in **Table 2**.

2. To install the shift drum segment, perform the following:

    a. Install the pin (A, **Figure 80**) into the shift drum.

    b. Install the shift drum segment—align the notch in the segment with the pin (**Figure 88**).

    c. Install the 6 pins (A, **Figure 79**) into the shift drum segment holes.

    d. Install the washer (B, **Figure 78**) and the shift drum segment bolt (A, **Figure 78**). Tighten the shift drum segment bolt to the torque specification in **Table 2**.

3. Install the stopper lever spring onto the bolt boss as shown in **Figure 77**.

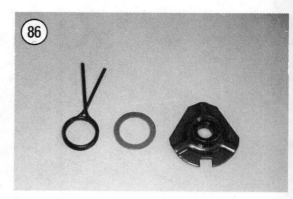

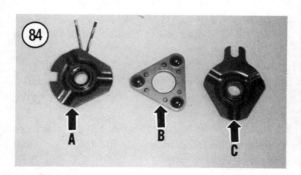

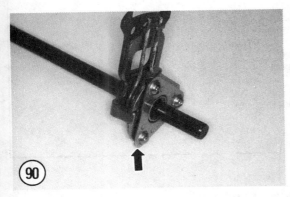

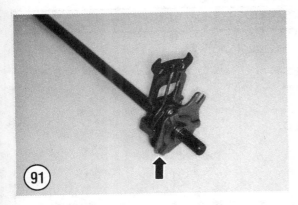

4. Install the stopper lever (B, **Figure 76**) and bolt (A, **Figure 76**). Tighten the bolt securely. Then move the stopper lever by hand, making sure it can move freely. The stopper lever roller should contact the shift drum segment as shown in **Figure 76**.

5A. On 2-wheel drive models, install the shift shaft as follows:

    a. Install the release bearing (**Figure 89**) onto the shift shaft and seat it against the inner release cam (**Figure 90**).

    b. Install the outer release cam and seat it against the release bearing (**Figure 91**).

    c. Slide the shift shaft (A, **Figure 92**) into the crankcase. Center the outer release cam notch (B, **Figure 92**) with the return spring bolt. Center the return spring (C, **Figure 92**) with the opposite return spring bolt.

5B. On 4-wheel drive models, install the shift shaft as follows:

    a. Slide the shift lever into the crankcase. Center the return spring with the return spring bolt.

    b. Apply some grease onto the shift lever splines.

    c. Install the clutch release lever onto the shift shaft splines. Position the clutch release lever so that it points toward the center of the secondary clutch as shown in **Figure 93**.

    d. Install the washer onto the shift shaft and seat it against the clutch release lever.

6. Install the shift lever and secure it with its pinch bolt. See **Figure 75**, typical.

7. Install the clutch as described in this chapter.

6

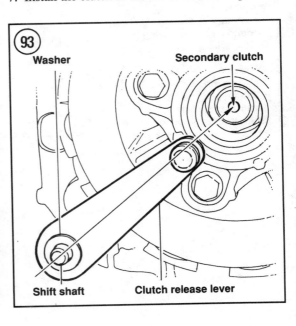

93

Washer   Secondary clutch

Shift shaft   Clutch release lever

Table 1 GENERAL CLUTCH SPECIFICATIONS

	New mm (in.)	Service limit mm (in.)
Primary clutch		
Primary clutch housing inside diameter	125.0-125.2 (4.921-4.929)	125.5 (4.941)
Primary clutch shoe groove depth	1.0 (0.039)	0.5 (0.020)
Secondary clutch		
Friction plate thickness	2.92-3.08 (0.115-0.121)	2.8 (0.110)
Friction plate warp	0-0.15 (0-0.006)	0.3 (0.012)
Steel plate warp	0-0.2 (0-0.008)	0.3 (0.012)
Clutch spring free length	30.38 (1.196)	28.8 (1.134)
Gear backlash	0.02-0.11 (0.001-0.004)	0.14 (0.006)
Primary clutch housing bushing inside diameter	27.000-27.021 (1.063-1.063)	27.03 (1.064)
Crankshaft diameter	26.959-26.980 (1.061-1.062)	26.94 (1.060)
Secondary clutch housing bushing inside diameter	25.000-25.021 (0.983-0.984)	25.03 (0.985)
Secondary clutch housing spacer outside diameter	24.970-24.985 (0.983-0.984)	24.95 (0.982)
Number of clutch plates		
Steel plates	4	—
Friction plates	5	—

Table 2 TIGHTENING TORQUES

	N•m	ft.-lb.
Oil pipe banjo bolts	20	15
Primary clutch nut		
2-wheel drive		
1986-1987	125	92
1988-on	83	61
4-wheel drive	125	92
Secondary clutch nut	78	58
Secondary clutch spring bolts		
New bolts	15	11
Used bolts	12	9
Oil pressure relief valve		
4-wheel drive	15	11
Oil drain plug	29	21
Return spring bolt(s)	17	12
Shift drum segment bolt	12	9

TRANSMISSION AND INTERNAL SHIFT MECHANISM

7

The transmission on all models provides 6 forward speeds and 1 reverse speed. To gain access to the transmission and internal shift mechanism, it is necessary to remove the engine and split the crankcase (Chapter Five). Once the crankcase has been split, removal of the transmission, reverse gears, shift drums and forks is a simple task of pulling the assemblies up and out of the crankcase.

Transmission gear ratios and general specifications are listed in **Table 1** and **Table 2. Tables 1-3** are at the end of this chapter.

TRANSMISSION/REVERSE SYSTEM IDENTIFICATION

With the forward and reverse systems, there are 5 different assemblies in the transmission that will be covered in this chapter. The different assemblies are identified in **Figure 1** and listed as follows:

a. Drive axle.

b. Output axle.

c. Reverse axle.

d. Shift drum.

e. Shift forks and shafts.

TRANSMISSION TROUBLESHOOTING

Refer to Chapter Two.

TRANSMISSION/REVERSE OVERHAUL

Removal/Installation

Remove and install the transmission and internal shift assemblies as described under *Crankcase Disassembly and Crankcase Assembly* in Chapter Five.

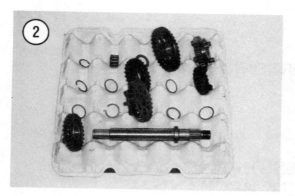

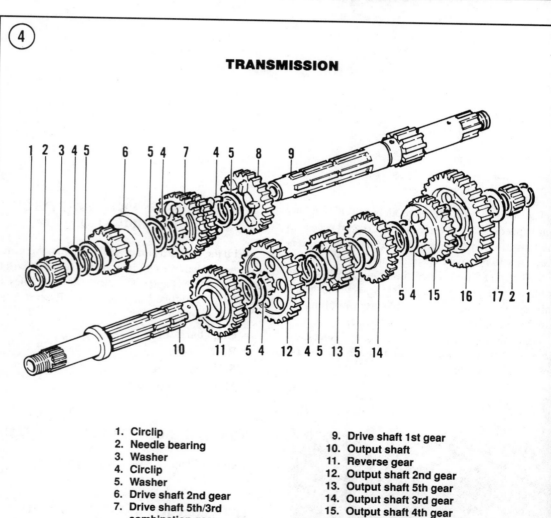

TRANSMISSION

1. Circlip
2. Needle bearing
3. Washer
4. Circlip
5. Washer
6. Drive shaft 2nd gear
7. Drive shaft 5th/3rd combination gear
8. Drive shaft 4th gear

9. Drive shaft 1st gear
10. Output shaft
11. Reverse gear
12. Output shaft 2nd gear
13. Output shaft 5th gear
14. Output shaft 3rd gear
15. Output shaft 4th gear
16. Output shaft 1st gear
17. Washer

Transmission Service Notes

1. A divided container such as an egg carton can be used to help maintain correct alignment and position of the parts as they are removed from the transmission and reverse shafts. See **Figure 2**, typical.

2. The circlips are a tight fit on the transmission axles. All circlips removed during disassembly should be discarded and new circlips installed.

3. Circlips will turn and fold over, making removal and installation difficult. To ease removal, open the circlip with a pair of circlip pliers while at the same time holding the back of the circlip with a pair of pliers, then remove it. See **Figure 3**, typical.

Drive Axle
Disassembly/Assembly

Refer to **Figure 4** and **Figure 5** for this procedure.

1. Clean the assembled axle in solvent. Dry with compressed air or let sit on rags to drip dry.
2. Remove the circlip, needle bearing and flat washer.
3. Remove the circlip and flat washer.
4. Slide off second gear.
5. Remove the flat washer and circlip.
6. Slide off the fifth/third gear cluster.
7. Remove the circlip and flat washer.
8. Slide off fourth gear.

NOTE
*Drive axle first gear (**Figure 6**) is an integral part of the drive axle.*

9. Inspect the drive axle assembly as described under *Transmission Inspection* in this chapter.
10. Install fourth gear (**Figure 7**) with its gear dogs facing away from first gear.
11. Install the flat washer and circlip (**Figure 8**). Seat the circlip in the groove next to fourth gear

7

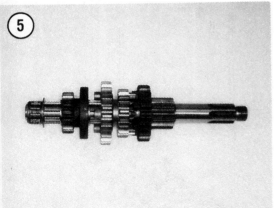

5

6

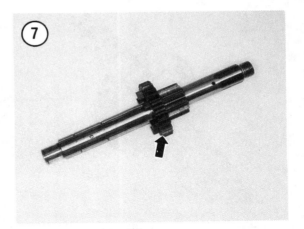

7

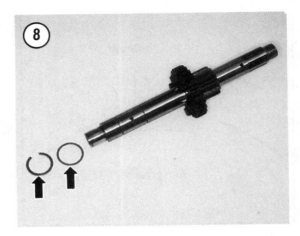

8

(**Figure 9**). Position the circlip so that its gap aligns with the axle groove (**Figure 10**).

12. Install the fifth/third gear cluster with third gear (the smaller gear) toward fourth gear; see **Figure 11**.

13. Install the circlip and flat washer (**Figure 12**). Seat the circlip in the groove shown in **Figure 13**. Position circlip so that its gap aligns with the axle groove (**Figure 10**).

14. Install second gear (**Figure 14**) with its dog engagement holes toward fifth gear.

15. Install the flat washer and circlip (**Figure 15**). Seat the circlip in the groove next to second gear (**Figure 16**). Position circlip so that its gap aligns with the axle groove (**Figure 10**).

16. Install the flat washer, needle bearing and circlip (**Figure 17**). Seat the circlip in the groove next to the bearing; see **Figure 18**.

17. Refer to **Figure 5** for the correct placement of the drive axle gears.

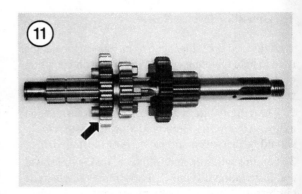

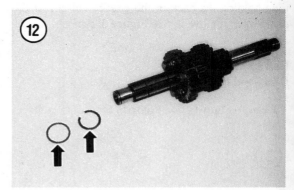

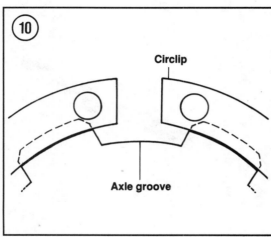

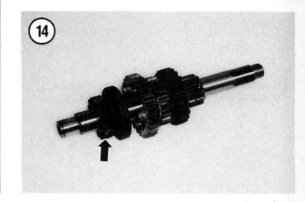

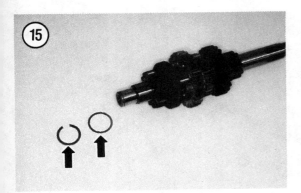

Output Axle
Disassembly/Assembly

Refer to **Figure 4** and **Figure 19** for this procedure.

1. Clean the assembled axle in solvent. Dry with compressed air or let sit on rags to drip dry.

2. Remove the circlip, needle bearing and flat washer.

3. Slide off first and fourth gears.

4. Remove the circlip and flat washer.

5. Slide off third gear.

6. Remove the flat washer.

7. Slide off fifth gear.

8. Remove the flat washer and circlip.

9. Slide off second gear.

10. Remove the circlip and flat washer.

11. Slide off reverse gear.

12. Inspect the output axle assembly as described under *Transmission Inspection* in this chapter.

13. Install reverse gear (**Figure 20**) with its gear dogs facing away from the shoulder on the output axle.

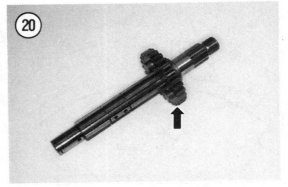

7

14. Install the flat washer and circlip (**Figure 21**). Seat the circlip in the groove next to reverse gear (**Figure 22**). Position circlip so that its gap aligns with the axle groove (**Figure 23**).

15. Install second gear (**Figure 24**) with its gear dogs facing away from reverse gear.

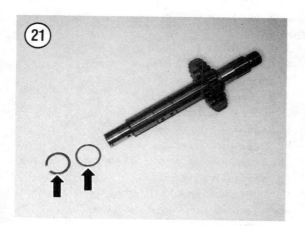

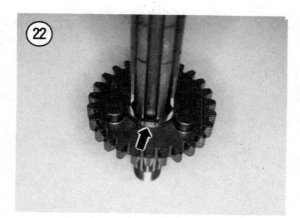

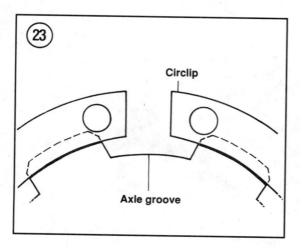

Circlip

Axle groove

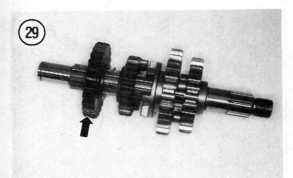

16. Install the circlip and seat it into the groove shown in **Figure 25**. Position circlip so that its gap aligns with the axle groove (**Figure 23**).

17. Install the flat washer (**Figure 26**) and seat it next to the circlip.

18. Install fifth gear (**Figure 27**) with its gear dogs toward second gear.

19. Install the flat washer (**Figure 28**) and seat it next to fifth gear.

20. Install third gear (**Figure 29**) with its shoulder toward fifth gear.

21. Install the flat washer and circlip (**Figure 30**). Seat the circlip in the groove next to third gear (**Figure 31**). Position the circlip so its gap aligns with the axle groove (**Figure 23**).

22. Install fourth gear (**Figure 32**) with its shift fork shoulder toward third gear.

23. Install first gear (**Figure 33**) with its flat side away from fourth gear.

7

24. Install the flat washer, needle bearing and circlip (**Figure 34**). Seat the circlip in the groove next to the bearing; see **Figure 35**.

25. Refer to **Figure 19** for the correct placement of the output axle gears.

REVERSE AXLE

The reverse axle assembly is shown in **Figure 36**.

Removal/Installation

Remove and install the reverse axle as described under *Crankcase Disassembly and Crankcase Assembly* in Chapter Five.

Disassembly/Reassembly

> *NOTE*
> *The outer left- and right-hand needle bearing assemblies are identical except for the 2 plate washers. See A, **Figure 37** (left-hand side) and B, **Figure 37** (right-hand side).*

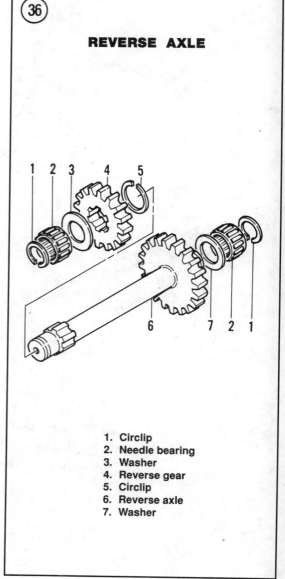

REVERSE AXLE

1. Circlip
2. Needle bearing
3. Washer
4. Reverse gear
5. Circlip
6. Reverse axle
7. Washer

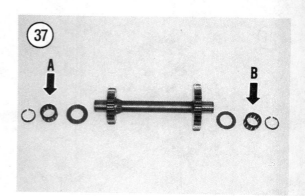

1. From the right-hand side, remove the circlip, needle bearing and plate washer (**Figure 38**).
2. From the left-hand side, remove the following:
   a. Circlip, needle bearing and plate washer (**Figure 39**).
   b. Reverse axle gear (**Figure 39**).
   c. Circlip (**Figure 40**).
3. Inspect reverse axle and gears as described under *Transmission Inspection* in this chapter.
4. To assemble the left-hand side reverse axle:
   a. Install a new circlip into the reverse axle groove (**Figure 40**).
   b. Install the reverse axle gear (**Figure 39**).
   c. Install the plate washer (17.3 × 30 × 1.4 mm). See **Figure 39**.
   d. Install the needle bearing and circlip (**Figure 39**).
5. To assemble the right-hand side reverse axle:
   a. Install the plate washer (17.3 × 28 × 1 mm). See **Figure 38**.
   b. Install the needle bearing and circlip (**Figure 38**).

NOTE
Figure 41 shows the reverse axle properly assembled.

TRANSMISSION INSPECTION

1. Clean all parts in solvent. Dry with compressed air.

NOTE
Maintain alignment of disassembled axles and gears when cleaning and drying them.

2. Check all axle splines for wear, cracks or other damage. Identify transmission axles as follows:
   a. Drive axle (**Figure 42**).

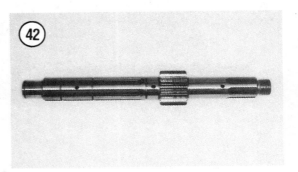

b. Output axle (**Figure 43**).

c. Reverse axle (**Figure 40**).

3. Check the drive axle first gear (**Figure 42**). If gear is damaged, replace drive axle.

4. Check reverse axle gear (**Figure 40**). If gear is damaged, replace reverse axle.

5. Check each gear for excessive wear, burrs, pitting, or chipped or missing teeth.

6. Check each stationary gear bore (**Figure 44**) and sliding gear splines (**Figure 45**) for scoring, cracks or other damage.

7. Check the gear dogs (A, **Figure 46**) for severe wear or damage.

8. Check each sliding gear groove (B, **Figure 46**) for wear, cracks or other damage.

9. Make sure that all gears slide or turn on their respective axles smoothly without binding.

NOTE
Defective gears should be replaced, and it is a good idea to replace the mating gear even though it may not show as much wear or damage.

10. Check needle bearings (**Figure 47**) for severe wear or damage.

11. Replace all circlips during reassembly. In addition, check the washers for burn marks, scoring or cracks. Replace if necessary.

INTERNAL SHIFT MECHANISM

The shift mechanism assembly is shown in **Figure 48**, **Figure 49** and **Figure 50**.

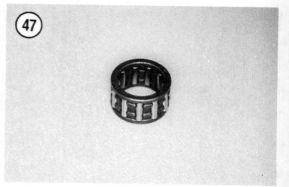

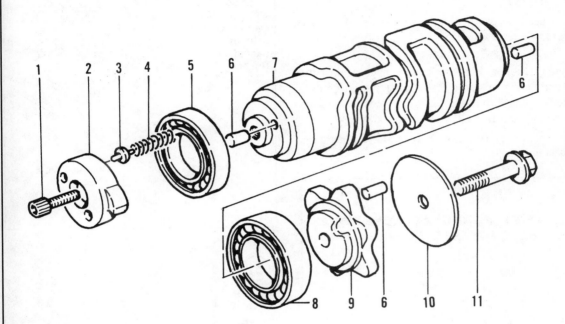

SHIFT DRUM

1. Allen bolt
2. Neutral switch holder
3. Pin
4. Spring
5. Bearing
6. Pins
7. Shift drum
8. Bearing
9. Shift drum cam
10. Washer
11. Bolt

Removal/Installation

Remove and install the transmission assembly as described under *Crankcase Disassembly and Crankcase Assembly* in Chapter Five.

Shift Drum
Inspection

Refer to **Figure 48** for this procedure.

1. Check the grooves in the shift drum (A, **Figure 51**) for wear or roughness.

2. Measure the shift drum groove width with a vernier caliper (**Figure 52**) and check against the specification in **Table 3**. Repeat for each groove. Replace the shift drum if any groove is worn to the service limit (**Table 3**).

3. Check the bearing (B, **Figure 51**) for roughness or damage.

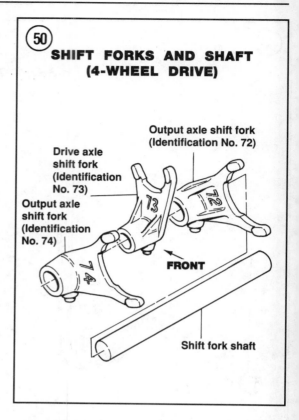

(50)

SHIFT FORKS AND SHAFT (4-WHEEL DRIVE)

Output axle shift fork (Identification No. 72)

Drive axle shift fork (Identification No. 73)

Output axle shift fork (Identification No. 74)

FRONT

Shift fork shaft

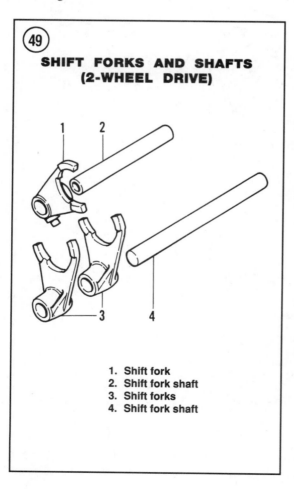

(49)

SHIFT FORKS AND SHAFTS (2-WHEEL DRIVE)

1. Shift fork
2. Shift fork shaft
3. Shift forks
4. Shift fork shaft

(51)

(52)

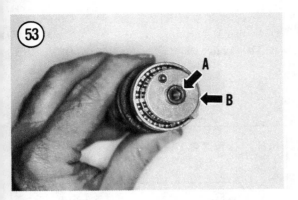

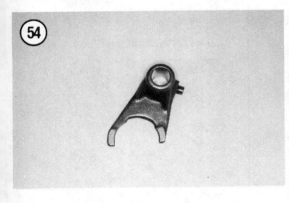

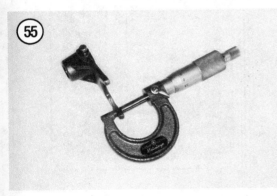

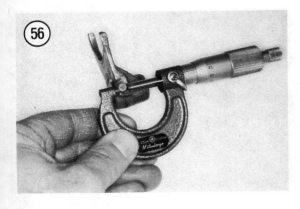

4. Check the neutral switch holder (C, **Figure 51**) for excessive wear or damage. Check the pin and spring for damage.

5. Check the shift drum cam (D, **Figure 51**) for excessive wear or damage.

6. Check the pins for flat spots or other damage.

7. To service the shift drum assembly, refer to *Shift Drum Disassembly/Reassembly* in this chapter.

8. Oil the bearing with clean engine oil.

Shift drum
Disassembly/Reassembly

All of the shift drum components (**Figure 48**), except the shift drum, can be purchased separately. If the shift drum is damaged, the entire shift drum assembly will have to be replaced as an assembly.

1. Hold the shift drum in a vise with soft jaws and remove the Allen bolt (A, **Figure 53**).

2. Remove the neutral switch holder (B, **Figure 53**), pin and spring.

3. Press off the bearing and remove the other small pin.

4. Clean all parts in solvent and dry thoroughly.

5. Replace severely worn or damaged parts.

6. Assemble by reversing these disassembly steps. Tighten the Allen bolt (A, **Figure 53**) to 12 N•m (104 in.-lb.).

Shift Fork
Inspection

Refer to **Figure 49** (2-wheel drive) or **Figure 50** (4-wheel drive) for this procedure.

1. Inspect each shift fork (**Figure 54**) for excessive wear or damage. Examine the shift forks at the points where they contact the slider gear. This surface should be smooth with no signs of wear or damage.

2. Check for any arc-shaped wear or burn marks on the shift forks. This indicates that the shift fork has excessive contact with the gear. If the shift fork fingers are excessively worn, the shift fork must be replaced.

3. Measure the shift fork finger thickness at the gear contact point (**Figure 55**) and check against the specification in **Table 3**. Replace if excessively worn.

4. Measure the shift fork guide pin diameter (**Figure 56**) and check against the specification in **Table 3**. Replace if worn to the service limit.

7

5. Measure the sliding gear shift fork groove width and check against the specification in **Table 3**. Replace if worn to the service limit.

6. Check the shift fork shafts for bending or other damage. Check that each shift fork slides smoothly on its respective shaft; see **Figure 57**, typical.

7. Replace all worn or damaged parts.

REVERSE CABLE

All KLF300 models are equipped with 5-forward gears and 1 reverse gear. Neutral is located between first gear and reverse gear. See the shift pattern decal on your vehicle or refer to **Figure 58**.

Reverse Operation

To shift the transmission in and out of REVERSE, perform the following.

1. Start the engine and allow to idle. If the engine is cold, allow to warm up to normal operating temperature.

> *WARNING*
> *Improper use of the reverse system can cause an accident and possible injury to yourself and to people near your vehicle. Observe all of the WARNING labels affixed to your vehicle and to the information listed in your vehicles Owners Manual.*

2. To shift into REVERSE, perform the following:
   a. Shift transmission into NEUTRAL.
   b. Stop the vehicle and allow engine to operate at idle speed.
   c. Turn the reverse knob (A, **Figure 59**) clockwise while pressing the shift pedal down and into

reverse (**Figure 58**). Then release the reverse knob and the shift pedal.
   d. The vehicle can now be operated in REVERSE gear.

3. To shift out of REVERSE, perform the following:

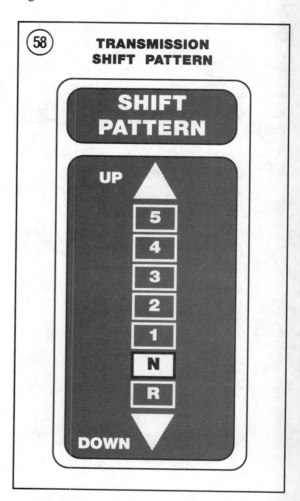

58 **TRANSMISSION SHIFT PATTERN**

SHIFT PATTERN

UP
5
4
3
2
1
N
R
DOWN

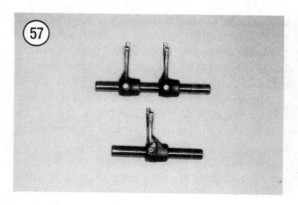

57

59

a. Stop the vehicle and allow engine to operate at idle speed.

b. Lift the shift pedal up and into NEUTRAL.

c. The vehicle can now be operated in the FORWARD gears.

Reverse Cable Adjustment

Reverse cable adjustment takes up slack caused by cable stretch.

1. Shift the transmission into NEUTRAL.

> *NOTE*
> *Free play is the amount of reverse knob movement before any reverse cable action takes place.*

2. Move the reverse knob (A, **Figure 59**) from side-to-side and measure free play. The standard reverse knob free play is 2-3 mm (7/64 in.). If the free play is incorrect, continue with Step 3.

3. Loosen the reverse cable adjust nuts and reposition the cable until the reverse knob has 2-3 mm (7/64 in.) of free play. See A, **Figure 60** (2-wheel drive) or **Figure 61** (4-wheel drive).

4. Tighten the adjust nuts and recheck free play.

Reverse Cable Replacement

1. Shift the transmission into NEUTRAL.

2. Remove the handlebar cover (B, **Figure 59**).

3. On 4-wheel drive models, remove the following:
   a. Front fender (Chapter Fourteen).
   b. Fuel tank (Chapter Eight).
   c. Front propeller shaft (Chapter Eleven).

4. Remove the screws (**Figure 62**) holding the reverse knob and reverse cable to the steering bracket.

5A. On 2-wheel drive models, loosen the 2 reverse cable adjust nuts and disconnect the cable from the reverse lever. See A, **Figure 60** (2-wheel drive) or **Figure 61** (4-wheel drive).

5B. On 4-wheel drive models, perform the following:
   a. Remove the reverse cable holder mounting bolt (**Figure 61**).
   b. Remove the reverse lever mounting bolt and remove the reverse lever (**Figure 61**).
   c. Loosen the 2 reverse cable adjust nuts and disconnect the cable from the lever.

6. On a piece of paper, note the reverse cable routing path from the steering bracket to the engine.

7. Remove the reverse cable.

8. Lubricate the new reverse cable as described under *Control Cable Lubrication* in Chapter Three.

9. Install the new reverse cable by reversing these steps.

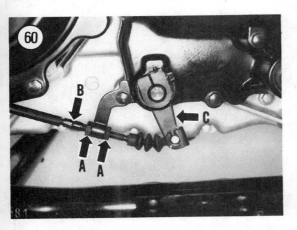

10. Adjust the reverse knob free play as described in the previous section.

11. Check reverse operation as described under *Reverse Operation* in this section.

Reverse Lever Alignment (2-Wheel Drive)

If the reverse lever (C, **Figure 60**) is removed, install it as follows:

1. Align the slot in the reverse lever with the mark on the front gear case (**Figure 63**) and slide the lever onto the reverse shaft. Install the pinch bolt and tighten securely.

2. Reattach the reverse cable and adjust it as described in this chapter.

3. If the reverse cable is difficult to adjust with the reverse lever in the position set in Step 1, remove the lever and rotate it one tooth counterclockwise on the reverse shaft.

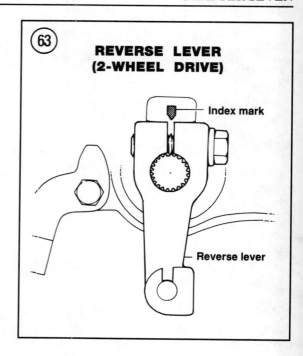

(63) REVERSE LEVER (2-WHEEL DRIVE)

Index mark — Reverse lever

Table 1 DRIVE TRAIN GENERAL SPECIFICATIONS—2-WHEEL DRIVE	
Primary reduction system	
Type	Gear
Reduction ratio	2.888 (78:27)
Primary	Auto centrifugal, wet
Secondary	Auto multidisc, wet
Transmission	
Type	5-speed plus reverse, constant mesh
Gear ratio	
1st	3.090 (34:11)
2nd	1.928 (27:14)
3rd	1.368 (26:19)
4th	1.000 (23:23)
5th	0.769 (20:26)
Reverse	3.072 (26:11 × 26:20)
Final drive	
Type	Shaft (2-wheel drive)
Reduction ratio	4.886 (20:16 × 43:11)
Overall drive ratio @ top gear	10.858

Table 2 DRIVE TRAIN GENERAL SPECIFICATIONS—4-WHEEL DRIVE

Primary reduction system	
Type	Gear
Reduction ratio	2.888 (78:27)
Primary	Auto centrifugal, wet
Secondary	Auto multidisc, wet
Transmission	
Type	10-speed plus reverse, constant mesh
Gear ratio	
1st	3.090 (34:11)
2nd	1.928 (27:14)
3rd	1.368 (26:19)
4th	1.000 (23:23)
5th	0.769 (20:26)
Reverse	3.072 (26:11 × 26:20)
Final drive	
Type	Shaft (4-wheel drive)
Reduction ratio	
High	5.416 (33:33 × 20:16 × 39:9)
Low	6.910 (37:29 × 20:16 × 39:9)
Overall drive ratio	
High	12.037
Low	15.357

7

Table 3 TRANSMISSION SERVICE SPECIFICATIONS

	New mm (in.)	Service limit mm (in.)
Shift fork finger thickness		
@ gear contact point	4.4-4.5 (0.173-0.177)	4.3 (0.169)
Sliding gear shift fork groove width	4.55-4.65 (0.179-0.183)	4.8 (0.189)
Shift fork guide pin diameter	5.9-6.0 (0.232-0.236)	5.8 (0.228)
Shift drum groove width	6.05-6.20 (0.238-0.244)	6.3 (0.248)

CHAPTER EIGHT

FUEL AND EXHAUST SYSTEMS

The fuel system consists of the fuel tank, fuel shutoff valve, a single carburetor and air filter.

The exhaust system consists of an exhaust pipe and muffler assembly.

This chapter includes service procedures for all parts of the fuel and exhaust systems. Air filter service is covered in Chapter Three.

Carburetor specifications are covered in **Tables 1-3**. **Tables 1-3** are at the end of this chapter.

CARBURETOR OPERATION

An understanding of the function of each of the carburetor components and their relation to one another is a valuable aid for pinpointing a source of carburetor trouble.

The carburetor's purpose is to supply and atomize fuel and mix it in correct proportions with air that is drawn in through the air intake. At the primary throttle opening (idle), a small amount of fuel is siphoned through the pilot jet by the incoming air. As the throttle is opened further, the air stream begins to siphon fuel through the main jet and needle jet. The tapered needle increases the effective flow capacity of the needle jet as it is lifted, in that it occupies progressively less of the area of the jet. At full throttle the carburetor venturi is fully open and the needle is lifted far enough to permit the main jet to flow at full capacity.

The choke circuit is a bystarter system in which the choke lever opens a valve rather than closing a butterfly in the venturi area as on many carburetors. In the open position, the slow jet discharges a stream of fuel into the carburetor venturi, to enrich the mixture when the engine is cold.

CARBURETOR

Removal/Installation

1. Place the vehicle on level ground and set the parking brake.
2. Remove the seat.
3. Remove the fuel tank as described in this chapter.

4. Loosen the 2 throttle cable nuts at the carburetor (**Figure 1**). Remove the throttle cable from the upper mounting bracket and then disconnect the cable ball from the throttle lever. Position the throttle cable along the upper frame rail to prevent its damage.

5. Unscrew the choke plunger nut (**Figure 2**) and pull the plunger out of the carburetor (**Figure 3**).

6. Loosen the front and rear carburetor clamp screws (**Figure 4**) and slide the clamps away from the carburetor.

7. Note the routing of the carburetor vent and overflow tubes prior to removing the carburetor.

8. Slide the carburetor back to free it from the intake manifold, then remove it from the air box boot.

9. Block off the intake manifold and air box boot openings to prevent the entry of foreign matter.

10. Drain all gas from the carburetor float bowl before storing or working on the carburetor.

11. Install by reversing these removal steps. Adjust the throttle cable as described in Chapter Three.

Disassembly

Refer to **Figure 5** when disassembling the carburetor.

1. Remove the carburetor as described in this chapter.

2. Disconnect the hoses (**Figure 6**) from the carburetor, noting their placement for reassembly.

3. To remove the vacuum piston and jet needle:
   a. Remove the cover screws and cover (**Figure 7**).
   b. Remove the spring and vacuum piston (**Figure 8**).
   c. Remove the spring (A, **Figure 9**) and spring seat (B, **Figure 9**) from the vacuum piston.
   d. Slide out the jet needle (C, **Figure 9**).

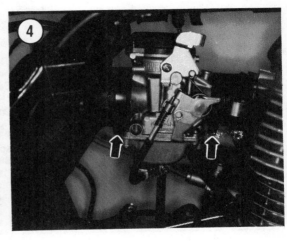

⑤ **CARBURETOR**

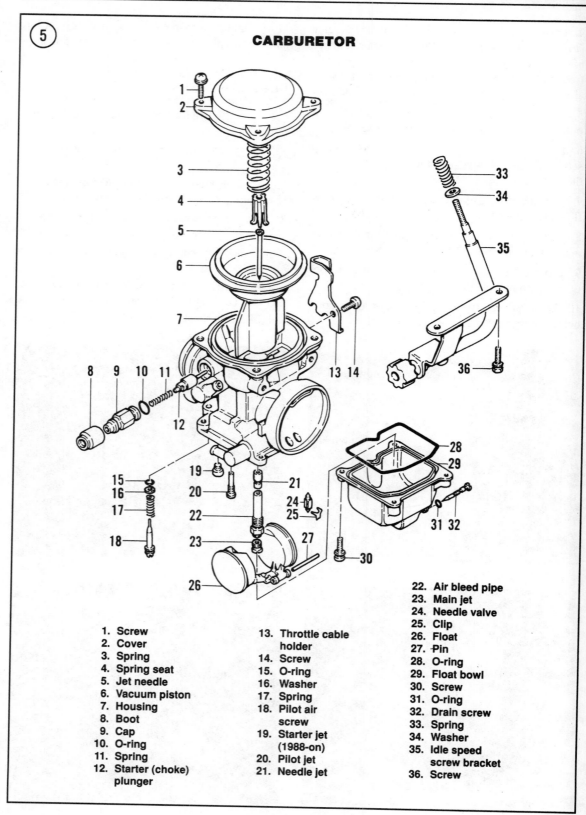

1. Screw
2. Cover
3. Spring
4. Spring seat
5. Jet needle
6. Vacuum piston
7. Housing
8. Boot
9. Cap
10. O-ring
11. Spring
12. Starter (choke) plunger
13. Throttle cable holder
14. Screw
15. O-ring
16. Washer
17. Spring
18. Pilot air screw
19. Starter jet (1988-on)
20. Pilot jet
21. Needle jet
22. Air bleed pipe
23. Main jet
24. Needle valve
25. Clip
26. Float
27. Pin
28. O-ring
29. Float bowl
30. Screw
31. O-ring
32. Drain screw
33. Spring
34. Washer
35. Idle speed screw bracket
36. Screw

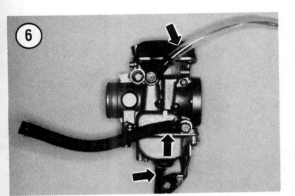

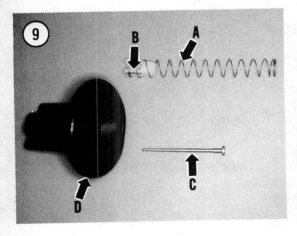

4. Remove the screws securing the idle speed screw bracket (A, **Figure 10**) and float bowl (B, **Figure 10**) to the carburetor housing. Remove the float bowl.

5. If necessary, disconnect the idle speed cable and remove it.

6. Remove the float pin, float (**Figure 11**) and needle valve (**Figure 12**).

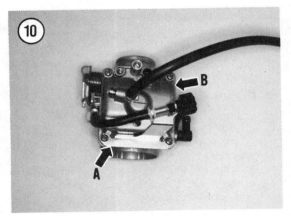

8

7. To remove the pilot air screw (**Figure 13**):

   a. Screw in the pilot air screw until it lightly seats, counting the number of turns so it can be installed in the same position.

   b. Unscrew the pilot air screw and remove it (A, **Figure 14**).

8. Unscrew the main jet (B, **Figure 14**).

9. Unscrew the air bleed pipe (**Figure 15**).

10. From inside the carburetor bore, push the needle jet down and remove it from the carburetor housing (**Figure 16**).

11. On 1988 and later models, unscrew the starter jet (**Figure 17**).

12. Unscrew the pilot jet (**Figure 18**).

> *NOTE*
> *Further disassembly is neither necessary nor recommended. Do not remove the throttle shaft and butterfly assembly (**Figure 19**). If these parts are damaged, the carburetor must be replaced as these items are not available separately.*

13. Clean and inspect all parts as described in this chapter.

Cleaning and Inspection

> *CAUTION*
> *The carburetor housing is equipped with plastic parts that cannot be removed. Do not dip the carburetor housing, O-rings, float, needle valve or vacuum piston in a carburetor cleaner or other harsh solution that can damage these parts. Use a high flash-point cleaning solution that is safe for these parts.*

1. Initially clean all parts in a mild cleaning solution. Then clean in hot soap and water and rinse with cold water. Blow dry with compressed air.

> *CAUTION*
> *If compressed air is not available, allow the parts to air dry or use a clean lint-free cloth. Do **not** use a paper towel to dry carburetor parts, as small paper particles may plug openings in the carburetor housing or jets.*

> *CAUTION*
> *Do **not** use wire or drill bits to clean jets as minor gouges in the jet can alter flow rate and upset the air/fuel mixture.*

2. Make sure the float bowl overflow tube is clear. Blow out with compressed air if necessary.

3. Inspect the float bowl O-ring (**Figure 20**). Replace the O-ring if it has become hard or is starting to deteriorate.

4. Inspect the vacuum piston diaphragm (D, **Figure 9**) for cracks, deterioration or other damage. Check the vacuum piston sides for excessive wear. Install the vacuum piston into the carburetor body and move it up and down in the bore. The vacuum piston should move smoothly with no binding or excessive play. If there is excessive play the vacuum piston and/or carburetor housing must be replaced.

5. Inspect the needle valve (**Figure 21**) as follows:
   a. Inspect the tapered end for steps, uneven wear or other damage. Replace if damaged.
   b. At the opposite end, push the needle in and release it. If the needle does not spring out, replace the needle valve.

6. Inspect the needle valve seat (**Figure 22**) for steps, uneven wear or other damage. The needle valve seat is an integral part of the carburetor hous-

8

ing. If the seat is severely worn or damaged, the carburetor housing must be replaced.

7. Inspect the pilot air screw (**Figure 23**) for damage. The tip must be straight without any visible damage. Replace if necessary.

NOTE
A worn or damaged pilot air screw tip will prevent the engine from idling smoothly.

8. Inspect the pilot air screw O-ring. Replace the O-ring if it has become hard or is starting to deteriorate.

9. Inspect all of the brass parts (**Figure 24**) for corrosion, excessive wear or other damage.

10. Inspect the float for deterioration or damage. If the float is suspected of leakage, place it in a container of water and push it down. If the float sinks or if bubbles appear (indicating a leak), the float must be replaced.

11. Make sure the butterfly screws (**Figure 19**) are tight. Tighten if necessary.

12. Move the throttle lever back and forth from stop-to-stop and check for free movement. The throttle lever should move smoothly and return under spring tension. If it does not move freely or if it sticks in any position, replace the carburetor housing.

13. Make sure all openings in the carburetor housing are clear. Clean out if they are plugged in any way.

Assembly

Refer to **Figure 5** when assembling the carburetor.

1. Install the pilot jet (**Figure 18**) and tighten securely.

2. On 1988 and later models, install the starter jet (**Figure 17**) and tighten securely.

3. Install the needle jet (A, **Figure 25**) and the air bleed pipe (B, **Figure 25**) as follows:

    a. Install the needle jet—small diameter end first—into the carburetor (**Figure 16**).

CAUTION
Do not overtighten the air bleed pipe. Doing so may damage the needle jet or carburetor housing.

    b. Install the air bleed pipe (**Figure 15**) and seat it against the needle jet. Then carefully tighten the

air bleed pipe so the air pipe pushes the end of the needle jet into the carburetor bore.

4. Install the main jet (B, **Figure 14**) and tighten securely.

5. Install the pilot air screw (A, **Figure 14**) and lightly seat it (**Figure 13**). Then back out the number of turns recorded during removal or set to the pilot air screw setting listed in **Table 1** or **Table 2**.

6. Put the needle valve onto the float and install the needle valve into its seat (**Figure 12**). Secure the float with the float pin (**Figure 11**).

7. Check the float height and adjust if necessary, as described in this chapter.

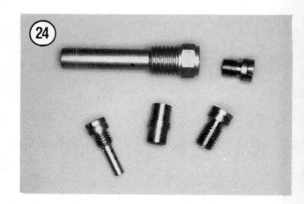

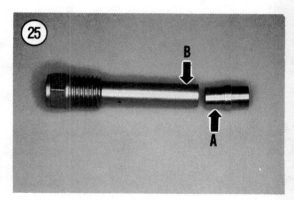

8. Make sure the O-ring is seated in the float bowl groove (**Figure 20**). Then install the float bowl (A, **Figure 10**) and the idle speed screw bracket (B, **Figure 10**). Install the mounting screws and tighten securely.

9. Install the vacuum piston and jet needle as follows:

   a. Drop the jet needle (C, **Figure 9**) into the vacuum piston.

   b. Install the spring seat (B, **Figure 9**) onto the end of the spring.

   c. Install the spring (A, **Figure 9**)—spring seat facing down—into the vacuum piston.

   d. Install the vacuum piston (**Figure 26**) into the carburetor housing.

   e. Seat the diaphragm lip into the carburetor housing groove (**Figure 8**).

   f. Install the cover onto the carburetor housing. Make sure the vacuum piston pin spring is centered in the cover, then install the screws and tighten securely.

10. Install the hoses (**Figure 6**) onto the carburetor. Secure each hose with its clip.

11. Install the carburetor as described in this chapter.

12. After assembly and installation are completed, adjust the carburetor as described in Chapter Three.

CARBURETOR ADJUSTMENTS

Idle speed and pilot screw adjustment are covered in Chapter Three.

Float Height
Check and Adjustment

The needle valve and float maintain a constant fuel level in the carburetor float bowl. Because the float height affects the fuel mixture throughout the engine's operating range, the height must be maintained within factory specifications.

The carburetor assembly has to be removed and partially disassembled for this adjustment.

1. Remove the carburetor as described in this chapter.

2. Remove the screws securing the idle speed screw bracket (A, **Figure 27**) and float bowl (B, **Figure 27**) to the carburetor housing. Remove the float bowl.

3. Hold the carburetor so the float arm tang is just touching the needle valve plunger—not pushing it down. Use a vernier caliper or small ruler and measure the distance from the float bowl mating surface to the top of the float (**Figure 28**). The correct float height is listed in **Table 3**.

4. If the float height is incorrect, adjust as follows:

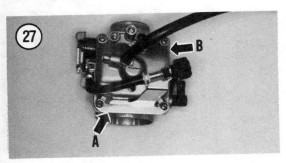

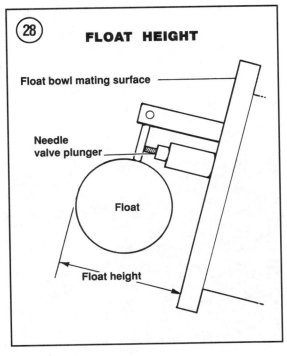

FLOAT HEIGHT

Float bowl mating surface

Needle valve plunger

Float

Float height

a. Push out the float pin and remove the float and needle valve (**Figure 29**). Remove the needle valve (**Figure 30**) from the float arm.

b. Carefully bend the float arm tang (**Figure 31**) with a screwdriver to adjust the float height.

NOTE
Decreasing the float height raises the fuel level. Increasing the float height lowers the fuel level.

c. Install the needle valve onto the float arm tang and install the float and float pin.

d. Recheck the float height as described in Step 3. Repeat until the float height adjustment is correct.

5. Reassemble and install the carburetor.

Fuel Level
Check and Adjustment

Kawasaki lists an actual fuel level specification, measured from the top edge of the float bowl with the carburetor mounted on the engine. The Kawasaki fuel level gauge (part No. 57001-1017) is required for this procedure.

The fuel level is adjusted by bending the float arm tang. You can approximate the proper fuel level by setting the initial float height as described under *Float Height Check and Adjustment* in this chapter.

WARNING
Some fuel may spill from the carburetor when performing this procedure. Because gasoline is extremely flammable, perform this procedure away from all open flames (including pilot lights) and sparks. Do not smoke or allow someone who is smoking in the work area as an

explosion and fire may occur. Always work in a well-ventilated area. Wipe up any spills immediately.

1. Park the vehicle on a level surface. Set the parking brake.

2. At the fuel tank, turn the fuel valve to the OFF position.

3. Pull the carburetor overflow hose (**Figure 32**) out from underneath the engine. Do not disconnect the hose from the carburetor.

4. Check the end of the overflow hose for contamination. Clean the hose if required.

5. Insert the fuel level gauge into the open end of the overflow hose.

6. Hold the gauge vertically against the carburetor so that the "0" gauge line is slightly higher than the bottom edge of the carburetor housing.

NOTE
The fuel level gauge must be held vertically against the carburetor housing when performing the following steps.

7. Turn the fuel valve to the ON position. Then open the carburetor drain plug (**Figure 33**) a few turns.

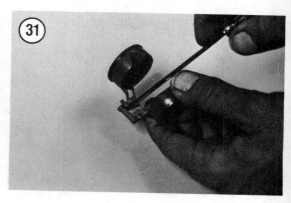

Fuel will begin to run through the overflow hose and into the fuel level gauge.

NOTE
When performing Steps 8 and 9, do not lower the fuel level gauge so the "0" gauge line drops below the bottom edge of the carburetor. Lowering the gauge past this point and then raising it will cause the gauge to show a higher than actual fuel level. If the gauge is lowered too far, turn the fuel valve off and empty

the fuel in the gauge into a gasoline storage container, then repeat the procedure.

8. Watch the fuel in the gauge. When the fuel level in the gauge settles, slowly lower the gauge (keeping it in a vertical position) until the "0" gauge line is even with the bottom edge of the carburetor housing (**Figure 33**).

9. Read the fuel level on the gauge (**Figure 33**) and compare to the specifications in **Table 3**. Note the following:

a. Tighten the drain plug (**Figure 33**) and remove the fuel level gauge from the carburetor overflow hose.

b. If the fuel level is correct, perform Step 10.

c. If the fuel level is incorrect, continue with Step 11.

10. Route the overflow hose (**Figure 32**) underneath the engine.

11. Remove the carburetor as described in this chapter.

12. Remove the screws securing the idle speed screw bracket (A, **Figure 27**) and float bowl (B, **Figure 27**) to the carburetor housing. Remove the float bowl.

13. Push out the float pin and remove the float and needle valve (**Figure 29**). Remove the needle valve (**Figure 30**) from the float arm.

14. Carefully bend the float arm tang (**Figure 31**) with a screwdriver to adjust the float height.

15. Install the needle valve onto the float arm and install the float and float pin.

16. Reinstall the carburetor and recheck the fuel level. Repeat until the fuel level is correct.

Jet Needle Adjustment

The stock jet needles are manufactured with a fixed height position. No adjustment is possible.

THROTTLE CABLE REPLACEMENT

A single throttle cable is used on all models.

1. Park the vehicle on level ground and set the parking brake.

2. Remove the seat.

3. Remove the front fender as described in Chapter Fourteen.

4. Remove the fuel tank as described in this chapter.

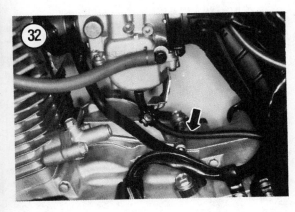

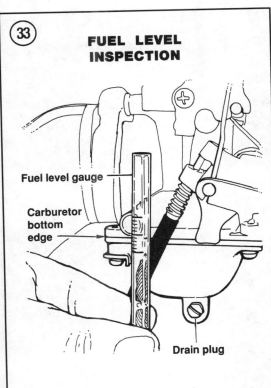

FUEL LEVEL INSPECTION

Fuel level gauge

Carburetor bottom edge

Drain plug

5. Loosen the 2 throttle cable nuts at the carburetor (**Figure 34**). Remove the throttle cable from the upper mounting bracket, then disconnect the cable ball from the throttle lever on the carburetor.

6. Slide the rubber cover away from the throttle cable adjuster at the handlebar.

7. Loosen the throttle cable adjuster locknut (A, **Figure 35**).

8. Remove the throttle lever housing screws and remove the top housing cover (B, **Figure 35**).

9. Unscrew the throttle cable adjuster (A, **Figure 36**) and disconnect the throttle cable from the throttle lever arm (B, **Figure 36**).

10. Disconnect the throttle cable from any clips holding the cable to the frame.

11. Make a note of the cable routing path through the frame, then remove it.

12. Lubricate the new cable as described in Chapter Three.

13. Reverse Steps 1-11 to install the new cable assembly, noting the following.

14. Apply grease to the front cable end (B, **Figure 36**).

15. Place the lower housing against the handlebar and operate the throttle lever (**Figure 37**). Make sure the throttle lever arm in the housing moves smoothly and does not contact the handlebar.

> *NOTE*
> *The upper and lower throttle housing covers must fit flush against the handlebar. If they do not, check the throttle housing cover(s) for a pin that must fit into a hole in the handlebar.*

16. Operate the throttle lever and make sure the carburetor throttle linkage is operating correctly without binding. If operation is incorrect or there is binding, carefully check that the cable is attached correctly with no tight bends.

17. Adjust the throttle cable as described in Chapter Three.

18. Start the engine and allow to idle. Then turn the handlebar from side to side, making sure the idle speed does not increase. If it does, the throttle cable is adjusted incorrectly or the throttle cable is improperly routed.

> *WARNING*
> *An improperly adjusted or incorrectly routed throttle cable can cause the throttle to hang open. This could cause*

you to crash. Do not ride the vehicle until the throttle cable operation is correct.

FUEL TANK

Removal/Installation

Refer to **Figure 38**, typical for this procedure.

> *WARNING*
> *Some fuel may spill from the carburetor when performing this procedure. Because gasoline is extremely flammable, perform this procedure away from all open flames (including pilot light) and sparks. Do not smoke or allow someone who is smoking in the work area as an explosion and fire may occur. Always work in a well-ventilated area. Wipe up any spills immediately.*

1. Park the vehicle on level ground and set the parking brake.

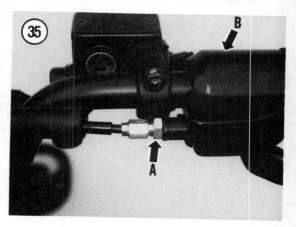

2. Remove the seat.

3. Disconnect the battery negative lead (**Figure 39**) from the battery.

4. Remove the fuel tank cover assembly as described in Chapter Fourteen.

5. Turn the fuel shutoff valve (**Figure 40**) to the OFF position and disconnect the fuel line from the valve. Plug the open end of the fuel line to prevent contamination.

6. Unwrap the hoses at the rear of the fuel tank (**Figure 41**).

7. Remove the fuel tank mounting bolts and remove the fuel tank.

8. Inspect the rubber cushion on each side of the fuel tank where the tank is held in place. Replace as a set if either is damaged or starting to deteriorate.

9. Install by reversing these removal steps. Check for fuel leakage after installation is completed. Tighten the fuel tank mounting bolts securely.

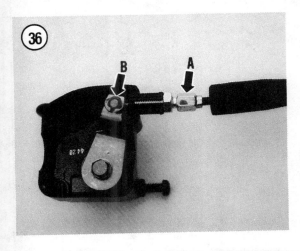

FUEL LEVEL GAUGE

Some fuel tanks are equipped with a fuel level gauge (**Figure 38**). The fuel level gauge can be replaced with the fuel tank mounted on the vehicle.

Removal/Installation

WARNING
Fuel vapors will be present when performing this procedure. Because gasoline is extremely flammable, perform this procedure away from all open flames (including pilot lights) and sparks. Do not smoke or allow someone who is smoking in the work area as an explosion and fire may occur. Always work in a well-ventilated area. Wipe up any spills immediately.

1. Park the vehicle on level ground and set the parking brake.

2. Remove the seat.

3. Disconnect the battery negative lead (**Figure 39**) from the battery.

4A. On 2-wheel drive models, perform the following:

   a. Remove the rear fuel tank cover (A, **Figure 42**).

   b. Remove the upper fuel tank cover screws.

   c. Remove the fuel tank cap (B, **Figure 42**) and remove the fuel tank cover (C, **Figure 42**). Reinstall the fuel tank cap.

4B. On 4-wheel drive models, perform the following:

   a. Remove the fuel tank cover mounting screws.

   b. Remove the fuel tank cap (A, **Figure 43**) and remove the fuel tank cover (B, **Figure 43**). Reinstall the fuel tank cap.

5. Pry the outer gauge cap (**Figure 44**) off the fuel gauge with a wide-blade screwdriver. Discard the outer gauge cap.

6. Lift the fuel gauge out of the fuel tank and remove it.

7. Install the new fuel gauge into the fuel tank.

8. Position the fuel gauge so that the 1/2 fuel mark faces to the front of the vehicle.

9. Place the new fuel gauge cap over the fuel gauge so that the notch mark on the cap aligns with the 1/2 fuel mark on the gauge. Push the fuel gauge cap into place. Then check that the gauge pins fit securely into the fuel tank boss grooves.

10. Reverse Steps 1-4 to complete installation.

8

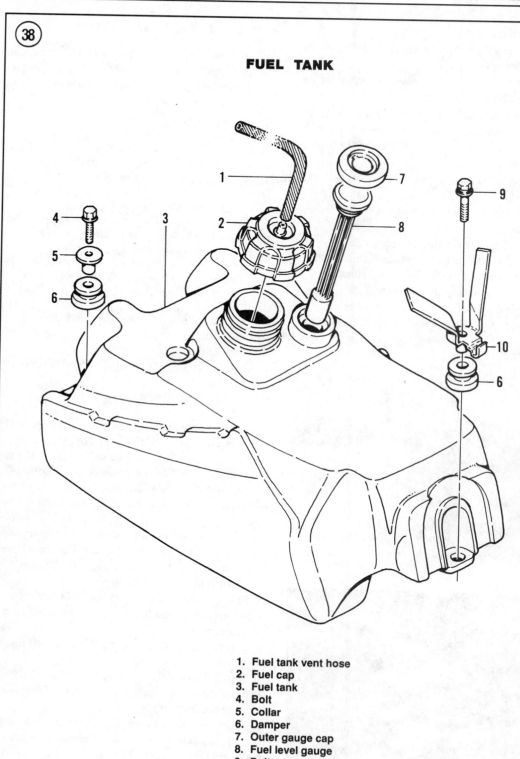

38

FUEL TANK

1. Fuel tank vent hose
2. Fuel cap
3. Fuel tank
4. Bolt
5. Collar
6. Damper
7. Outer gauge cap
8. Fuel level gauge
9. Bolt
10. Hose guide

Fuel Level Gauge Check

1. Remove the fuel level gauge as described in this chapter.
2. Inspect the fuel level gauge for damage.
3. Move the float up and down on the gauge runners. The float should move with no roughness or binding.
4. Replace the fuel level gauge if necessary.

FUEL SHUTOFF VALVE

The fuel shutoff valve is shown in **Figure 45**.

Removal/Installation

WARNING
Some fuel may spill from the carburetor, fuel line and fuel tank when performing this procedure. Because gasoline is extremely flammable, perform this procedure away from all open flames (including pilot lights) and sparks. Do not smoke or allow someone who is smoking in the work area as an explo-

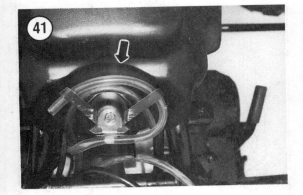

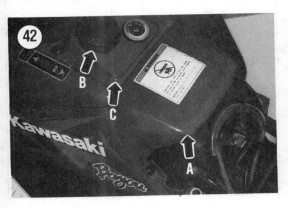

sion and fire may occur. Always work in a well-ventilated area. Wipe up any spills immediately.

1. Remove the fuel tank as described in this chapter.
2. Drain the fuel tank of all gas. Store the fuel in a can approved for gasoline storage.
3. Remove the bolts securing the fuel shutoff valve to the fuel tank and remove the valve (**Figure 45**) and O-ring.
4. To replace the fuel shutoff valve packing (5, **Figure 45**):
   a. Remove the 2 cover screws and disassemble the valve in the order shown in **Figure 45**.
   b. Replace the packing and reassemble the valve. Replace the O-ring (4, **Figure 45**) if leaking or damaged.
5. Install by reversing these steps. If necessary, install a new fuel shutoff valve O-ring (7, **Figure 45**). Tighten the screws securely.
6. Check for fuel leakage after installation is completed.

AIR BOX

The air box is mounted underneath the seat.

Removal/Installation

Refer to the exploded view drawing for your model:
   a. **Figure 46** (1986-1987).
   b. **Figure 47** (1988).
   c. **Figure 48** (1989-on).
1. Place the vehicle on level ground and set the parking brake.
2. Remove the seat as described in Chapter Fourteen.
3. Loosen the air box-to-carburetor hose clamp.
4. Remove the air box mounting bolts and lift the air box out of the frame and remove it. See **Figure 49**, typical.
5. Plug the hose opening to prevent abrasive dust from entering the carburetor.
6. Inspect all rubber components of the air box assembly and replace any that are damaged or starting to deteriorate.
7. Install by reversing these removal steps. Make sure the air box-to-carburetor hose clamp is seated properly and tightened securely.

EXHAUST SYSTEM

Check the exhaust system for deep dents and fractures and repair them or replace parts immediately. Check the muffler frame mounting flanges for fractures and loose bolts. Check the cylinder head mounting flange for tightness. A loose exhaust pipe connection will cause excessive exhaust noise and rob the engine of power.

The stock exhaust systems are shown in the following exploded drawings:

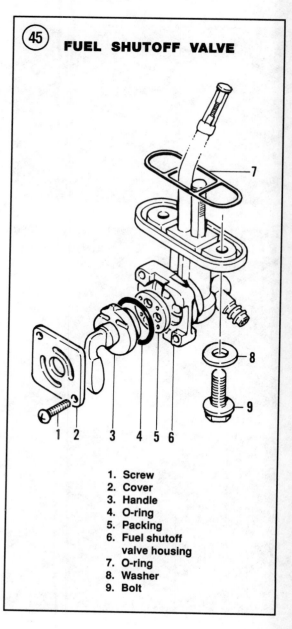

45

FUEL SHUTOFF VALVE

1. Screw
2. Cover
3. Handle
4. O-ring
5. Packing
6. Fuel shutoff valve housing
7. O-ring
8. Washer
9. Bolt

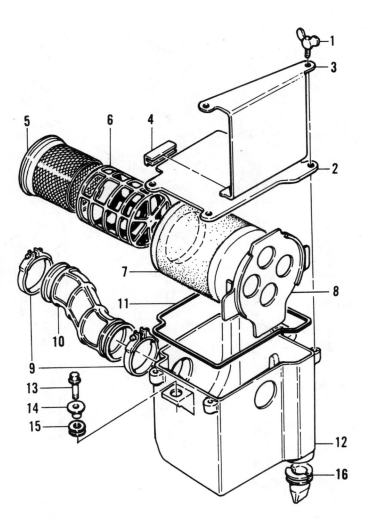

AIR BOX
(1986-1987)

1. **Wing screw**
2. **Baffle cover**
3. **Cover**
4. **Grommet**
5. **Screen**
6. **Frame**
7. **Air filter element**
8. **Filter holder**
9. **Clamps**
10. **Boot**
11. **Gasket**
12. **Air box**
13. **Bolt**
14. **Collar**
15. **Grommet**
16. **Drain hose**

8

(47)

AIR BOX
(1988)

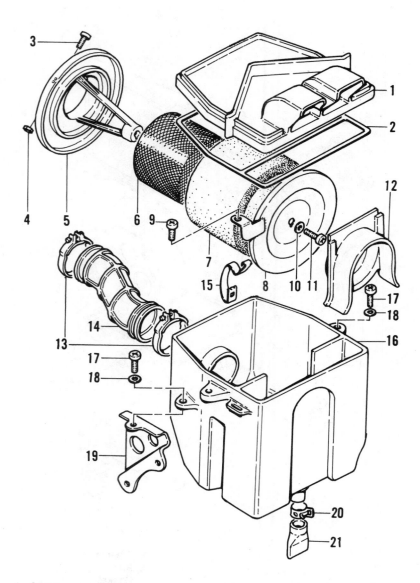

1. Cover
2. Gasket
3. Screw
4. Nut
5. Filter holder
6. Screen
7. Air filter element
8. Filter holder
9. Screw
10. Washer
11. Screw
12. Front holder
13. Clamps
14. Boot
15. Cover snap
16. Air box
17. Screw
18. Washer
19. Bracket
20. Clamp
21. Drain hose

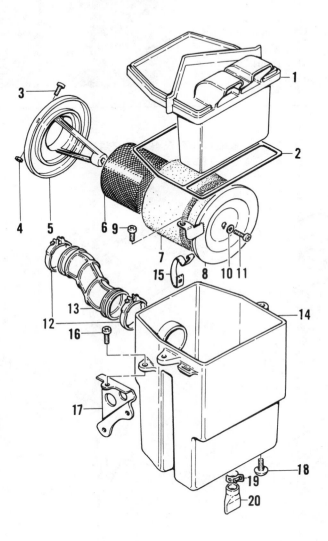

**AIR BOX
(1989-ON)**

8

1. Cover
2. Gasket
3. Screw
4. Nut
5. Filter holder
6. Screen
7. Air filter element
8. Filter holder
9. Screw
10. Washer
11. Screw
12. Clamps
13. Boot
14. Air box
15. Cover snap
16. Screw
17. Bracket
18. Screw
19. Clamp
20. Drain hose

a. **Figure 50** (1986-1987).
b. **Figure 51** (1988-on 2-wheel drive).
c. **Figure 52** (1989-on 4-wheel drive).

Removal/Installation

1. Park the vehicle on level ground and set the parking brake.

2. If necessary, remove the front and/or rear fender(s) as described in Chapter Fourteen.

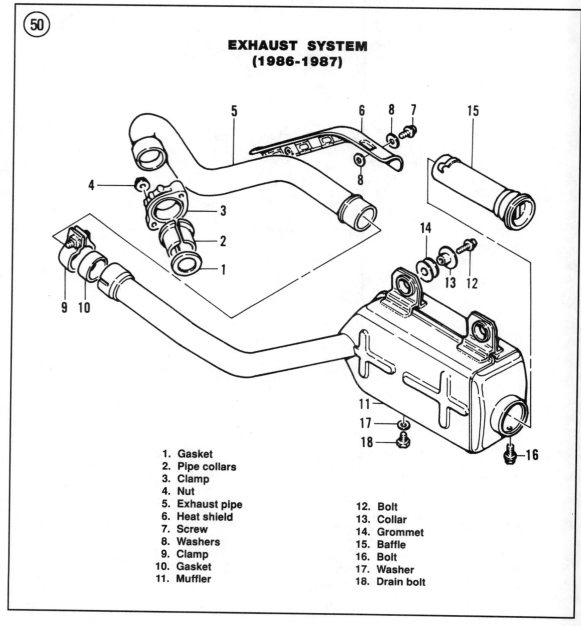

EXHAUST SYSTEM (1986-1987)

1. Gasket
2. Pipe collars
3. Clamp
4. Nut
5. Exhaust pipe
6. Heat shield
7. Screw
8. Washers
9. Clamp
10. Gasket
11. Muffler
12. Bolt
13. Collar
14. Grommet
15. Baffle
16. Bolt
17. Washer
18. Drain bolt

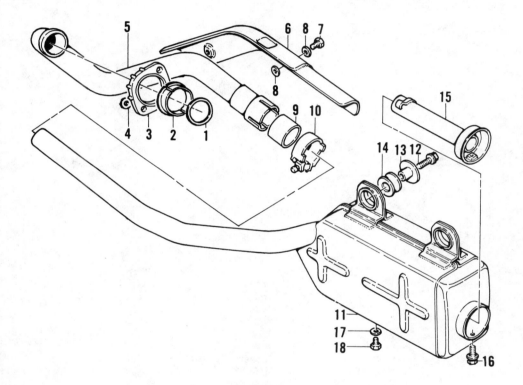

⑤¹

EXHAUST SYSTEM
(1988-ON 2-WHEEL DRIVE)

1. Gasket
2. Pipe collars
3. Clamp
4. Nut
5. Exhaust pipe
6. Heat shield
7. Screw
8. Washers
9. Gasket
10. Clamp
11. Muffler
12. Bolt
13. Collar
14. Grommet
15. Baffle
16. Bolt
17. Washer
18. Drain bolt

8

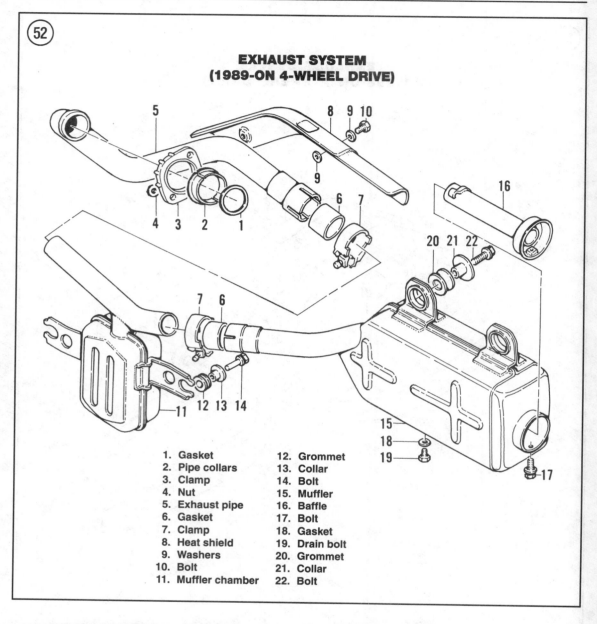

**EXHAUST SYSTEM
(1989-ON 4-WHEEL DRIVE)**

1. Gasket
2. Pipe collars
3. Clamp
4. Nut
5. Exhaust pipe
6. Gasket
7. Clamp
8. Heat shield
9. Washers
10. Bolt
11. Muffler chamber
12. Grommet
13. Collar
14. Bolt
15. Muffler
16. Baffle
17. Bolt
18. Gasket
19. Drain bolt
20. Grommet
21. Collar
22. Bolt

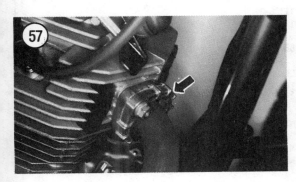

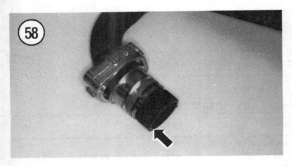

3. Remove the heat shield (**Figure 53**) screws and washers and remove the heat shield. Dont loose the washers installed behind the heat shield.

4A. On 2-wheel drive models, loosen the muffler-to-exhaust pipe clamp bolt (**Figure 54**).

4B. On 4-wheel drive models, loosen the muffler-to-muffler chamber clamp bolt.

5. Remove the bolts that hold the muffler (**Figure 55**) to the frame. Then withdraw the muffler from the pipe and remove the muffler.

6. On 4-wheel drive models, remove the muffler chamber (**Figure 56**) as follows:

    a. Loosen the muffler chamber-to-exhaust pipe clamp bolt.

    b. Remove the muffler chamber mounting bolts and withdraw the muffler chamber from the exhaust pipe.

7. Remove the nuts that hold the exhaust pipe clamp ring (**Figure 57**) to the cylinder head. Pull the exhaust pipe out of the cylinder head and remove the 2 pipe collars. Then remove the exhaust pipe from the vehicle.

8. Replace the worn or damaged exhaust pipe and muffler gaskets.

9. When installing or replacing the exhaust pipe gasket (**Figure 58**), insert it into the exhaust pipe so that the chamfered side faces out.

10. Replace missing or damaged muffler grommets.

11. Install by reversing these removal steps, noting the following.

12. Install the clamps (**Figure 54**, typical) so the gasket stopper on the clamp faces toward the back of the vehicle.

13. To minimize the chances of an exhaust leak at the cylinder head, tighten bolts in the following order:

    a. Exhaust pipe-to-cylinder head nuts.

    b. Muffler mounting bolts.

    c. On 4-wheel drive models, the muffler chamber-to-exhaust pipe clamp bolt.

    d. On 4-wheel drive models, the muffler chamber mounting bolts.

    e. On 2-wheel drive models, the exhaust pipe-to-muffler clamp bolt.

14. After installation is complete, start the engine and make sure there are no exhaust leaks.

Tables 1-3 are on the following page.

Table 1 CARBURETOR SPECIFICATIONS—2-WHEEL DRIVE

Carburetor type	Keihin
Model	CVK32
Main jet	
1986-1987; 1988-1995	130
1988	128
1996-on	125
Main air jet	
1986-1987	100
Needle jet	6
Jet needle	
1986-1988	N27Q
1989-1995	N36X
1996-on	N74T
Pilot jet	38
Starter jet	
1986-1988; 1996-on	55
1989-1995	58
1996-on	65
Pilot air screw (turns out)	
1986-1988; 1996-on	2 1/8
1989-1995	2 1/4

Table 2 CARBURETOR SPECIFICATIONS—4-WHEEL DRIVE

Carburetor type	Keihin
Model	CVK32
Main jet	
1989-1996	125
1997-on	
California models	125
All other models	138
Main air jet	
1989-1996	50
1997-on	
California models	50
All other models	70
Needle jet	6
Jet needle	
1989-1996	N36W
1997-on	
California models	N36W
All other models	N24G
Pilot jet	38
Starter jet	
1989-1995	58
1996-on	65
Pilot air screw (turns out)	
1989-1995	2 1/8 turns out
1996-on	2 turns out

Table 3 FLOAT HEIGHT AND FUEL LEVEL SPECIFICATIONS

	mm	in.
Float height		
2-wheel drive	15-19	0.591-0.748
4-wheel drive	16-18	0.630-0.709
Fuel level		
Below carburetor body bottom edge	0.5	0.020
Above carburetor body bottom edge	1.5	0.059

CHAPTER NINE

ELECTRICAL SYSTEM

This chapter contains service and test procedures for all electrical and ignition components. Since this type of vehicle may be subjected to moisture and during operation, it is important to keep all electrical connections completely coupled to each other. It is also suggested that you apply dielectric grease (available from automotive parts stores) to all electrical connectors whenever they are disconnected and reconnected. This helps seal out moisture to prevent corrosion of the electrical connector terminals. Information regarding the battery, spark plugs and ignition timing is covered in Chapter Three.

The electrical system includes the following systems:

   a. Charging system.
   b. Ignition system.
   c. Starting system.
   d. Lighting system.
   e. Electrical components.

Tables 1-5 are at the end of this chapter.

CHARGING SYSTEM

The charging system consists of the battery, alternator, fuse and a voltage regulator/rectifier (**Figure 1**). Alternating current generated by the alternator is rectified to direct current. The voltage regulator maintains the voltage to the battery and additional electrical loads (lights, ignition, etc.) at a constant voltage regardless of variations in engine speed and load.

Charging System Output Test

If charging system trouble is suspected, make sure the battery is fully charged and in good condition before going any further. Clean and test the battery as described under *Battery* in Chapter Three.

Also make sure all electrical connectors within the charging system are tight and free of corrosion prior to making this test.

1. Remove the seat.

2. Check the main fuse. Locate the fuse holder adjacent to the battery. Open the fuse holder and pull the fuse out and visually inspect it (**Figure 2**). If the fuse is blown, refer to *Fuse* in this chapter. If the main fuse is okay, reinstall it, or install a new one, then proceed to the next step.

NOTE
Make sure the fuse is secure in its holder.

3. Test the battery specific gravity as described under *Battery* in Chapter Three. Note the following:
   a. If the specific gravity reading is correct, perform Step 4.
   b. If the specific gravity reading is not within the specified range, clean and recharge the battery as described in Chapter Three. If the battery is damaged or if it will not hold a charge, replace it.

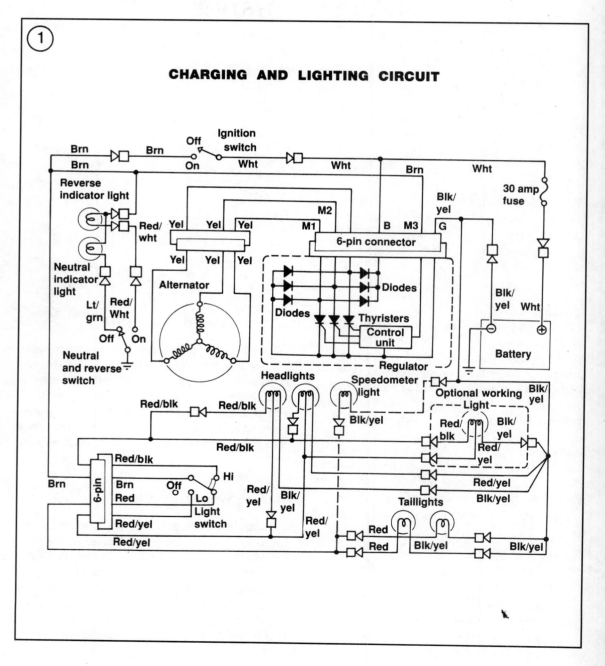

4. Connect a 0-20 DC voltmeter to the battery terminals as shown in **Figure 3**.

5. Start the engine and allow it to warm up to normal operating temperature.

6. With the engine running at idle speed, read the voltage indicated on the voltmeter. It should be approximately 12 volts. Now slowly increase engine rpm while reading the voltmeter. The voltage reading should increase with the rpm to a maximum voltage reading of 15 volts. Repeat the test with the lights on; test results should remain the same. Note the following:

    a. If the voltage readings are within the specified range, the charging system is operating correctly.

    b. Charging voltage incorrect: Test the stator coil as described under *Stator Coil* in this chapter. Replace the stator coil if faulty. If the stator coil test reading is correct, perform Step 7.

7. Check the charging system wiring harness and connectors (**Figure 4**) for dirty or loose-fitting terminals; clean and repair as required. If the wiring harness and connectors are okay, and you have not found the problem after performing the previous tests, the regulator/rectifier is probably faulty. Perform the *Regulator/Rectifier Circuit Test* in this chapter.

NOTE
Most ATV dealers and parts suppliers will not accept the return of any electrical part. If you have been unable to determine the cause of the charging system malfunction, have a Kawasaki dealer retest the charging system to verify your test results. If you purchase a new regulator/rectifier, install it, and then find that the charging system still does not work properly, you will, in most cases, be unable to return the unit for a refund.

8. Disconnect and remove the voltmeter.

9. Install the seat.

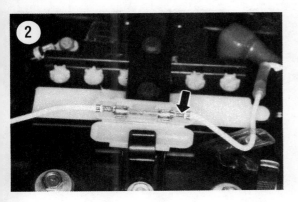

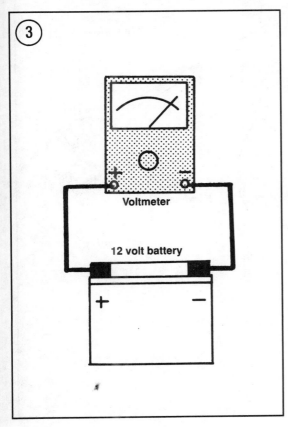

Voltmeter

12 volt battery

+   −

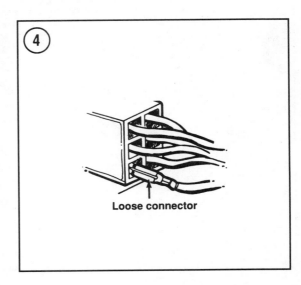

Loose connector

STATOR COIL

Stator coil and pickup coil (**Figure 5**) removal and installation procedures are covered under *Stator Coil and Left-Hand Side Cover* in Chapter Five.

Stator Coil Testing

The following test can be made with the stator coil assembled and mounted on the engine. To get accu-rate resistance measurements, the stator coil tem-perature must be approximately 20° C (68° F).

1. Remove the seat.

2. Disconnect the stator coil 3-pin electrical con-nector (**Figure 5**). All of the stator coil connector wires are yellow.

3. Use an ohmmeter set at R × 1 and check resis-tance between each yellow wire on the alternator side of the connector. See **Figure 5** and **Figure 6**.

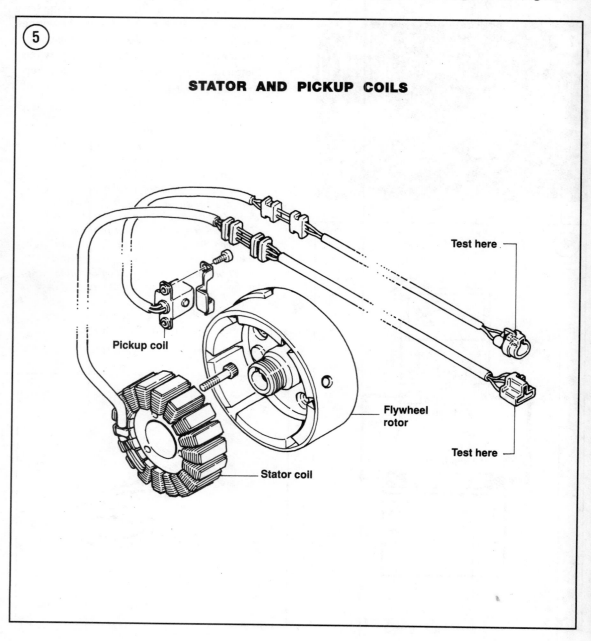

(5)

STATOR AND PICKUP COILS

Pickup coil

Flywheel rotor

Stator coil

Test here

Test here

4. The specified resistance is listed in **Table 2**. If there is continuity (indicated resistance) and it is within the specified resistance, the stator coil is good. If there is no continuity (infinite resistance) or the resistance is less than specified, the stator coil is faulty and must be replaced.

5. Apply dielectric grease (available from an automotive parts store) to the electrical connectors prior to reconnecting them. This helps seal out moisture.

6. Make sure the electrical connectors are free of corrosion and are completely coupled to each other.

REGULATOR/RECTIFIER

The regulator/rectifier (**Figure 7**) is mounted on the left-hand side of the vehicle.

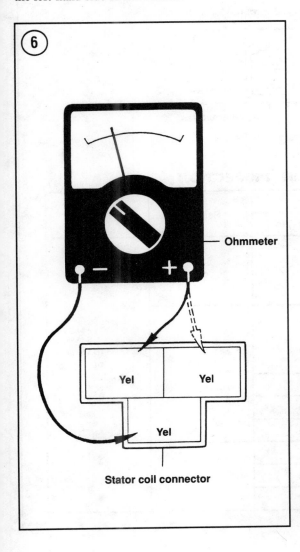

Ohmmeter

Yel Yel

Yel

Stator coil connector

Regulator Circuit Test

1. Remove the seat.
2. Remove the regulator/rectifier unit (**Figure 7**).
3. Set the ohmmeter on the R × 10 or R × 100 scale.
4. Refer to **Figure 8** for test connections and values. Make each connection and compare the meter reading to the value in **Figure 8**. If any meter reading differs from the stated value, replace the regulator/rectifier unit (**Figure 7**).

Rectifier Circuit Test

The following equipment is required to test the rectifier circuit:
 a. Two 12-volt batteries.
 b. 5 jumper wires.
 c. Test light—12-volt (3-6W) bulb.

CAUTION
The test light limits the current flow through the regulator/rectifier when making the following tests. Do not substitute the test light with an ohmmeter or ammeter; otherwise, excessive current will damage the regulator/rectifier.

1. Remove the seat.
2. Remove the regulator/rectifier unit (**Figure 7**).
3. Connect the test light and a 12-volt battery to the regulator/rectifier connector as shown in **Figure 9**.

Repeat for each alternator terminal (A1, A2 and A3). The test light should *not* light when testing each alternator terminal connector. Note the following:
 a. If the test light does not come on, continue with Step 4.
 b. If the test light comes on at any terminal, the regulator/rectifier unit is faulty.

9

4. Connect the test light and a 12-volt battery to the regulator/rectifier connector as shown in **Figure 10**. Repeat for each alternator terminal (A1, A2 and A3). The test light should *not* light when testing each alternator connector. Note the following:

    a. If the test light does not come on, continue with Step 5.

    b. If the test light comes on, the regulator/rectifier unit is faulty.

CAUTION
Do not apply more than 24 volts to the regulator/rectifier or leave the voltage applied to the unit for more than a few seconds when performing Step 5. Doing so will damage the regulator/rectifier unit.

5. Connect the test light and two 12-volt batteries (24 volts total) to the regulator/rectifier connector as

RECTIFIER CIRCUIT TEST

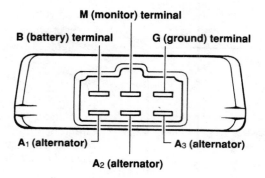

M (monitor) terminal

B (battery) terminal   G (ground) terminal

A₁ (alternator)   A₃ (alternator)

A₂ (alternator)

RECTIFIER CIRCUIT INSPECTION

No.	Connections		Reading	Meter range
	Meter (+) to	Meter (−) to		
1	A1		∞	×10 Ω or ×100 Ω
2	A2	B		
3	A3			
4	A1		0 −1/2 scale	
5	A2	G		
6	A3			
7		A1		
8	B	A2		
9		A3		
10		A1	∞	
11	G	A2		
12		A3		

shown in **Figure 11**. Quickly repeat the test for each alternator terminal (A1, A2 and A3), then disconnect the battery supply. The test light *should* light at each alternator terminal connector. Note the following:

a. If the test light comes on, continue with Step 6.

b. If the test light does not come on, the regulator/rectifier unit is faulty.

6. If the regulator/rectifier unit passes all of the tests in Steps 3-5, it may still be defective. If the charging system still does not work properly and the battery and stator coil check out okay, install a new regulator/rectifier unit into the charging system. Then start the engine and see if the problem still exists.

Removal/Installation

1. Place the vehicle on level ground and set the parking brake.

2. Disconnect the voltage regulator/rectifier electrical connector (**Figure 7**).

3. Remove the voltage regulator/rectifier mounting bolts and remove the unit from the frame; see **Figure 7**.

4. Install by reversing these removal steps, noting the following.

5. Apply dielectric grease to the electrical connectors prior to reconnecting them. This helps seal out moisture.

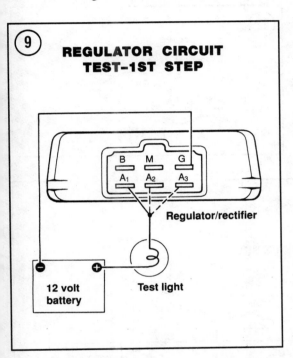

9

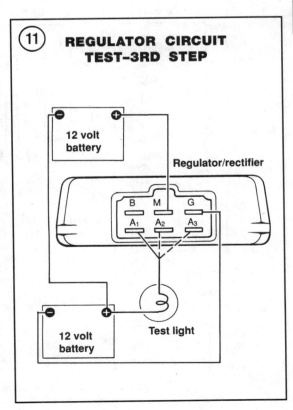

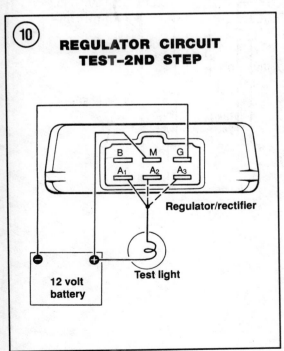

6. Make sure all electrical connectors are free of corrosion and are completely coupled to each other.

CAPACITOR DISCHARGE IGNITION

All models are equipped with a capacitor discharge ignition system. The ignition system is shown in **Figure 12**.

CDI Precautions

Certain measures must be taken to protect the capacitor discharge system.

1. Never disconnect any of the electrical connections while the engine is running.

2. Apply dielectric grease to all electrical connectors to seal out moisture.

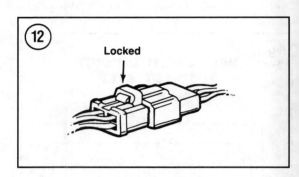

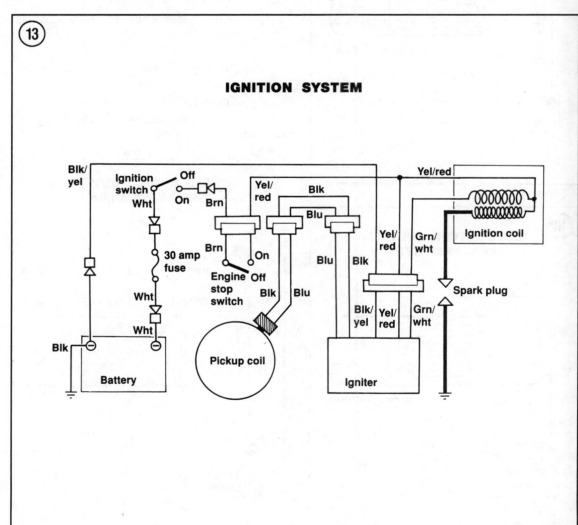

3. Make sure all electrical connectors (**Figure 13**) are free of corrosion and are completely coupled to each other.

4. The IC Igniter unit is mounted within a rubber vibration isolator. Always be sure that the isolator is in place when installing the unit.

Troubleshooting

Refer to Chapter Two.

IC IGNITER

The IC Igniter is mounted on the battery box; see **Figure 14**.

IC Igniter Testing

The resistance values provided by Kawasaki are based on the use of its ohmmeter (part No. 57001-983). If another ohmmeter is used, the readings obtained may not agree with those specified due to the different internal resistance of the individual ohmmeters.

1. Remove the IC Igniter unit.
2. Set the ohmmeter on the R × 1,000 scale.
3. Refer to **Figure 15** (1986-1987) or **Figure 16A** (1988), **Figure 16B** (1989-on) or **Figure 16C**

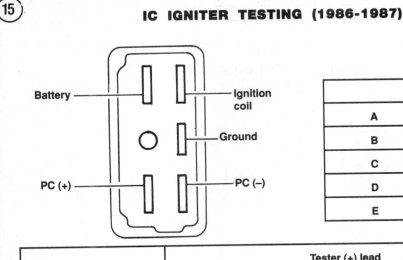

IC IGNITER TESTING (1986-1987)

Battery — Ignition coil
— Ground
PC (+) — PC (−)

	Value
A	1.8 – 2.6 kΩ
B	200 – 1,000 kΩ
C	3 – 4.2 kΩ
D	2.3 – 3.2 kΩ
E	80 – 150 kΩ

		Tester (+) lead				
		Battery	Ig. coil	Ground	PC (+)	PC (−)
Tester (−) lead	Battery		C	A	E	A
	Ig. coil	∞		∞	∞	∞
	Ground	A	D		E	0 Ω
	PC (+)	B	B	B		B
	PC (−)	A	D	0 Ω	E	

9

A

IC IGNITER TESTING (1988)

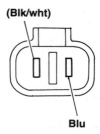

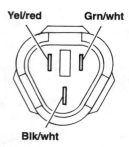

Unit: × kΩ

Scale R × 1 kΩ		Tester positive (+) lead connection				
		Grn/wht	Yel/red	Blk/wht	Blu	(Blk/wht)
Tester negative (-) lead connection	Grn/wht		∞	∞	∞	∞
	Yel/red	3 – 30		2 – 15	60 – 500	2 – 15
	Blk/wht	0.8 – 8.0	1.2 – 12.0		30 – 300	0
	Blu	50 – 500	70 – 550	30 – 300		30 – 300
	(Blk/wht)	0.8-8.0	1.2-12.0	0	30-300	

 B

IC IGNITER TESTING (1989-ON)

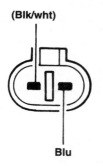

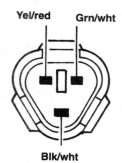

Unit: × kΩ

Scale R × 1 kΩ		Tester positive (+) lead connection				
		Grn/wht	Yel/red	Blk/wht	Blu	(Blk/wht)
Tester negative (-) lead connection	Grn/wht		∞	∞	∞	∞
	Yel/red	5-15		1-10	∞	1-10
	Blk/wht	1-5	1-10		∞	0
	Blu	50 – 150	∞	50-150		50-150
	(Blk/wht)	1-5	1-10	0	∞	

(Europe) for test connections and values. If any of the meter readings differ from the stated values, replace the IC Igniter unit.

IC Igniter
Removal/Installation

1. Park the vehicle on level ground and set the parking brake.

2. Disconnect the electrical connector from the IC Igniter unit (**Figure 14**).

3. Remove the IC Igniter mounting bolts and remove the IC Igniter from the battery box (**Figure 14**).

4. Install by reversing these removal steps, noting the following.

5. Apply dielectric grease to the electrical connector pins prior to connecting the connector block. This helps seal out moisture.

IGNITION COIL

The ignition coil is mounted underneath the front upper frame rails; see **Figure 17**.

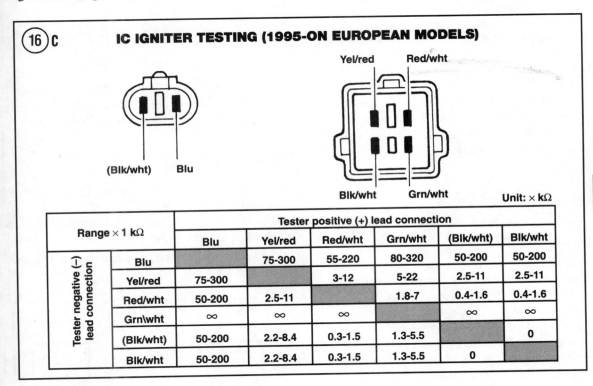

16 C   IC IGNITER TESTING (1995-ON EUROPEAN MODELS)

Yel/red   Red/wht

(Blk/wht)   Blu

Blk/wht   Grn/wht

Unit: × kΩ

Range × 1 kΩ		Tester positive (+) lead connection					
		Blu	Yel/red	Red/wht	Grn/wht	(Blk/wht)	Blk/wht
Tester negative (−) lead connection	Blu		75-300	55-220	80-320	50-200	50-200
	Yel/red	75-300		3-12	5-22	2.5-11	2.5-11
	Red/wht	50-200	2.5-11		1.8-7	0.4-1.6	0.4-1.6
	Grn\wht	∞	∞	∞		∞	∞
	(Blk/wht)	50-200	2.2-8.4	0.3-1.5	1.3-5.5		0
	Blk/wht	50-200	2.2-8.4	0.3-1.5	1.3-5.5	0	

17

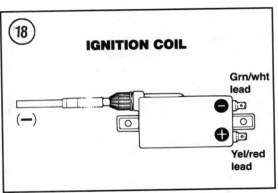

18   IGNITION COIL

Grn/wht
lead

(−)

Yel/red
lead

Testing

The ignition coil (**Figure 18**) is a form of transformer which develops the high voltage required to jump the spark plug gap. The only maintenance required is that of keeping the electrical connections clean and tight and occasionally checking to see that the coil is mounted securely.

If the condition of the coil is doubtful, there are several checks which may be made.

NOTE
To get accurate resistance measurements, the coil temperature must be approximately 20° C (68° F).

1. Remove the front fender as described in Chapter Fourteen.
2. Disconnect the spark plug cap from the spark plug.
3. Disconnect the green/white and yellow/red leads from the ignition coil (**Figure 18**).
4. Carefully remove the spark plug cap from the ignition coil secondary wire.

NOTE
When switching between ohmmeter scales (analog ohmmeter), always cross the test leads and zero the needle to assure a correct reading.

5. Measure the coil primary resistance using an ohmmeter set at R × 1. Measure resistance between the primary terminals shown in **Figure 19**. See **Table 3** for test specifications.
6. Measure the secondary resistance using an ohmmeter set at R × 1,000. Measure the resistance between the secondary lead (spark plug lead) and the ignition coil green/white terminal plug as shown in **Figure 19**. See **Table 3** for test specifications.
7. If the coil resistance does not meet either of these specifications, the coil must be replaced. If the coil exhibits visible damage, it should be replaced.
8. Install the spark plug cap onto the ignition coil secondary wire.
9. Reconnect the ignition coil leads (**Figure 18**).

Removal/Installation

1. Place the vehicle on level ground and set the parking brake.

2. Remove the front fender as described in Chapter Fourteen.
3. Remove the fuel tank as described in Chapter Eight.
4. Disconnect the spark plug cap (secondary lead) from the spark plug.
5. Disconnect the green/white and yellow/red leads from the ignition coil (**Figure 18**).
6. Remove the ignition coil mounting screws and remove the ignition coil (**Figure 17**).
7. Install by reversing these removal steps. Make sure all electrical connections are tight and free of corrosion.

PICKUP COIL

Stator coil and pickup coil (**Figure 20**) removal and installation procedures are covered under *Stator Coil and Left-Hand Side Cover* in Chapter Five.

Pickup Coil Testing

The following test can be made with the pickup coil mounted on the engine. To get accurate resistance measurements, the stator assembly must be at approximately 20° C (68° F).

1. Remove the rear fender as described in Chapter Fourteen.

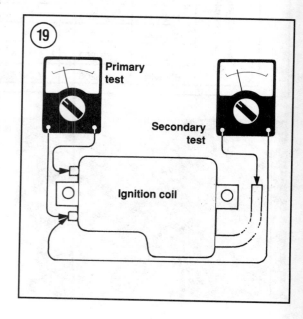

Primary test

Secondary test

Ignition coil

2. Disconnect the 2-pin pickup coil electrical connector (blue and black wires) from the pickup coil; see **Figure 20**, typical.

3. Set an ohmmeter to the R × 100 scale and cross the test leads to zero the meter (analog meters only).

4. Connect the ohmmeter between the black lead and the blue lead on the pickup coil connector side, not on the IC Igniter connector side; see **Figure 20**.

5. Note the ohmmeter reading and compare to **Table 3**. If not within specification, replace the pickup coil. See Chapter Five.

6. Apply dielectric grease to the electrical connector to seal out moisture.

7. Install the rear fender as described in Chapter Fourteen.

STARTING SYSTEM

The starting system consists of the starter motor, starter gears, solenoid and the starter button. An electrical diagram of the starting system is shown in **Figure 21**. When the starter button is pressed, it engages the starter solenoid switch that completes the circuit allowing electricity to flow from the battery to the starter motor.

CAUTION
Do not operate the starter for more than 5 seconds at a time. Let it rest approximately 10 seconds, then use it again.

The starter gears are covered in Chapter Five.

Troubleshooting

Refer to Chapter Two.

**Starter
Removal/Installation**

1. Park the vehicle on level ground and set the parking brake.

2. Remove the seat.

3. Disconnect the negative lead (**Figure 22**) from the battery.

4. Remove the left-hand side cover as described under *Stator and Left-Hand Side Cover* in Chapter Five.

5. Pull back the rubber boot on the electrical connector.

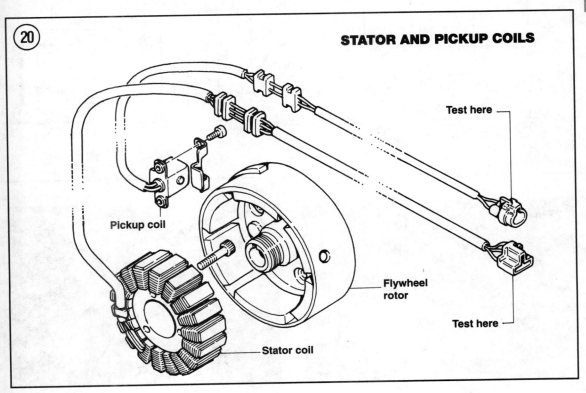

STATOR AND PICKUP COILS

Test here

Pickup coil

Flywheel rotor

Test here

Stator coil

6. Disconnect the black electric starter cable from the starter (**Figure 23**).

7. Remove the bolts (**Figure 24**) securing the starter to the crankcase.

8. Pull the starter (**Figure 25**) toward the right-hand side and remove it from the engine.

9. Install by reversing these removal steps while noting the following.

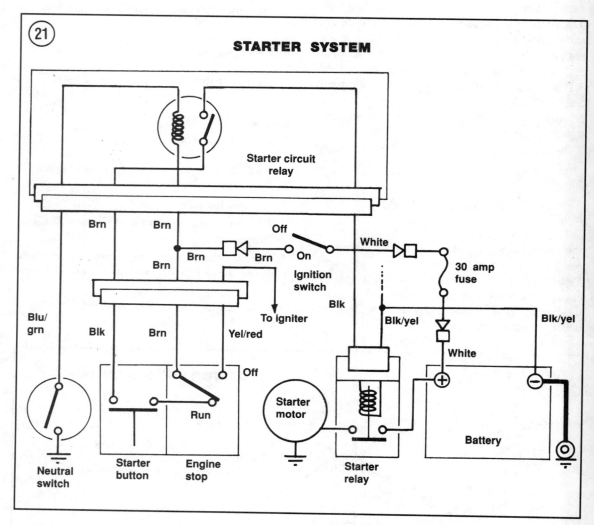

STARTER SYSTEM

10. Clean the starter motor lugs and their contact points on the crankcase.

11. Inspect the starter motor O-ring. Replace the O-ring if it has become hard or is starting to deteriorate.

12. Push the starter motor into the crankcase while guiding the starter motor sprocket onto the starter motor shaft; see **Figure 25**.

13. If the starter motor sprocket is removed on 1986-1987 models, install it with its shoulder facing toward the starter motor.

14. Install the starter motor mounting bolts and tighten securely.

Disassembly/Reassembly (1986-1991 2-Wheel Drive)

Refer to **Figure 26** for this procedure.

1. Locate the index marks on both end covers and armature housing (**Figure 27**). If there are no marks, scribe an alignment mark across both end covers and the armature housing for reassembly.

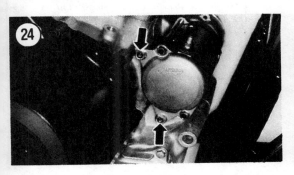

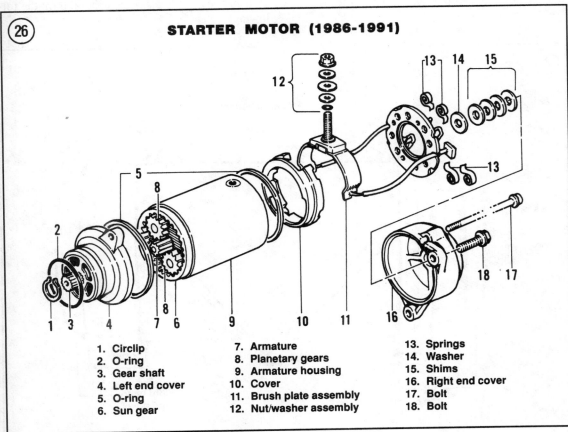

STARTER MOTOR (1986-1991)

1. Circlip	7. Armature	13. Springs
2. O-ring	8. Planetary gears	14. Washer
3. Gear shaft	9. Armature housing	15. Shims
4. Left end cover	10. Cover	16. Right end cover
5. O-ring	11. Brush plate assembly	17. Bolt
6. Sun gear	12. Nut/washer assembly	18. Bolt

9

NOTE
Record the thickness and number of shims used on the shaft next to the left and right end covers as they are removed in the following steps. Be sure to install these shims in their same position when reassembling the starter.

2. Remove the 2 case bolts and remove the left end cover and the 2 planetary gears (**Figure 28**).

3. Remove the right end cover.

4. Remove the brush plate.

5. Remove the bearing plate (**Figure 28**) from the starter housing.

6. Slide the armature out of the housing and remove it.

7. To remove the gear shaft from the left end cover:
   a. Remove the circlip from the gear shaft.
   b. Pull the gear shaft and sun gear out of the left end cover.
   c. Remove the shims from the gear shaft.

8. To remove the brush plate:
   a. Remove the terminal nut and the washer assembly.

   b. Push the terminal through the end cover and remove the brush plate.
   c. Note the O-rings installed on the terminal. Remove the O-rings if necessary.

9. Pull back the brush springs and pull the brushes out of their holders.

10. Clean all grease, dirt and carbon from the armature, case and end covers.

CAUTION
Do not immerse the wire windings in the case or the armature coil in solvent as the insulation may be damaged. Wipe the windings with a cloth lightly moistened with solvent and thoroughly dry.

11. Inspect the starter components as described under *Starter Inspection* in this chapter.

Assembly
(1986-1991 2-Wheel Drive)

1. If the gear set is disassembled, perform the following:

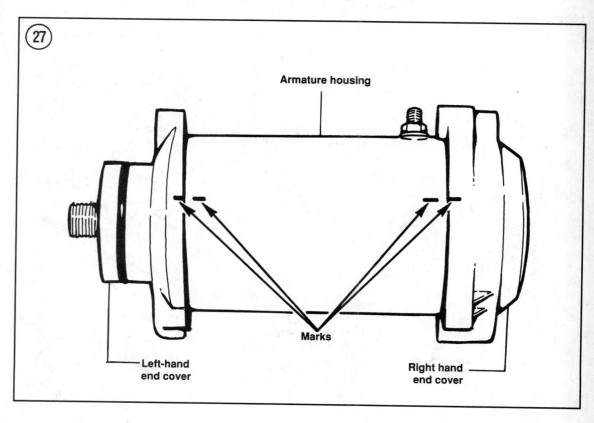

a. Grease the gears, shaft and bearing plate (**Figure 28**).

b. Install the shims onto the gear shaft.

c. Insert the gear shaft through the left end cover.

d. Install the circlip into the gear shaft groove.

e. Align the notch in the sun gear with the key in the left end cover and slide the sun gear into position next to the gear shaft.

f. Install the 2 planetary gears onto the gear shaft knobs.

g. Align the notch in the bearing plate with the key in the left end cover (**Figure 28**) and slide the bearing plate into position so that its shoulder faces out.

2. Slide the armature into the armature housing.

3. Slide the negative brushes into the holders, clockwise from the point where the brush leads are mounted to the brush plate.

4. Position the brush plate over the starter housing—align the tab in the brush plate with the notch in the housing.

5. Install the brush springs, if removed.

6. Install the shims onto the end of the armature shaft, next to the brush plate.

7. Install the right end cover onto the housing—align the index marks on the outside of the housing (**Figure 27**).

8. Install the left end cover onto the housing—align the index marks on the outside of the housing (**Figure 27**).

9. Install the 2 housing bolts and tighten securely.

Disassembly
(1992-on 2-Wheel Drive and all 4-Wheel Drive)

Refer to **Figure 29** for this procedure.

1. Locate the index marks on both end covers and armature housing. If there are no marks, scribe an alignment mark across both end covers and the armature housing for reassembly.

NOTE
Record the thickness and number of shims used on the shaft next to the left and right end covers as they are removed in the following steps. Be sure to install these shims in their same position when reassembling the starter.

2. Remove the 2 case bolts (**Figure 30**).

3. Remove the left end cover and the 2 planetary gears (A, **Figure 31**).

4. Remove the sun gear and yoke assembly (**Figure 32**).

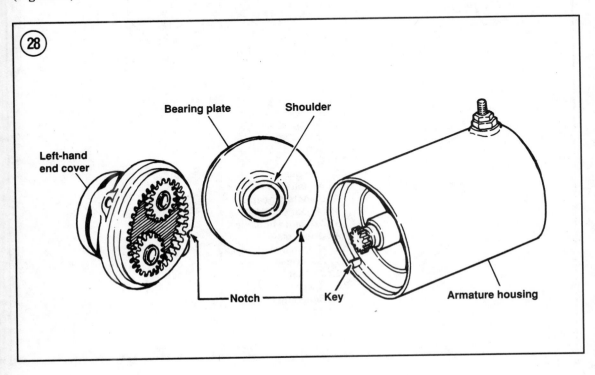

Figure 28

Left-hand end cover

Bearing plate

Shoulder

Notch

Key

Armature housing

(29)

STARTER MOTOR
(1992-ON 2-WHEEL DRIVE; ALL 4-WHEEL DRIVE)

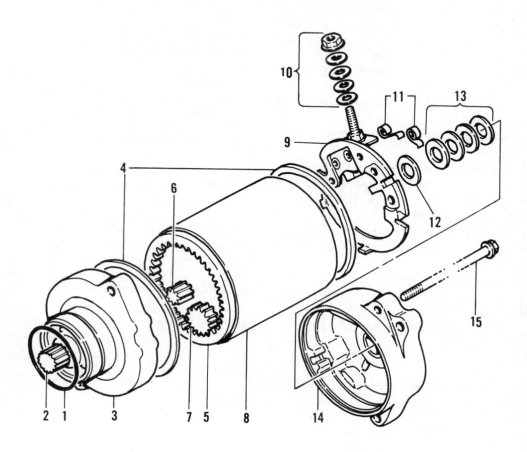

1. O-ring
2. Gear shaft
3. Left end cover
4. O-ring
5. Sun gear
6. Armature
7. Planetary gears
   (1 gear shown)
8. Armature housing
9. Brush plate
10. Nut/washer assembly
11. Springs
12. Washer
13. Shims
14. Right end cover
15. Bolt

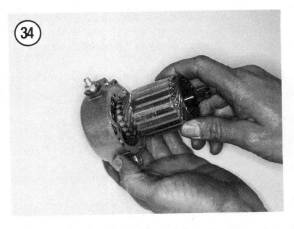

5. Hold the armature housing and remove the right end cover (**Figure 33**).

6. Remove the armature from the right end cover or from the armature housing; see **Figure 34**.

7. To remove the brush plate:

    a. Remove the terminal nut (**Figure 35**) and the washer assembly (**Figure 36**).

    b. Push the terminal through the end cover and remove the brush plate (**Figure 36**).

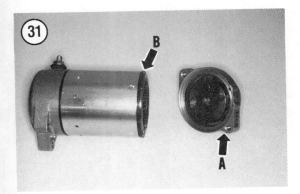

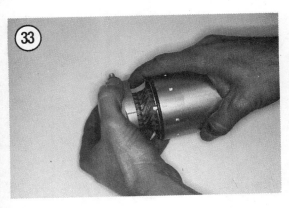

9

c. Note the O-rings (**Figure 37**) installed on the terminal. Remove the O-rings if necessary.

8. Pull back the brush springs and pull the brushes out of their holders (**Figure 38**).

9. Clean all grease, dirt and carbon from the armature, case and end covers.

> *CAUTION*
> *Do not immerse the wire windings in the case or the armature coil in solvent as the insulation may be damaged. Wipe the windings with a cloth lightly moistened with solvent and thoroughly dry.*

10. Inspect the starter components as described under *Starter Inspection* in this chapter.

Reassembly
(1992-on 2-Wheel Drive and all 4-Wheel Drive)

1. Pull back the brush springs and insert the brushes into their holders (**Figure 38**).

2. Install the brush plate as follows:
   a. Install the O-rings onto the terminal bolt, if removed. See **Figure 37**.
   b. Insert the terminal bolt through the end cover (**Figure 36**).
   c. Install the washer assembly in the order shown in **Figure 36**.
   d. Install the nut (**Figure 35**) and tighten securely.

3. Install the washers onto the commutator end of the armature (**Figure 39**).

4. Insert the armature (**Figure 40**) through the brush plate and past the brushes. See **Figure 34**.

5. Install the O-ring (A, **Figure 41**) onto the armature housing groove.

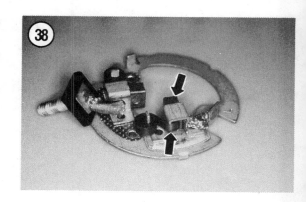

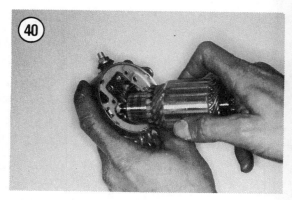

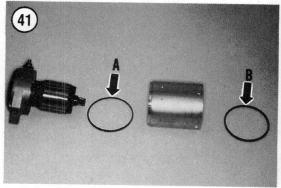

6. Slide the armature housing over the armature (**Figure 33**). Align the index mark on the end cover with the mark on the armature housing.

7. Align the notch in the sun gear yoke with the key in the armature housing (**Figure 32**) and slide the yoke into the housing (**Figure 42**).

8. Install the O-ring (B, **Figure 41**) onto the yoke shoulder.

9. If removed, install the 2 planetary gears into the left end cover (A, **Figure 31**).

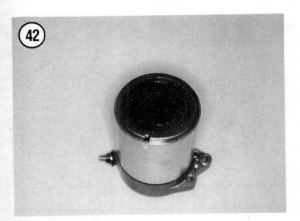

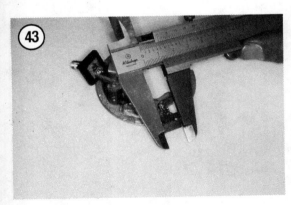

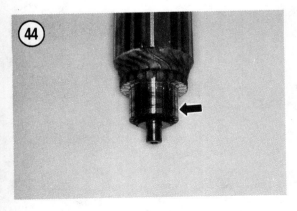

10. Install the left end cover onto the armature housing (**Figure 30**). Align the index mark on the cover and housing.

11. Install the starter bolts and tighten securely.

Starter Inspection
(All Models)

Starter motor specifications are listed in **Table 4**.

1. Measure the length of each brush with a vernier caliper (**Figure 43**). If the length is equal to or less than the service limit in **Table 4**, replace both brushes as a set.

2. Inspect the brush springs (**Figure 38**) for damage or weakness. If necessary, replace brush springs as follows:

    a. Make a drawing of the brush springs as they are installed on the brush plate, noting the direction in which the spring coils turn.

    b. Remove and replace both brush springs as a set.

3. Inspect the commutator (**Figure 44**). The mica in a good commentator is below the surface of the copper bars. On a worn commutator the mica and copper bars may be worn to the same level (**Figure 45**). If necessary, have the commutator serviced by a dealer or electrical repair shop.

4. Inspect the commutator copper bars for discoloration. If a pair of bars are discolored, grounded armature coils are indicated.

5. Use an ohmmeter and perform the following:

9

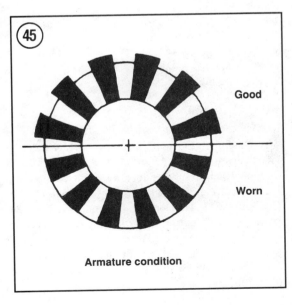

Good

Worn

Armature condition

a. Check for continuity between the commutator bars (**Figure 46**); there should be continuity (indicated resistance) between pairs of bars.

b. Check for continuity between the commutator bars and the shaft (**Figure 47**); there should be no continuity (infinite resistance).

c. If the unit fails either of these tests, the starter assembly must be replaced. The armature cannot be replaced individually.

6. Inspect the gear set (**Figure 48**) for excessive wear or damage.

7. Inspect the bushing (**Figure 49**) in the right end cover for severe wear or damage. If it is damaged, replace the starter assembly as this part is not available separately.

8. Inspect the starter housing (**Figure 50**) for cracks or other damage. Then inspect for loose, chipped or damaged magnets.

9. Inspect all of the starter O-rings. Replace worn or damaged O-rings.

STARTER RELAY

The starter relay is mounted on the battery box; see A, **Figure 51**.

System Test

System testing of the starter relay is found under *Engine Starting System* in Chapter Two.

Starter Relay
Resistance Test

The starter relay can be tested with an ohmmeter as follows.

1. Remove the rear fender as described in Chapter Fourteen.

2. Turn the ignition switch OFF.

3. Shift the transmission into NEUTRAL.

4. Disconnect the starter motor-to-starter relay black cable from the starter relay (B, **Figure 51**).

5. Switch an ohmmeter to R × 1 and connect its leads across the 2 large starter relay terminals (B and C, **Figure 51**). Turn on the ignition switch. Then push the starter button while reading the resistance scale on the ohmmeter. When the starter button is pressed, the starter relay (A, **Figure 51**) should click once and the ohmmeter should read 0 ohms. Note the following.

a. If the starter relay does not click or if the ohmmeter reads more than 0 ohms, the starter relay is defective. Replace the starter solenoid.

b. If the starter relay clicked once but the ohmmeter reads more than 0 ohms, the starter relay is defective. Replace the starter relay.

c. Turn the ignition switch off and disconnect the ohmmeter leads from the starter relay.

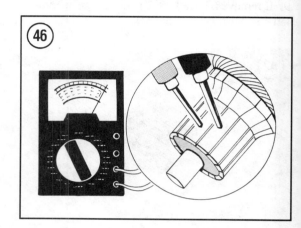

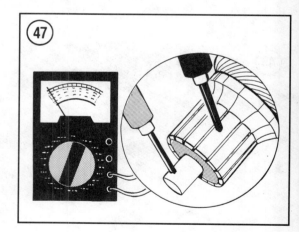

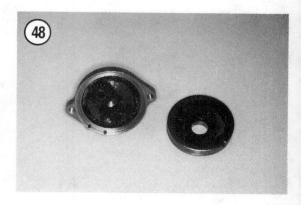

d. If the starter relay operates correctly, continue with Step 6.

6. Disconnect the small electrical connector (D, **Figure 51**) from the bottom of the starter relay.

7. Set the ohmmeter to the R × 1 scale and cross the test leads to zero the meter (analog meters only). Connect the ohmmeter between the 2 connector pins (D, **Figure 51**) on the starter relay. The ohmmeter should read approximately 0 ohms. Note the following:

    a. Disconnect the ohmmeter leads from the starter relay.

    b. If the ohmmeter reads more than 0 ohms, the starter relay is defective. Replace the starter relay.

    c. If the ohmmeter reads approximately 0 ohms, continue with Step 8.

8. Reconnect the electrical connector and starter motor lead at the starter relay.

9. Check starter circuit voltage as follows:

    a. Connect a DC voltmeter across the black and brown wires in the starting circuit; see **Figure 21** and the wiring diagram for your model at the end of this book.

    b. Turn the ignition switch on. Then depress the starter button while reading the voltage scale on the voltmeter. The voltmeter should read battery voltage (12 volts).

    c. Turn the ignition switch off and disconnect the voltmeter leads from the wiring harness.

    d. If the voltmeter reads less than 12 volts and the battery is fully charged, check the starting system wiring harness for damage. If the wiring harness is okay, test the starter circuit relay and the starter switch as described in this chapter.

Starter Relay
Removal/Installation

1. Remove the seat.

2. Disconnect the negative battery lead (**Figure 52**) from the battery.

3. Disconnect the starter relay electrical connector (D, **Figure 51**).

4. Disconnect the red (from battery) and black (from starter motor) relay leads from the top of the relay (**Figure 51**).

5. Remove the relay from the rubber mount on the frame.

6. Replace by reversing these removal steps, noting the following.

7. Install both electrical wires to the relay and tighten the nuts securely.

8. Make sure the electrical connectors are on tight and that the rubber boot is properly installed to keep out moisture.

Starter Circuit Relay Test
Testing and Replacement

A fully charged 12-volt battery and an ohmmeter are required for this test.

1. Disconnect and remove the starter circuit relay from its mounting position on the battery case; see **Figure 53**.

2. Switch an ohmmeter to its R × 1 scale. Then connect the ohmmeter to the starter circuit relay as shown in **Figure 54**. The ohmmeter should read infinity (high resistance).

3. Connect a 12-volt battery to the starter circuit relay as shown in **Figure 54** and note the ohmmeter reading. With the battery connected, the ohmmeter should read 0 ohms (low resistance).

4. Disconnect the battery and ohmmeter leads.

5. If the starter circuit relay fails to provide the test results as described in Step 2 and/or Step 3, the relay is defective. Replace the starter circuit relay.

6. Install the starter circuit relay into its mounting position. Reconnect the electrical connector to the starter circuit relay.

LIGHTING SYSTEM

The lighting system consists of a headlight, tail-light and indicator lights. **Table 5** lists replacement bulbs for these components.

Always use the correct wattage bulb as indicated in this section. The use of a larger wattage bulb will give a dim light and a smaller wattage bulb will burn out prematurely.

Single Headlight Bulb Replacement
(1986-1994 2-Wheel Drive)

Refer to **Figure 55**.

CAUTION
All models are equipped with quartz-halogen bulbs. Do not touch the bulb glass with your fingers because traces of oil from your fingers will drastically reduce the life of the bulb. Clean any traces of oil or other chemicals from the bulb with a cloth moistened in alcohol or lacquer thinner.

WARNING
If the headlight has just burned out or just been turned off, it will be hot! Do not touch the bulb until it cools off.

1. Loosen and then remove the 2 headlight mounting knobs (**Figure 55**) and lift off the headlight housing.

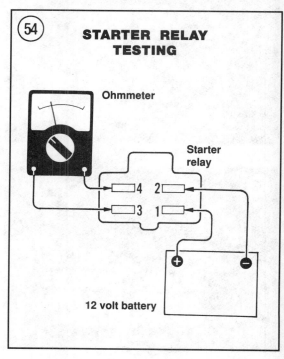

STARTER RELAY TESTING

Ohmmeter

Starter relay

4 2

3 1

12 volt battery

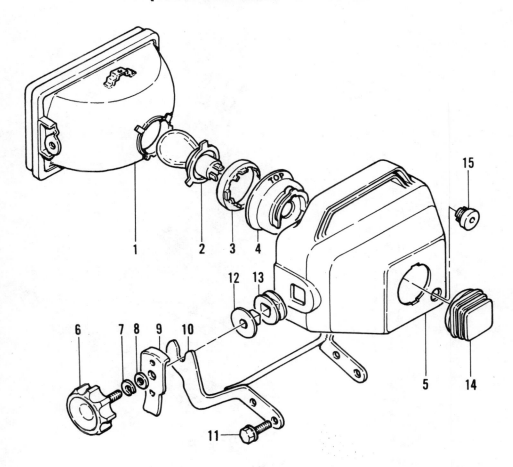

HEADLIGHT
(1986-1994 2-WHEEL DRIVE)

1. Lens assembly
2. Bulb
3. Bulb socket
4. Cover
5. Headlight housing
6. Knob
7. Lockwasher
8. Flat washer
9. Bracket
10. Stay bracket
11. Bolt
12. Collar
13. Damper
14. Plug
15. Damper (1986)

9

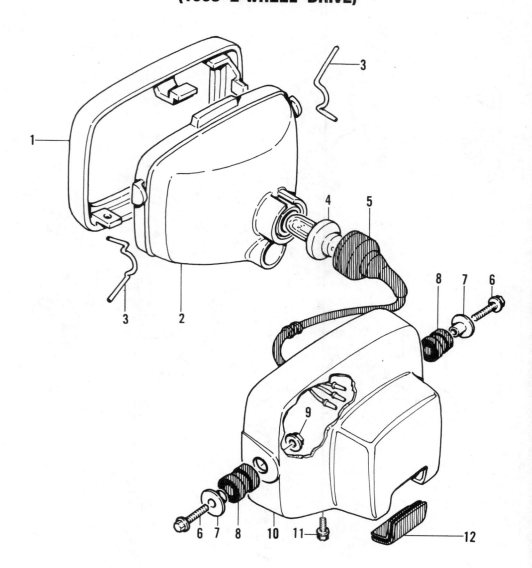

**HEADLIGHT
(1995 2-WHEEL DRIVE)**

1. Headlight rim
2. Lens assembly
3. Clip
4. Bulb
5. Connector
6. Bolt
7. Collar
8. Damper
9. Nut
10. Housing
11. Screw
12. Cover

2. Disconnect the electrical connector from the bulb.

3. Slide the headlight lens assembly out of the headlight housing.

3. Pry the dust cover off the headlight lens assembly.

4. Turn the bulb holder counterclockwise and remove it.

5. Remove and discard the blown bulb.

6. Align the tangs on the new bulb with the notches in the headlight housing and install the bulb.

7. Install the bulb holder over the bulb, push it in, then turn it clockwise until it locks.

8. Slide the dust cover over the bulb with the "TOP" mark on the cover positioned at the top of the bulb.

9. Slide the headlight lens assembly into the headlight housing. The "TOP" mark on the lens must be toward the top of the headlight housing.

10. Reconnect the electrical connector to the bulb.

11. Position the headlight housing between its mounting bracket—the "TOP" mark on the lens must be toward the top. Install the 2 headlight mounting knobs.

12. Check headlight operation.

13. Adjust the headlight as described in this section.

Headlight Bulb Replacement
Dual Headlights
(1995 2-Wheel Drive and All 4-Wheel Drive)

Refer to **Figure 56** (1995 2-wheel drive) or **Figure 57** (4-wheel drive).

CAUTION
All models are equipped with quartz-halogen bulbs. Do not touch the bulb glass with your fingers because traces of oil from your fingers will drastically reduce the life of the bulb. Clean any traces of oil or other chemicals from the bulb with a cloth moistened in alcohol or lacquer thinner.

WARNING
If the headlight has just burned out or just been turned off, it will be hot! Do not touch the bulb until it cools off.

1. Remove the side and bottom headlight lens screws (**Figure 58**, typical).

2. Pivot the headlight lens out and remove it from the headlight housing.

3. Slide the dust cover away from the connector.

4. Turn the bulb holder counterclockwise (**Figure 59**) and remove it.

5. Remove and discard the blown bulb.

6. Align the tangs on the new bulb with the notches in the headlight housing and install the bulb (**Figure 60**).

7. Install the bulb holder over the bulb, push it in, then turn it clockwise until it locks.

8. Slide the dust cover over the bulb.

9. Position the headlight lens assembly into the headlight housing. Install and tighten the side and bottom headlight lens screws.

10. Check headlight operation.

11. Check headlight adjustment as described in this section.

Headlight Adjustment
(2-Wheel Drive)

Loosen the headlight mounting knobs and move the headlight up or down to adjust the headlight vertically. See **Figure 55** or **Figure 56**. On 1995 models, adjust both headlights to the same setting.

Headlight Adjustment
(Dual Headlights)

The headlights are equipped with a vertical adjust screw located at the base of the headlight (**Figure 61**).

To adjust the headlight vertically, turn the screw clockwise to move the light up and counterclockwise to move the light down. Adjust both headlights to the same setting.

Taillight Bulb Replacement
(2-Wheel Drive)

Refer to **Figure 62** for this procedure.

1. If the rear fender is mounted on the vehicle, remove the taillight mounting screws and remove the taillight (**Figure 63**).

2. Turn the bulb socket (**Figure 64**) counterclockwise and remove it from the housing.

3. Push the bulb in, turn it counterclockwise, and remove it. Discard the blown bulb.

4. Align the bulb pins with the bulb socket grooves. Then push the bulb in, turn it clockwise, and release it. Make sure the bulb is locked in the bulb socket.

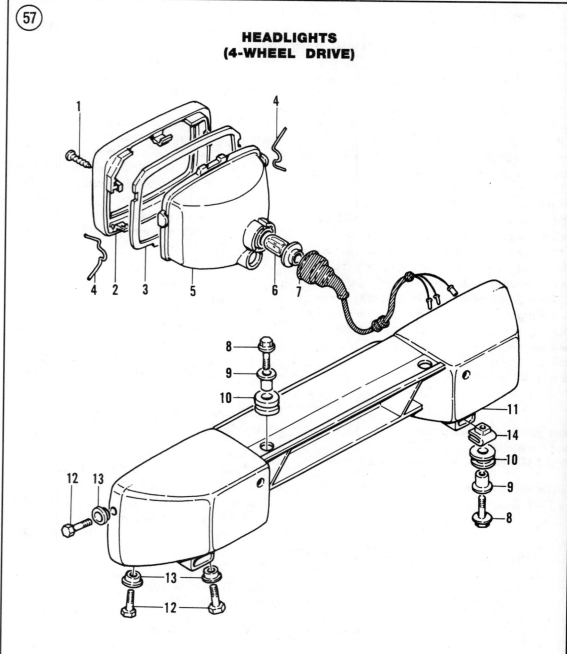

**HEADLIGHTS
(4-WHEEL DRIVE)**

1. Screw
2. Rim
3. Gasket
4. Spring
5. Headlight housing
6. Bulb
7. Bulb socket
8. Bolt
9. Collar
10. Damper
11. Headlight body
12. Bolt
13. Collar
14. Clamp nut

5. Insert the bulb socket—triangular mark on socket facing up—into the housing. Turn the bulb socket clockwise to lock it.

6. Install the taillight onto the frame and secure it with its mounting bolts.

7. Check taillight operation.

Taillight Bulb Replacement (4-Wheel Drive)

Refer to **Figure 65** for this procedure.

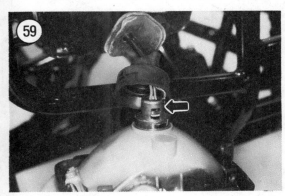

1. Remove the Phillips screws and remove the taillight lens (**Figure 66**) and its gasket from the housing.

2. Push the bulb in (**Figure 67**), turn it counterclockwise, and remove it. Discard the blown bulb.

3. Clean the lens in a mild detergent and rinse with clear water.

4. Replace the gasket if damaged or missing.

5. Align the bulb pins with the bulb socket grooves. Then push the bulb in, turn it clockwise, and release it. Make sure the bulb is locked in the bulb socket.

6. Install the lens and gasket. Secure with the 2 Phillips screws.

7. Check taillight operation.

Indicator Lights Lamp Replacement

Reverse and neutral indicator lights (**Figure 68**) are used on all models. The lights operate as follows:

   a. *NEUTRAL light*: When the transmission is in neutral, the neutral light is lit.

   b. *REVERSE light*: When the transmission is in reverse, the reverse light is lit.

9

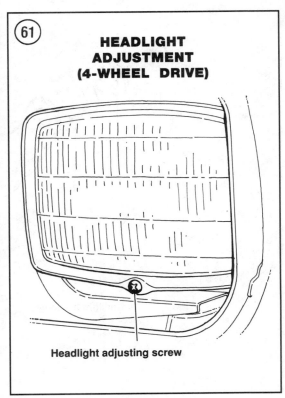

HEADLIGHT ADJUSTMENT (4-WHEEL DRIVE)

Headlight adjusting screw

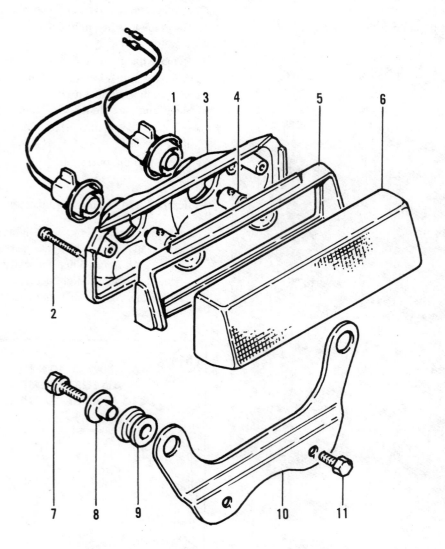

**TAILLIGHT
(2-WHEEL DRIVE)**

1. Bulb socket
2. Screw
3. Taillight housing
4. Bulb
5. Gasket
6. Lens

7. Bolt
8. Collar
9. Damper
10. Bracket
11. Bolt

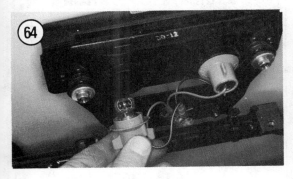

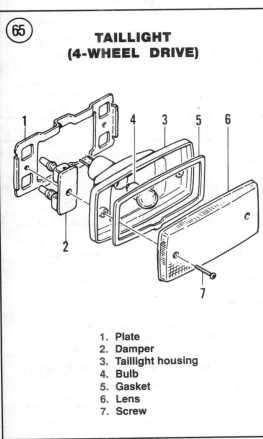

**TAILLIGHT
(4-WHEEL DRIVE)**

1. Plate
2. Damper
3. Taillight housing
4. Bulb
5. Gasket
6. Lens
7. Screw

1. Remove the ignition switch ring nut (A, **Figure 68**).

2. Remove the steering stem cover mounting screws (B, **Figure 68**) and lift off the cover. On 1986-1987 models, do not remove the rubber damper installed over the ignition switch.

3A. On 1986-1987 models, perform the following:

   a. Remove the rubber boot from around the blown bulb.

   b. Push the bulb down, turn it counterclockwise, and remove it. Discard the blown bulb.

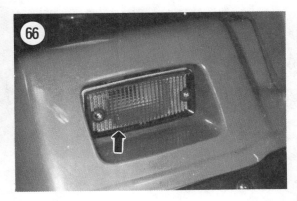

c. Align the bulb pins with the socket wall grooves. Then push the bulb down, turn it clockwise, and release it. Make sure the bulb is locked in place.

d. Slide the rubber boot over the new bulb.

3B. On 1988-on models, perform the following:

a. Pull the bulb socket and bulb (**Figure 69**) out of the steering stem cover.

b. Push the bulb down, turn it counterclockwise, and remove it. Discard the blown bulb.

c. Align the bulb pins with the socket wall grooves. Then push the bulb down, turn it clockwise, and release it. Make sure the bulb is locked in place.

d. Install the bulb socket and bulb into its mounting hole in the steering stem cover.

4. Install the steering stem cover over the ignition switch.

5. Install the ignition switch ring nut (A, **Figure 68**) and tighten securely.

6. Install the steering stem cover mounting screws and tighten securely.

7. Check the ignition switch and each indicator light for proper operation.

SWITCHES

Testing

Switches can be tested for continuity with an ohmmeter (see Chapter One) or a test light at the switch connector plug by operating the switch in each of its operating positions and comparing results with its switch operating diagram. For example, **Figure 70** shows a continuity diagram for the starter

---

(70) STARTER BUTTON

	Blk	Yel/red
Pushed	●———————●	
Released		↑

To engine stop

---

(71) ENGINE STOP SWITCH

	Yel/red	Brn
Off		
Run	●———————●	

↑
To starter button

---

(72) IGNITION SWITCH (1986-1987)

	Wht	Brn
Off		
On	●———————●	
Off		

---

(73) IGNITION SWITCH (1988-ON)

	Wht	Brn
Off		
On	●———————●	

---

(74) LIGHT SWITCH (1986-1987)

	Brn	Red
On	●———————●	
Off		

(75)

**LIGHT SWITCH
(1988-ON)**

	Red	Brn	Red/yel	Red/blk
Off				
Lo	●——————●——————●			
Hi	●——————●———————————————●			

(76)

**NEUTRAL AND
REVERSE SWITCH
(2-WHEEL DRIVE)**

Gear position	Grn	Ground	Red
1st – 5th			
Neutral	●————————●		
Reverse		●————————●	

(77)

**NEUTRAL AND
REVERSE SWITCH
(4-WHEEL DRIVE)**

Gear position	Grn	Ground	Red
1st – 5th			
Neutral	●————————●		
Reverse		●————————●	

(78)

**FAN SWITCH
(U.K. MODEL)**

	Brn	Blu
Off		
On	●————————●	

switch. It shows which terminals should show continuity when the switch is in a given position.

When the starter switch is in the ON position, there should be continuity between the black and yellow/red terminals. This is indicated by the line on the continuity diagram. An ohmmeter connected between these 2 terminals should indicate little or no resistance, or a test light should light. When the starter switch is OFF, there should be no continuity between the same terminals.

When testing switches, note the following:

a. First check the fuse as described under *Fuse* in this chapter.

b. Check the battery as described under *Battery* in Chapter Three; charge the battery to the correct state of charge, if required.

c. Disconnect the negative battery lead (**Figure 52**) from the battery if the switch connectors are not disconnected in the circuit.

CAUTION
Do not attempt to start the engine with the battery disconnected.

d. When separating 2 connectors, pull on the connector housings and not the wires.

e. After locating a defective circuit, check the connectors to make sure they are clean and properly connected. Check all wires going into a connector housing to make sure each wire is properly positioned and that the wire end is not loose.

f. When reconnecting connector halves, push them together until they click or snap into place.

If the switch or button does not perform properly, replace it. Refer to the following figures when testing the switch:

a. Starter switch: **Figure 70**.

b. Engine stop switch: **Figure 71**.

c. Ignition switch: **Figure 72** (1986-1987) or **Figure 73** (1988-on).

d. Light switch: **Figure 74** (1986-1987) or **Figure 75** (1988-on).

e. Neutral/reverse switch assembly: **Figure 76** (2-wheel drive) or **Figure 77** (4-wheel drive).

f. Fan switch (U.K. models): **Figure 78**.

Left-Hand Handlebar Switch Housing Replacement

The left-hand handlebar switch housing is equipped with the following switches:

   a. Light/dimmer switch (A, **Figure 79**).
   b. Engine stop switch (B, **Figure 79**).
   c. Starter switch (C, **Figure 79**).

> *NOTE*
> *The switches mounted in the left-hand handlebar switch housing are not available separately. If one switch is damaged, replace the housing assembly.*

1. On 4-wheel drive models, remove the front fuel tank cover as described in Chapter Fourteen.

2. Open the electrical connector vinyl cover to access the electrical connectors. See **Figure 80**, typical.

3. Disconnect the left-hand handlebar switch electrical connectors.

4. Remove or cut any clamps securing the switch wiring harness to the handlebar.

5. Remove the screws securing the switch (**Figure 79**) to the handlebar and remove the switch assembly.

6. Remove the choke assembly from the lower switch housing. See **Figure 81**, typical.

7. Install by reversing these removal steps, noting the following.

8. When installing the switch housing onto the handlebar, insert the round knob on the lower switch housing (**Figure 82**) into the hole in the handlebar.

9. Check the operation of each switch mounted in the left-hand switch housing.

10. Adjust the choke as described in Chapter Three.

Ignition Switch Replacement

The ignition switch (**Figure 83**) is mounted in the steering stem cover.

1. Remove the ignition switch ring nut (A, **Figure 83**).

2. Remove the steering stem cover mounting screws (B, **Figure 83**) and lift off the cover. On 1986-1987 models, remove the rubber damper installed over the ignition switch.

3. Remove the fuel tank cover as described in Chapter Fourteen.

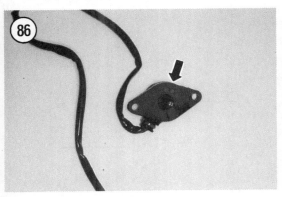

4. Open the electrical connector vinyl cover to access the electrical connectors.

5. Disconnect the ignition switch electrical connector and remove the switch (**Figure 84**).

6. Install a new ignition switch by reversing these removal steps.

7. Check the ignition switch in each of its operating positions.

Neutral/Reverse Switch Replacement

The combination neutral/reverse switch is mounted on the left side of the crankcase, behind the front gear case. See **Figure 85**.

1A. On 2-wheel drive models, remove the front gear case as described in Chapter Twelve.

1B. On 4-wheel drive models, remove the sub-transmission case as described in Chapter Eleven.

2. Remove the seat.

3. Disconnect the neutral/reverse switch electrical connectors.

4. Remove the neutral/reverse switch mounting screws and remove the switch assembly (**Figure 85**).

5. Installation is the reverse of these steps while noting the following.

6. Prior to installation, clean the switch contacts (**Figure 86**).

7. Carefully route the switch wiring harness through the crankcase as shown in **Figure 87**, typical. Insert the switch grommets into the crankcase notches.

8. Apply Loctite 242 (blue) to the switch mounting screws. Install screws and tighten securely.

9. Check switch operation with transmission in neutral and reverse.

9

COOLING FAN
(U.K MODEL)

A cooling fan system is used on certain models sold in the U.K. The cooling fan assembly is shown in **Figure 88**. **Figure 89** shows the fan system wiring diagram.

Testing

1. If the cooling fan does not work, check the fan circuit 10 amp fuse. See *Fuse* in this chapter. If the fuse is okay, continue with Step 2.
2. Remove the fan from the vehicle.

WARNING
Do not touch the fan blades when sup-
plying battery power to the fan motor.

3. Connect a 12-volt battery to the fan electrical connectors—connect the positive battery cable to the blue terminal and the negative battery cable to the black/yellow terminal. The fan should rotate counterclockwise when viewed from the rear.
4. Disconnect the battery from the fan.
5. If the fan does not rotate, replace the fan. If the fan rotates, check the fan switch and the fan wiring circuit (**Figure 89**) for damage. Refer to *Switches* in this chapter when testing the fan switch.

FUSE

All models are equipped with a 30 amp main fuse that is located next to the battery (**Figure 90**). To replace the fuse, open the fuse holder and remove the fuse. Replace the blown fuse and install the fuse holder.

On U.K. models, a 10 amp fuse is installed in the fan circuit (**Figure 89**).

NOTE
Always carry a spare fuse.

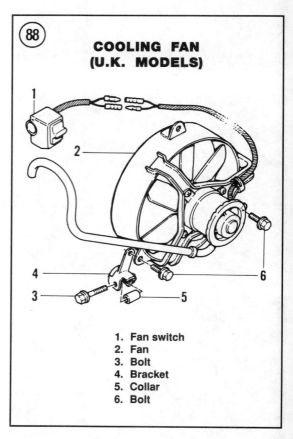

88

**COOLING FAN
(U.K. MODELS)**

1. Fan switch
2. Fan
3. Bolt
4. Bracket
5. Collar
6. Bolt

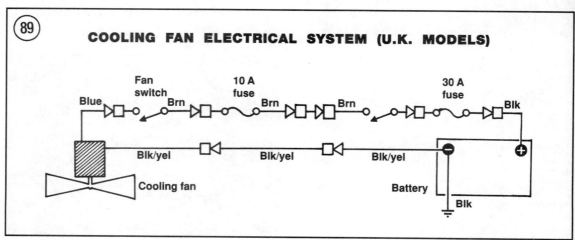

89

COOLING FAN ELECTRICAL SYSTEM (U.K. MODELS)

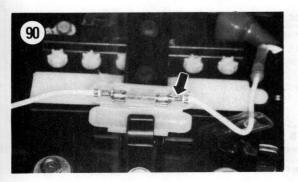

If the fuse blows, find out the reason for the failure before replacing the fuse. Usually, the trouble is a short circuit in the wiring. This may be caused by worn-through insulation or a disconnected wire shorted to ground.

WIRING DIAGRAMS

Wiring diagrams for all models are located at the end of this book.

Table 1 ELECTRICAL SYSTEM GENERAL SPECIFICATIONS

Battery capacity	
2-wheel drive	
1986-1987	12 volts, 19 amp hours
1988-1991	12 volts, 14 amp hours
1992	
U.S. and Australia	12 volts, 14 amp hours
All other models	12 volts, 19 amp hours
1993-on	
U.S.	12 volts, 14 amp hours
All other models	12 volts, 19 amp hours
4-wheel drive	
1989	12 volts, 14 amp hours
1990-on	
U.S.	12 volts, 14 amp hours
All other models	12 volts, 19 amp hours
Alternator	
Type	Three-phase AC
Rated output	23.5 amps @ 9,000 rpm, 14 volts

Table 2 CHARGING SYSTEM TEST SPECIFICATIONS

Regulator/rectifier output voltage (maximum)	15 volts
Stator coil resistance	
1986-1987	0.2-0.8 ohms
1988-on	0.1-0.7 ohms

Table 3 IGNITION SYSTEM TEST SPECIFICATIONS

Ignition coil spark gap distance	7 mm (9/32 in.) or more
Pickup coil air gap	0.9 mm (0.035 in.)
Pickup coil resistance	390-590 ohms
Spark plug cap resistance	
1986-1987	Not specified
1988-on	3.75-6.25 K ohms
Ignition coil resistance*	
Primary winding resistance	1.8-2.8 ohms
Secondary winding resistance	10-16 K ohms
IC igniter resistance	See text

* Remove the spark plug cap from the ignition coil when measuring the secondary winding resistance. See text for procedure.

Table 4 STARTER MOTOR TEST SPECIFICATIONS

Brush length	
New	12.0-12.5 mm (0.472-0.492 in.)
Service limit	6 mm (0.236 in.)

Table 5 REPLACEMENT BULBS

Headlight	
Type	Semi-sealed beam
Bulb	
2-wheel drive	
1986-1987	12 volt, 60 watt
1988-1994	12 volt, 65/60 watt
1995-on	12 volt, 25/25 watt
4-wheel drive	12 volt, 25/25 watt
Taillight	12 volt, 8 watt

CHAPTER TEN

FRONT SUSPENSION AND STEERING

This chapter describes repair and maintenance of the front wheels, hubs, front suspension arms and steering components.

On 4-wheel drive models, the front drive axles, drive mechanism and sub-transmission are covered in Chapter Eleven.

Table 1 lists front suspension and steering specifications. **Table 2** lists stock tire and wheel specifi-

cations. **Tables 1-5** are located at the end of this chapter.

WHEEL ALIGNMENT

Toe-in is a condition where the front of the tires are closer together than the back; see **Figure 1**. Toe-in is adjusted by changing the length of the tie rods.

Steering Inspection

Before the toe-in can be adjusted, the steering centering adjustment must be checked and adjusted.

Test ride the vehicle on a smooth, level road. Hold the handlebar so that it is pointed straight ahead. Note the following:

a. If the vehicle travels in a straight line with the handlebar pointed straight ahead, the steering centering position is correct. Refer to *Toe-in Adjustment* in this chapter.

b. If the vehicle does not travel in a straight line, the steering centering position must be ad-

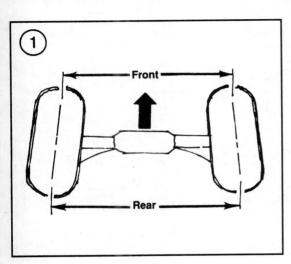

justed. Refer to *Steering Centering Adjustment* in this chapter.

Steering Centering Adjustment

1. Inflate all 4 tires to the recommended tire pressure specified in **Table 3**.

2. Park the vehicle on level ground and set the parking brake. Support the vehicle so both front wheels are off the ground. In addition, the vehicle should be positioned so that the front axles are at about the same height from the ground as the rear axle.

3. Turn the handlebar so it is pointing straight ahead.

4. Hold a straightedge across the rear wheel rim, at axle height, as shown in **Figure 2**.

5. Check the position of the front wheel in relationship to the straightedge. The front wheel should be parallel to the straightedge. If not, perform Step 6.

6A. On 1986-1987 2-wheel drive models, perform the following:

   a. Loosen the tie rod adjusting sleeve locknuts (**Figure 3**) for the right- and left-hand sides.

> *NOTE*
> *The outside locknut on each tie rod uses left-hand threads (**Figure 3**). Turn the locknuts clockwise to loosen them.*

   b. Turn both tie rod adjusting sleeves the same number of turns until the front wheel for the side being checked is parallel to the straightedge as shown in **Figure 1**.

   c. Tighten the tie rod adjusting sleeve locknuts to the torque specification in **Table 4** or **Table 5**.

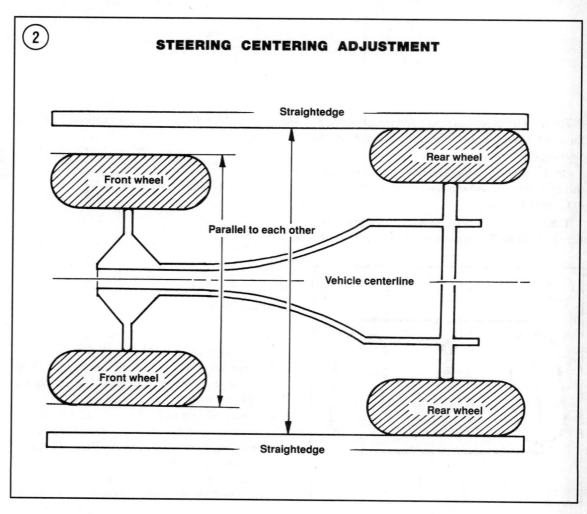

② STEERING CENTERING ADJUSTMENT

③

TIE ROD LENGTH ADJUSTMENT
(1986-1987 2-WHEEL DRIVE)

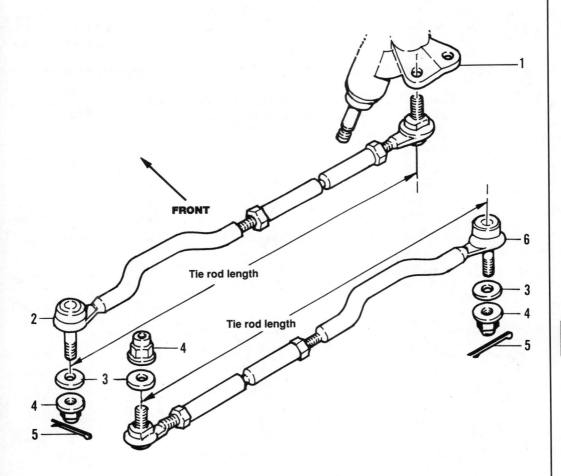

FRONT

Tie rod length

Tie rod length

10

1. Steering shaft
2. Left-hand tie rod
3. Washer
4. Nut
5. Cotter pin
6. Right-hand tie rod

6B. On 1988-on 2-wheel drive models, perform the following:

  a. Loosen the tie rod adjusting sleeve locknuts (**Figure 4**) for the right- and left-hand sides.

> *NOTE*
> *The outside locknut (painted yellow) on each tie rod has left-hand threads (**Figure 4**). Turn the locknuts clockwise to loosen them.*

  b. Turn both tie rod adjusting sleeves the same number of turns until the front wheel for the side being checked is parallel to the straightedge as shown in **Figure 2**.

  c. Tighten the tie rod adjusting sleeve locknuts to the torque specification in **Table 4** or **Table 5**.

6C. On 1988-on 4-wheel drive models, perform the following:

  a. Loosen the tie rod adjusting sleeve locknuts (**Figure 5**) for the right- and left-hand sides.

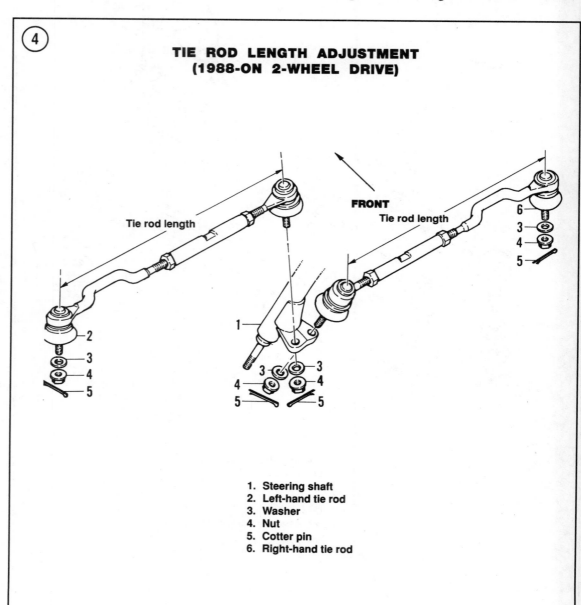

(4)

TIE ROD LENGTH ADJUSTMENT
(1988-ON 2-WHEEL DRIVE)

FRONT

Tie rod length

1. Steering shaft
2. Left-hand tie rod
3. Washer
4. Nut
5. Cotter pin
6. Right-hand tie rod

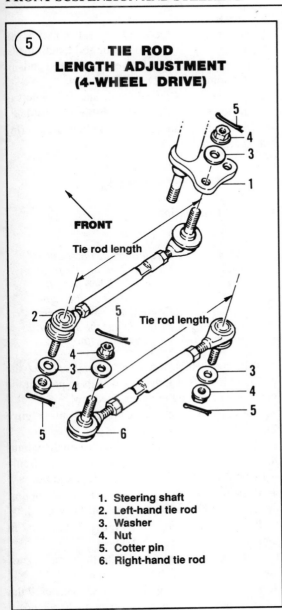

TIE ROD LENGTH ADJUSTMENT (4-WHEEL DRIVE)

FRONT

Tie rod length

Tie rod length

1. Steering shaft
2. Left-hand tie rod
3. Washer
4. Nut
5. Cotter pin
6. Right-hand tie rod

NOTE
The outside locknut (painted white) on each tie rod has left-hand threads (Figure 5). Turn the locknuts clockwise to loosen them.

b. Turn both tie rod adjusting sleeves the same number of turns until the front wheel for the side being checked is parallel to the straightedge as shown in **Figure 2**.

c. Tighten the tie rod adjusting sleeve locknuts to the torque specification in **Table 4** or **Table 5**.

7. Lower the front wheels to the ground.

Toe-in Adjustment

1. Inflate all 4 tires to the recommended tire pressure specified in **Table 3**.

2. Park the vehicle on level ground and set the parking brake. Raise and support the front end so that the front tires just clear the ground.

3. Turn the handlebar so the wheels are at the straight-ahead position.

4. Using a ruler, carefully measure the distance between the center of both front tires as shown in A, **Figure 6**. Mark the tires with a piece of chalk at these points. Write down the measurement.

5. Turn each tire exactly 180° and measure the distance between the center of both front tires at the points marked B in **Figure 6**. Write down the measurement.

6. Subtract the measurement in Step 4 from Step 5 as shown in **Figure 6**. Toe-in is correct if the difference is as follows:

  a. 2-wheel drive: 27 mm (1.06 in.).
  b. 4-wheel drive: 20 mm (0.78 in.).
  c. If the toe-in is incorrect, proceed to Step 7.

NOTE
When performing Step 7, it is important to turn both tie rods the same number of turns. This ensures that both tie rods are the same length.

WARNING
If the tie rod lengths are different, the vehicle will tend to drift to the left or right, even though the handlebar is pointed straight ahead. This may cause you to lose control and crash. If you cannot adjust the toe-in properly, have a dealer inspect the front end and then adjust the toe-in for you.

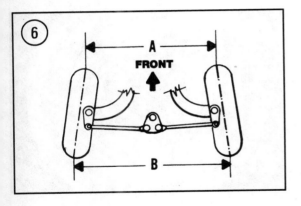

A

FRONT

B

10

7A. On 1986-1987 2-wheel drive models, perform the following:

a. Loosen the tie rod adjusting sleeve locknuts (**Figure 3**) for the right- and left-hand sides.

NOTE
*The outside locknut on each tie rod has left-hand threads (**Figure 3**). Turn the locknuts clockwise to loosen them.*

b. Use a wrench on the flat portion of the tie rods and slowly turn both tie rod adjusting sleeves the same amount until the tie rod measurement is correct. The toe-in adjustment should be approximately correct if the tie rod length measurement, measured between the tie rod ends, is 380 mm (14.96 in.).

c. Tighten the tie rod adjusting sleeve locknuts to the torque specification in **Table 4** or **Table 5**.

7B. On 1988-on 2-wheel drive models, perform the following:

a. Loosen the tie rod adjusting sleeve locknuts (**Figure 4**) for the right- and left-hand sides.

NOTE
*The outside locknut (painted yellow) on each tie rod has left-hand threads (**Figure 4**). Turn the locknuts clockwise to loosen them.*

b. Use a wrench on the flat portion of the tie rods and slowly turn both tie rod adjusting sleeves the same amount until the tie rod measurement is correct. The toe-in adjustment should be approximately correct if the tie rod length measurement, measured between the tie rod ends, is 380 mm (14.96 in.).

c. Tighten the tie rod adjusting sleeve locknuts to the torque specification in **Table 4** or **Table 5**.

7C. On 1988-on 4-wheel drive models, perform the following:

a. Loosen the tie rod adjusting sleeve locknuts (**Figure 5**) for the right- and left-hand sides.

NOTE
*The outside locknut (painted white) on each tie rod has left-hand threads (**Figure 5**). Turn the locknuts clockwise to loosen them.*

b. Use a wrench on the flat portion of the tie rods and slowly turn both tie rod adjusting sleeves the same amount until the tie rod measurement

is correct. The toe-in adjustment should be approximately correct if the tie rod length measurement, measured between the tie rod ends, is 305 mm (12.00 in.).

c. Tighten the tie rod adjusting sleeve locknuts to the torque specification in **Table 4** or **Table 5**.

8. Test ride the vehicle slowly, checking the steering and handling.

FRONT WHEEL

Removal/Installation

NOTE
All models are equipped at the factory with directional-type tires on the front and rear of the vehicle. Therefore, the wheels must be reinstalled on the same side of the ATV from which they were removed. Before removing wheels, mark them for reference during installation.

1. Park the vehicle on level ground and set the parking brake. Block the rear wheels to prevent the vehicle from rolling in either direction.

2. Loosen but do not remove the wheel nuts (**Figure 7**).

3. Raise the front of the vehicle with a small hydraulic or scissor jack. Place the jack under the frame with a piece of wood between the jack and frame.

4. Place wooden blocks under the frame to support the vehicle with the front wheels off the ground.

5. Remove the wheel nuts (**Figure 7**) loosened in Step 2 and remove the front wheel.

6. Install the tire and wheel onto the same side of the vehicle from which it was removed.

7. Install and finger tighten the wheel nuts until the wheel is positioned correctly on all 4 wheel studs.

10

WARNING
Always tighten the wheel nuts to the correct torque specification or the lug nuts may work loose and the wheel could fall off.

8. Tighten the lug nuts to the torque specification listed in **Table 4** or **Table 5**.

9. After the wheel is installed completely, rotate it. Apply the brake several times to make sure that the wheel rotates freely and that the brake is operating correctly.

10. Raise the front of the vehicle a little and remove the wooden block(s).

11. Let the jack down, and remove the jack and wooden block.

FRONT HUB/BRAKE DRUM (1986-1987 2-WHEEL DRIVE)

Refer to **Figure 8** when servicing the front hub/brake drum.

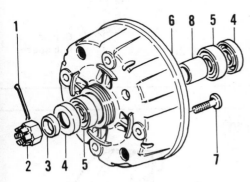

8 **FRONT HUB/BRAKE DRUM (1986-1987 2-WHEEL DRIVE)**

1. Cotter pin
2. Nut
3. Collar
4. Oil seal
5. Bearing
6. Front hub/brake drum
7. Stud
8. Distance collar

Inspection

Inspect each wheel bearing prior to removing it from the wheel hub.

CAUTION
Do not remove the wheel bearings for inspection purposes. The wheel bearings are damaged during the removal process. Remove the wheel bearings only if they reqire replacement.

1. Perform Steps 1-5 of *Front Hub/Brake Drum Disassembly* in this section.
2. Turn each bearing by hand. Make sure each bearing turns smoothly.

NOTE
Some axial play is normal, but radial play should be negligible. The bearing should turn smoothly.

3. On non-sealed bearings, check the balls for evidence of wear, pitting or excessive heat (bluish tint). Replace bearings if necessary; always replace as a complete set. When replacing, be sure to take your old bearings along to ensure a perfect match.

NOTE
Fully sealed bearings are available from many good specialty bearing shops. Fully sealed bearings provide better protection from dirt and moisture that may get into the hub.

4. Inspect the oil seals. Replace if they are deteriorating or starting to harden.
5. Inspect the threaded studs on the front hub/brake drum assembly. Replace as necessary.

Front Hub/Brake Drum Disassembly

Refer to **Figure 8** for this procedure.
1. Remove the front wheel as described in this chapter.

WARNING
Do not inhale brake dust. It may contain asbestos, which can cause lung injury and cancer.

2. Remove the cotter pin and hub nut securing the front hub/brake drum assembly and remove the front hub/brake drum assembly.

3. Remove the collar from the outside surface of the hub/brake drum.

4. Remove the oil seal from the outside surface of the hub/brake drum.

5. Remove the oil seal from the inside surface of the hub/brake drum.

6. Before proceeding any further, inspect the wheel bearings as described in this chapter.

7. To remove the inner and outer bearings and distance collar, insert a soft aluminum or brass drift into one side of the hub. Push the distance collar over to one side and place the drift on the inner race of the outer bearing. Tap the bearing out of the hub with a hammer working around the perimeter of the inner race (**Figure 9**).

8. Remove the distance collar and tap out the inner bearing.

9. Thoroughly clean out the inside of the hub with solvent and dry with compressed air or a shop cloth.

Front Hub/Brake Drum Assembly

1. On non-sealed bearings, pack the bearings with a good quality bearing grease. Work the grease in between the balls thoroughly. Turn the bearing by hand a couple of times to make sure the grease is distributed evenly inside the bearing.

2. Pack the wheel hub and distance collar with bearing grease.

CAUTION
Install the wheel bearings with the sealed side facing out. During installation, tap the bearings squarely into place. Tap on the outer race only. Use a socket that matches the outer race diameter. Do not tap on the inner race or the bearing may be damaged. Be sure that the bearings are completely seated.

3. Install the outer bearing.

4. Install the distance collar and the inner bearing.

5. Apply a light coat of bearing grease to both oil seals.

6. Install both oil seals.

7. Install the collar into the outside surface of the hub/brake drum.

WARNING
Do not allow any grease to get on the brake drum surface. Grease will contaminate the brake shoes and greatly

reduce braking ability. If necessary, thoroughly clean off all grease with lacquer thinner.

8. Install the front hub/brake drum onto the steering knuckle.

9. Install the hub nut and tighten to the torque specification listed in **Table 4**.

NOTE
Install a new cotter pin. Never reuse an old one as it may break and fall out.

10. Install a new cotter pin and bend the ends over completely (**Figure 10**).

11. Install the front wheel as described in this chapter.

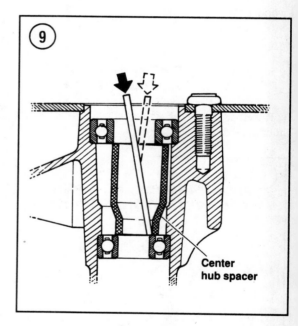

Center
hub spacer

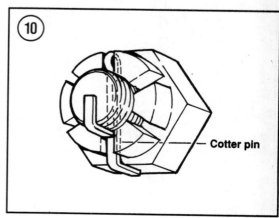

Cotter pin

FRONT HUB
(1988-ON 2-WHEEL DRIVE)

Refer to **Figure 11** when servicing the front hub.

Inspection

Inspect each wheel bearing prior to removing it from the wheel hub.

> *CAUTION*
> *Do not remove the wheel bearings for inspection purposes. The bearings are damaged during the removal process. Remove the wheel bearings only if replacement is necessary.*

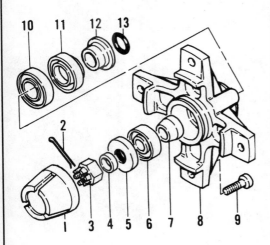

**FRONT HUB
(1988-ON 2-WHEEL DRIVE)**

1. Cover
2. Cotter pin
3. Nut
4. Collar
5. Oil seal
6. Bearing
7. Distance collar
8. Hub
9. Stud
10. Bearing
11. Oil seal
12. Collar
13. O-ring

1. Perform Steps 1-9 of *Front Hub Removal/Disassembly* in this section.
2. Turn each bearing by hand. Make sure each bearing turns smoothly.

> *NOTE*
> *Some axial play is normal, but radial play should be negligible. The bearing should turn smoothly.*

3. On non-sealed bearings, check the balls for evidence of wear, pitting or excessive heat (bluish tint). Replace bearings if necessary; always replace as a complete set. When replacing, be sure to take your old bearings along to ensure a perfect matchup.

> *NOTE*
> *Fully sealed bearings are available from many specialty bearing shops. Fully sealed bearings provide better protection from dirt and moisture that may get into the hub.*

4. Inspect the oil seals. Replace if they are deteriorating or starting to harden.

Front Hub
Removal/Disassembly

Refer to **Figure 11** for this procedure.
1. Remove the front wheel as described in this chapter.

> *WARNING*
> *Do not inhale brake dust. It may contain asbestos, which can cause lung injury and cancer.*

2. Remove the front brake caliper as described in Chapter Thirteen.
3. Remove the cotter pin and hub nut (**Figure 12**) securing the front hub assembly to the steering knuckle.

10

4. Remove the collar (**Figure 13**).

5. Remove the front hub assembly (**Figure 14**).

6. Remove the collar (**Figure 15**).

7. Remove the oil seal from the outside surface of the front hub.

8. Remove the oil seal (**Figure 16**) from the inside surface of the front hub. See **Figure 17**.

9. Before proceeding any further, inspect the wheel bearings (**Figure 18**) as described in this chapter.

10. To remove the inner and outer bearings and distance collar, insert a soft aluminum or brass drift into one side of the hub. Push the distance collar over to one side and place the drift on the inner race of the outer bearing. Tap the bearing out of the hub with a hammer working around the perimeter of the inner race (**Figure 9**).

11. Remove the distance collar and tap out the inner bearing.

12. Thoroughly clean the inside of the hub with solvent and dry with compressed air or a shop cloth.

Front Hub
Assembly/Installation

1. On non-sealed bearings, pack the bearings with a good quality bearing grease. Work the grease in between the balls thoroughly. Turn the bearing by hand a couple of times to make sure the grease is distributed evenly inside the bearing.

2. Wipe the distance collar with bearing grease.

> *CAUTION*
> *Install the wheel bearings with the sealed side facing out. During installation, drive the bearings squarely into place by tapping on the outer race only. Use a socket that matches the outer race diameter. Do not tap on the inner race*

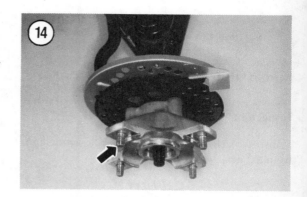

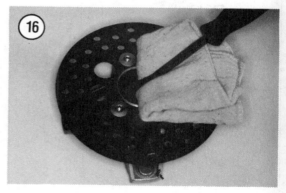

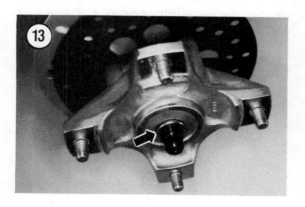

*or the bearing may be damaged. Be sure
that the bearings are completely seated.*

3. Install the outer bearing.

4. Install the distance collar and the inner bearing.

5. Apply a light coat of multipurpose grease to the inner oil seal at the points shown in **Figure 19**.

6. Install the inner oil seal (**Figure 20**).

7. Install the collar (**Figure 15**) into the inner oil seal.

8. If removed, install the O-ring (13, **Figure 11**) onto the knuckle shaft.

9. Slide the front hub (**Figure 14**) onto the knuckle shaft.

10. Slide the collar (**Figure 21**) onto the knuckle shaft.

11. Install the oil seal (**Figure 22**) over the collar and seat it into the front hub. See **Figure 13**.

12. Install the front hub nut (**Figure 12**) and tighten to the torque specification listed in **Table 4**.

*NOTE
Install a new cotter pin. Never reuse an
old one as it may break and fall out.*

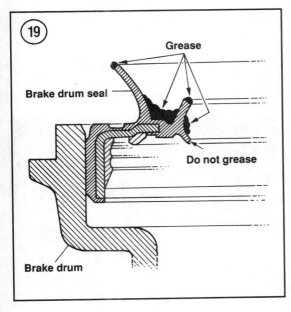

10

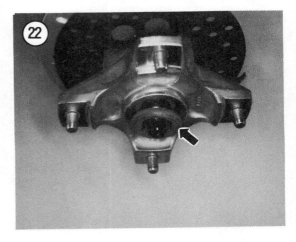

13. Install a new cotter pin and bend the ends over completely (**Figure 23**).

14. Install the front brake caliper as described in Chapter Thirteen.

15. Install the front wheel as described in this chapter.

FRONT HUB
(4-WHEEL DRIVE)

Refer to **Figure 24** when servicing the front hub.

Removal/Installation

1. Remove the front wheel as described in this chapter.

> *WARNING*
> *Do not inhale brake dust. It may contain asbestos, which can cause lung injury and cancer.*

2. Remove the front brake caliper as described in Chapter Thirteen.

3. Remove the cotter pin (**Figure 25**).

4. Remove the hub nut and washer (**Figure 26**) securing the front hub assembly to the steering knuckle.

5. Slide the front hub (**Figure 27**) off the knuckle shaft.

6. Inspect the front hub (**Figure 28**) for damage. Replace the hub studs if damaged.

7. Install by reversing these removal steps, noting the following.

8. Grease the axle splines (A, **Figure 29**).

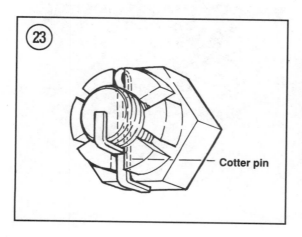

Cotter pin

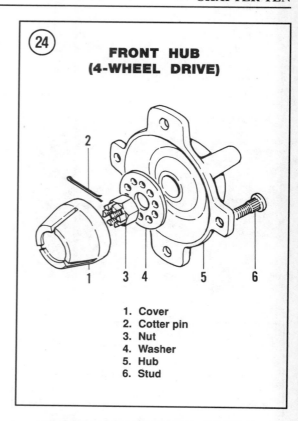

FRONT HUB (4-WHEEL DRIVE)

1. Cover
2. Cotter pin
3. Nut
4. Washer
5. Hub
6. Stud

9. Pack the oil seal lips (B, **Figure 29**) with a multipurpose grease.

10. Install the flat washer and hub nut (**Figure 26**). Tighten the front hub nut to the torque specification in **Table 5**.

> *NOTE*
> *Install a new cotter pin. Never reuse an old one as it may break and fall out.*

11. Install a new cotter pin and bend the ends over completely (**Figure 23**).

12. Install the front brake caliper as described in Chapter Thirteen.

13. Install the front wheel as described in this chapter.

HANDLEBAR

Removal

Refer to **Figure 30** for this procedure.

> *CAUTION*
> *Cover the seat, fuel tank and front fender with a heavy cloth or plastic tarp to protect it from the accidental spilling of brake fluid. Wash any spilled brake fluid off any painted or plated surface immediately as it will destroy the finish. Use soapy water and rinse thoroughly.*

1. Remove the bolts (A, **Figure 31**) securing the front master cylinder to the handlebar. Remove the master cylinder and lay it over the front fender. Keep the reservoir in the upright position to minimize loss of brake fluid and to keep air from entering the brake system. It is not necessary to remove the hydraulic brake line from the master cylinder.

2. Remove the screws and clamp securing the throttle assembly (B, **Figure 31**) to the handlebar and remove the assembly. Lay the assembly over the front fender. Be careful that the cable does not get crimped or damaged.

3. Remove the screws securing the left-hand switch assembly (**Figure 32**) to the handlebar and set the switch assembly aside.

4. On 4-wheel drive models, remove the screws and clamp securing the parking brake lever assembly (**Figure 33**) to the handlebar. Remove the parking brake assembly and lay it over the front fender. Be careful that the cable does not get crimped or damaged.

5. To remove the steering stem cover:

   a. Remove the ignition switch ring nut (A, **Figure 34**).

   b. Remove the steering stem cover mounting screws (B, **Figure 34**) and lift off the cover.

6. Remove the handlebar holder bolts (A, **Figure 35**), steering stem cover mounting brackets (B, **Figure 35**) and the handlebar holders (C, **Figure 35**).

7. Remove the handlebar.

8. To maintain a good grip on the handlebar and to prevent it from slipping down, clean the knurled

10

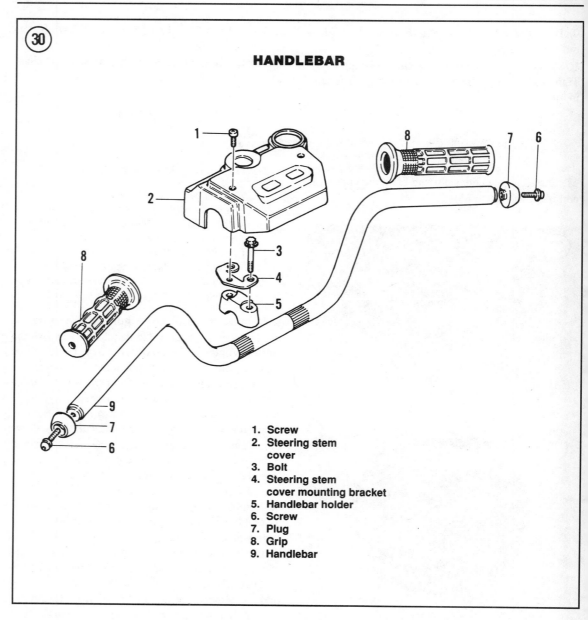

HANDLEBAR

1. Screw
2. Steering stem
   cover
3. Bolt
4. Steering stem
   cover mounting bracket
5. Handlebar holder
6. Screw
7. Plug
8. Grip
9. Handlebar

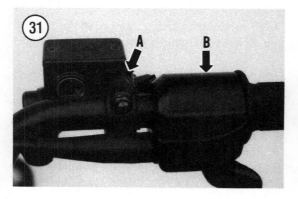

section of the handlebar with a wire brush. It should be kept rough so it will be held securely by the holders. The holders should also be kept clean and free of any metal that may have been gouged loose by handlebar slippage.

Installation

1. Install the handlebar on the lower holders. Then install the handlebar holders (C, **Figure 35**), ignition

stem cover mounting brackets (B, **Figure 35**) and the handlebar holder bolts (A, **Figure 35**).

2. Position the handlebar so the handlebar angle matches the steering stem angle as shown in **Figure 36**.

3. Tighten the 2 rear handlebar holder bolts first, then tighten the 2 front bolts. Tighten all 4 bolts to the torque specification in **Table 4** or **Table 5**. When the bolts are properly tightened, there will be an even gap at the front of the handlebar holders and no gap at the rear of the handlebar holders.

4. On 4-wheel drive models, install the parking brake lever assembly onto the handlebar (**Figure 33**).

5. Install the left-hand switch assembly (**Figure 32**). Insert the round knob in the lower switch housing (**Figure 37**) into the hole in the handlebar.

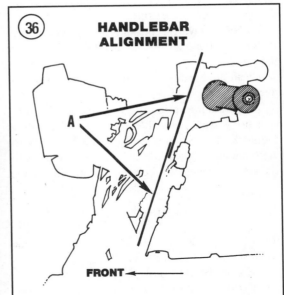

10

6. Position the master cylinder (A, **Figure 31**) onto the handlebar. Then install its clamp—arrow mark facing up—and install the 2 clamp bolts. Tighten the bolts to the torque specification in **Table 4** or **Table 5**.

7. Install the throttle assembly (B, **Figure 31**) onto the handlebar.

8. After all assemblies have been installed, test each one to make sure it operates correctly with no binding. Correct any problem at this time.

Handlebar Grip Replacement

Refer to **Figure 30**.

1. Remove the screw and remove the plug (A, **Figure 38**) from the end of the handlebar.

2. Slide a thin screwdriver between the grip and handlebar. Then spray electrical contact cleaner into the opening under the grip.

3. Pull the screwdriver out and quickly twist the grip to break its bond against the handlebar. Then slide the grip off.

4. Clean the handlebar of all rubber or sealer residue.

5. Install the new grip following its manufacturers directions. Apply an adhesive, such as ThreeBond Griplock, between the grip and handlebar. When applying an adhesive, follow its manufacturers directions for drying time before operating the vehicle.

STEERING SHAFT

Refer to the exploded view drawing for your model when servicing the steering shaft:
  a. **Figure 39**: 1986-1987 2-wheel drive.
  b. **Figure 40**: 1988-on 2-wheel drive.
  c. **Figure 41**: 4-wheel drive.

Removal

1. Park the vehicle on level ground and set the parking brake. Block the rear wheels so the vehicle will not roll in either direction.

2. Remove both front wheels as described in this chapter.

3. Remove the seat and front fender as described in Chapter Fourteen.

4. Remove the fuel tank as described in Chapter Eight.

5. Remove the handlebar as described in this chapter.

6. Remove the reverse knob and cable from the steering stem head.

7. Remove the ignition switch from the steering stem head.

8. On 1986-1987 models, perform the following:
  a. Remove the headlight and brackets from the steering stem head.
  b. Remove the neutral and reverse indicator light sockets from the steering stem head.

9. Remove the cotter pin, nut and washer securing the tie rod to the steering shaft. See **Figure 42** (2-wheel drive) or A, **Figure 43** (4-wheel drive).

10. Disconnect the tie rod from the steering shaft.

11. Repeat Steps 9 and 10 for the other tie rod.

12. Remove the bolts securing the bottom of the steering shaft to the frame. See **Figure 44** (2-wheel drive) or B, **Figure 43** (4-wheel drive).

13. Remove the bolts securing the upper steering shaft bearing clamp to the frame. See **Figure 45**, typical. Then remove the bearing clamp halves.

14. Remove the steering shaft from the frame.

Inspection

1. Carefully inspect the entire steering shaft assembly, especially if the vehicle has been involved in a collision or spill. If the shaft is bent or twisted in any way it must be replaced. If a damaged shaft is installed in the vehicle, it will cause rapid and excessive wear to the bearings as well as place undue stress on other components in the frame and steering system.

2. Inspect the tie rod attachment holes in the lower section of the steering shaft. Check for hole elonga-

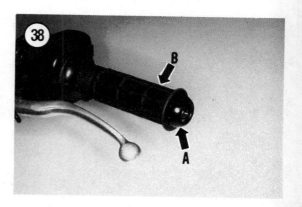

39

STEERING SHAFT
(1986-1987 2-WHEEL DRIVE)

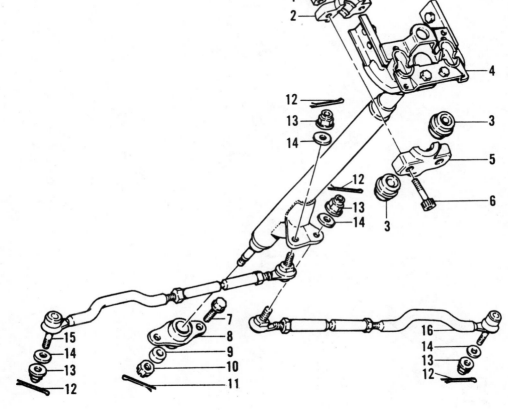

10

1. Nut
2. Bearing clamp
3. Oil seals
4. Steering shaft
5. Bearing clamp
6. Bolt
7. Bolt
8. Steering shaft bearing
9. Collar
10. Nut
11. Cotter pin
12. Cotter pin
13. Nut
14. Washer
15. Left-hand tie rod
16. Right-hand tie rod

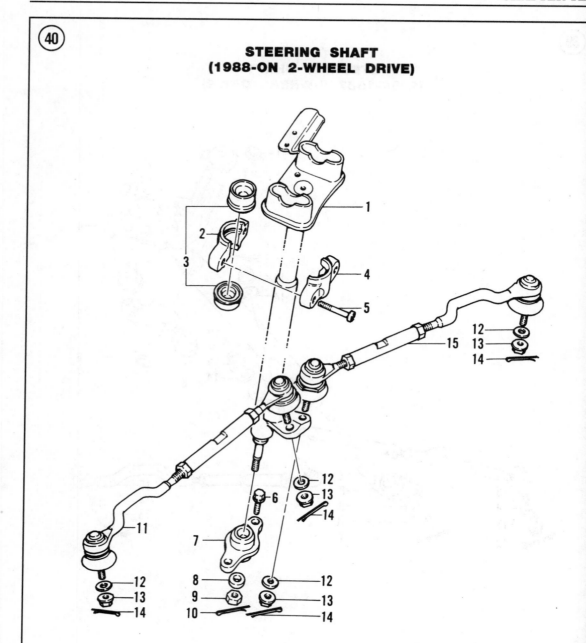

40

STEERING SHAFT
(1988-ON 2-WHEEL DRIVE)

1. Steering shaft
2. Bearing clamp
3. Oil seals
4. Bearing clamp
5. Bolt
6. Bolt
7. Steering shaft bearing
8. Collar
9. Nut
10. Cotter pin
11. Left-hand tie rod
12. Washer
13. Nut
14. Cotter pin
15. Right-hand tie rod

STEERING SHAFT (4-WHEEL DRIVE)

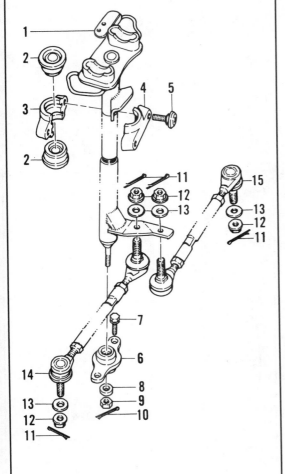

1. Steering shaft
2. Oil seals
3. Bearing clamp
4. Bearing clamp
5. Bolt
6. Steering shaft bearing
7. Bolt
8. Collar
9. Nut
10. Cotter pin
11. Cotter pin
12. Nut
13. Washer
14. Left-hand tie rod
15. Right-hand tie rod

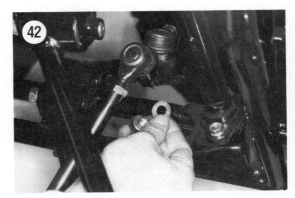

10

tion, cracks or wear. Replace the steering shaft if necessary.

3. Inspect the steering shaft bearing clamps for wear or damage. Replace if necessary.

NOTE
On 1988 and later models, the steering shaft bearing clamps must be replaced as a set.

4. Replace the upper steering shaft oil seals if severely worn or damaged.

5. Hold the steering shaft and turn the lower bearing (**Figure 46**) back and forth by hand. The bearing should turn freely with no roughness or binding. If necessary, replace the lower bearing as described in this chapter.

Steering Shaft Bearing Lubrication and/or Replacement

The steering shaft bearing (**Figure 46**) is mounted on the bottom of the steering shaft.

1. Remove and discard the cotter pin.

2. Remove the nut, washer and bearing from the bottom of the steering shaft.

3. Remove the 2 oil seals from the bearing.

4. If you are going to lubricate the bearing, perform the following:
   a. Remove the 2 oil seals from the steering shaft bearing.
   b. Wipe all the old grease out of the oil seals and steering stem.
   c. Pack the oil seals with grease and install the oil seals onto the bearing.

5. Replace the bearing and oil seals if severely worn or damaged.

6. Install by reversing these removal steps, noting the following.

7. Tighten the steering shaft bearing nut to the torque specification listed in **Table 4** or **Table 5**.

8. Secure the nut with a new cotter pin. Bend the cotter pin over to lock it.

Installation

1. Install the steering shaft into the frame.

2. Install the upper steering shaft oil seals. Position the oil seals with their open ends facing toward the rear.

3. Apply grease to the seal grooves.

4. Apply grease to the steering shaft bearing clamp halves.

5A. On 1986-1987 models, install the steering shaft bearing clamp halves by aligning the marks made on the bearing clamps prior to removing them. Install the bolts and nuts finger-tight.

5B. On 1988 and later models, install the steering shaft bearing clamp halves, aligning the marks on the sides of both clamps. Install the bolts finger-tight.

6. Install the bolts securing the bottom of the steering shaft to the frame. See **Figure 44** (2-wheel drive) or B, **Figure 43** (4-wheel drive).

7. Tighten the steering stem bearing clamp bolts (and nuts on 1986-1987) to the torque specification in **Table 4** or **Table 5**. See **Figure 45**.

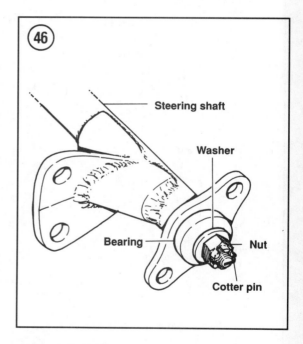

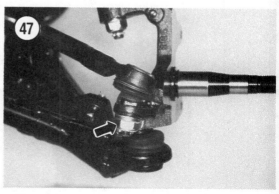

8. Tighten the bottom steering shaft bolts to the torque specification in **Table 4** or **Table 5**. See **Figure 44** (2-wheel drive) or B, **Figure 43** (4-wheel drive).

9. Reconnect the tie rod at the steering shaft. See **Figure 42** (2-wheel drive) or A, **Figure 43** (4-wheel drive). Then install the washer and nut. Tighten the tie rod end nut to the torque specification listed in **Table 4** or **Table 5**. Install a new cotter pin through the nut and bend the ends over completely.

10. Repeat Step 9 for the other tie rod.

11. On 1986-1987 models, perform the following:
   a. Install the neutral and reverse indicator light sockets onto the steering stem head.
   b. Install the headlight and brackets onto the steering stem head.

12. Install the ignition switch onto the steering stem head.

13. Install the reverse knob and cable onto the steering stem head.

14. Install the handlebar as described in this chapter.

15. Install the fuel tank as described in Chapter Eight.

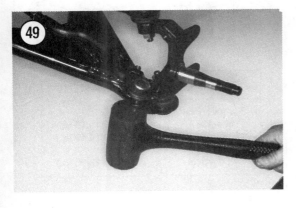

16. Install the front fender and seat as described in Chapter Fourteen.

17. Install the front wheels as described in this chapter.

18. If the tie rods were replaced, adjust the toe-in as described in this chapter.

TIE ROD

Refer to the exploded view drawing for your model when servicing the tie rods:
   a. **Figure 39**: 1986-1987 2-wheel drive.
   b. **Figure 40**: 1988-on 4-wheel drive.
   c. **Figure 41**: 4-wheel drive.

Removal

Both tie rod assemblies are the same.

1. Place the vehicle on level ground and set the parking brake. Block the rear wheels so the vehicle will not roll in either direction.

2. Remove both front wheels as described in this chapter.

3. Remove the front fender as described in Chapter Fourteen.

4. To disconnect the tie rod from the steering knuckle:
   a. Remove the cotter pin from the tie rod ball joint stud nut. Discard the cotter pin.
   b. Remove the nut from the ball joint stud. See **Figure 47** (2-wheel drive) or **Figure 48** (4-wheel drive).
   c. Install a nut onto the tie rod stud and tap the nut to disconnect the tie rod from the steering knuckle. See **Figure 49**, typical.

5. To disconnect the tie rod from the steering shaft:
   a. Remove the cotter pin from the tie rod ball joint stud nut. Discard the cotter pin.
   b. Remove the nut from the ball joint stud. See **Figure 42** (2-wheel drive) or A, **Figure 43** (4-wheel drive).
   c. Disconnect the tie rod from the steering shaft.

6. Remove the tie rod.

Inspection

NOTE
When cleaning a tie rod with solvent, work carefully to prevent the solvent

10

from contaminating the grease in the rubber boot.

1. Inspect the tie rod shaft (**Figure 50**) for damage. There should be no creases or bends along the shaft.

2. Inspect the rubber boot at each end of the tie rod end swivel joint (A, **Figure 51**). The swivel joints are permanently packed with grease. If the rubber boot is damaged, dirt and moisture can enter the swivel joint and destroy it. If the boot is damaged in any way, disassemble the tie rod and replace the tie rod end(s). Refer to *Tie Rod Disassembly/Reassembly* in the following procedure.

3. Pivot the tie rod stud (B, **Figure 51**) back and forth by hand. If the tie rod end moves roughly or with excessive play, replace it as described in the following procedure.

Tie Rod
Disassembly/Reassembly

Refer to **Figure 52** when performing this procedure.

1. Hold the tie rod with a wrench across the shaft flat and loosen the locknut for the ball joint end being replaced.

NOTE
The locknut securing the outside tie rod end has left-hand threads. The inside tie rod end locknut has right-hand threads.

2. Unscrew and remove the damaged tie rod end(s).
3. Clean the mating shaft and tie rod end threads with contact cleaner.
4. Thread the tie rod end (with locknut) into the tie rod shaft.

5. Adjust the tie rod length to the measurement listed for your model in **Figure 52**.

6. Install the tie rod and adjust the toe-in as described in this chapter.

Installation

1. Oil the tie rod stud at the point indicated in B, **Figure 51**.

2. Attach the tie rod end to the steering shaft. See **Figure 42** (2-wheel drive) or A, **Figure 43** (4-wheel drive).

3. Attach the tie rod to the steering knuckle. See **Figure 47** (2-wheel drive) or **Figure 48** (4-wheel drive).

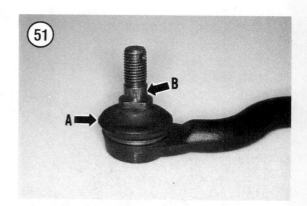

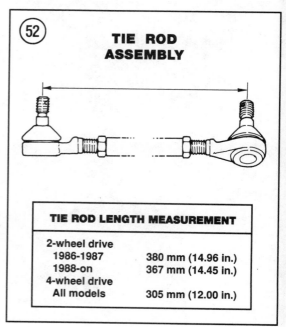

TIE ROD ASSEMBLY

TIE ROD LENGTH MEASUREMENT	
2-wheel drive	
1986-1987	380 mm (14.96 in.)
1988-on	367 mm (14.45 in.)
4-wheel drive	
All models	305 mm (12.00 in.)

4. Thread the nut onto each ball joint stud and tighten to the torque specification in **Table 4** or **Table 5**.

5. Tighten the nut(s), if necessary, to align the cotter pin hole with the nut slot.

6. Install new cotter pins through all ball joint nuts and studs. Open and bend the cotter pin ends to lock them in place.

7. Install the front fender as described in Chapter Fourteen.

8. Install the front wheels as described in this chapter.

9. Check the toe-in adjustment, and adjust if necessary, as described in this chapter.

STEERING KNUCKLE (2-WHEEL DRIVE)

Refer to **Figure 53** (1986-1987) or **Figure 54** (1988-on) when servicing the steering knuckle.

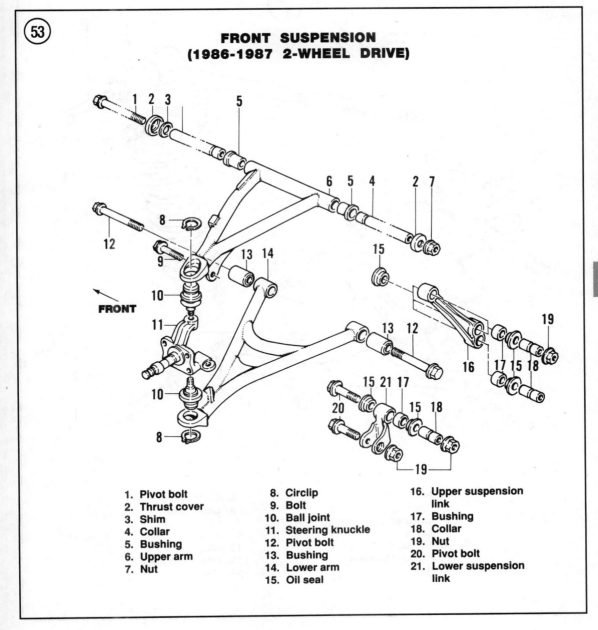

(53)

FRONT SUSPENSION (1986-1987 2-WHEEL DRIVE)

FRONT

10

1. Pivot bolt	8. Circlip	16. Upper suspension link
2. Thrust cover	9. Bolt	17. Bushing
3. Shim	10. Ball joint	18. Collar
4. Collar	11. Steering knuckle	19. Nut
5. Bushing	12. Pivot bolt	20. Pivot bolt
6. Upper arm	13. Bushing	21. Lower suspension link
7. Nut	14. Lower arm	
	15. Oil seal	

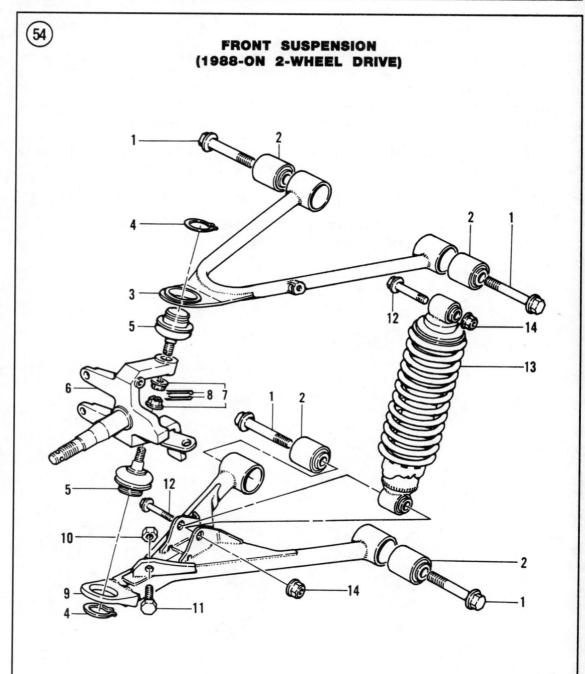

**FRONT SUSPENSION
(1988-ON 2-WHEEL DRIVE)**

1. Pivot bolt
2. Bushing
3. Upper arm
4. Circlip
5. Ball joint
6. Steering knuckle
7. Nut
8. Cotter pin
9. Lower arm
10. Nut
11. Bolt
12. Bolt
13. Shock absorber
14. Nut

Steering Knuckle Tool

Separating the control arms from the steering knuckle can be difficult because of the confined working area. However, a special removal tool can be made quite easily. The tool shown in **Figure 55** is made from a discarded motorcycle flywheel puller, a 2 1/4 in. length of 1/2-13 threaded rod and two 1/2-13 nuts. The flywheel puller is drilled and tapped to accept national coarse (USS) 1/2-13 threads. Basic dimensions for the tool are shown in **Figure 56**.

NOTE
When machining the tool body from a piece of steel, either machine it with hex or square stock or cut 2 opposite flats on a round piece of steel so that you can hold it with a wrench when using it.

Removal

1. Remove the front wheels as described in this chapter.
2A. On 1986-1987 models, remove the front brake drum and brake panel assembly as described in Chapter Thirteen.
2B. On 1988 and later models, perform the following:
   a. Remove the front hub as described in this chapter.
   b. Remove the bolt securing the brake hose to the upper control arm (**Figure 57**).
   c. Remove the inner disc cover bolts and remove the disc cover (**Figure 58**).
3. Remove the shock absorber as described in this chapter.

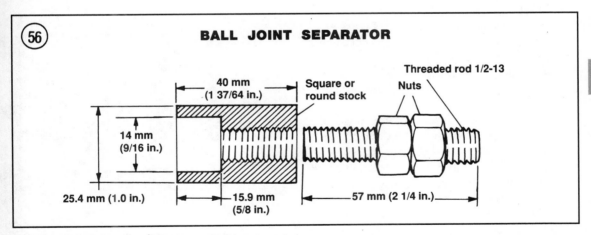

BALL JOINT SEPARATOR

40 mm (1 37/64 in.)
Square or round stock
Threaded rod 1/2-13
Nuts
14 mm (9/16 in.)
25.4 mm (1.0 in.)
15.9 mm (5/8 in.)
57 mm (2 1/4 in.)

10

4. To disconnect the tie rod from the steering knuckle:

   a. Remove the cotter pin from the tie rod ball joint stud nut. Discard the cotter pin.

   b. Remove the nut from the ball joint stud. See **Figure 47** (2-wheel drive) or **Figure 48** (4-wheel drive).

   c. Install a nut onto the tie rod stud and tap the nut to disconnect the tie rod from the steering knuckle. See **Figure 49**, typical.

5. To disconnect the upper and lower control arm ball joints from the steering knuckle:

   a. Remove the cotter pins from the upper (A, **Figure 59**) and lower (B, **Figure 59**) control arm ball joint stud nuts. Discard the cotter pins.

   b. Remove the castellated nuts that hold the ball joint in each control arm to the steering knuckle.

NOTE
*Refer to **Steering Knuckle Tool** in this section for a description of the tool used to separate the control arm ball joints from the steering knuckle.*

   c. To separate the upper control arm, attach the special tool between upper and lower control arm ball joint studs as shown in **Figure 60**—center the tool's pressure bolt against the upper control arm stud. Tighten the tool's pressure bolt to apply pressure against the ball joint stud. Continue until the ball joint pops free. See **Figure 61**.

   d. To separate the lower control arm, attach the special tool between the control arm ball joint stud and steering knuckle arm as shown in **Figure 62**—center the tool's pressure bolt against the lower control arm stud. Tighten the tool's pressure bolt to apply pressure against the ball joint stud. Continue until the ball joint pops free.

6. Remove the steering knuckle.

Inspection

1. Clean the steering knuckle in solvent and dry with compressed air.

2. Inspect the steering knuckle (**Figure 63**) for bending, thread damage, cracks or other damage.

3. Inspect the spindle portion where the front wheel bearings ride for wear or damage. A hard spill or collision may cause the spindle portion to bend or fracture. If the spindle is damaged in any way, replace the steering knuckle.

4. Check the hole at the end of the spindle where the cotter pin fits. Make sure there are no fractures or cracks leading out toward the end of the steering knuckle. If any are present, replace the steering knuckle.

Installation

1. Position the steering knuckle between the control arms. Then install the upper and lower control arm ball joint studs through the steering knuckle. See **Figure 59**.

2. Thread the castellated nuts onto the upper and lower ball joint studs. Then tighten the control arm-to-steering knuckle stud nuts to the torque specification in **Table 4**. Tighten the nuts, if necessary, to align the cotter pin holes with the nut slots.

3. To attach the tie rod to the steering knuckle:

   a. Oil the tie rod stud at the point indicated in B, **Figure 51**.

   b. Attach the tie rod to the steering knuckle. See **Figure 47**.

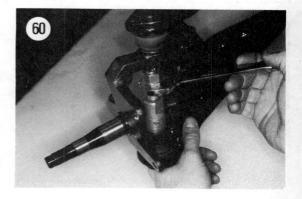

c. Install the tie rod end nut and tighten to the torque specification in **Table 4**. Tighten the nut, if necessary, to align the cotter pin hole with the nut slot.

4. Install new cotter pins through all ball joint studs. Open the cotter pins arms to lock them in place.

5. Install the shock absorber as described in this chapter.

6. Turn handlebar from side to side. Check that steering knuckle moves smoothly with no binding or roughness.

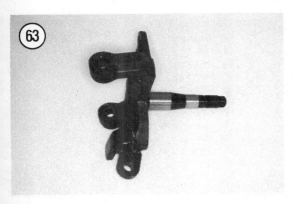

7A. On 1986-1987 models, install the front brake panel and brake drum assembly as described in Chapter Thirteen.

7B. On 1988 and later models, perform the following:

    a. Install the inner disc cover (**Figure 58**).

    b. Secure the brake hose to the upper control arm (**Figure 57**).

    c. Install the front hub as described in this chapter.

8. Install the front wheels as described in this chapter.

STEERING KNUCKLE (4-WHEEL DRIVE)

Refer to **Figure 64** when servicing the steering knuckle.

Removal

1. Remove the front wheels as described in this chapter.

2. Remove the front hub as described in this chapter.

3. Remove the inner disc cover bolts and remove the disc cover (**Figure 65**).

4. Remove the lower shock absorber mounting bolt and nut (**Figure 66**).

5. To disconnect the tie rod arm (A, **Figure 67**) from the steering knuckle:

    a. Remove the cotter pins from the tie rod arm bolts (B, **Figure 67**).

    b. Remove the tie rod arm locknuts.

    c. Loosen and remove the tie rod arm bolts.

    d. Separate the tie rod arm from the steering knuckle.

6. To disconnect the upper and lower control arm ball joints from the steering knuckle:

    a. Remove the cotter pins from the upper (**Figure 68**) and lower (**Figure 69**) control arm ball joint stud nuts. Discard the cotter pins.

    b. Remove the upper control arm stud nut.

    c. Remove the lower control arm stud nut, washer and bolt.

    d. Tap the steering knuckle to separate it from the upper and lower control arms.

7. Remove the steering knuckle.

10

⑭

STEERING KNUCKLE AND CONTROL ARMS
(4-WHEEL DRIVE)

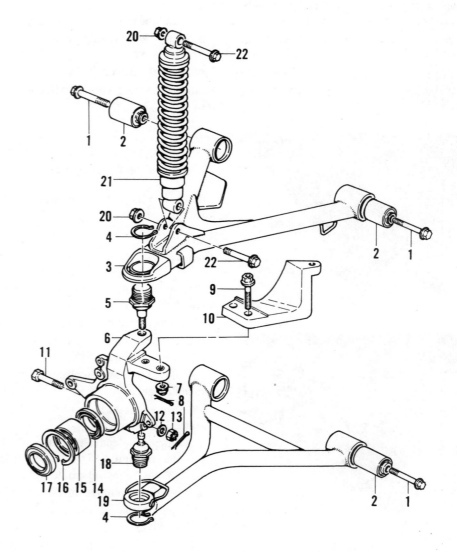

1. Bolt
2. Bushing
3. Upper arm
4. Circlip
5. Upper ball joint
6. Steering knuckle
7. Nut
8. Cotter pin
9. Bolt
10. Tie rod arm
11. Bolt

12. Washer
13. Nut
14. Oil seal
15. Bearing
16. Circlip
17. Oil seal
18. Lower ball joint
19. Lower arm
20. Nut
21. Shock absorber
22. Bolt

Inspection

1. Clean the steering knuckle in solvent and dry with compressed air.

2. Inspect the steering knuckle for bending, thread damage, cracks or other damage.

3. Turn the bearing (15, **Figure 64**) inner race with your finger. It should turn smoothly and quietly with no signs of roughness or damage. If necessary, replace the bearing as described in this chapter.

4. Check the bearing seals for tearing or damage. If the seals are damaged, or if the bearing is leaking, replace the bearing as described in this chapter. Do not attempt to repack the bearing.

5. Inspect the inner (14, **Figure 64**) and outer (17, **Figure 64**) oil seals. Replace damaged oil seals as described in this chapter.

Bearing and Oil Seal Replacement

A double-sealed bearing is used.

> *NOTE*
> *The inner and outer oil seals are different. Identify the oil seals prior to removing them so the new seals can be correctly installed.*

1. Remove the inner and outer oil seals. Discard both oil seals as new ones must be installed.

2. Remove the circlip (16, **Figure 64**) from the groove in the steering knuckle.

3. Press or drive the bearing out of the steering knuckle. Remove the bearing from the circlip side of the steering knuckle.

> *NOTE*
> *Install the bearing with the manufacturers name and size code facing out.*

10

4. Tap or press the bearing squarely into the steering knuckle. Use a socket that matches the outer bearing race diameter. Do not tap on the inner race or the bearing might be damaged. Make sure the bearing is completely seated so the circlip can be installed above it.

5. Install the circlip in the steering knuckle groove. Make sure the circlip is fully seated in the groove.

6. Pack the lip of each oil seal with waterproof bearing grease prior to installation.

NOTE
Install both oil seals with their closed side facing out.

7. Press in the inner oil seal (14, **Figure 64**) until its outer surface is flush with the steering knuckle bearing bore surface.

8. Press in the outer oil seal (17, **Figure 64**) until its outer surface is flush with the steering knuckle bearing bore surface.

Installation

1. Position the steering knuckle through the front axle and between the control arms. Then install the upper and lower control arm ball joint studs through the steering knuckle. See **Figure 70**.

2. Thread the nut onto the upper ball joint stud (**Figure 68**). Then tighten the upper control arm-to-steering knuckle stud nut to the torque specification in **Table 5**. Tighten the nut, if necessary, to align the cotter pin hole with the nut slot.

3. Install the lower control arm bolt through the front side of the steering knuckle. Then install the washer and nut (**Figure 69**). Tighten the lower control arm-to-steering knuckle bolt and nut to the torque specification in **Table 5**. Tighten the nut, if necessary, to align the cotter pin hole with the nut slot.

4. To attach the tie rod arm (A, **Figure 67**) to the steering knuckle:

   a. Position the tie rod arm onto the steering knuckle and align both sets of holes.

   b. Apply Loctite 242 (blue) to the tie rod arm bolts and thread the bolts (B, **Figure 67**) into the steering knuckle. Tighten the tie rod arm bolts to the torque specification in **Table 5**.

   c. Install the tie rod arm locknuts and tighten to the torque specification in **Table 5**. Tighten the

nuts, if necessary, to align the cotter pin holes with the nut slots.

5. Install new cotter pins through all ball joint studs and through both tie rod arm locknuts. Open the cotter pin ends to lock them in place.

6. Install the lower shock absorber bolt and nut (**Figure 66**) and tighten to the torque specification in **Table 5**.

7. Turn handlebar from side to side, and make sure the steering knuckle moves smoothly with no binding or roughness.

8. Install the inner disc cover (**Figure 65**).

9. Install the front hub as described in this chapter.

10. Install the front wheels as described in this chapter.

CONTROL ARMS

Refer to the exploded view drawing for your model when servicing the control arms:

   a. **Figure 71**: 1986-1987 2-wheel drive.

   b. **Figure 72**: 1988-on 2-wheel drive.

   c. **Figure 64**: 4-wheel drive.

Removal/Installation

1. Disconnect the control arm(s) from the steering knuckle as described under *Steering Knuckle* for 2- or 4-wheel drive models in this chapter.

2. Remove the nut from each pivot bolt that secures the upper control arm to the frame. Remove the upper control arm assembly. See **Figure 73** (2-wheel drive) or **Figure 74** (4-wheel drive). On 1986-1987 models, remove the thrust covers (2, **Figure 71**) and shim (3).

(70)

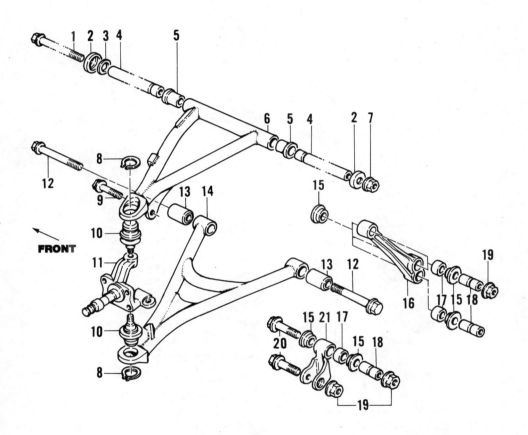

**FRONT SUSPENSION
(1986-1987 2-WHEEL DRIVE)**

FRONT

10

1. Pivot bolt	13. Bushing
2. Thrust cover	14. Lower arm
3. Shim	15. Oil seal
4. Collar	16. Upper suspension link
5. Bushing	17. Bushing
6. Upper arm	18. Collar
7. Nut	19. Nut
8. Circlip	20. Pivot bolt
9. Bolt	21. Lower suspension link
10. Ball joint	
11. Steering knuckle	
12. Pivot bolt	

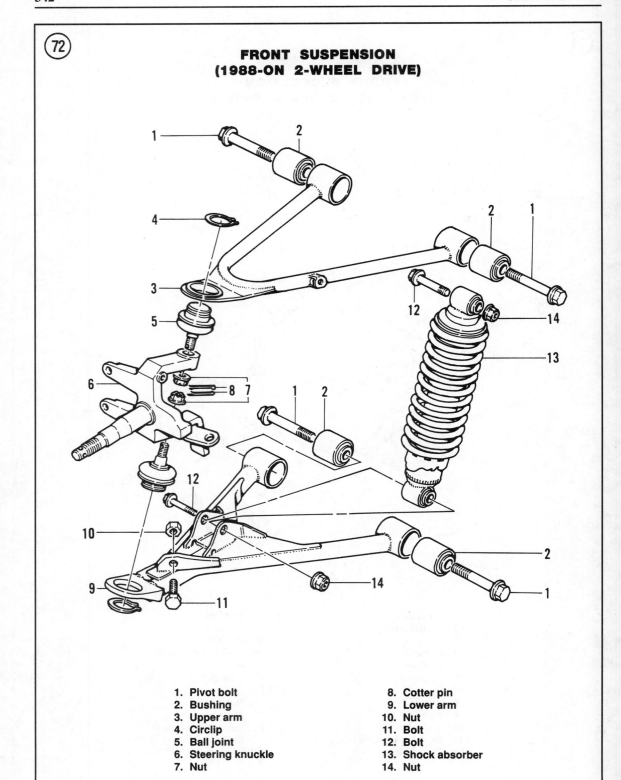

**FRONT SUSPENSION
(1988-ON 2-WHEEL DRIVE)**

1. Pivot bolt
2. Bushing
3. Upper arm
4. Circlip
5. Ball joint
6. Steering knuckle
7. Nut

8. Cotter pin
9. Lower arm
10. Nut
11. Bolt
12. Bolt
13. Shock absorber
14. Nut

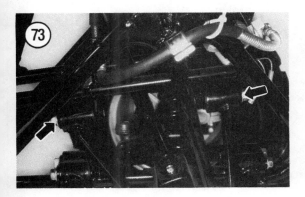

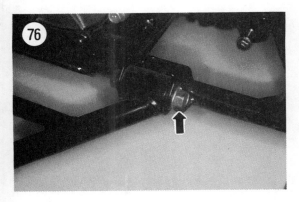

3. Remove the nut from each pivot bolt that secures the lower control arm to the frame. Remove the upper control arm assembly. See **Figure 75** (2-wheel drive) or **Figure 76** (4-wheel drive).

4. On 1986-1987 2-wheel drive models, remove the upper and lower suspension link assembly (**Figure 71**).

5. Install by reversing these removal steps, noting the following.

6. Lubricate the collars and pivot bolts with water-proof grease.

7. On 4-wheel drive models, install the control arms so that the "F" mark on each arm faces up and points forward.

8. Tighten the upper and lower control arm pivot bolts to the torque specification in **Table 4** or **Table 5**.

9. Raise and lower both control arms by hand. Control arms should pivot smoothly with no roughness or binding.

Control Arm
Cleaning and Inspection

> *NOTE*
> *Do not intermix the pivot bolts, nuts, bushings and thrust covers when disassembling and cleaning the upper and lower control arms. Separate the parts so that they can be installed in their original mounting positions.*

1. On 1986-1987 2-wheel drive models, remove the thrust covers, shim and collar from the upper control arm.

> *NOTE*
> *When cleaning the control arms, do not wash the ball joints (**Figure 77**) in sol-*

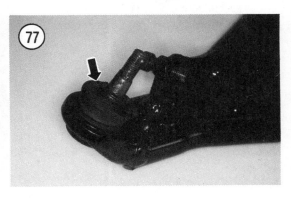

10

vent. Handle the ball joints carefully to avoid contaminating the grease or damaging them.

2. Clean parts in solvent and dry with compressed air.

3. Inspect both control arms for cracks, fractures and dents. If damage is noted, replace the control arm. Never try to straighten a damaged or dented control arm as it cannot be straightened properly. See **Figure 78**, typical.

4. Inspect each bushing (**Figure 79**) for excessive wear or damage. Replace bushings as described in Step 5.

5A. To replace the upper control arm bushings on 1986-1987 models:

   a. Remove the collar from the control arm.

   b. Support the control arm and drive or press out the bushing. Repeat this step for each bushing.

   c. Clean the control arm bushing bores in solvent and dry thoroughly. Remove all rust and dirt residue.

   d. Support the control arm and the press bushing into the bore until the bushing shoulder bottoms.

5B. To replace the bushings (**Figure 79**) on all other models and control arms:

   a. Support the control arm and drive or press out the bushing. Repeat this step for each bushing.

   b. Clean the control arm bushing bores in solvent and dry thoroughly. Remove all rust and dirt residue.

   c. Support the control arm and press the bushing into the bore. Center the bushing in the bore.

6. On 1986-1987 models, inspect the upper control arm and both suspension link collars for severe wear or damage. Replace if necessary.

7. Inspect pivot bolts for bending or other damage. Replace damaged bolts.

8. Inspect ball joints (**Figure 77**) as described under *Ball Joint Inspection and Replacement* in this chapter.

Ball Joint
Inspection and Replacement

1. Inspect the ball joint rubber boot (**Figure 77**). The swivel joint is packed with grease. If the rubber boot or ball joint is damaged, replace the ball joint as follows.

2. Remove the circlip (**Figure 80**).

3. Unscrew and remove the ball joint from the control arm.

4. Clean the control arm threads.

5A. On 2-wheel drive models, hand thread the ball joint into the control arm. Then tighten the ball joint securely.

5B. On 4-wheel drive models, hand thread the ball joint into the control arm. Then torque the ball joint to the torque specification in **Table 5**.

6. Install the circlip (**Figure 80**).

STEERING STOPPER ADJUSTMENT (2-WHEEL DRIVE)

1. Turn the handlebar to the left until the edge of the steering shaft stop bracket touches the frame bracket (at the top of the steering shaft).

2. Loosen the steering knuckle stopper bolt (**Figure 81**) and turn the stopper bolt until its head just touches the bracket on the lower suspension arm. Tighten the locknut.

3. Turn the handlebar to the right and repeat Step 2.

STEERING STOPPER ADJUSTMENT (4-WHEEL DRIVE)

1. Turn the handlebar all the way to the left.

2. With the tie rod arm stopper against the control arm stopper, measure the clearance between the stopper bolt and the frame stopper. The clearance must be less than 1.0 mm (0.039 in.). See **Figure 82**.

3. To correct the clearance, add or subtract shims on the steering stopper bolt (**Figure 82**).

4. Repeat Steps 1-3 for the right-hand side.

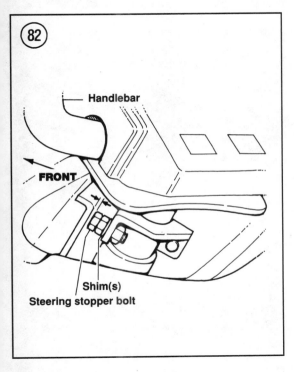

Handlebar

FRONT

Shim(s)

Steering stopper bolt

SHOCK ABSORBER

Refer to the exploded view drawing for your model when servicing the shock absorbers:

a. **Figure 71**: 1986-1987 2-wheel drive.

b. **Figure 72**: 1988-on 2-wheel drive.

c. **Figure 64**: 4-wheel drive.

Spring Preload Adjustment

The front shock absorber springs are provided with 3 (4-wheel drive) or 5 (2-wheel drive) preload positions. See **Figure 83**, typical. The No. 1 position is soft and the No. 3 (4-wheel drive) or No. 5 (2-wheel drive) position is hard. The spring preload can be changed by rotating the cam at the end of the spring. Set both front shock absorbers to the same preload position.

Removal/Installation

1. Remove the front wheel(s) as described in this chapter.

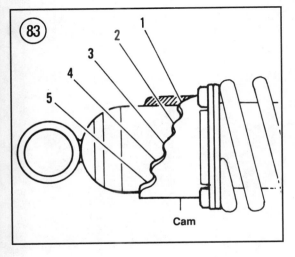

Cam

10

2. Remove the upper and lower shock absorber mounting nuts and bolts and remove the shock absorber. See **Figure 84** and **Figure 85**, typical.

3. Install by reversing these removal steps, while noting the following.

4. Inspect each damper unit (**Figure 86**) for fluid leakage or other damage. Replace the shock if leakage is found.

> *WARNING*
> *Do not attempt to disassemble the damper unit. Disassembly can release high-pressure gas and cause personal injury.*

5. Clean the upper and lower mounting bolts and nuts in solvent and dry thoroughly.

6. Install by reversing these removal steps, noting the following.

7. Apply a waterproof grease to the upper and lower mounting bolts prior to installation.

8. Tighten the upper and lower shock mounting bolts and nuts to the torque specification in **Table 4** or **Table 5**.

9. Repeat for the other side as required.

Shock Spring Replacement

The shock is spring-controlled and hydraulically damped. The shock damper unit is sealed and cannot be serviced. Service is limited to removal and replacement of the damper unit, spring and mounting bushings.

Kawasaki does not list spring free length specifications for the front shock absorbers.

1. Mount the lower shock mount in a vise with soft jaws and turn the spring adjuster (**Figure 87**) to its softest position.

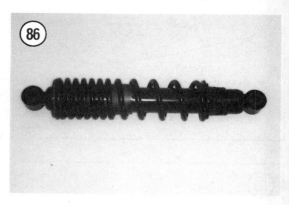

> *WARNING*
> *Do not remove the spring without a spring compressor. The spring is under considerable pressure and may fly off and cause injury.*

2. Mount a spring compressor onto the shock absorber and compress the spring. Then remove the upper spring seat (**Figure 88**) and remove the spring.

> *NOTE*
> *The damper unit cannot be rebuilt; it must be replaced as a unit.*

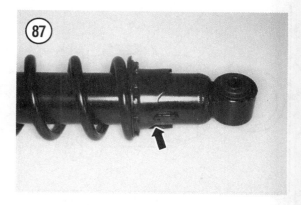

3. Check the damper unit for leakage and make sure the damper rod is straight. Replace the damper unit if necessary.

4. Assemble the shock by reversing these steps, while noting the following.

5. If installing progressive rate springs, install the spring with closer wound coils toward the top of the shock.

6. Make sure the spring seat is properly seated in the spring (**Figure 88**).

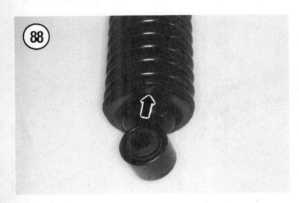

7. Turn the spring adjuster to adjust spring preload (**Figure 87**). Adjust both shocks to the same spring preload setting.

Shock Bushing Replacement

1. Check the shock bushings (**Figure 89**) for deterioration, severe wear or other damage. If necessary, replace bushings as follows:

2. Support damper unit in a press and press out the damaged bushing.

3. Clean shock bushing bore to remove dirt, rust and other debris.

4. Press in the new bushing until its outer surface is flush with the bushing bore inside surface as shown in **Figure 89**.

TIRES AND WHEELS

All models are equipped with tubeless, low pressure tires (**Figure 90**) designed specifically for off-road use only. Rapid tire wear will occur if the vehicle is ridden on paved surfaces.

> *CAUTION*
> *Do not overinflate the stock tires as they will be permanently distorted and damaged. If overinflated they will bulge out similar to an inner tube that is not within the constraints of a tire and **will not** return to their original contour.*

Tire Changing

The front and rear tire rims used on all models are of the 1-piece type and have a very deep built-in ridge to keep the tire bead seated on the rim under severe riding conditions. Unfortunately it also tends to keep the tire on the rim during tire removal as well.

To change the tires on your Kawasaki, the following tools are required:

  a. Bead breaker tool.

  b. Tire irons.

1. Remove the valve stem cap and core and deflate the tire. Do not reinstall the core at this time.

2. Lubricate the tire bead and rim flanges with a liquid dish detergent or any rubber lubricant. Press the tire sidewall/bead down to allow the liquid to run into and around the bead area. Also apply lubricant to the area where the bead breaker arm will come in contact with the tire sidewall.

10

⑨¹

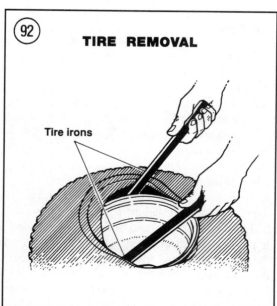

⁹² **TIRE REMOVAL**

Tire irons

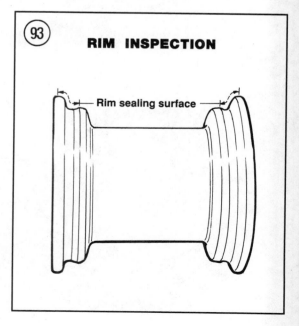

⁹³ **RIM INSPECTION**

Rim sealing surface

3. Position the wheel into the bead breaker tool (**Figure 91**).

4. Slowly work the bead breaker, making sure the tool is up against the inside of the rim, and force the tire bead away from the rim.

5. Using your hands, press down on the tire on either side of the tool and try to break the rest of the bead free from the rim.

6. If the rest of the tire bead cannot be broken loose by hand, raise the tool, rotate the tire/rim assembly and repeat Steps 4 and 5 until the entire bead is broken loose from the rim.

7. Turn the wheel over and repeat steps 2-6 to break the opposite side loose.

> *CAUTION*
> *When using tire irons in the following steps, work carefully so you do not damage the tire or rim sealing surfaces. Damage to these areas may cause an air leak.*

8. Lubricate the tire bead and rim flanges as described in Step 2. Then pry the bead over the rim with 2 tire irons as shown in **Figure 92**. Take small "bites" with the tire irons.

9. When the top tire bead is free, lift the second bead up into the center rim well and remove it as described in Step 8.

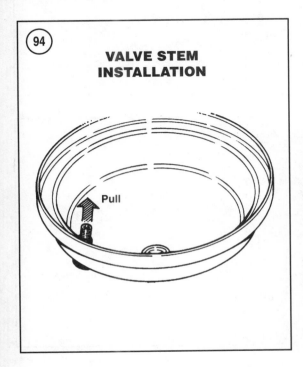

94

VALVE STEM INSTALLATION

Pull

10. Inspect the sealing surface on both sides of the rim (**Figure 93**). If the rim has been severely hit, it will probably leak air.

11. To replace the air valve, perform the following:

    a. Support the rim and pull the valve stem out of the rim. Discard the valve stem.

    b. Lubricate the new valve stem with soap and water.

    c. Pull the new valve stem into the rim, from the inside out, until it snaps in place (**Figure 94**).

> *NOTE*
> *There are special tools available for installing valve stems into the rims. See your dealer or an automotive parts store.*

12. Inspect the tire for cuts, tears, abrasions or any other defects.

13. Wipe the tire beads and rims free of any lubricant agent used in Step 2.

14. Apply clean water to the rim flanges, tire rim beads and outer rim.

> *NOTE*
> *Use only clean water and make sure the rim flange is clean. Wipe with a lint-free cloth prior to wetting down the tire.*

15. The tire tread on the factory equipped tires, for both the front and rear wheels, is directional. Position the tire onto the rim so the rotation arrow on the side wall (**Figure 95**) is pointing in the correct direction of wheel rotation.

16. Install the tire onto the rim starting with the side opposite the valve stem. Push the first bead over the

10

95

rim flange. Force the bead into the center of the rim to help installation (**Figure 96**).

17. Install the rest of the bead with tire irons (**Figure 97**).

18. Repeat to install the second bead onto the rim.

19. Install the valve stem core.

> *WARNING*
> *Do not inflate the tire past the maximum inflation pressure (for seating tires) listed in **Table 3**. Doing so can explode the tire and cause severe personal injury.*

20. Apply tire mounting lubricant or a liquid dish detergent to the tire bead and inflate the tire to the maximum tire pressure (for seating tires) listed in **Table 3**.

21. Make sure the rim lines on both sides of the tire are parallel with the rim flanges as shown in **Figure 98**. If the rim flanges are not parallel, deflate the tire and break the bead. Then lubricate the tire bead and reinflate the tire.

> *NOTE*
> *If there are air bubbles visible around the tire, the tire bead is leaking.*

22. Deflate the tire to the operating tire pressure listed in **Table 3**.

23. Install the air valve cap.

Cold Patch Repair

The rubber plug type of repair is recommended only for an emergency repair, or until the tire can be patched correctly with the cold patch method.

Use the manufacturer's instructions for the tire repair kit you are using. If there are no instructions, use the following procedure.

1. Remove the tire as described in this chapter.

2. Prior to removing the object that punctured the tire, mark the location of the puncture with chalk or crayon on the outside of the tire. Remove the object (**Figure 99**).

3. On the inside of the tire, roughen an area around the hole slightly larger than the patch (**Figure 100**). Use the cap from the tire repair kit or pocket knife. Do not scrape too vigorously or you may cause additional damage.

TIRE INSTALLATION

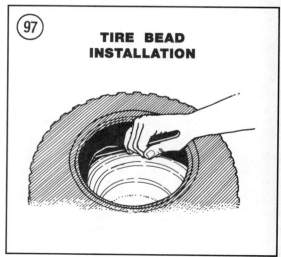

TIRE BEAD INSTALLATION

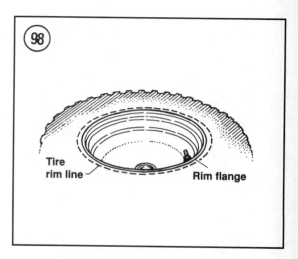

Tire rim line — Rim flange

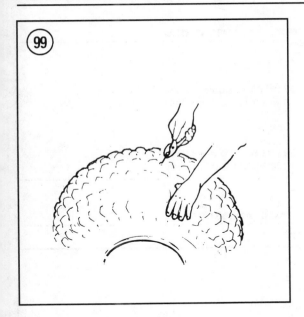

4. Clean the area with a nonflammable solvent. Do not use an oil base solvent as it leaves a residue rendering the patch useless.

5. Apply a small amount of special cement to the puncture and spread it with your finger.

6. Allow the cement to dry until tacky—usually 30 seconds or so is sufficient.

7. Remove the backing from the patch.

CAUTION
Do not touch the newly exposed rubber with your fingers or the patch will not stick firmly.

8. Center the patch over the hole. Hold the patch firmly in place for about 30 seconds to allow the cement to dry. If you have a roller, use it to help press the patch into place (**Figure 101**).

9. Dust the area with talcum powder.

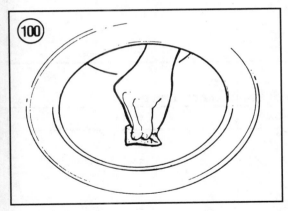

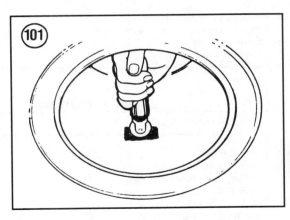

Table 1 FRONT SUSPENSION AND STEERING GENERAL SPECIFICATIONS

Caster (rake angle)	
2-wheel drive	
1986-1987	4°
1988-on	3°
4-wheel drive	1°
Camber	
2-wheel drive	
1986-1987	0.8°
1988-on	1.0°
4-wheel drive	0°
Front suspension	
Type	**Double wishbone**
Wheel travel	
2-wheel drive	
1986-1987	115 mm (4.5 in.)
1988-on	125 mm (4.9 in.)
4-wheel drive	110 mm (4.3 in.)

Table 2 TIRE AND WHEEL SPECIFICATIONS

Front tire	
Type	Tubeless
Size/Manufacturer	
2-wheel drive	22 × 9.00-10/Dunlop KT761
4-wheel drive	AT24 × 8-11/Dunlop KT962
Rear tire	
Type	Tubeless
Size	
2-wheel drive	24 × 11.00-10/Dunlop KT761
4-wheel drive	AT24 × 10-11/Dunlop KT962

Table 3 TIRE INFLATION PRESSURE

	kPa	psi
Operating tire pressure (cold)		
2-wheel drive		
Front and rear	21	3
4-wheel drive		
Front	35	5
Rear	28	4
Maximum tire pressure		
(cold, to seat beads when installing tire)		
2-wheel drive	137	20
4-wheel drive	250	36

Table 4 TIGHTENING TORQUES—2-WHEEL DRIVE

	N•m	ft.-lb.
Wheel nuts	34	25
Front hub nut	34	25
Handlebar holder bolts	20	15
Steering stem bearing clamp		
1986-1987 (nuts)	20	15
1988-on (bolts)	25	18
Steering shaft bearing nut	29	21
Steering shaft bottom bolts	20	15
Tie rod end nuts	41	30
Tie rod adjusting sleeve locknuts		
1986-1987	29	21
1988-on	27	20
Control arm-to-steering knuckle stud nuts	41	30
Front master cylinder clamp bolts		
1986-1987	11	97 in.-lb.
1988-on	8.8	78 in.-lb.
Shock absorber nuts and bolts	34	25
Ball joints	Not specified	
Control arm pivot bolts	88	65

Table 5 TIGHTENING TORQUES—4-WHEEL DRIVE

	N•m	ft.-lb.
Wheel nuts	34	25
Front hub nut	145	107
Handlebar holder bolts	20	15
(continued)		

Table 5 TIGHTENING TORQUES—4-WHEEL DRIVE (continued)

	N·m	ft.-lb.
Steering stopper nut	8.8	78 in.-lb.
Steering stem bearing clamp bolts	25	18
Steering shaft bearing nut	29	21
Steering shaft bottom bolts	20	15
Tie rod end nuts	41	30
Tie rod adjusting sleeve locknuts	27	20
Tie rod arm		
Bolts	49	36
Locknuts	34	25
Control arm-to-steering knuckle	52	38
Front master cylinder clamp bolts		
1986-1987	11	97 in.-lb.
1988-on	8.8	78 in.-lb.
Shock absorber bolts and nuts	34	25
Ball joints	49	36
Control arm pivot bolts	88	65

10

FRONT DRIVE MECHANISM FOUR-WHEEL DRIVE

This chapter contains repair and replacement procedures for the front drive mechanism. This includes the front propeller shaft, front axles and front final gear case.

Table 1 lists tightening torques for the front drive mechanism and sub-transmission assembly. **Table 1** is found at the end of this chapter.

FRONT PROPELLER SHAFT

The front propeller shaft (**Figure 1**) connects the front final gear case to the sub-transmission.

Removal

1. Park the vehicle on a level surface and set the parking brake.
2. Remove the shift lever (A, **Figure 2**).
3. Remove the front propeller shaft cover mounting bolts and remove the cover (B, **Figure 2**).
4. Remove the circlip (A, **Figure 3**) from the groove in the propeller shaft sliding joint, then slide the circlip down the propeller shaft.

5. Pull the front propeller shaft coupling (B, **Figure 3**) back and disconnect it from the universal joint. The spring installed inside the coupling will come off with the universal joint.
6. Pull the propeller shaft (C, **Figure 3**) out of the sub-transmission and remove it from the vehicle.
7. Remove the universal joints. See **Figure 4** (front) and **Figure 5** (rear).
8. Install by reversing these removal steps, noting the following.
9. Perform the *Inspection* procedures.
10. Apply new grease to the front propeller shaft, propeller shaft joint and universal joint splines.
11. Install a new front propeller shaft circlip.
12. Align the yoke angle of the front propeller shaft and output shaft when sliding the coupling into position.

Inspection

1. Wipe the old grease off the propeller shaft, propeller shaft joint and universal joint splines.

①

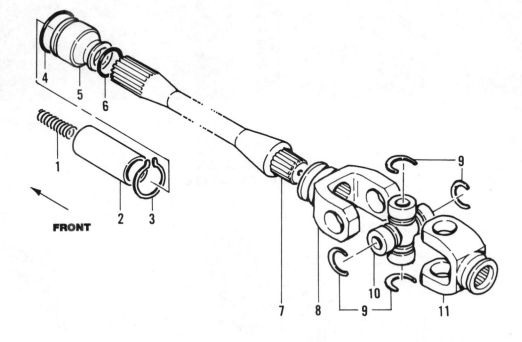

**FRONT PROPELLER SHAFT
(4-WHEEL DRIVE)**

FRONT

1. Spring
2. Coupling
3. Circlip
4. O-ring
5. Boot
6. O-ring

7. Propeller shaft
8. Yoke
9. Snap ring
10. Spider
11. Yoke

11

②

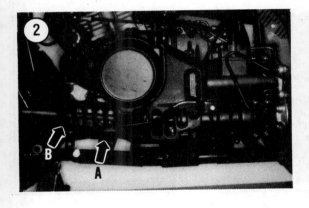

③

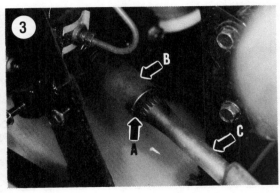

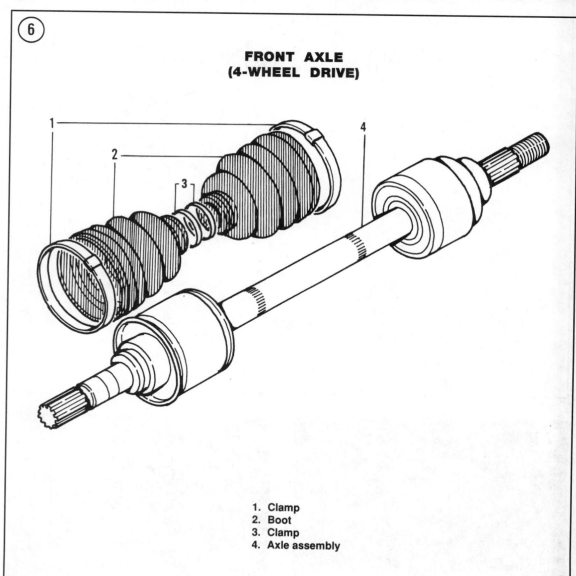

**FRONT AXLE
(4-WHEEL DRIVE)**

1. Clamp
2. Boot
3. Clamp
4. Axle assembly

2. Inspect the splines for severe wear or damage. Replace any component with damaged splines.

3. Replace a weak or damaged coupling spring.

FRONT AXLE

Figure 6 is an exploded view of the left- and right-hand front axles.

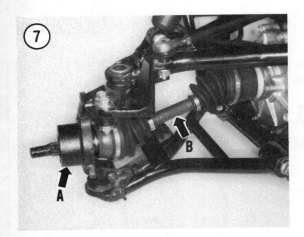

Removal/Installation

1. Remove the steering knuckle (A, **Figure 7**) as described in Chapter Ten.

2. Remove the bolts that hold the front axle cap to the front final gear case. See **Figure 8** (left-hand) or **Figure 9** (right-hand).

> *CAUTION*
> *Handle the front axle carefully to prevent the boots from catching on an object and tearing.*

3. Pull the front axle (B, **Figure 7**) out of the front final gear case and remove it from the vehicle.

4. Remove the spacer (**Figure 10**) from inside the recess in the front final gear case.

5. Install by reversing these removal steps, noting the following.

6. Install the spacer into the recess in the front final gear case.

7. Tighten the front axle cap bolts to the torque specification in **Table 1**.

8. Install the steering knuckle as described in Chapter Ten.

Inspection

> *NOTE*
> *The axle boots are subjected to much abuse. Damaged boots allow dirt, mud and moisture to enter the boot and contaminate the grease and bearing.*

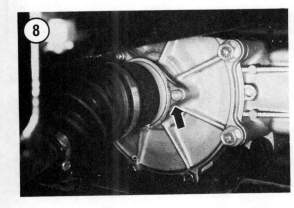

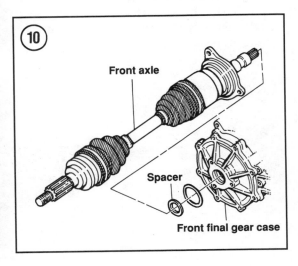

Front axle

Spacer

Front final gear case

1. Inspect the rubber boots (A, **Figure 11**) for wear, cuts or damage. Replace if necessary as described under *Front Axle Boot Replacement* in this chapter.

2. Move each end of the drive shaft in a circular motion and check the constant velocity joints for excessive wear or play.

Front Axle Boots
Removal

It is not possible to replace the inboard or outboard constant velocity joints as these items are not available separately. If either joint is damaged or if the front axle is damaged, replace the front axle assembly. The inboard joint, however, can be removed to allow replacement of the axle boots.

The front axle boot replacement kit includes both rubber boots, 4 new clamps and grease.

Refer to **Figure 6** for this procedure.

1. Remove the front axle as described in this chapter.

2. Open the boot band clamps (B, **Figure 11**) on the inboard joint, then remove boot band clamps. Discard the boot band. Open the clamps with a screwdriver.

3. Carefully slide the boot (A, **Figure 12**) onto the front axle and off the inboard joint.

4. Wipe out all of the grease within the inboard joint cavity (B, **Figure 12**).

5. Remove the retaining ring (**Figure 13**) from the inboard joint.

6. Remove the inboard joint (**Figure 14**).

7. Remove the circlip (**Figure 15**) and slide off the bearing assembly (**Figure 16**). Be careful not to drop any of the steel balls from the bearing cage.

8. Slide the inboard boot off the front axle and discard the boot band clamp.

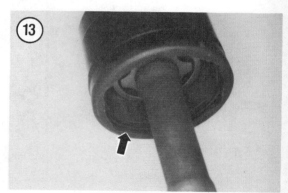

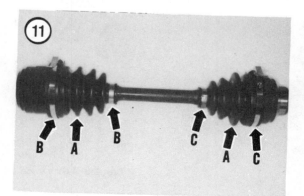

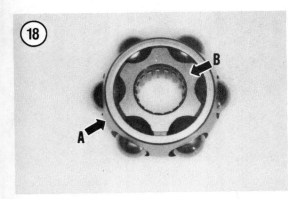

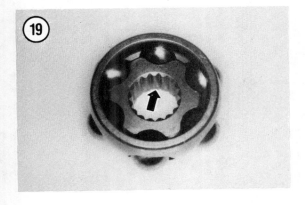

NOTE
To remove the outboard boot, continue with Step 9.

9. Open the clamps (C, **Figure 11**) on the outboard joint, then remove clamp. Discard the boot band as it cannot be reused.

10. Slide the outboard boot off the front axle and discard clamp.

11. Inspect the front axle as described in this chapter.

Inspection

Refer to **Figure 6** for this procedure.

CAUTION
Before cleaning the rubber boots in solvent, make sure the solvent will not damage rubber products. Gasoline and other chemicals will cause the rubber to deteriorate, destroying the boot.

1. Clean the bearing assembly in solvent. Dry the bearings with compressed air or allow to air dry.

2. Inspect the steel balls (**Figure 17**), bearing case (A, **Figure 18**) and the bearing race (B, **Figure 18**) for wear.

3. Check the bearing race inner splines (**Figure 19**) for wear or damage.

4. Clean the inboard joint in solvent and dry thoroughly.

5. Inspect the inboard joint ball guides (A, **Figure 20**) for wear or damage.

6. Inspect the inboard joint retaining ring groove (B, **Figure 20**) for wear or damage.

11

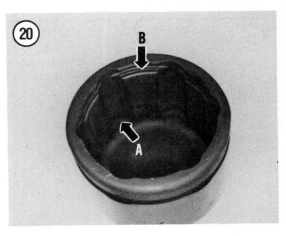

7. Inspect the splines on the axle and inboard joint (A, **Figure 21**) wear or damage.

8. Check the circlip groove (B, **Figure 21**) in the inboard joint shaft for excessive wear or damage.

9. Inspect the exterior of the inboard joint (**Figure 22**) for cracks or damage.

10. Check the outboard joint for excessive play or noise (**Figure 23**) by moving the axle in a circular direction.

11. Inspect the front axle for bending, wear or damage.

12. Inspect the inner end splines, the outer end splines and the front hub cotter pin hole for wear or damage.

13. Replace the front axle assembly if any of the components are worn or damaged. Individual replacement parts for the front axle, other than the rubber boots and clamps, are not available.

Front Axle Boots
Installation

Before installing the rubber boots, note the following:

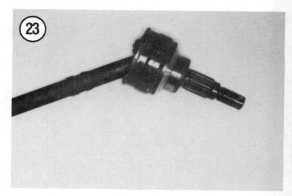

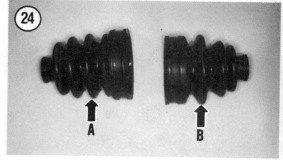

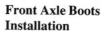

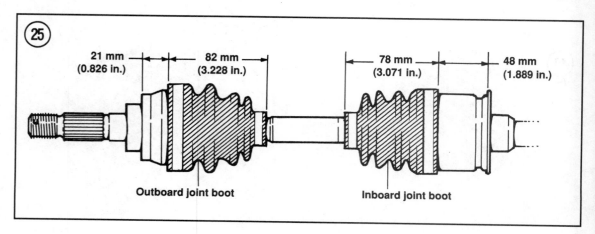

Outboard joint boot   Inboard joint boot

21 mm (0.826 in.)   82 mm (3.228 in.)   78 mm (3.071 in.)   48 mm (1.889 in.)

a. The inboard and outboard rubber boots (A and B, **Figure 24**) are identical and can be installed on either side.

b. A special grease is supplied with the Kawasaki replacement boot kit. When grease is called for in the following steps, use this grease. If you did not buy a replacement boot kit, use molybdenum disulfide grease.

c. Do not assemble the bearing assembly until the parts are clean and dry. The bearing assembly must be dry when greasing it.

Refer to **Figure 6** for this procedure.

1. If the outboard boot was removed, install a new boot onto the front axle. Position the boot to the dimensions shown in **Figure 25**.

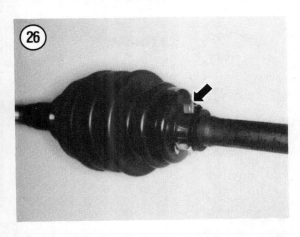

2. Install 2 new small boot clamps onto the front axle.

3. Install the inboard boot and move the small boot clamp onto the boot (**Figure 26**). Do not lock the boot band at this time.

4. If the inboard bearing assembly (**Figure 27**) was disassembled, assemble the bearing as follows:

a. Position the bearing race with the wide inner diameter (I.D.) going on first and install the race into the bearing case. Align the steel ball receptacles in both parts.

b. Install the steel balls into their receptacles in the bearing case.

c. Pack the bearing assembly with grease included in the boot replacement kit. Grease will help hold the steel balls in place.

5. Align the bearing assembly, with the *small end* of the bearing going on first, and install the bearing onto the front axle (**Figure 16**).

6. Push the bearing assembly on until it stops, then install the circlip (**Figure 27**) into the groove in the shaft. Make sure the circlip is fully seated in the groove.

7. Apply a liberal amount of grease to the bearing assembly (**Figure 28**). Work the grease between the balls, race, and case. Check for voids and fill with grease.

8. Apply a liberal amount of grease to the inner surfaces of the inboard joint.

9. Install the inboard joint over the bearing assembly (**Figure 27**) and install the retaining ring (**Figure 27**). Make sure the retaining ring is fully seated in the groove. Position the retaining ring so that its

11

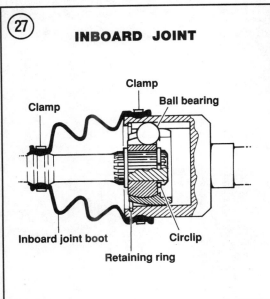

INBOARD JOINT

Clamp

Clamp

Ball bearing

Inboard joint boot

Circlip

Retaining ring

opening aligns with one of the outer race projections as shown in **Figure 29**.

10. After the retaining ring is in place, fill the inboard joint cavity behind the bearing assembly with grease; see B, **Figure 12**.

11. Pack each boot with the following amounts of grease:

　　a. Inboard joint: 25 grams (0.87 oz.)

　　b. Outboard joint: 40 grams (1.4 oz.)

12. Move the inboard boot over the inboard joint (**Figure 30**).

13. Move the outboard boot over the outboard joint.

14. Position the inboard and outboard boots on the axle to the dimensions shown in **Figure 25**.

15. Crack open the large end of each boot to equalize the air pressure inside the boots.

16. Move the small boot clamps onto each boot as shown in **Figure 31**. Bend down the tab on the boot band and secure the tab with the locking clips (**Figure 32**). If necessary, tap the clips with a plastic hammer. Make sure they are locked in place.

17. Install the large boot clamps onto each boot. Make sure the boots are not twisted on the axle.

> *CAUTION*
> *Make sure the inboard joint does not move while installing the boot clamps. The boot dimensions set in Step 14 must be maintained. This dimension is critical to avoid undue stress on the rubber boots after the front axle is installed and the vehicle is run.*

18. Refer to **Figure 33** and secure both large boot clamps. Bend down the tab (**Figure 34**) on the boot clamps and secure the tab with the locking clips, then tap them with a plastic hammer. Make sure they are locked in place (**Figure 35**).

19. Apply grease to the end of the axle splines.

20. Install the front axle as described in this chapter.

FRONT FINAL GEAR CASE

Removal

Refer to **Figure 36** for this procedure.

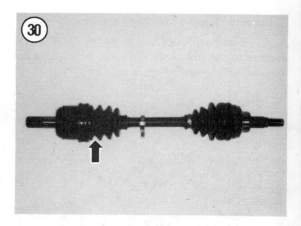

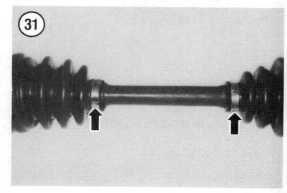

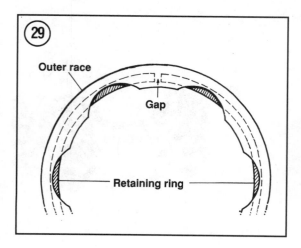

1. Drain the oil from the front final gear case as described in Chapter Three.

2. Remove the front propeller shaft as described in this chapter.

3. Remove the left- and right-hand front axles as described in this chapter.

4. Remove the skid plate (**Figure 37**).

5. Place a small jack underneath the front final gear case. Place a block of wood on top of the jack.

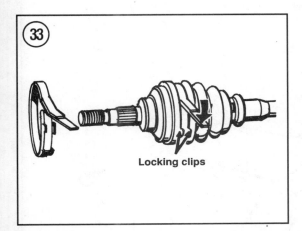

Locking clips

6. Loosen, but do not remove, the left- and right-hand suspension arm pivot bolts. See A, **Figure 38**.

7. Remove the nuts and bolts securing the front final gear case to the frame. See B and C, **Figure 38** and **Figure 39**.

8. Disconnect the vent hose from the front final gear case.

9. Remove the front final gear case from the vehicles right-hand side.

10. Installation is the reverse of these removal steps. Note the following.

11. Apply molybdenum disulfide grease to the splines on each shaft.

12. Position the front final gear case in the frame.

13. Reconnect the vent hose to the gear case.

14. Install, but do not tighten, the gear case bolts and nuts. Apply a non-permanent thread locking compound to the 2 case bolts (B, **Figure 38**) on the front side.

15. Tighten the suspension arm pivot bolts to the torque specification in **Table 1**.

16. Tighten the front final gear case mounting bolts to the torque specification in **Table 1**.

17. Fill the front final gear case with the recommended type and quantity of oil as described in Chapter Three.

Disassembly/Inspection/Assembly

The front final gear case requires a number of special Kawasaki special tools for disassembly and reassembly. The price of these tools could be more than the cost of most repairs or seal replacement by a dealer.

1. Check the entire front final drive unit for oil leakage.

2. Inspect the pinion gear splines (**Figure 40**) for severe wear or damage. If damaged, refer repair to a Kawasaki dealer.

3. Rotate the drive pinion (**Figure 40**) by hand. It should turn smoothly and quietly. If the rotation is rough or noisy, have the unit serviced by a Kawasaki dealer.

4. Make sure the ring gear cover bolts (**Figure 41**) and the pinion gear bearing housing nuts (**Figure 40**) are tight. Tighten, if necessary, to the torque specifications listed in **Table 1**.

11

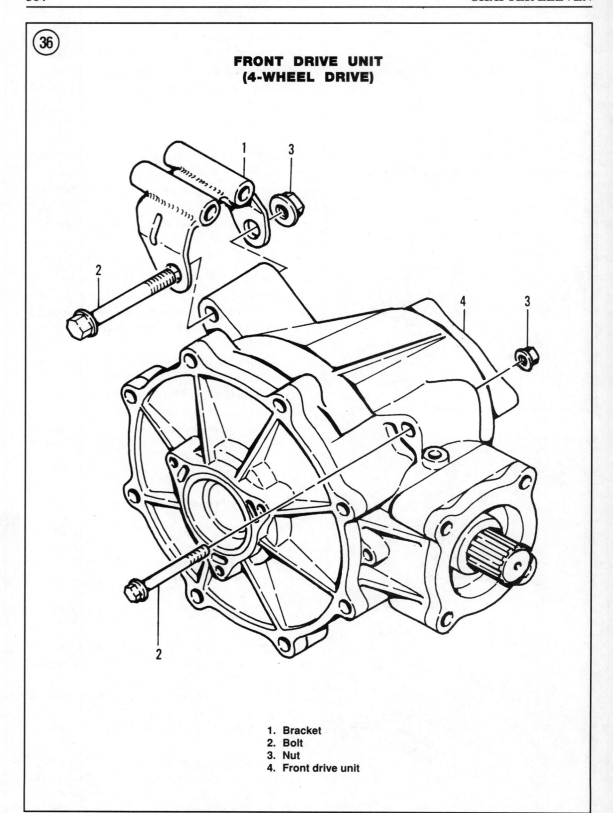

36

**FRONT DRIVE UNIT
(4-WHEEL DRIVE)**

1. Bracket
2. Bolt
3. Nut
4. Front drive unit

SUB-TRANSMISSION

Refer to **Figure 42** when servicing the sub-transmission assembly.

Sub-Transmission Shift Lever

The sub-transmission assembly provides maximum transmission efficiency by allowing the transmission to work in low and high gear ranges. Low range allows the engine to operate at maximum

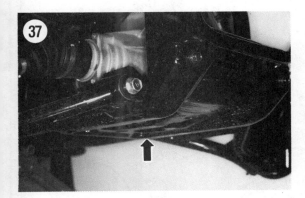

torque for trailer pulling, hill climbing and general agricultural use. High range allows the vehicle to operate at higher speeds for general off-road use.

To shift the sub-transmission shift lever into low and high gear ranges (A, **Figure 43**), perform the following:

1. Start the engine and shift the transmission into NEUTRAL.

> *CAUTION*
> *Do not shift the sub-transmission lever (A, **Figure 43**) if the vehicle is moving. The vehicle must be stopped when changing gear ranges.*

2. To shift into low range, push in the shift lever knob (B, **Figure 43**) and hold it against the shift

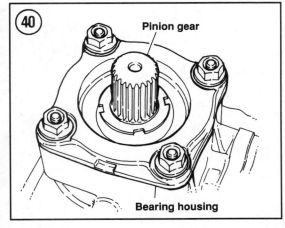

Pinion gear

Bearing housing

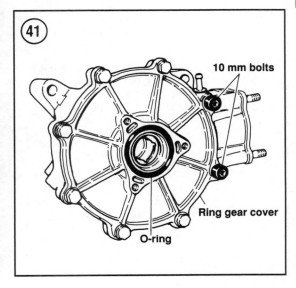

10 mm bolts

Ring gear cover

O-ring

11

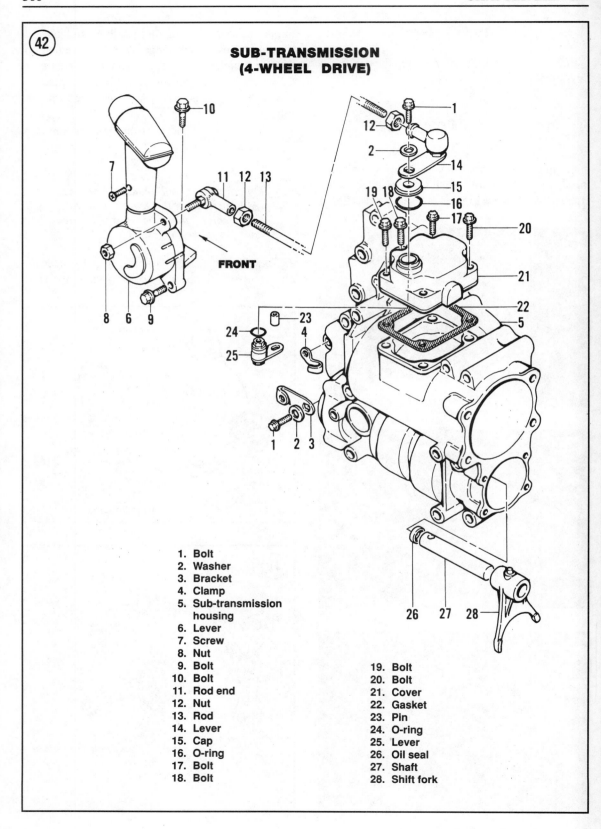

**SUB-TRANSMISSION
(4-WHEEL DRIVE)**

FRONT

1. Bolt
2. Washer
3. Bracket
4. Clamp
5. Sub-transmission
   housing
6. Lever
7. Screw
8. Nut
9. Bolt
10. Bolt
11. Rod end
12. Nut
13. Rod
14. Lever
15. Cap
16. O-ring
17. Bolt
18. Bolt

19. Bolt
20. Bolt
21. Cover
22. Gasket
23. Pin
24. O-ring
25. Lever
26. Oil seal
27. Shaft
28. Shift fork

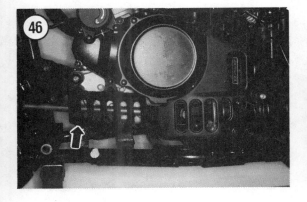

lever. Then move the shift lever rearward into low range.

3. To shift into high range, push in and hold the shift lever knob (B, **Figure 43**). Then move the shift lever forward into high range. Then check that each line on the shift lever lines up with the lines on the shift lever holder (**Figure 44**).

Sub-Transmission
Removal/Installation

1. Park the vehicle on level ground and set the parking brake.

2. Remove the rear fender as described in Chapter Fourteen.

3. Remove the left-hand footpeg and guard.

4. Remove the shift shaft.

5. Disconnect the sub-transmission shift fork lever bolt and lever (**Figure 45**).

6. Remove the sub-transmission cover (**Figure 46**).

7. Remove the oil pipe and oil pipe cap (**Figure 47**).

8. Support the rear of the frame so the rear suspension arms are free of any weight load. Then support the final drive unit separately.

9. Disconnect the parking brake and rear brake cables (**Figure 48**) from the rear brake panel.

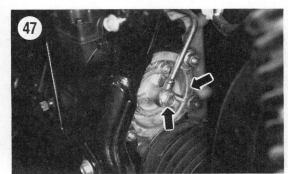

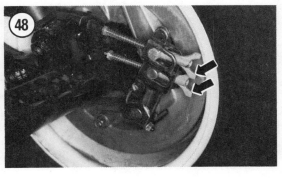

11

10. Remove the upper rear shock mounting bolts and nuts.

11. Remove the suspension arm pivot shafts.

12. Remove the rear propeller shaft joint boot clamp screw.

13. Carefully slide the rear propeller shaft and rear axle rearward to disconnect the propeller shaft from the sub-transmission shaft.

14. Remove the sub-transmission output shaft oil seal housing.

15. Pry back the toothed washer tabs on the 2 sub-transmission shaft slotted nuts (**Figure 49**).

16. Remove the drive shaft and the output shaft slotted nuts (**Figure 49**) with the Kawasaki socket wrench (part No. 57001-1282). See **Figure 50**.

17. Tie the front brake lever so that the front brake is applied.

18. Remove the front propeller shaft as described in this chapter.

19. Remove the left-hand side cover as described under *Stator and Left-Hand Side Cover* in Chapter Five.

20. Disconnect the reverse cable from the reverse lever (**Figure 51**).

21. Remove the sub-transmission 8 mm bolts.

22. Remove the sub-transmission 6 mm bolts. Then remove the sub-transmission assembly.

NOTE
To replace the sub-transmission gasket, the drive bevel gear and output shaft left-hand bearing housing must be removed as described in Step 23.

23. To remove the drive bevel gear and output shaft left-hand bearing housing from the crankcase, perform the following (**Figure 52**):

a. Hold the flywheel bolt to prevent the engine from turning.

b. Remove the drive bevel gear nut and remove the gear and shim(s).

c. Remove the bolts that hold the left-hand bearing housing to the crankshaft. Then remove the bearing housing.

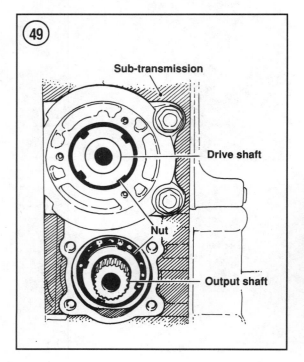

52

DRIVE BEVEL GEAR
AND LEFT-HAND BEARING HOUSING

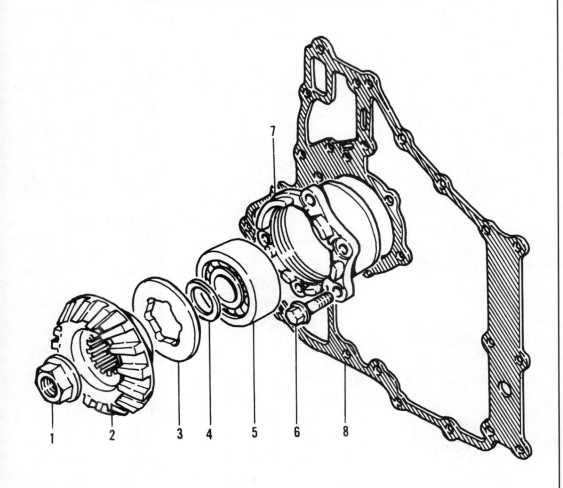

1. Nut
2. Drive bevel gear
3. Bearing holder
4. Shim
5. Bearing
6. Bolt
7. Bearing housing
8. Gasket

11

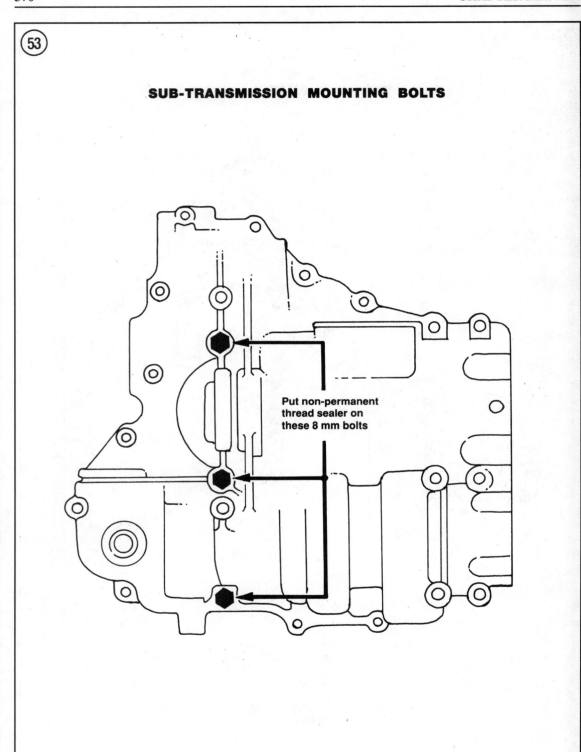

(53)

SUB-TRANSMISSION MOUNTING BOLTS

Put non-permanent
thread sealer on
these 8 mm bolts

d. Remove the gasket and dowel pins from the crankshaft.

24. Install by reversing these removal steps, noting the following.

25. If any parts in the sub-transmission assembly were replaced, have a Kawasaki dealer check and adjust the bevel gear backlash and tooth contact.

26. To install the output shaft left-hand bearing housing and drive bevel gear, perform the following:

    a. Install a new sub-transmission gasket.

    b. Tighten the left-hand bearing housing mounting bolts to the torque specification in **Table 1**.

    c. Coat the bearing holder (3, **Figure 52**) with clean engine oil and install it with its flat side facing out (away from bearing).

    d. Install the shim(s) and the drive bevel gear (2, **Figure 52**) onto the output shaft.

27. Install the sub-transmission housing onto the engine.

28. Apply a non-permanent thread locking compound to the 8 mm bolts identified in **Figure 53**. Then install the remaining 8 mm bolts. Tighten all the sub-transmission 8 mm bolts to the torque specification in **Table 1**.

29. Install the sub-transmission 6 mm bolts and tighten securely.

30. Install and tighten the drive and output shaft nuts (**Figure 49**) as follows:

    a. Install a tooth lockwasher and flat washer onto the drive and output shafts.

    b. Apply engine oil to the drive and output shaft nuts and thread them onto the shafts.

    c. Using the Kawasaki socket wrench (part No. 57001-1282 [**Figure 50**]), tighten the drive and output shaft locknuts (**Figure 49**) to the torque specification in **Table 1**.

    d. Bend one of the lockwasher tabs into one of the nut slots as shown in **Figure 54**. Tighten the nut,

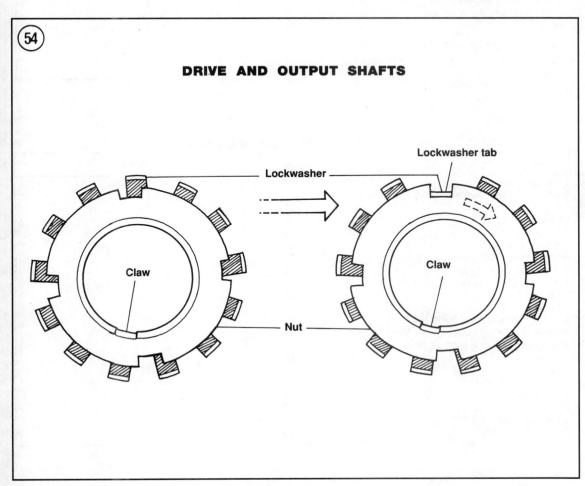

54

DRIVE AND OUTPUT SHAFTS

Lockwasher

Lockwasher tab

Claw

Claw

Nut

11

if necessary, to align the nut slot with a lock-washer tab.

31. To install the oil seal housing (**Figure 55**):
   a. If removed, install the large O-ring into the oil seal housing.
   b. Install the oil seal housing into the sub-transmission housing.
   c. Tighten the oil seal housing mounting nuts to the torque specification in **Table 1**.

32. Install the oil pipe cap and O-ring (**Figure 55**) onto the oil seal housing. Tighten the oil pipe cap screws to the torque specification in **Table 1**.

33. Install the oil pipe banjo bolts and tighten to the torque specification in **Table 1**.

34. Install the front propeller shaft as described in this chapter.

35. Install the rear propeller shaft as described in Chapter Twelve.

36. Adjust the reverse cable as described under *Reverse Cable Adjustment* in Chapter Seven.

37. Refill the engine with oil as described in Chapter Three.

38. Start the engine and check the transmission forward and reverse operations in the high- and low-gear ranges.

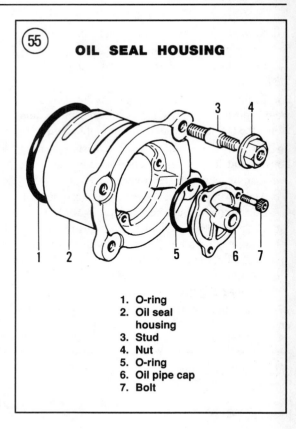

OIL SEAL HOUSING

1. O-ring
2. Oil seal housing
3. Stud
4. Nut
5. O-ring
6. Oil pipe cap
7. Bolt

Table 1 TORQUE SPECIFICATIONS

	N·m	ft.-lb.
Front axle cap bolts	8.8	78 in.-lb.
Front final gear case mounting bolts and nuts		
8 mm	25	18
10 mm	37	27
Oil drain plug	20	15
Oil filler cap	29	21
Pinion gear bearing housing nuts	25	18
Pinion gear slotted nut	120	88
Ring gear cover bolts		
8 mm	25	18
10 mm	47	35
Suspension arm pivot bolts	88	65
Left-hand bearing housing mounting bolts	12	9
Sub-transmission mounting bolts		
6 mm	see text	
8 mm	25	18
Drive shaft locknut	180	133
Output shaft locknut	180	133
Oil seal housing nuts	25	18
Oil pipe cap screws	7.8	69 in.-lb.
Oil pipe banjo bolts	20	15

CHAPTER TWELVE

REAR AXLE, SUSPENSION AND FINAL DRIVE

This chapter contains repair and replacement procedures for the rear wheels, rear suspension, propeller shaft, rear axles and the front gear case on 2-wheel drive models. Service to the rear suspension consists of periodically checking bolt tightness, replacing suspension bushings and checking the condition of the rear shock absorbers. Tire removal from the rim and tire repair are covered in Chapter Ten.

Rear suspension specifications are listed in **Table 1** and rear suspension torque specifications are listed in **Table 2** and **Table 3**. **Tables 1-3** are located at the end of this chapter.

REAR WHEEL

Removal/Installation

1. The tire and wheels are directional and must be installed on the correct side of the vehicle. Note the directional arrow mark on each tire (**Figure 1**).

2. Place the vehicle on level ground and set the parking brake. Block the front wheels so the vehicle will not roll in either direction.

3. Raise the rear of the vehicle with a small hydraulic or scissor jack. Place the jack under the frame with a piece of wood between the jack and the frame.

4. Place wooden block(s) under the frame to support the vehicle securely with the rear wheels off the ground.

5. Remove the rear wheel nuts (**Figure 2**) securing the rear wheel to the rear hub. Remove the tire and wheel assembly.

6. Install the rear wheel onto the same side of the vehicle from which it was removed.

7. Install the wheel nuts (**Figure 2**) finger-tight until the wheel is positioned correctly onto all 4 studs.

8. Tighten the wheel nuts to the torque specification listed in **Table 2** or **Table 3**.

9. After the wheel is installed, rotate it and apply the brake several times. Make sure the wheel rotates freely and the brake is operating correctly.

12

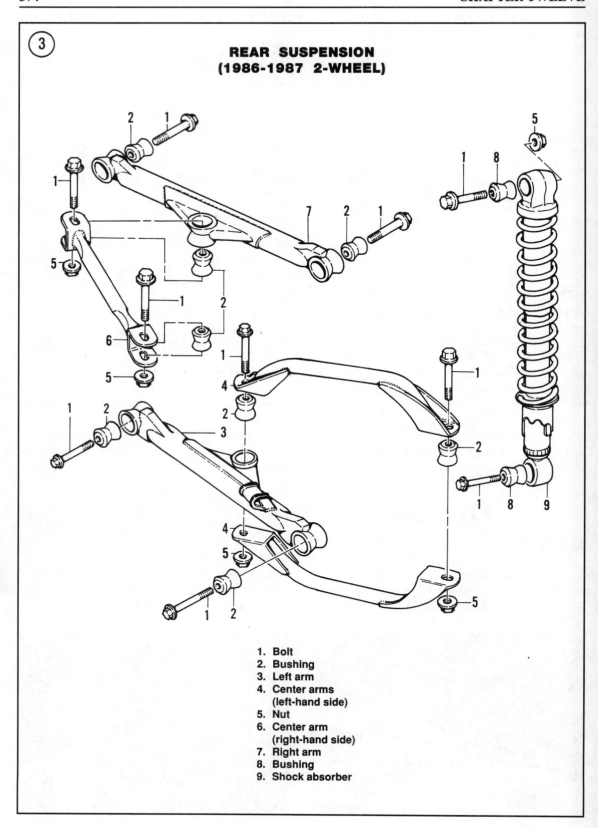

③ **REAR SUSPENSION
(1986-1987 2-WHEEL)**

1. Bolt
2. Bushing
3. Left arm
4. Center arms
   (left-hand side)
5. Nut
6. Center arm
   (right-hand side)
7. Right arm
8. Bushing
9. Shock absorber

10. Lower the vehicle so that both rear tires are on the ground.

REAR SUSPENSION ARMS

Torque tube rear suspension arms are used on all models. The pivot end of each arm is equipped with a rubber bushing. Refer to the exploded view drawing for your model when servicing the rear suspension arms:

a. **Figure 3**: 1986-1987.
b. **Figure 4**: 1988-on.

Removal/Installation

1. Place the vehicle on level ground and set the parking brake. Block the front wheels so the vehicle will not roll in either direction.

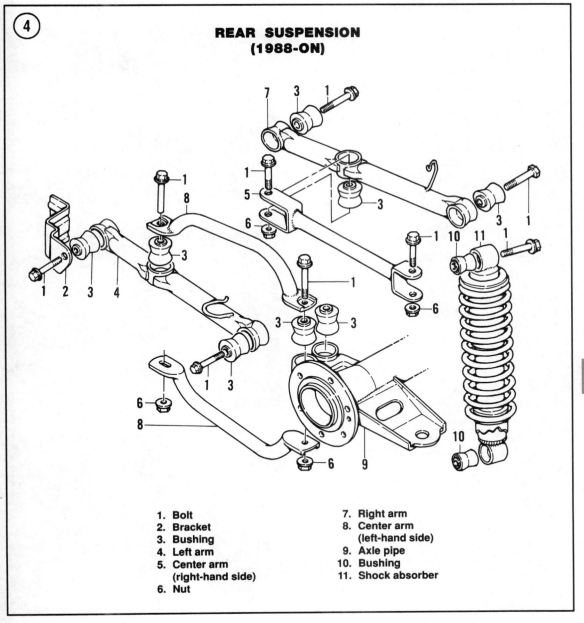

**REAR SUSPENSION
(1988-ON)**

1. Bolt
2. Bracket
3. Bushing
4. Left arm
5. Center arm
   (right-hand side)
6. Nut
7. Right arm
8. Center arm
   (left-hand side)
9. Axle pipe
10. Bushing
11. Shock absorber

12

2. Raise the rear of the vehicle with a small hydraulic or scissor jack. Place the jack under the frame with a piece of wood between the jack and the frame.

3. Place wooden block(s) under the frame to support the vehicle securely with the rear wheels off the ground.

4. Remove the final gear case skid plate (**Figure 5**, typical).

5. Support the final gear case with a jack or wooden blocks.

6. Remove the nuts and bolts securing the rear suspension arm to the frame or final drive unit. Refer to the following:

    a. Center arms (**Figure 6**).

    b. Left arm (**Figure 7**).

    c. Right arm (**Figure 8**).

7. Install by reversing these removal steps, noting the following.

8. Lubricate the pivot bolts with waterproof grease.

9. Install all the pivot bolts from the direction shown in **Figure 3** or **Figure 4**.

10. On 1988-on models, install the right-hand center arm (A, **Figure 9**) so the end with the longer mounting bracket (B, **Figure 9**) faces forward.

11. On 4-wheel drive models, install the left arm with its "F" mark facing up and pointing forward.

12. Tighten the suspension arm pivot bolts to the torque specification in **Table 2** or **Table 3**.

Suspension Arm
Cleaning and Inspection

1. Clean parts in solvent and dry with compressed air.

2. Inspect the suspension arms for cracks, fractures and dents. If damage is noted, replace the suspension. Never try to straighten a damaged or dented suspension arm as it cannot be straightened properly.

3. Inspect each bushing for severe wear or damage. Replace damaged parts. See **Figure 10** and **Figure 11**.

4. To replace the suspension arm bushings.

    a. Support the suspension arm and drive or press out the bushing. Repeat this step for each bushing.

    b. Clean the suspension arm bushing bores in solvent and dry thoroughly. Remove all rust and dirt residue.

    c. Support the suspension arm and press the bushing into the bore. Center bushing in bore.

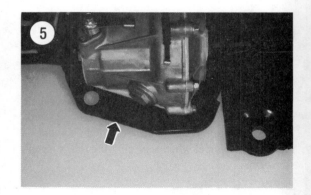

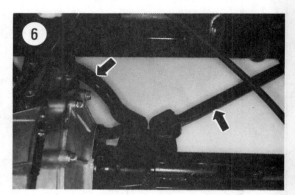

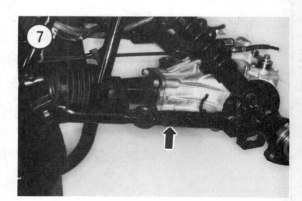

5. Inspect pivot bolts for bending or other damage. Replace damaged bolts.

REAR SHOCK ABSORBERS

Refer to the exploded view drawing for your model when servicing the rear shock absorbers:
  a. **Figure 3**: 1986-1987.
  b. **Figure 4**: 1988-on.

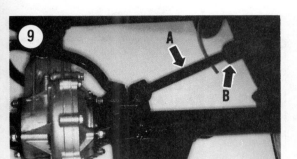

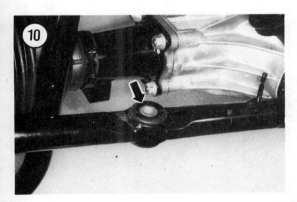

Spring Preload Adjustment

The rear shock absorber springs are provided with 3 (4-wheel drive) or 5 (2-wheel drive) preload positions. See **Figure 12**, typical. The No. 1 position is soft and the No. 3 (4-wheel drive) or No. 5 (2-wheel drive) position is hard. The spring preload can be changed by rotating the cam at the end of the spring. Set both rear shock absorbers to the same preload position.

Removal/Installation

1. Park the vehicle on level ground.
2. Support the vehicle securely with the rear wheels off the ground. Block the front wheels so that the vehicle cannot roll in either direction.
3. Remove the upper and lower shock absorber mounting nuts and bolts and remove the shock absorber. See **Figure 13**, typical.

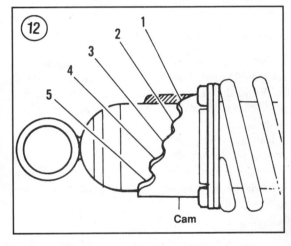

Cam

12

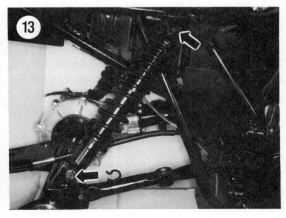

4. Install by reversing these removal steps, while noting the following.

5. Inspect each damper unit (**Figure 14**) for fluid leakage or other damage. Replace the shock if leakage is found.

> *WARNING*
> *Do not attempt to disassemble the damper unit. Disassembly can release high-pressure gas and cause personal injury.*

6. Clean the upper and lower mounting bolts and nuts in solvent and dry thoroughly.

7. Install by reversing these removal steps, noting the following.

8. Apply waterproof grease to the upper and lower mounting bolts prior to installation.

9. Tighten the upper and lower shock mounting bolts and nuts to the torque specification in **Table 2** or **Table 3**.

10. Repeat for the other side as required.

Shock Spring Replacement

The shock is spring-controlled and hydraulically damped. The shock damper unit is sealed and cannot be serviced. Service is limited to removal and replacement of the damper unit, spring and mounting bushings.

Kawasaki does not list spring free length specifications for the rear shock absorbers.

1. Mount the lower shock mount in a vise with soft jaws and turn the spring adjuster (**Figure 12**) to its softest position.

> *WARNING*
> *Do not remove the spring without a spring compressor. The spring is under considerable pressure and may fly off and cause injury.*

2. Mount a spring compressor onto the shock absorber and compress the spring. Then remove the upper spring seat and remove the spring.

> *NOTE*
> *The damper unit cannot be rebuilt; it must be replaced as a unit.*

3. Check the damper unit for leakage and make sure the damper rod is straight. Replace the damper unit if necessary.

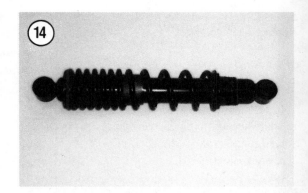

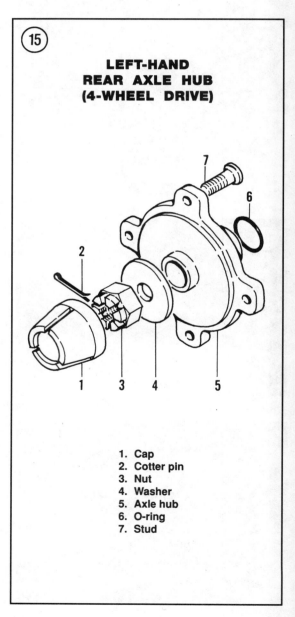

**LEFT-HAND
REAR AXLE HUB
(4-WHEEL DRIVE)**

1. Cap
2. Cotter pin
3. Nut
4. Washer
5. Axle hub
6. O-ring
7. Stud

4. Assemble the shock by reversing these steps, while noting the following.

5. If installing progressive rate springs, install spring with closer wound coils toward the top of the shock.

6. Make sure the spring seat is properly seated in the spring.

7. Turn the spring adjuster to adjust spring preload (**Figure 12**). Adjust both shocks to the same spring preload setting.

Shock Bushing Replacement

1. Check the shock bushings for deterioration, severe wear or other damage. If necessary, replace bushings as follows:

2. Support the damper unit in a press and press out the damaged bushing.

3. Clean the shock bushing bore to remove dirt, rust and other debris.

4. Press in the new bushing until its outer surface is flush with the bushing bore inside surface.

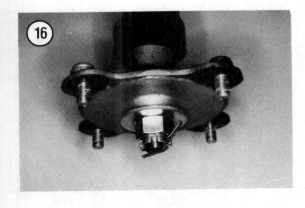

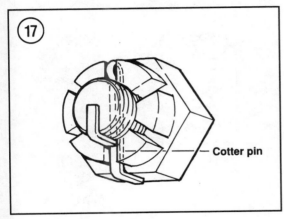

Cotter pin

LEFT-HAND REAR HUB (4-WHEEL DRIVE)

Removal/Installation

Refer to **Figure 15** when servicing the left-hand rear hub.

1. Remove the left-hand rear wheel as described in this chapter.

2. Remove the cotter pin and the left-hand axle hub nut. See **Figure 16**.

3. Remove the washer and slide off the left-hand rear hub.

4. Remove the O-ring.

5. Inspect the wheel studs on the hub. If the studs are damaged, replace the hub assembly. Kawasaki does not recommend replacing individual studs.

6. Apply grease to the O-ring and install it.

7. Apply grease to the axle splines.

8. Slide the hub onto the rear axle (**Figure 16**).

9. Install the washer onto the axle and seat it against the hub (**Figure 16**).

10. Install the left-hand axle hub nut (**Figure 16**) and tighten to the torque specification listed in **Table 3**.

NOTE
Install a new cotter pin. Never reuse an old one as it may break and fall out.

11. Install a new cotter pin and bend the ends over completely (**Figure 17**).

12. Install the rear wheel as described in this chapter.

FINAL DRIVE UNIT

Removal

This procedure describes removal of the final drive unit and propeller shaft.

1. Park the vehicle on level ground and set the parking brake.

2. Remove the rear fender as described in Chapter Fourteen.

3. Remove the final gear case skid plate (**Figure 5**, typical).

4. Drain the final drive unit oil as described in Chapter Three.

5. Remove the rear wheels as described in this chapter.

6. Remove the rear brake drum(s) as described in Chapter Thirteen.

7. Remove the rear brake panel(s) as described in Chapter Thirteen.

8. Loosen the propeller shaft boot clamp. See **Figure 18** (2-wheel drive) or **Figure 19** (4-wheel drive).

9. On 2-wheel drive models, perform the following:

   a. Remove the shift cable bracket bolts and bracket (A, **Figure 20**) from the final drive unit.

   b. Disconnect the shift cable from the shift lever (B, **Figure 20**).

   c. Disconnect the vent hose (C, **Figure 20**) from the final drive unit.

10. Support the final drive unit with wooden blocks.

11A. On 2-wheel drive models, perform the following:

   a. Remove the left center suspension arm assembly (A, **Figure 21**).

   b. Remove the bolt and nut securing the right center suspension arm (B, **Figure 21**) to the final drive unit.

   c. Disconnect the left-hand suspension arm (A, **Figure 22**) from the final drive unit.

   d. Disconnect the left-hand shock (B, **Figure 22**) from the final drive unit.

   e. Disconnect the right-hand suspension arm (A, **Figure 23**) from the final drive unit.

   f. Disconnect the right-hand shock (B, **Figure 23**) from the final drive unit.

11B. On 4-wheel drive models, perform the following:

   a. Remove the left center suspension arm (A, **Figure 24**) assembly.

   b. Remove the bolt and nut securing the right center suspension arm (B, **Figure 24**) to the final drive unit.

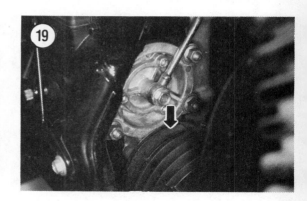

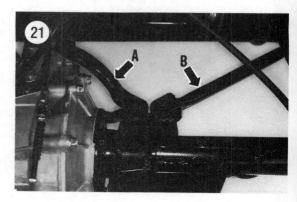

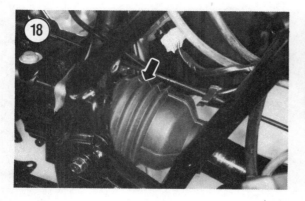

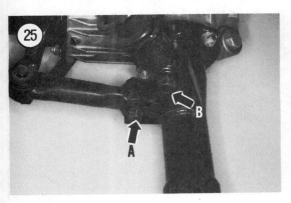

c. Disconnect the left-hand suspension arm (A, **Figure 25**) from the final drive unit.

d. Disconnect the left-hand shock (B, **Figure 25**) from the final drive unit.

e. Disconnect the right-hand suspension arm from the final drive unit.

f. Disconnect the right-hand shock from the final drive unit.

12. Pull the final drive unit toward the rear and disengage the propeller shaft from the engine. See **Figure 26**, typical.

13. If necessary, service the propeller shaft as described in this chapter.

14. If necessary, service the rear axles as described in this chapter.

Installation

1. Apply grease to the drive gear (**Figure 27**) and propeller shaft splines.

2. Carefully align the drive gear and propeller shaft splines (**Figure 28**), then slide the final drive gear unit forward.

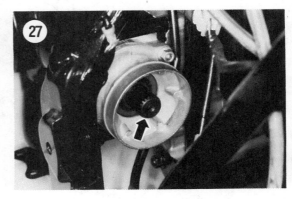

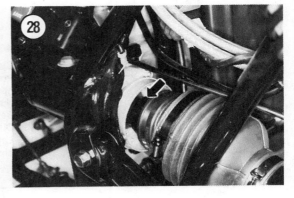

12

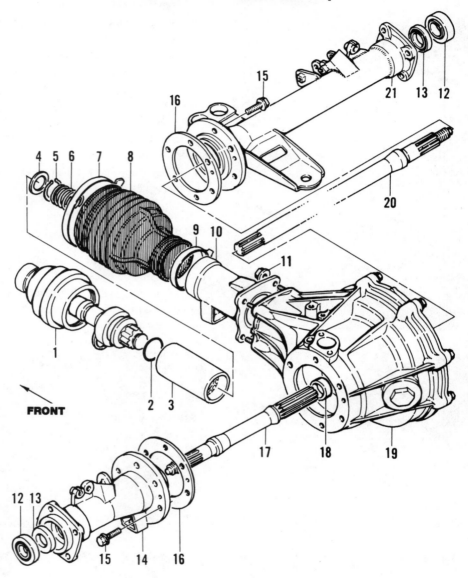

**FINAL DRIVE UNIT
(1986-1987 2-WHEEL DRIVE)**

FRONT

1. Propeller shaft
2. O-ring
3. Coupling
4. Spacer
5. Circlip
6. Spring
7. Clamp
8. Boot
9. Clamp
10. Propeller shaft
    housing
11. Nut
12. Bearing
13. Oil seal
14. Left-hand axle
    pipe
15. Bolt
16. Gasket
17. Left-hand axle
18. Spacer
19. Final drive unit
20. Right-hand axle
21. Right-hand axle
    pipe

3. Support the final drive gear unit with a jack or wooden blocks.

4A. On 2-wheel drive models, perform the following:

    a. Reconnect the left-hand suspension arm (A, **Figure 22**) to the final drive unit.

    b. Reconnect the right-hand suspension arm (A, **Figure 23**) to the final drive unit.

    c. Reconnect the right center suspension arm (B, **Figure 21**) to the final drive unit.

    d. Reinstall the left center suspension arm (A, **Figure 21**).

    e. Reconnect the left-hand shock (B, **Figure 22**) to the final drive unit.

    f. Reconnect the right-hand shock (B, **Figure 23**) to the final drive unit.

4B. On 4-wheel drive models, perform the following:

    a. Reconnect the left-hand suspension arm (A, **Figure 25**) to the final drive unit.

    b. Reconnect the right-hand suspension arm to the final drive unit.

    c. Reconnect the right center suspension arm (B, **Figure 24**) to the final drive unit.

    d. Reinstall the left center suspension arm (A, **Figure 24**).

    e. Reconnect the left-hand shock (B, **Figure 25**) to the final drive unit.

    f. Reconnect the right-hand shock to the final drive unit.

5. Tighten the suspension arm and shock absorber mounting bolts and nuts to the torque specifications listed in **Table 2** or **Table 3**.

6. On 2-wheel drive models, perform the following:

    a. Reconnect the vent hose (C, **Figure 20**) to the final drive unit.

    b. Reconnect the shift cable to the shift lever (B, **Figure 20**).

    c. Bolt the shift cable bracket (A, **Figure 20**) to the final drive unit.

7. Slide the front propeller shaft boot into place. Then tighten the boot clamp securely. See **Figure 18** (2-wheel drive) or **Figure 19** (4-wheel drive).

8. Reinstall the rear brake panel(s) as described in Chapter Thirteen.

9. Reinstall the rear brake drum(s) as described in Chapter Thirteen.

10. Install the rear wheels as described in this chapter.

11. Lower the rear wheels to the ground. Set the parking brake.

12. Refill the final drive unit with the recommended type and quantity of oil as described in Chapter Three.

13. Install the final gear case skid plate (**Figure 5**, typical).

14. Install the rear fender as described in Chapter Fourteen.

Disassembly/Inspection/Assembly

The final drive unit requires a considerable number of special Kawasaki tools for disassembly and reassembly. The price of all of these tools could be more than the cost of most repairs or seal replacement by a dealer. However, the propeller shaft and rear axle shaft assemblies can be serviced with basic hand tools as described in this chapter.

Figures 29-31 show the final drive units.

1. Check the entire unit for oil leakage (**Figure 32**).

2. Remove the propeller shaft as described in this chapter.

3. Check the pinion gear splines (**Figure 33**) for wear or damage. If damaged, repair should be referred to a Kawasaki dealer.

4. Inspect the threaded studs (**Figure 33**) for damage. Chase the threads with the correct size thread die or replace them.

5. Make sure the ring gear cover bolts are tight. Tighten, if necessary, to the torque specification(s) in **Table 2** or **Table 3**.

6. Install the propeller shaft as described in this chapter.

PROPELLER SHAFT

Refer to the exploded view drawing for your model when servicing the propeller shaft assembly:

    a. **Figure 29**: 1986-1987 2-wheel drive.

    b. **Figure 30**: 1988-on 2-wheel drive.

    c. **Figure 31**: 4-wheel drive.

Removal/Installation.

The propeller shaft is removed and installed with the final drive unit. Refer to *Final Drive Unit Removal and Installation* in this chapter.

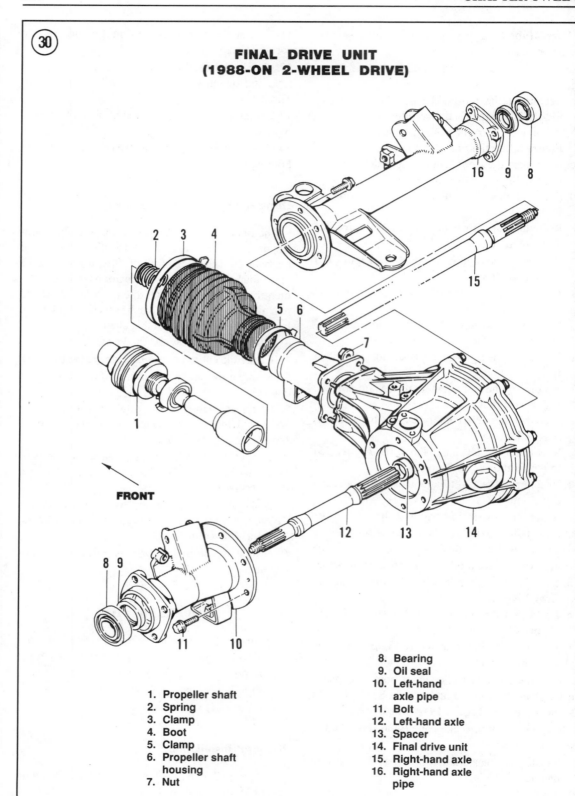

30

FINAL DRIVE UNIT
(1988-ON 2-WHEEL DRIVE)

FRONT

1. Propeller shaft
2. Spring
3. Clamp
4. Boot
5. Clamp
6. Propeller shaft
   housing
7. Nut
8. Bearing
9. Oil seal
10. Left-hand
    axle pipe
11. Bolt
12. Left-hand axle
13. Spacer
14. Final drive unit
15. Right-hand axle
16. Right-hand axle
    pipe

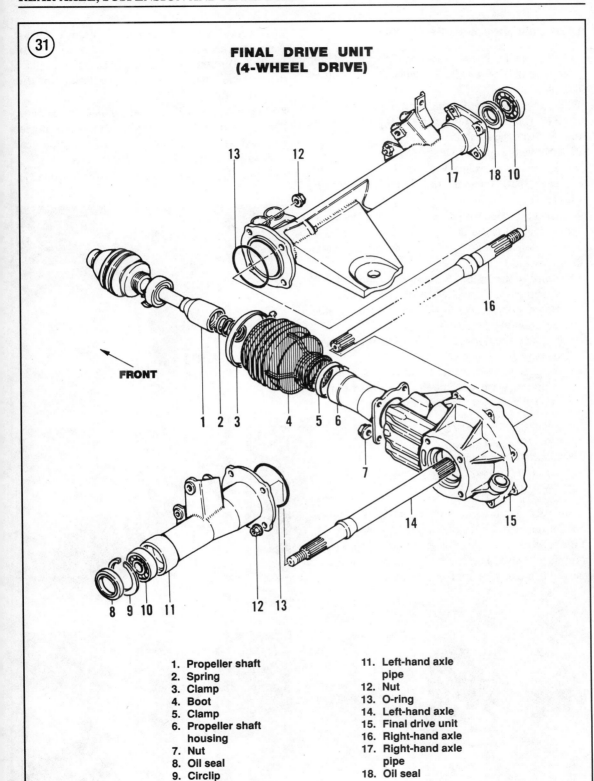

**FINAL DRIVE UNIT
(4-WHEEL DRIVE)**

FRONT

1. Propeller shaft
2. Spring
3. Clamp
4. Boot
5. Clamp
6. Propeller shaft
   housing
7. Nut
8. Oil seal
9. Circlip
10. Bearing

11. Left-hand axle
    pipe
12. Nut
13. O-ring
14. Left-hand axle
15. Final drive unit
16. Right-hand axle
17. Right-hand axle
    pipe
18. Oil seal

12

Disassembly/Inspection/Reassembly

The propeller shaft is an integral unit. Do not attempt to disassemble it (remove universal joint or its center bearing).

1. Remove the propeller shaft housing nuts (A, **Figure 34**). Then withdraw the propeller shaft (B, **Figure 34**) from the final drive unit.

2. Remove the spring (**Figure 35**).

3. Remove the circlip (**Figure 36**) and pull the propeller shaft assembly out of its housing. See **Figure 37**.

4. Inspect the outer boot for tearing or other damage. Replace if necessary.

5. On 1986-1987 2-wheel drive models, perform the following:

  a. Remove the circlip (5, **Figure 29**) and slide the coupling (3, **Figure 29**) off the propeller shaft. Remove the spacer (4, **Figure 29**) from inside the coupling.

  b. Replace the O-ring (2, **Figure 29**) if worn or damaged.

  c. Reverse sub-step a and b to install the O-ring, coupling, washer and circlip. Grease the O-ring and splines prior to reassembly.

> *NOTE*
> *On 1988 and later 2- and 4-wheel drive models, the coupling (A, **Figure 38**) is an integral part of the propeller shaft assembly.*

6. Inspect the universal joint assembly (B, **Figure 38**) for damage. Check the universal joint boot (B, **Figure 38**) for leakage or other damage. Replace the propeller shaft if necessary. Do not attempt to remove the universal joint from the propeller shaft.

7. Inspect the center bearing (C, **Figure 38**) for damage. Check the bearing seals for damage or leakage. Turn the bearing slowly by hand. Replace the propeller shaft if the bearing is leaking or if it turns roughly.

8. Check the propeller shaft splines for damage. Replace the propeller shaft if damage is noted. Check the mating output (engine) and pinion gear joint splines (final drive unit) for damage.

9. Slide the outer boot over the housing (**Figure 37**).

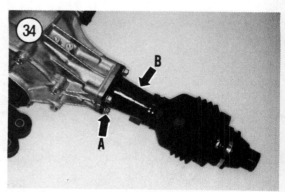

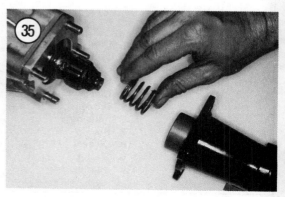

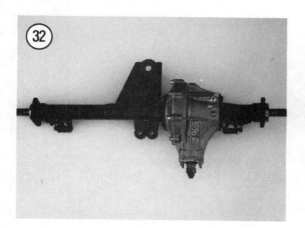

10. Slide the propeller shaft into its housing as shown in **Figure 37** and **Figure 39**.

11. Slide the center bearing into the housing (**Figure 36**).

12. Install the circlip (**Figure 36**) into the housing groove. Make sure the circlip is fully seated in the groove.

13. Grease the pinion shaft (**Figure 33**) and pinion shaft splines.

14. Grease the spring and slide it onto the pinion shaft (**Figure 35**).

15. Slide the pinion shaft forward and engage its splines with the output shaft splines (B, **Figure 34**).

16. Install the propeller shaft housing nuts (A, **Figure 34**) and tighten in a crisscross pattern to the torque specification in **Table 2** or **Table 3**.

REAR AXLE

Refer to the exploded view drawing for your model when servicing the rear axles:

a. **Figure 29**: 1986-1987 2-wheel drive.
b. **Figure 30**: 1988-on 2-wheel drive.
c. **Figure 31**: 4-wheel drive.

Left-Hand Axle Removal

> *NOTE*
> *In this procedure, the final drive unit used on 1988-on 2-wheel drive models is shown in the photographs. Where differences occur that relate to the procedure, they are identified in the text. When removing the rear axles, refer to the exploded view drawing for your model.*

1. Drain the final drive unit oil as described in Chapter Three.

2. Remove the final drive unit as described under *Final Drive Unit Removal* in this chapter.

3. If necessary, remove the propeller shaft assembly as described under *Propeller Shaft Disassembly/Inspection/Reassembly* in this chapter.

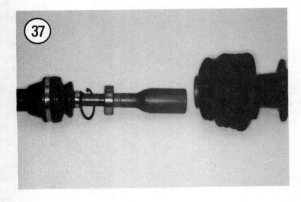

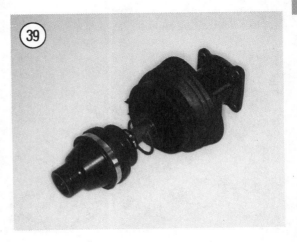

12

4. Remove the bolts (2-wheel drive) or nuts (4-wheel drive) that hold the left-hand axle pipe (**Figure 40**) to the final drive unit. Then withdraw the axle pipe and left-hand axle assembly. See A, **Figure 41**.

.5. On 1986-1987 2-wheel drive models, remove and discard the axle pipe gasket.

6. On 4-wheel drive models, remove the O-ring from the axle pipe flange.

7. Slide the axle (A, **Figure 42**) out of the axle pipe. See **Figure 43**. On 2-wheel drive models, slide the collar (B, **Figure 42**) off the axle.

Inspection, Bearing and Oil Seal Replacement (Left-Hand Axle)

1. On 2-wheel drive models, remove all gasket and/or sealer residue from the axle pipe-to-final drive unit mating surfaces.

2. Clean the axle pipe, axle and collar in solvent. Dry thoroughly.

3. Inspect the axle splines (**Figure 44**) for twisting, cracks or other damage. Replace the axle if necessary.

4. Check the cotter pin hole at the end of the axle. Make sure there are no fractures or cracks leading out toward the end of the axle. If any are found, replace the axle.

5. Inspect the axle pipe bearing and oil seal. **Figure 45** shows the bearing used on 2-wheel drive models. On 4-wheel drive models, an oil seal is installed on the outside of the bearing; see **Figure 31**. On 2-wheel drive models, the oil seal is installed behind the bearing. Turn the bearing with your finger. The bearing should turn smoothly with no roughness, catching, binding or excessive noise. If damaged, replace the bearing and oil seals as follows:

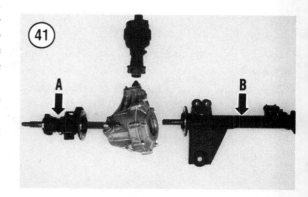

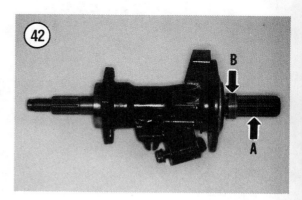

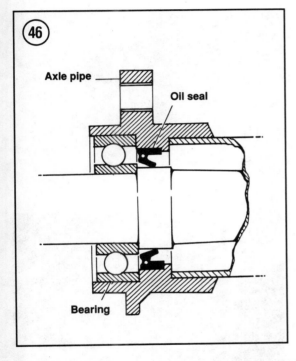

Axle pipe

Oil seal

Bearing

6A. To replace the bearing and oil seal (**Figure 46**) on 2-wheel drive models:

a. Support the axle pipe in a vise with soft jaws.

b. Remove the bearing with a slide hammer type bearing removal tool (**Figure 47**).

c. Repeat to remove the oil seal.

d. Clean the axle pipe bearing and oil seal bores thoroughly.

e. Pack the oil seal lips with waterproof bearing grease prior to installation

f. Drive the oil seal—closed side facing out—into the axle pipe until it bottoms out. See **Figure 46**.

g. Drive the bearing into the axle pipe until it bottoms out. Install the bearing with its manufacturers name and size code facing out. See **Figure 45** and **Figure 46**.

6B. To replace the bearing and oil seal (**Figure 48**) on 4-wheel drive models:

a. Support the axle pipe in a vise with soft jaws.

b. Pry the oil seal out of the axle pipe with a wide-blade screwdriver.

c. Remove the circlip.

d. Remove the bearing with a slide hammer type bearing removal tool (**Figure 47**).

e. Clean the axle pipe bearing and oil seal bores thoroughly.

f. Drive the bearing into the axle pipe until it bottoms out. Install the bearing with its manufacturers name and size code facing out.

g. Install the circlip into the axle pipe groove. Make sure the circlip is fully seated in the groove.

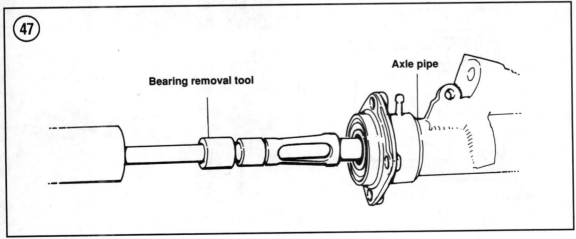

Bearing removal tool

Axle pipe

h. Pack the oil seal lips with a waterproof bearing grease prior to installation

i. Drive the oil seal—closed side facing out—into the axle pipe until it bottoms out. See **Figure 48**.

Left-Hand Axle Installation

1. On 2-wheel drive models, make sure the differential collar (**Figure 49**) is in place.

2. Apply a light coat of grease to the splines and bearing contact area on the axle.

3. Pack the oil seal lips with waterproof bearing grease. See **Figure 46** or **Figure 48**.

4. Slide the axle (A, **Figure 42**) into the axle pipe.

5. On 2-wheel drive models, slide the collar (B, **Figure 42**) onto the axle.

6A. On 1986-1987 2-wheel drive models, install a new axle pipe gasket.

6B. On 1988-on 2-wheel drive models, apply Kawasaki Bond (RTV sealant) to the axle pipe mating surface (**Figure 50**).

6C. On 4-wheel drive models, apply clean engine oil to the new O-ring and install it on the axle pipe flange.

7. Align the axle pipe with the final drive unit and install it (**Figure 40**). Turn the axle shaft, if necessary, to engage the shaft splines.

8. Install the left-hand axle pipe bolts (2-wheel drive) or nuts (4-wheel drive) and tighten to the torque specification in **Table 2** or **Table 3**.

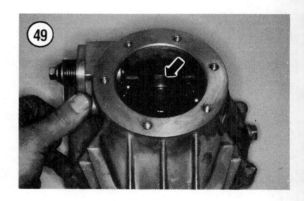

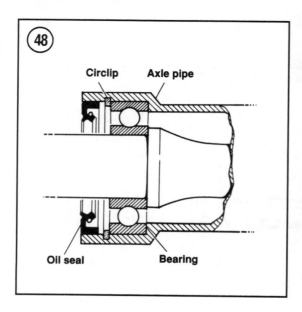

Circlip　　Axle pipe

Oil seal　　Bearing

9. If removed, install the propeller shaft assembly as described under *Propeller Shaft Disassembly/Inspection/Reassembly* in this chapter.

10. Install the final drive unit as described under *Final Drive Unit Installation* in this chapter.

11. Refill the final drive unit with the recommended type and quantity of oil as described in Chapter Three.

Right-Hand Axle Removal

> *NOTE*
> *In this procedure, the final drive unit used on 1988-on 2-wheel drive models is shown in the photographs. Where differences occur that relate to the procedure, they are identified in the text. When removing the rear axles, refer to the exploded view drawing for your model.*

1. Drain the final drive unit oil as described in Chapter Three.

2. Remove the final drive unit as described under *Final Drive Unit Removal* in this chapter.

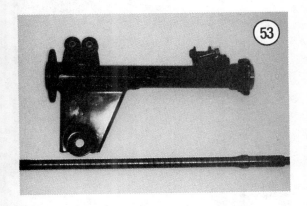

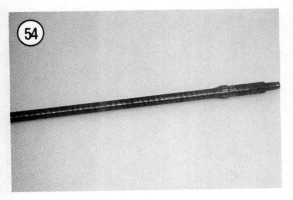

3. If necessary, remove the propeller shaft assembly as described under *Propeller Shaft Disassembly/Inspection/Reassembly* in this chapter.

4. Remove the bolts (2-wheel drive) or nuts (4-wheel drive) that hold the right-hand axle pipe (**Figure 51**) to the final drive unit. Then withdraw the axle pipe and left-hand axle assembly. See B, **Figure 41**.

5. On 1986-1987 2-wheel drive models, remove and discard the axle pipe gasket.

6. On 4-wheel drive models, remove the O-ring from the axle pipe flange.

7. Slide the axle (**Figure 52**) out of the axle pipe. See **Figure 53**.

Inspection and Bearing and Oil Seal Replacement (Right-Hand Axle)

1. On 2-wheel drive models, remove all gasket and/or sealer residue from the axle pipe-to-final drive unit mating surfaces.

2. Clean the axle pipe, axle and collar in solvent. Dry thoroughly.

3. Inspect the axle splines (**Figure 54**) for twisting, cracks or other damage. Replace the axle if necessary.

4. Check the cotter pin hole at the end of the axle. Make sure there are no fractures or cracks leading out toward the end of the axle. If any are found, replace the axle.

5. Inspect the axle pipe bearing (**Figure 55**) and oil seal. The oil seal is installed behind the bearing (**Figure 46**). Turn the bearing with your finger. The bearing should turn smoothly with no roughness, catching, binding or excessive nose. If damaged, replace the bearing and oil seal as follows:

12

6. To replace the bearing and oil seal (**Figure 46**):

   a. Support the axle pipe in a vise with soft jaws.

   b. Remove the bearing with a slide hammer type bearing removal tool (**Figure 47**).

   c. Repeat to remove the oil seal.

   d. Clean the axle pipe bearing and oil seal bores thoroughly.

   e. Pack the oil seal lips with waterproof bearing grease prior to installation

   f. Drive the oil seal—closed side facing out—into the axle pipe until it bottoms out. See **Figure 46**.

   g. Drive the bearing into the axle pipe until it bottoms out. Install the bearing with its manufacturers name and size code facing out. See **Figure 55** and **Figure 46**.

Right-Hand Axle Installation

1. Apply a light coat of grease to the splines and bearing contact area on the axle.

2. Pack the oil seal lips with waterproof bearing grease. See **Figure 46**.

3. Slide the axle (**Figure 52**) into the axle pipe.

4A. On 1986-1987 2-wheel drive models, install a new axle pipe gasket.

4B. On 1988-on 2-wheel drive models, apply Kawasaki Bond (RTV sealant) to the axle pipe mating surface (**Figure 56**)

4C. On 4-wheel drive models, apply clean engine oil to the new O-ring and install it on the axle pipe flange.

5. Align the axle pipe with the final drive unit and install it (**Figure 51**). Turn the axle shaft, if necessary, to engage the shaft splines.

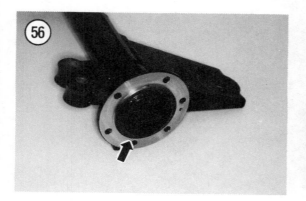

6. Install the right-hand axle pipe bolts (2-wheel drive) or nuts (4-wheel drive) and tighten to the torque specification in **Table 2** or **Table 3**.

7. If removed, install the propeller shaft assembly as described under *Propeller Shaft Disassembly/Inspection/Reassembly* in this chapter.

8. Install the final drive unit as described under *Final Drive Unit Installation* in this chapter.

9. Refill the final drive unit with the recommended type and quantity of oil as described in Chapter Three.

DIFFERENTIAL SHIFT LEVER AND CABLE (2-WHEEL DRIVE)

Two-wheel drive models can be operated in one of two rear axle operation modes: locked-axle or differential (unlocked axle). The differential shift lever assembly is mounted on the left-hand side of the engine; see A, **Figure 57**.

Differential Shift Lever Operation

Locked-axle mode

The locked-axle mode is useful for sport riding, climbing hills, riding in rough terrain and when maximum pulling power is needed.

To shift into the locked-axle mode:
1. Bring the vehicle to a complete stop with the transmission in NEUTRAL.
2. Slide the differential shift lever (B, **Figure 57**) to the left and push it all the way down.

> *NOTE*
> *If the differential shift lever moves roughly, turn the handlebar to the left- or right-hand side. Then roll the vehicle slightly while moving the shift lever.*

Differential mode

The differential or unlocked axle mode is useful when minimum surface disturbance is desired (operating on lawns, golf course fairways, etc.)

To shift into the differential mode:

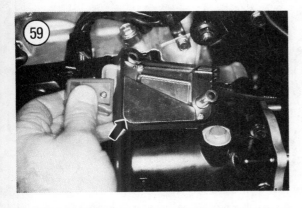

1. Bring the vehicle to a complete stop with the transmission in NEUTRAL.
2. Pull the differential shift lever (B, **Figure 57**) all the way up.

> *NOTE*
> *If the differential shift lever moves roughly, turn the handlebar to the left- or right-hand side. Then roll the vehicle slightly while moving the shift lever.*

Differential Lever Case and Cable Removal/Installation

1. Park the vehicle on a level surface and set the parking brake.
2. Remove the bolts (C, **Figure 57**) holding the differential shift lever case to the engine.

> *NOTE*
> *To remove the differential shift lever cable, continue with Step 3.*

3. To disconnect the differential shift lever cable from the final drive unit:
   a. Remove the bracket bolts and bracket (A, **Figure 58**).
   b. Disconnect the differential shift lever cable from the shift lever (B, **Figure 58**).
4. To disconnect the differential shift lever cable from the differential case:
   a. Remove the case screws and remove the case (**Figure 59**).
   b. Pry open the cable bracket (A, **Figure 60**) and free the cable from the cable bracket.

> *CAUTION*
> *Do not loosen the pivot bolt (B, **Figure 60**). Doing so will change the position of a special collar installed underneath the lever. This could cause the differential lever to malfunction.*

   c. Free the cable end from inside the differential lever case. Then remove the cable. Do not lose the rubber seals.
5. Install by reversing these removal steps, noting the following.
6. Lubricate the differential cable as described in Chapter Three.
7. Tighten the differential lever case mounting bolts (C, **Figure 57**) to the torque specification in **Table 2**.

12

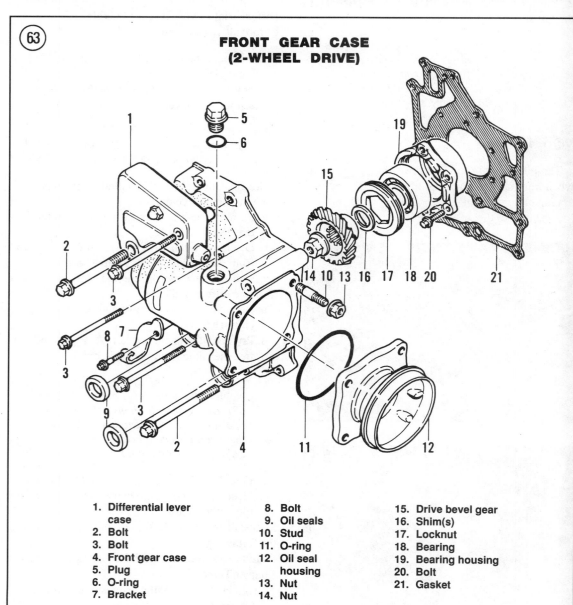

**FRONT GEAR CASE
(2-WHEEL DRIVE)**

1. Differential lever
   case
2. Bolt
3. Bolt
4. Front gear case
5. Plug
6. O-ring
7. Bracket
8. Bolt
9. Oil seals
10. Stud
11. O-ring
12. Oil seal
    housing
13. Nut
14. Nut
15. Drive bevel gear
16. Shim(s)
17. Locknut
18. Bearing
19. Bearing housing
20. Bolt
21. Gasket

8. Adjust the differential lever cable as described in this chapter.

Differential Lever Cable Adjustment

1. Support the vehicle with the rear wheels off the ground.
2. Slide the differential shift lever (B, **Figure 57**) to the left and push it all the way down.
3. Unhook the shift fork lever return spring mounted on the shift fork lever (A, **Figure 61**).

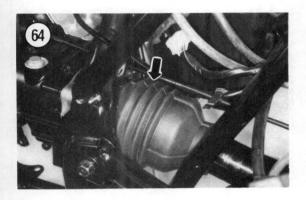

4. Remove the shift fork lever nut and remove the lever (A, **Figure 61**) from the shift fork.
5. Loosen the cable adjuster mounting nuts (B, **Figure 61**).
6. Slide the cable housing forward until the front end of the cable (**Figure 62**) seats fully into the holder on the case. Then tighten the cable adjuster mounting nuts (B, **Figure 61**), making sure you do not change the position of the cable housing.
7. Rotate the rear wheels and shift the rear axle into the locked-axle mode by turning the shift fork shaft (C, **Figure 61**) clockwise.
8. Install the rear of the shift lever cable into the shift fork lever (A, **Figure 61**). Then pull the cable rearward so it is tight and install the shift fork lever onto the shift fork shaft. Install the shift fork lever nut and tighten securely. Reconnect the shift fork lever return spring onto the shift fork lever (A, **Figure 61**).
9. Remove the jack and lower the rear wheels to the ground.
10. Check differential shift lever operation as described under *Differential Shift Lever Operation* in this chapter.

FRONT GEAR CASE AND DRIVE GEAR (2-WHEEL DRIVE)

Refer to **Figure 63** when servicing the front gear case.

Front Gear Case Removal/Installation

1. Park the vehicle on level ground.
2. Support the vehicle so the rear wheels are off the ground.
3. Loosen the front propeller cover clamp screw (**Figure 64**).
4. Remove the pivot bolts at the front of the left- and right-hand suspension arms. **Figure 65** shows the left-hand suspension arm pivot bolt.
5. Remove the upper shock absorber mounting bolts for the left- and right-hand shock absorbers.
6. Pull the rear axle and propeller shaft toward the rear to disconnect the propeller shaft from the front drive gear shaft at the front gear case. See **Figure 66**.
7. Remove the differential lever case (A, **Figure 57**) as described under *Differential Lever Case and Ca-*

12

ble in this chapter. Do not disconnect or remove the cable from the case.

8. Remove the shift lever from the front gear case.

9. Remove reverse lever from the front gear case (**Figure 67**).

10. Place an oil pan underneath the front gear case.

11. Remove the nuts holding the oil seal housing to the front gear case. Then remove the oil seal housing (**Figure 68**). See **Figure 69**.

12. Remove the bolts that hold the front gear case (**Figure 70**) to the engine. Then withdraw the front gear case from the engine and remove it. Remove the dowel pin.

13. Remove the reverse shaft and spring (A, **Figure 71**) from the crankcase.

14. To remove the drive bevel gear and output shaft left-hand bearing housing from the crankcase, perform the following:

    a. Hold the flywheel bolt or shift the transmission into gear, to prevent the engine from turning.

    b. Remove the drive bevel gear nut (B, **Figure 71**).

    c. Remove the gear (C, **Figure 71**) and shim(s). See **Figure 72**.

    d. Remove the bolts that hold the left-hand bearing housing (**Figure 73**) to the crankshaft. Then remove the bearing housing. See **Figure 74**.

15. Remove the gasket from the crankcase.

16. Install by reversing these removal steps, noting the following.

17. If any parts in the front gear case assembly are replaced, have a Kawasaki dealer check and adjust the bevel gear backlash and tooth contact.

18. To install the output shaft left-hand bearing housing and drive bevel gear, perform the following:

    a. Install the bearing housing (**Figure 73**) and its mounting bolts. Tighten the output shaft left-

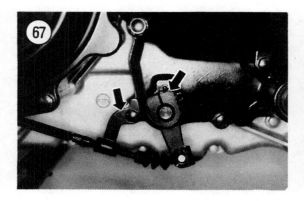

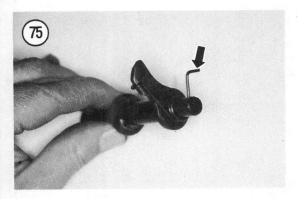

hand bearing housing bolts to the torque specification in **Table 2**.

   b. Install the shim(s) and the drive bevel gear (C, **Figure 71**) onto the output shaft.

   c. Apply new engine oil to the output shaft threads.

   d. Install the drive bevel gear nut (B, **Figure 71**) and tighten to the torque specification in **Table 2**.

19. Hook the spring onto the reverse shaft as shown in **Figure 75**.

20. Install the reverse shaft and spring into the crankcase. Insert the free spring end into the hole in the crankcase as shown in **Figure 76**.

21. Apply grease to the oil seals (**Figure 77**) mounted in the front gear case.

22. Install a new front gear case gasket.

23. Tighten the front gear case mounting bolts to the torque specification in **Table 2**.

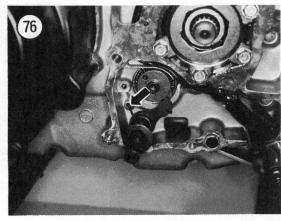

12

24. Apply high-temperature grease to the oil seal (A, **Figure 78**) and O-ring (B, **Figure 78**) mounted in the oil seal housing.

25. Install the oil seal housing (**Figure 69**) and tighten its mounting nuts to the torque specification in **Table 2**.

26. Apply grease to the propeller shaft and drive gear (**Figure 79**) shaft splines.

27. Tighten the upper rear shock absorber mounting bolts and nuts to the torque specification in **Table 2**.

28. Tighten the front suspension arm bolts to the torque specification in **Table 2**.

29. Adjust the reverse lever angle as described under *Reverse Cable* in Chapter Seven.

30. Adjust the reverse cable as described under *Reverse Cable* in Chapter Seven.

31. Check the engine oil and refill as necessary.

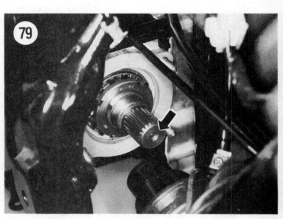

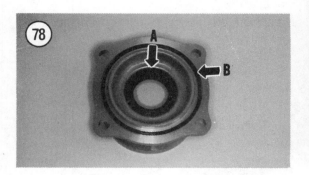

Table 1 REAR SUSPENSION GENERAL SPECIFICATIONS

Rear suspension type	Torque tube
Wheel travel	120 mm (4.724 in.)

Table 2 TIGHTENING TORQUES—2-WHEEL DRIVE

	N·m	ft.-lb.
Wheel nuts	34	25
Shock absorber mounting bolts/nuts	34	25
Suspension arm pivot bolts		
10 mm	34	25
12 mm	88	65
Propeller shaft housing nuts	25	18
Axle shaft pipe bolts		
1986-1987	20	15
1988-on	25	18
Ring gear cover and differential		
gear housing bolts	29	21
Final gear case drain plug	20	15
Final gear case filler cap	29	21
Final gear case bolts	25	18
Differential lever case		
mounting bolts	25	18
Output shaft left-hand		
bearing housing bolts	12	9
Oil seal housing nuts	25	18
Drive bevel gear nut		
14 mm nut	88	65
16 mm nut	93	69

Table 3 TIGHTENING TORQUES—4-WHEEL DRIVE

	N·m	ft.-lb.
Wheel nuts	34	25
Left-hand axle hub nut	145	107
Shock absorber mounting bolts/nuts	34	25
Suspension arm pivot bolts		
10 mm	34	25
12 mm	88	65
Oil drain plug	20	15
Oil filler cap	29	21
Propeller shaft housing nuts	34	25
Axle pipe nuts	34	25
Rear gear cover bolts		
8 mm	25	18
10 mm	47	35

12

CHAPTER THIRTEEN

BRAKES

This chapter describes service procedures for the front and rear brakes. Brake specifications are listed in **Tables 1-6** at the end of this chapter.

FRONT DRUM BRAKE
(1986-1987)

The front drum brake is operated by hydraulic brake fluid and a master cylinder.

> *WARNING*
> *When working on the brake system, never blow off brake components or use compressed air. Do **not** inhale any airborne brake dust as it may contain asbestos, which can cause lung injury and cancer. As an added precaution, wear an approved filtering face mask and thoroughly wash your hands and forearms with warm water and soap after completing any brake work.*

Front Brake Drum
Removal/Installation

Refer to **Figure 1** when performing this procedure.

1. Remove the front wheels as described in Chapter Ten.

2. Remove the hub nut cotter pin and discard it.

3. Remove the hub nut and collar.

4. Remove the front brake drum

5. Install by reversing these removal steps, noting the following.

6. Tighten the front hub nut to the torque specification in **Table 4**. Secure the hub nut with a new cotter

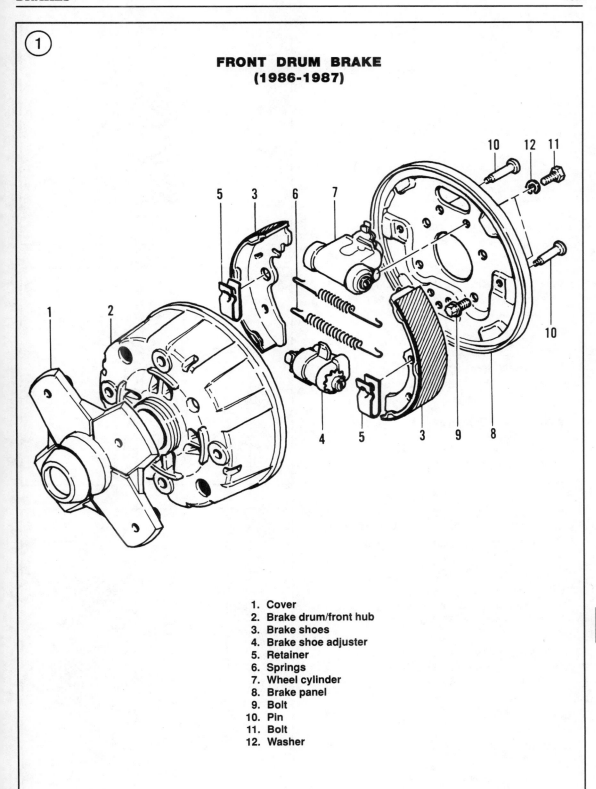

①

FRONT DRUM BRAKE
(1986-1987)

1. Cover
2. Brake drum/front hub
3. Brake shoes
4. Brake shoe adjuster
5. Retainer
6. Springs
7. Wheel cylinder
8. Brake panel
9. Bolt
10. Pin
11. Bolt
12. Washer

13

pin. Bend the cotter pin ends over to lock it (**Figure 2**).

Front Brake Drum
Inspection

1. Clean the brake drum in a detergent solution, then allow to dry.

> *NOTE*
> *Immediately discard the detergent solu-*
> *tion and wash your hands.*

2. Check the drum contact surface for scoring or other damage.

> *NOTE*
> *If oil or grease is on the drum surface,*
> *clean it off with a clean rag soaked in*
> *lacquer thinner—do not use any solvent*
> *that may leave an oil residue.*

3. Measure the brake drum inside diameter and check against the specification in **Table 1**. Replace if measurement exceeds the service limit.

Front Brake Shoe Replacement

Refer to **Figure 1** for this procedure.
1. Remove the front brake drum as described in this section.
2. Measure the brake shoe lining thickness with a vernier caliper (**Figure 3**) and check against the dimension in **Table 1**. Replace if worn to the service limit. If replacement is necessary, continue with this procedure.
3. Disconnect the brake shoe springs (**Figure 4**) from the brake shoes.
4. Push the retainer and then twist the pin (**Figure 4**) to remove the retainer. Repeat for the other side.
5. Remove the brake shoes.
6. Replace the springs if weak or damaged.
7. Install the new brake shoes—insert the pins through the brake shoes and secure with the retainers.
8. Connect the brake shoe springs to the brake shoes.
9. Install the front brake drum as described in this chapter.
10. Adjust the brake shoes as described under *Front and Rear Brake Shoe Adjustment (1986-1987 Drum Brake)* in Chapter Three.

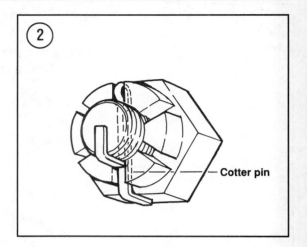
Cotter pin

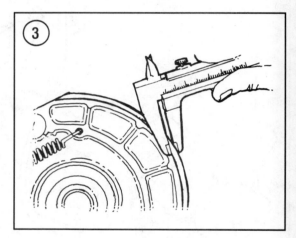

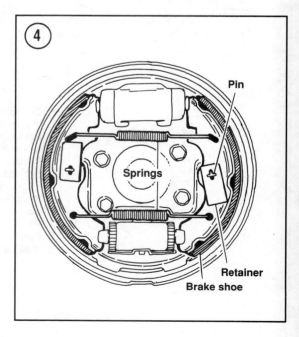
Pin
Springs
Retainer
Brake shoe

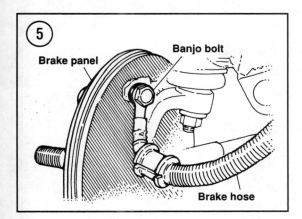

(5)

Brake panel

Banjo bolt

Brake hose

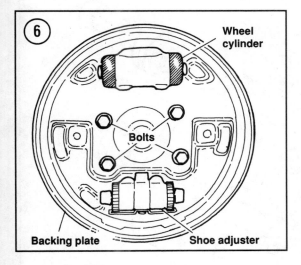

(6)

Wheel cylinder

Bolts

Backing plate

Shoe adjuster

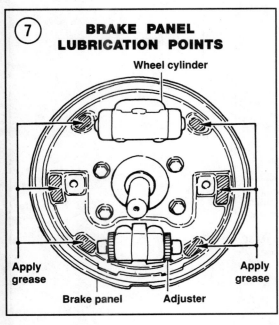

(7) **BRAKE PANEL LUBRICATION POINTS**

Wheel cylinder

Apply grease

Apply grease

Brake panel

Adjuster

Brake Panel Removal

Refer to **Figure 1** for this procedure.

1. Remove the brake shoes as described in this section.

2. Remove the brake hose banjo bolt and washers at the back of the brake panel (**Figure 5**).

> *CAUTION*
> *Wash brake fluid off any painted or plated surfaces immediately as it will destroy the finish. Use soapy water and rinse completely.*

3. Remove the bolts (**Figure 6**) that hold the brake panel to the steering knuckle. Then remove the brake panel.

4. Remove the brake shoe adjuster mounting bolts and remove the brake shoe adjuster (**Figure 6**).

5. Remove the wheel cylinder mounting bolts and remove the wheel cylinder (**Figure 6**).

6. Wipe off all old grease from all of the brake panel parts.

7. If necessary, service the wheel cylinder as described in this chapter.

Brake Panel Installation

Refer to **Figure 1** for this procedure.

1. Install the brake shoe adjuster onto the brake panel. Install the mounting bolts and tighten to the torque specification in **Table 4**.

2. Install the wheel cylinder onto the brake panel. Install the mounting bolts and tighten to the torque specification in **Table 4**.

3. Install the brake panel (**Figure 6**) and its mounting bolts. Tighten the mounting bolts to the torque specification in **Table 4**.

4. Apply a high-temperature grease to the following brake panel parts (**Figure 7**):

   a. Wheel cylinder piston ends.

   b. Brake shoe adjuster ends.

   c. Brake panel and brake shoe contact points.

5. Reconnect the brake hose banjo bolt (**Figure 5**). Install a washer on each side of the brake hose. Tighten the banjo bolt to the torque specification in **Table 4**.

6. Install the brake shoes as described in this section.

13

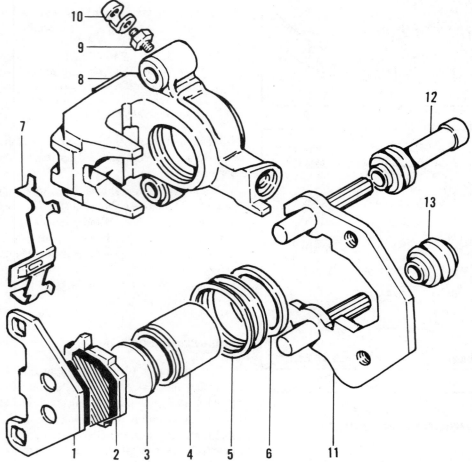

**FRONT BRAKE CALIPER
(1988-ON 2-WHEEL DRIVE)**

1. Brake pad
2. Brake pad
3. Insulator
4. Piston
5. Dust seal
6. Piston seal
7. Pad spring
8. Caliper housing
9. Bleed screw
10. Cover
11. Caliper bracket
12. Friction boot
13. Friction boot

7. Bleed the brake system as described in this chapter.

Wheel Cylinder
Disassembly/Inspection/Reassembly

Parts that make up the wheel cylinder assembly are not available separately.

1. Pull the dust covers out of the cylinder.
2. Pull the pistons and piston cups out of the cylinder.
3. Inspect the pistons and cylinder bore for severe wear or damage.
4. Inspect the dust covers and piston cups for severe wear or damage.
5. If a part is severely worn or damaged, or if the dust covers are leaking, replace the wheel cylinder assembly.
6. Coat the piston cups and pistons with new DOT 3 brake fluid.
7. Install the piston cups and pistons into the cylinder bore.
8. Install the dust covers over the pistons and install them into the wheel cylinder.

DISC BRAKE

The front disc brakes are actuated by hydraulic fluid and controlled by a hand lever on the master cylinder. As the brake pads wear, the brake fluid level drops in the reservoir and automatically adjusts for wear.

When working on a hydraulic brake system, it is essential that the work area and all tools be absolutely clean. Any tiny particles of foreign material or grit in the caliper assembly or master cylinder can damage the components.

Consider the following when servicing the front disc brake.

1. Use only DOT 3 brake fluid from a sealed container.
2. Do not allow disc brake fluid to contact any plastic parts or painted surfaces as damage will result.
3. Always keep the master cylinder reservoir and spare cans of brake fluid closed to prevent dust or moisture from entering. Brake fluid contamination can result in brake system failure.
4. Use only disc brake fluid (DOT 3) to wash parts. Never clean any internal brake components with solvent or any other petroleum-base cleaners.
5. Whenever any component is removed from the brake system, the system is considered *opened* and must be bled to remove air bubbles. Also, if the brake feels *spongy*, this usually means there are air bubbles in the system, and it must be bled. For safe brake operation, refer to *Brake Bleeding* in this chapter for complete details.

> *CAUTION*
> *Disc brake components rarely require disassembly, so do not disassemble unless absolutely necessary. Do not use solvents of any kind on the brake system's internal components. Solvents will cause the seals to swell and distort. When disassembling and cleaning brake components (except brake pads) use new DOT 3 brake fluid.*

> *CAUTION*
> *Never reuse brake fluid. Contaminated brake fluid can cause brake failure. Dispose of brake fluid according to local EPA regulations.*

FRONT CALIPER
(1988-ON 2-WHEEL DRIVE)

Refer to **Figure 8** when replacing the front brake pads or servicing the front brake caliper.

Brake Pad Inspection

You can measure brake pad wear with the brake caliper installed on the vehicle.

1. Remove the front wheels as described in Chapter Ten.
2. Measure the distance from the disc surface to the back of the pad's friction material (**Figure 9**) with a small ruler. The brake pads should be replaced if the

13

friction material thickness is equal to or less than the service limit specification in **Table 2**.

3. Install the front wheels as described in Chapter Ten, or replace the brake pads as described in the following section.

Front Brake Pad Replacement

There is no recommended time interval for changing the friction pads in the front brakes. Pad wear depends greatly on riding habits and conditions.

To maintain even brake pressure on the disc, always replace both pads in both calipers at the same time.

1. Read the information listed under *Disc Brake* in this chapter.

2. Remove the front wheel as described in Chapter Ten.

3. Loosen the brake caliper mounting bolts (A, **Figure 10**) and remove them from the caliper. Lift the caliper off of the brake disc.

4. Push in the caliper bracket (A, **Figure 11**) and remove the outer (B, **Figure 11**) and inner brake pads.

5. Check the pad spring (**Figure 12**) in the caliper. Replace the pad spring if corroded or damaged.

6. Support the brake caliper with a Bunjee cord or heavy wire hook.

7. Measure the thickness of each brake pad (**Figure 13**). Replace the brake pads if the thickness of any one pad is equal to or less than the service limit in **Table 2**. Replace all 4 brake pads as a set.

8. Inspect the brake pads (**Figure 14**) for uneven wear, damage or grease contamination. Replace all 4 brake pads as a set.

9. Check the end of the piston (**Figure 15**) for fluid leakage. If the dust seal is damaged and/or if there is fluid leaking from the caliper, overhaul the brake caliper as described in this chapter.

10. Check the brake disc for wear as described in this chapter.

11. To make room for the new pads, the piston (**Figure 15**) must be pushed back into the caliper. This will force brake fluid back through the hose and into the master cylinder reservoir. To prevent the reservoir from overflowing, remove some brake fluid as follows:

   a. Clean the top of the master cylinder of all dirt.

   b. Remove the cap and diaphragm from the master cylinder.

c. Temporarily install the inside brake pad into the caliper and slowly push the piston back into the caliper.

d. Constantly check the reservoir to make sure brake fluid does not overflow. Siphon fluid, if necessary, before it overflows.

WARNING
Brake fluid is poisonous. Do not siphon with your mouth.

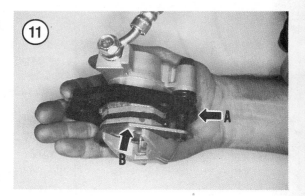

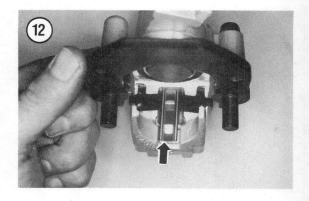

e. The caliper piston should move freely. If not, the caliper should be removed and overhauled as described in this chapter.

f. Push the caliper piston in all the way to allow room for the new pads.

g. Remove the inside pad.

BRAKE PAD LINING THICKNESS

1 mm

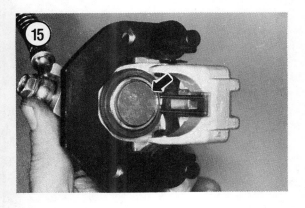

12. Install the pad spring into the caliper as shown in **Figure 12**.

13. Install the inside and outside brake pads as shown in **Figure 11**. The outer brake pad holes should ride on the bracket arms (A, **Figure 11**).

14. Slide the brake caliper over the brake disc. Then install the brake caliper mounting bolts (A, **Figure 10**) and tighten to the torque specification in **Table 5**.

15. Repeat for the other brake caliper.

> *WARNING*
> *Use new brake fluid clearly marked DOT 3 from a sealed container.*

16. Install the master cylinder reservoir diaphragm and top cover. Tighten the cover screws securely.

17. Pull and release the brake lever a few times to seat the pads against each disc, then recheck the brake fluid level in the reservoir. If necessary, add fresh DOT 3 brake fluid.

18. Install the front wheels as described in Chapter Ten.

> *WARNING*
> *Do not ride the vehicle until you are sure that both front brakes are operating correctly with full hydraulic advantage. If necessary, bleed the front brakes as described in this chapter.*

Removal/Installation (Caliper Will Not Be Disassembled)

If the brake caliper is to be removed without disassembling it, perform this procedure. If the caliper is to be disassembled, refer to *Caliper Removal/Piston Removal* in this chapter.

1. Remove the front wheel(s) as described in Chapter Ten.

2A. If the caliper is to be completely removed from the vehicle, perform the following:

   a. Loosen the brake hose banjo bolt (B, **Figure 10**) at the caliper.

   b. Remove the bolts (A, **Figure 10**) that hold the brake caliper to the steering knuckle. Then lift the caliper off the brake disc.

   c. Remove the banjo bolt and the 2 washers and remove the brake caliper. Seal the hose so that brake fluid does not drip out.

13

2B. If the caliper is only being partially removed and it is not necessary to disconnect the brake line at the caliper, perform the following:

a. Remove the bolts (A, **Figure 10**) that hold the brake caliper to the steering knuckle. Then lift the caliper off the brake disc.

b. Insert a wooden or plastic spacer block in the caliper between the brake pads.

NOTE
The spacer block prevents the piston from being forced out of the caliper if the brake lever is squeezed while the caliper is removed from the brake disc. If the brake lever is squeezed, the piston will be forced out. If this happens, the caliper will have to be disassembled to properly reseat the piston. After reassembly, bleeding air from the system will also be required.

c. Support the caliper with a Bunjee cord or a wire hook. Do not allow the caliper to hang by its hose.

3. Install the caliper by reversing these steps, while noting the following.

4A. If the caliper is completely removed from the vehicle:

a. Make sure the brake pads are not contaminated with brake fluid. Wipe the caliper housing off with a clean rag.

b. Position the brake hose against the caliper as shown in **Figure 10**.

c. Place a washer on each side of the brake hose. Then install the bolt into the caliper (B, **Figure 10**). Tighten the banjo bolt finger-tight at this time.

d. Carefully install the caliper assembly over the brake disc so the leading edge of the pads are not damaged.

e. Install the 2 bolts (A, **Figure 10**) that hold the brake caliper to the steering knuckle. Then torque the bolts to the specification in **Table 5**.

f. Torque the brake hose banjo bolt to the specification in **Table 5**.

g. Refill the master cylinder with DOT 3 brake fluid and bleed the front brake as described in this chapter.

4B. If the caliper is only partially removed from the vehicle:

a. Remove the spacer block from between the brake pads.

b. Disconnect the caliper from its hanger and carefully install the caliper over the brake disc. Be careful not to damage the leading edge of the pads during installation.

c. Install the 2 bolts (A, **Figure 10**) that hold the brake caliper to the steering knuckle. Then torque the bolts to the specification in **Table 5**.

d. Operate the brake lever a few times to seat the pads against the brake disc.

WARNING
Do not ride the vehicle until you are sure that both front brakes are operating correctly with full hydraulic advantage. If necessary, bleed the front brakes as described in this chapter.

Caliper Removal/Piston Removal (Caliper Will Be Disassembled)

Force is required to remove the piston from the caliper. This force can be supplied by hydraulic pressure in the brake system itself, or compressed air. If you are going to use hydraulic pressure, you must do so before the brake hose is disconnected from the caliper. This procedure describes how to remove the piston while the caliper is still connected to the hydraulic system.

1. Remove the brake pads as described in this chapter.
2. Wrap a large cloth around the brake caliper.
3. Hold the caliper so your hand and fingers are placed away from the piston and brake pad areas.

4. Operate the front brake lever to force the piston (**Figure 16**) out of the caliper cylinder. Remove the piston.

> *NOTE*
> *If the piston will not come out, you will have to use compressed air to remove it. Refer to **Disassembly** in this chapter.*

5. Loosen the caliper banjo bolt (B, **Figure 10**) and remove the bolt and its 2 washers from the caliper. Seal the brake hose to prevent brake fluid from dripping out.
6. Take the caliper to a workbench for further disassembly.

Disassembly

1. Remove the caliper as described in this chapter.

> *WARNING*
> *The piston is forced out of the caliper with considerable force in Step 2. Do not try to cushion the piston with your fingers, as injury could result.*

2. Cushion the caliper piston with a shop rag, making sure to keep your fingers and hand away from the piston area. Then apply compressed air through the brake line port (**Figure 17**) to remove the piston.
3. Remove the support bracket from the caliper.
4. Remove the dust seal (**Figure 18**) and piston seal (**Figure 19**) from the caliper bore grooves.
5. If necessary, remove the friction boots (A, **Figure 20**) from the caliper body.
6. Remove the bleed valve and its cover from the caliper.

Inspection

1. Clean the caliper housing in solvent. Remove stubborn dirt with a soft brush, but do not brush the cylinder bore. Clean the dust and piston seal grooves with a plastic-tipped tool so you do not damage them or the cylinder bore. Then clean the caliper in hot soapy water and rinse in clear, cold water. Dry with compressed air.
2. Clean the piston in new DOT 3 brake fluid.
3. Check the piston and cylinder bore (B, **Figure 20**) for deep scratches or other obvious wear marks. Do not hone the cylinder. If the piston or cylinder is damaged, replace the caliper assembly.

13

4. Clean the bleed valve with compressed air. Check the valve threads for damage. Replace the dust cap if missing or damaged.

5. Clean the banjo bolt with compressed air. Check the threads for damage. Replace worn or damaged washers.

6. Check the friction boots (A, **Figure 20**). Replace if swollen, cracked or severely worn.

7. Check the support bracket shafts for severe wear, damage or uneven wear (steps). The shafts must be in good condition for the caliper to slide back and forth. Remove all grease residue from the bracket. If the support bracket is damaged, the entire brake caliper must be replaced.

8. Measure the thickness of each brake pad (**Figure 13**) with a vernier caliper or ruler and compare to the specification listed in **Table 2**. If the pad thickness is equal to or less than the wear limit, replace the pads. Replace all 4 pads as a set.

9. Inspect the brake pads (**Figure 14**) for uneven wear, damage or grease contamination. Replace the pads as a set, if necessary.

10. Replace the piston seal and dust seal as a set.

NOTE
Kawasaki recommends replacing the piston and dust seals at the same time.

Assembly

NOTE
Use new, DOT 3 brake fluid in the following steps.

1. If removed, install the friction boots (A, **Figure 20**).

2. Soak the piston seal and dust seal in brake fluid for approximately 5 minutes.

3. Lightly coat the piston and cylinder bore with brake fluid.

4. Install a new piston seal into the second groove in the cylinder bore (**Figure 19**).

5. Install the piston as follows:

a. Slide a new dust seal over the rear piston end (A, **Figure 21**).

NOTE
The piston ends can be identified by the insulator. The insulator is installed in the front side of the piston; see B, Figure 21.

b. Place the piston between the caliper arms as shown in **Figure 22**. The front of the piston should be pointing out (away from the caliper bore).

c. Slide the piston into the caliper bore (**Figure 23**). Stop before the groove in the front of the piston enters the dust seal.

d. Pull the seal out and install its lip into the piston groove, then push the piston all the way into the caliper bore (**Figure 24**).

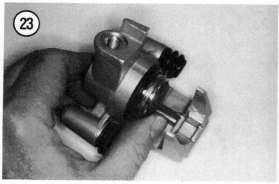

6. If the support bracket is removed, perform the following:

   a. Apply a thin coat of PBC (Poly Butyl Cuprysil) grease (or equivalent) to the caliper bracket shafts.

> *CAUTION*
> *PBC grease (or equivalent) is a special high-temperature, water-resistant grease that is used in braking systems. Do not use any other kind of lubricant as it may thin out and contaminate the brake pads.*

   b. Slide the support bracket shafts into the caliper (**Figure 25**). Slide the bracket back and forth, without removing it, to distribute the grease and to check the shafts for binding. The bracket must move smoothly; if any binding is noted, remove the bracket and inspect the shafts for damage. Wipe off any excess grease from the outside of the caliper or bracket.

7. If necessary, install the bleed screw and its dust cover. Tighten securely.

8. Install the brake caliper assembly and brake pads as described in this chapter.

FRONT CALIPER
(4-WHEEL DRIVE)

Refer to **Figure 26** when replacing the front brake pads or servicing the front brake caliper.

Brake Pad Inspection

You can measure brake pad wear with the brake caliper installed on the vehicle as follows.
1. Remove the front wheels as described in Chapter Ten.
2. Measure the distance from the disc surface to the back of the pad's friction material (**Figure 27**) with a small ruler. The brake pads should be replaced if the friction material thickness is equal to or less than the service limit specification in **Table 3**.
3. Install the front wheels as described in Chapter Ten, or replace the brake pads as described in the following section.

Front Brake Pad Replacement

There is no recommended time interval for changing the friction pads in the front brakes. Pad wear depends greatly on riding habits and conditions.

To maintain even brake pressure on the disc, always replace both pads in both calipers at the same time.
1. Read the information listed under *Disc Brake* in this chapter.
2. Remove the front wheel as described in Chapter Ten.
3. Loosen, but do not remove, the 2 pad pin bolts (A, **Figure 28**) that hold the brake pads to the caliper.
4. Remove the 2 brake caliper mounting bolts (B, **Figure 28**). Then slide the brake caliper off of the brake disc.
5. Remove the 2 brake pad pin bolts (**Figure 29**).
6. Push the caliper bracket (A, **Figure 30**) toward the caliper and remove the 2 brake pads (B, **Figure 30**).
7. Support the brake caliper with a Bunjee cord or heavy wire hook.
8. Check the pad spring (**Figure 31**) in the caliper.
9. Measure the thickness of each brake pad (**Figure 32**). Replace the brake pads if the thickness of any

13

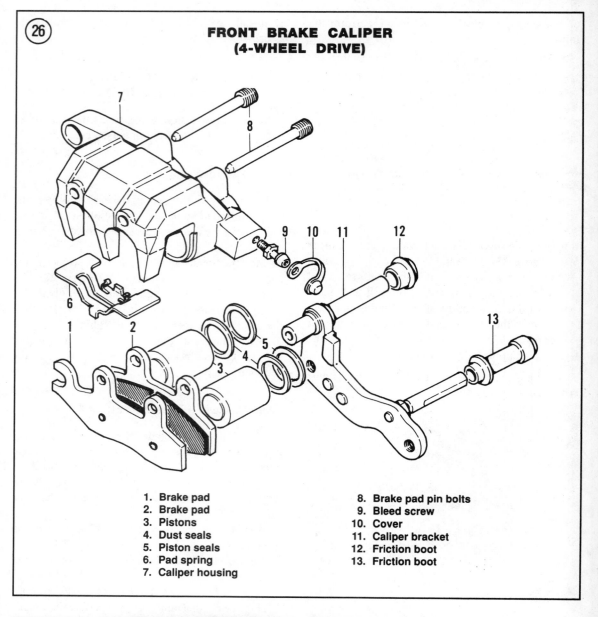

**FRONT BRAKE CALIPER
(4-WHEEL DRIVE)**

1. Brake pad
2. Brake pad
3. Pistons
4. Dust seals
5. Piston seals
6. Pad spring
7. Caliper housing
8. Brake pad pin bolts
9. Bleed screw
10. Cover
11. Caliper bracket
12. Friction boot
13. Friction boot

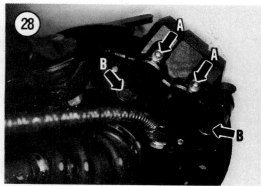

one pad is equal to or is less than the service limit in **Table 3**. Replace all 4 brake pads as a set.

10. Inspect the brake pads (**Figure 33**) for uneven wear, damage or grease contamination. Replace all 4 brake pads as a set.

11. Check the end of the piston for fluid leakage. If the dust seal is damaged and/or if there is fluid leaking from the caliper, overhaul the brake caliper as described in this chapter.

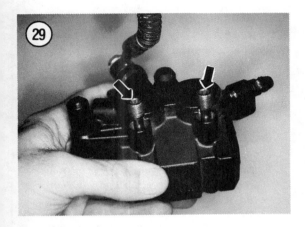

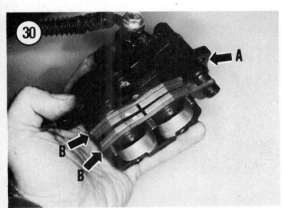

12. Check the pad pin bolts for corrosion, bending or other damage.

13. Check the brake disc for wear as described in this chapter.

14. To make room for the new pads, the pistons must be pushed back into the caliper. This forces brake fluid back through the hose and into the master cylinder reservoir. To prevent the reservoir from overflowing, remove some of the brake fluid as follows:

    a. Clean the top of the master cylinder of all dirt.

    b. Remove the cap and diaphragm from the master cylinder.

    c. Temporarily install the inside brake pad into the caliper and slowly push the pistons back into the caliper.

    d. Constantly check the reservoir to make sure brake fluid does not overflow. Siphon fluid, if necessary, before it overflows.

> *WARNING*
> *Brake fluid is poisonous. Do not siphon with your mouth.*

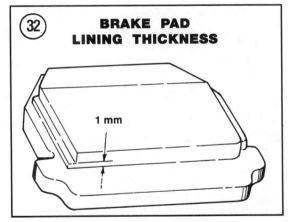

BRAKE PAD
LINING THICKNESS

1 mm

13

e. Both pistons should move freely. If not, the caliper should be removed and overhauled as described in this chapter.

f. Push the pistons in to allow room for the new pads.

g. Remove the inside pad.

15. Install the inside brake pad (A, **Figure 34**).

16. Hook the outside brake pad onto the bracket arm and install the outside brake pad (B, **Figure 34**). The friction material on both brake pads must face toward each other.

17. Compress both brake pads, then install the 2 pad pin bolts (**Figure 29**) through the brake pads. Using an Allen wrench, tighten the pad pin bolts securely.

18. Slide the brake caliper over the brake disc. Then install the brake caliper mounting bolts (B, **Figure 28**) and tighten to the torque specification in **Table 6**.

19. Torque the caliper pad pin Allen bolts (A, **Figure 28**) to the specification in **Table 6**.

20. Repeat for the other brake caliper.

WARNING
Use new brake fluid clearly marked DOT 3 from a sealed container.

21. Install the master cylinder reservoir diaphragm and top cover. Tighten the cover screws securely.

22. Pull and release the brake lever a few times to seat the pads against each disc, then recheck the brake fluid level in the reservoir. If necessary, add fresh DOT 3 brake fluid.

23. Install the front wheels as described in Chapter Ten.

WARNING
Do not ride the vehicle until you are sure that both front brakes are operating correctly with full hydraulic advantage. If necessary, bleed the front brakes as described in this chapter.

Removal/Installation
(Caliper Will Not Be Disassembled)

If the brake caliper is to be removed without disassembling it, perform this procedure. If the caliper is to be disassembled, refer to *Caliper Removal/Piston Removal* in this chapter.

1. Remove the front wheel(s) as described in Chapter Ten.

2A. If the caliper is to be completely removed from the vehicle, perform the following:

a. Loosen the brake hose banjo bolt (A, **Figure 35**) at the caliper.

b. Remove the brake caliper mounting bolts (B, **Figure 35**). Then lift the caliper off the brake disc.

c. Remove the banjo bolt and the 2 washers and remove the brake caliper. Seal the hose so that brake fluid does not drip out.

2B. If the caliper is only being partially removed and it is not necessary to disconnect the brake line at the caliper, perform the following:

a. Remove the brake caliper mounting bolts (B, **Figure 35**). Then lift the caliper off the brake disc.

b. Insert a wooden or plastic spacer block in the caliper between the brake pads.

NOTE
The spacer block prevents the piston from being forced out of the caliper if the brake lever is squeezed while the caliper is removed from the brake disc. If the brake lever is squeezed, the piston

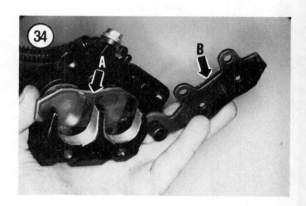

will be forced out. If this happens, the caliper will have to be disassembled to properly reseat the piston. Bleeding the system will also be required after reassembly.

c. Support the caliper with a Bunjee cord or a wire hook. Do not allow the caliper to hang by its hose.

3. Install the caliper by reversing these steps, while noting the following.

4A. If the caliper is completely removed from the vehicle:

a. Make sure the brake pads are not contaminated with brake fluid. Wipe off the caliper housing with a clean rag.

b. Place a washer on each side of the brake hose. Then install the banjo bolt into the caliper (A, **Figure 35**). Tighten the banjo bolt finger-tight at this time.

c. Carefully install the caliper assembly over the brake disc so that the brake pad leading edges are not damaged.

d. Install the brake caliper mounting bolts (B, **Figure 35**) Then torque the bolts to the specification in **Table 6**.

f. Torque the brake hose banjo bolt to the specification in **Table 6**.

g. Refill the master cylinder and bleed the front brake system as described in this chapter.

4B. If the caliper was only partially removed from the vehicle:

a. Remove the spacer block from between the brake pads.

b. Disconnect the caliper from its hanger and carefully install the caliper over the brake disc. Be careful not to damage the leading edge of the pads during installation.

c. Install the brake caliper mounting bolts (B, **Figure 35**) that hold the brake caliper to the steering knuckle. Then torque the bolts to the specification in **Table 6**.

d. Operate the brake lever a few times to seat the pads against the brake disc.

WARNING
Do not ride the vehicle until you are sure that both front brakes are operating correctly with full hydraulic advantage. If necessary, bleed the front brakes as described in this chapter.

Caliper Removal/Piston Removal (Caliper Will Be Disassembled)

Force is required to remove the pistons from the caliper. This force can be supplied by hydraulic pressure in the brake system itself, or compressed air. If you are going to use hydraulic pressure, you must do so before the brake hose is disconnected from the caliper. This procedure describes how to remove the piston while the caliper is still connected to the hydraulic system.

1. Remove the brake pads as described in this chapter.

2. Wrap a large cloth around the brake caliper.

3. Hold the caliper so that your hand and fingers are placed away from the piston and brake pad areas.

4. Operate the front brake lever to force the pistons (**Figure 36**) out of the caliper. Remove the pistons.

NOTE
*If the pistons will not come out, you will have to use compressed air to remove them. Refer to **Disassembly** in this chapter.*

5. Support the caliper. Then loosen the caliper banjo bolt (**Figure 37**) and remove the bolt and its 2

13

washers from the caliper. Seal the brake hose to prevent brake fluid from dripping out.

6. Take the caliper to a workbench for further disassembly.

Disassembly

1. Remove the caliper as described in this chapter.

> *WARNING*
> *The piston is forced out of the caliper with considerable force in Step 2. Do not try to cushion the piston with your fingers, as injury could result.*

2. Cushion the caliper piston with a shop rag, making sure to keep your fingers and hand away from the piston area. Then apply compressed air through the brake line port (**Figure 38**) to remove the piston.

3. Remove the dust seals (A, **Figure 39**) and piston seals (B, **Figure 39**) from the inside of the cylinder.

4. Remove the support bracket from the caliper.

5. If necessary, remove the friction boots (12 and 13, **Figure 26**) from the caliper body.

6. Remove the bleed valve and its cover from the caliper.

7. Remove the pad spring (**Figure 31**) from the caliper.

Inspection

1. Clean the caliper housing in solvent. Remove stubborn dirt with a soft brush, but do not brush the cylinder bores as this may damage them. Clean the dust and piston seal grooves with a plastic tipped tool so that you do not damage them or the cylinder bore. Then clean the caliper in hot soapy water and rinse in clear, cold water. Dry with compressed air.

2. Clean the pistons using DOT 3 brake fluid.

3. Check the pistons and cylinder bores for deep scratches or other obvious wear marks. Do not hone the cylinder. If the pistons or cylinder bores are damaged, replace the caliper assembly.

4. Clean the bleed valve with compressed air. Check the valve threads for damage. Replace the dust cap if missing or damaged.

5. Clean the banjo bolt with compressed air. Check the threads for damage. Replace worn or damaged washers.

6. Check the friction boots. Replace if swollen, cracked or severely worn.

7. Check the support bracket shafts for severe wear, damage or uneven wear (steps). The shafts must be in good condition for the caliper to slide back and forth. Remove all grease residue from the bracket. If the support bracket is damaged, the entire brake caliper will have to be replaced.

8. Measure the thickness of each brake pad (**Figure 32**) with a vernier caliper or ruler and compare to the service limit in **Table 1**. If the pad thickness is equal to or less than the service limit, replace all 4 pads as a set.

9. Inspect the brake pads (**Figure 40**) for uneven wear, damage or grease contamination. Replace the pads as a set, if necessary.

10. Replace the piston seals and dust seals as a set.

Assembly

> *NOTE*
> *Use new, DOT 3 brake fluid when brake fluid is called for in the following steps.*

1. Soak the piston seals and dust seals in brake fluid for approximately 5 minutes.

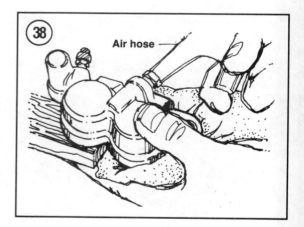

2. Lightly coat the pistons and cylinder bores with brake fluid.

3. Install a new piston seal (B, **Figure 39**) into the second groove in the cylinder bore.

4. Install a new dust seal (A, **Figure 39**) into the front groove in the cylinder bore.

> *NOTE*
> *Make sure both seals fit squarely into their respective cylinder bore grooves. If a seal is not installed properly, the caliper assembly will leak and braking performance will be reduced.*

5. Repeat Steps 3 and 4 for the other cylinder.

6. Install the pistons—steel side facing out—into the cylinder bores (**Figure 36**).

7. If the support bracket is removed, perform the following:

  a. Apply a thin coat of PBC (Poly Butyl Cuprysil) grease (or equivalent) to the caliper bracket shafts.

> *CAUTION*
> *PBC grease (or equivalent) is a special high-temperature, water-resistant grease that is used in braking systems. Do not use any other kind of lubricant as it may thin out and contaminate the brake pads.*

  b. Slide the support bracket shafts into the caliper. Slide the bracket back and forth, without removing it, to distribute the grease and to check the shafts for binding. The bracket must move smoothly; if any binding is noted, remove the bracket and inspect the shafts for damage. Wipe off any excess grease from the outside of the caliper or bracket.

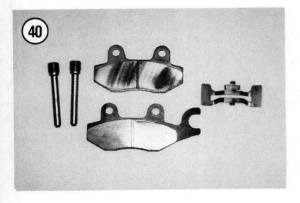

8. If necessary, install the bleed screw and its dust cover. Tighten securely.

9. Install the pad spring (**Figure 31**) into the brake caliper.

10. Install the brake caliper assembly and brake pads as described in this chapter.

FRONT MASTER CYLINDER

The front master cylinder is bolted to the handlebar with 2 bolts and a removable clamp.

Refer to **Figure 41** (1986-1987) or **Figure 42** (1988-on) when servicing the master cylinder in the following sections.

Read the information listed under *Disc Brake* in this chapter before servicing the front master cylinder.

Removal/Installation

1. Park the vehicle on level ground and set the parking brake.

2. Cover the area under the master cylinder to prevent brake fluid from damaging any component that it might contact.

> *CAUTION*
> *If brake fluid should contact any surface, wash the area immediately with soapy water and rinse completely. Brake fluid will damage plastic, painted and plated surfaces.*

3. To remove brake fluid from the reservoir:

  a. Remove the master cylinder cap and diaphragm.

  b. Use a clean syringe and remove the brake fluid from the reservoir. Discard the brake fluid.

4. Pull the rubber cover away from the brake hose at the master cylinder.

5. Remove the banjo bolt (**Figure 43**) and the washers securing the brake hose to the master cylinder. Seal the brake hose to prevent brake fluid from dripping out.

6. Remove the 2 bolts and the clamp holding the master cylinder to the handlebar and remove the master cylinder (A, **Figure 44**).

7. If necessary, service the master cylinder as described in this chapter.

8. Clean the handlebar, master cylinder and clamp mating surfaces.

13

(41)

FRONT MASTER CYLINDER
(1986-1987)

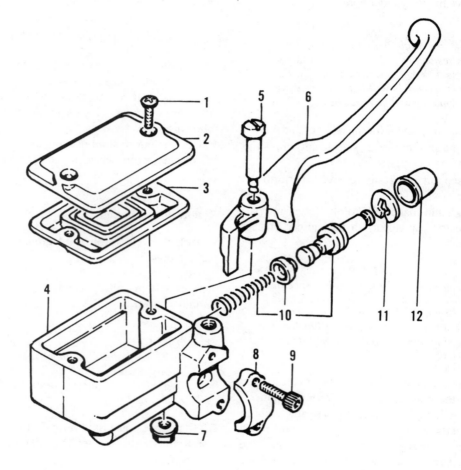

1. Screw
2. Cover
3. Diaphragm
4. Master cylinder housing
5. Pivot bolt
6. Brake lever
7. Nut
8. Clamp
9. Bolt
10. Piston assembly
11. Circlip
12. Boot

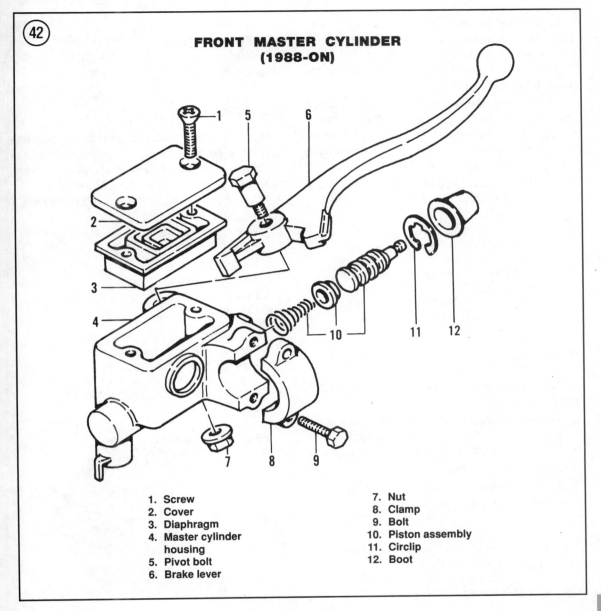

FRONT MASTER CYLINDER (1988-ON)

1. Screw
2. Cover
3. Diaphragm
4. Master cylinder housing
5. Pivot bolt
6. Brake lever
7. Nut
8. Clamp
9. Bolt
10. Piston assembly
11. Circlip
12. Boot

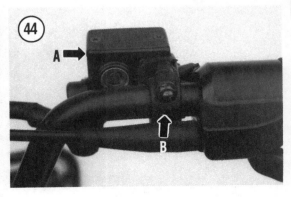

13

9. Position the master cylinder onto the handlebar. Then install its clamp—arrow mark facing up (B, **Figure 44**)—and install the 2 mounting bolts. Tighten the bolts to the torque specification in **Tables 4-6** for your model.

10. Install the brake hose onto the master cylinder, using the banjo bolt (**Figure 43**) and the 2 washers; a washer should be installed on each side of the hose. Tighten the banjo bolt to the torque specification listed in **Tables 4-6** for your model.

11. Refill the master cylinder with DOT 3 brake fluid and bleed the brake as described in this chapter.

> *WARNING*
> *Do not ride the vehicle until the front brakes are working properly. Make sure that the brake lever travel is not excessive and that the lever does not feel spongy—both indicate that the bleeding operation needs to be repeated.*

Disassembly

1. Remove the master cylinder as described in this chapter.

2. Remove the master cylinder cap screws and remove the cap and diaphragm from the caliper.

3. Remove the brake lever pivot bolt, nut and lever (**Figure 45**) from the master cylinder.

4. Carefully remove the dust cover (**Figure 46**) from the groove in the end of the piston.

> *NOTE*
> *If there is brake fluid leaking at the front of the piston bore, the piston cups are worn or damaged. Replace the piston assembly during reassembly.*

5. Compress the piston and remove the circlip (**Figure 47**) from the groove in the master cylinder. Then withdraw the circlip, washer and piston assembly (**Figure 48**) from the master cylinder.

Inspection

Worn or damaged master cylinder components prevent proper brake fluid pressure from building in the brake line. Reduced pressure will cause the brake to feel weak, and it will not hold properly.

1. Wash the piston and cylinder with clean DOT 3 brake fluid.

2. The piston assembly is identified in **Figure 49**:
   a. Spring.
   b. Primary cup.
   c. Secondary cup.
   d. Piston.
   e. Circlip.

> *CAUTION*
> *Do not attempt to remove the secondary cup (C, **Figure 49**) from the piston. Removal will damage the cup, requiring replacement of the piston assembly.*

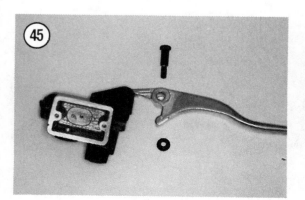

3. Check the piston assembly (**Figure 49**) for the following defects:

   a. Broken, distorted or collapsed piston return spring (A, **Figure 49**).

   b. Worn, cracked, damaged or swollen primary (B, **Figure 49**) and secondary cups (C, **Figure 49**).

   c. Scratched, scored or damaged piston (D, **Figure 49**).

   d. Corroded, weak or damaged circlip (E, **Figure 49**).

   e. Worn or damaged boot.

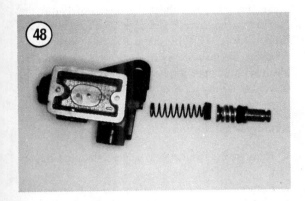

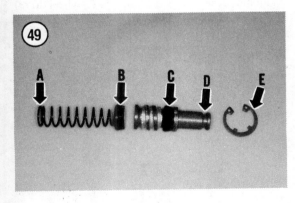

If any of these parts are worn or damaged, replace the piston assembly.

4. Inspect the master cylinder bore (**Figure 50**). If the bore is corroded, scored or damaged in any way, replace the master cylinder assembly. Do not hone the master cylinder bore to remove scratches or other damage.

5. Check for plugged supply and relief ports in the master cylinder. Clean with compressed air.

> *NOTE*
> *A plugged relief port will cause the pads to drag on the disc.*

6. Check the brake lever and pivot bolt for severely worn or damaged parts.

7. Check the reservoir cap and diaphragm for damage. Check the diaphragm for cracks or deterioration. Replace damaged parts as required.

8. Check all the threaded holes in the master cylinder. Clean with compressed air. The small Phillips screws used to secure the reservoir cap strip easily; check the screw heads and threads for damage and replace or repair if necessary.

Assembly

Use new, DOT 3 brake fluid when brake fluid is called for in the following steps.

1. If you are installing a piston repair kit, note the following:

   a. Check the repair kit to make sure that it contains all of the necessary new parts.

   b. Coat the new parts with new brake fluid.

2. Lightly coat the piston assembly and cylinder bore with brake fluid.

3. Assemble the piston assembly as shown in **Figure 49**. The primary cup fits onto the return spring.

> *CAUTION*
> *When installing the piston assembly in Step 4, make sure the primary and secondary cups do not tear or turn inside out; both cups are slightly larger than the bore.*

4. Insert the piston assembly into the master cylinder bore in the direction shown in **Figure 48**.

5. Compress the piston assembly and install the washer and circlip. Make sure the circlip seats in the master cylinder groove (**Figure 47**). Push and re-

13

lease the piston a few times to make sure it moves smoothly in the cylinder bore.

6. Slide the boot (**Figure 46**) over the piston. Seat the cover in the cylinder bore groove.

7. Install the brake lever onto the master cylinder. Lightly grease the pivot bolt shoulder and install the bolt through the master cylinder and brake lever. Install the nut and tighten securely. Then, operate the hand lever, making sure the lever moves freely without binding, and that the adjust screw on the lever contacts the piston correctly.

8. Install the master cylinder as described in this chapter.

BRAKE DISC

The front brake discs are mounted onto the front hubs. See **Figure 51** (2-wheel drive) or **Figure 52** (4-wheel drive).

Inspection

It is not necessary to remove the disc to inspect it. Small marks on the disc are not important, but radial scratches deep enough to snag a fingernail reduce braking effectiveness and increase brake pad wear. If these grooves are evident, and the brake pads are wearing rapidly, the disc should be replaced.

Kawasaki lists standard and wear limit specifications for the brake discs; see **Table 2** and **Table 3**. When servicing the brake discs, do not have the discs reconditioned (ground) to compensate for warpage. The discs are thin and grinding will only reduce their thickness, causing them to warp quite rapidly. If a disc is warped, the brake pads may be dragging on the disc, causing the disc to overheat. Overheating is also caused if there is unequal brake pad pressure on both sides of the disc. Four main causes of unequal pad pressure are:

a. The floating caliper is binding on the caliper bracket shafts, thus preventing the caliper from floating (side-to-side) on the disc.

b. The brake caliper piston seal is worn or damaged.

c. The small master cylinder relief port is plugged.

d. The primary cup on the master cylinder piston is worn or damaged.

1. Support the vehicle with both front wheels off the ground. Set the parking brake and block the rear wheels so that the vehicle cannot roll in either direction.

2. Remove the front wheels as described in Chapter Ten.

3. Measure the thickness around the disc at several locations (**Figure 53**) and compare to the dimension listed in **Table 2** or **Table 3**. Replace the disc if the thickness at any point is less than the service limit specified in **Table 2** or **Table 3**.

4. Make sure the disc bolts are tight prior to performing this check. Using a magnetic stand, install a dial indicator and position its stem against the brake disc. Then zero the dial gauge. Slowly turn the hub to measure runout. If the runout exceeds service limit in **Table 2** or **Table 3**, the disc must be replaced.

5. Clean the disc of any rust or corrosion and wipe clean with lacquer thinner. Never use an oil-based solvent that may leave an oil residue on the disc.

Removal/Installation

1. Remove the front hub(s) as described in Chapter Ten.

2. Remove the screws securing the disc to the hub and remove the disc. See **Figure 54** (2-wheel drive) or **Figure 55** (4-wheel drive).

3. Install by reversing these removal steps. Tighten the disc mounting screws to the torque specification in **Table 5** or **Table 6**.

CAUTION
The disc mounting screws are made of a hard material. When replacing these screws, make sure to purchase the correct type.

REAR DRUM BRAKE

All models are equipped with a rear drum brake(s). On 2-wheel drive models, left- and right-hand rear drum brake units are used. On 4-wheel drive models, a rear drum brake is used on the right-hand side. See **Figure 56** (2-wheel drive) or **Figure 57** (4-wheel drive).

WARNING
*When working on the brake system, never blow off brake components or use compressed air. Do **not** inhale any airborne brake dust as it may contain asbestos, which can cause lung injury and cancer. As an added precaution, wear*

an approved filtering face mask and thoroughly wash your hands and forearms with warm water and soap after completing any brake work.

Rear Brake Drum
Removal/Installation

Refer to **Figure 56** or **Figure 57** when performing this procedure.

1A. On 2-wheel drive models, remove the rear wheels as described in Chapter Twelve.

1B. On 4-wheel drive models, remove the right-hand rear wheel as described in Chapter Twelve.

2. Remove the rear axle nut cotter pin and discard it. See **Figure 58** (2-wheel drive) or **Figure 59** (4-wheel drive).

3. Remove the rear axle nut and washer (**Figure 60**).

4. Remove the rear brake drum.

5. Install by reversing these removal steps, noting the following.

6. Inspect the brake drum seal (**Figure 61**) as described in this chapter. Make sure it is in place before installing the brake drum.

7. Check the brake drum seal for lubrication. Grease should be applied to the 2 seal areas shown in **Figure 62**. If necessary, apply a low-temperature grease to the brake drum seal lip at the 2 areas shown in **Figure 62**. Do not overgrease the seal or the brake shoes may become contaminated.

8. Slide the rear brake drum into position. Then install the washer and nut (**Figure 60**).

9. Tighten the rear axle nut to the torque specification in **Tables 4-6** for your model. Secure the axle nut with a new cotter pin. Bend the cotter pin arms over to lock it (**Figure 63**).

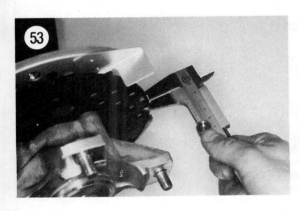

13

(56)

**REAR DRUM BRAKE
(2-WHEEL DRIVE)**

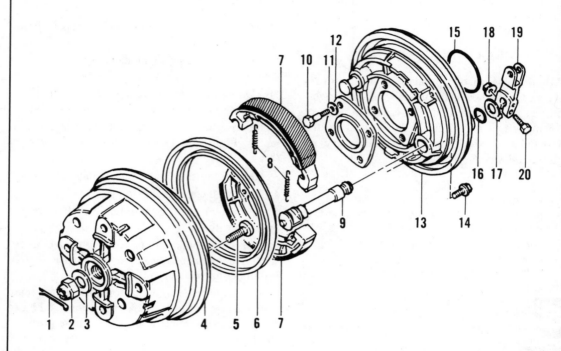

1. Cotter pin
2. Nut
3. Washer
4. Brake drum/rear hub
5. Stud
6. Oil seal
7. Brake shoes
8. Springs
9. Brake cam
10. Bolt
11. Washer
12. Position plate
13. Brake panel
14. Bolt
15. O-ring
16. O-ring
17. Brake wear
    indicator plate
18. Nut
19. Brake cam lever
20. Bolt

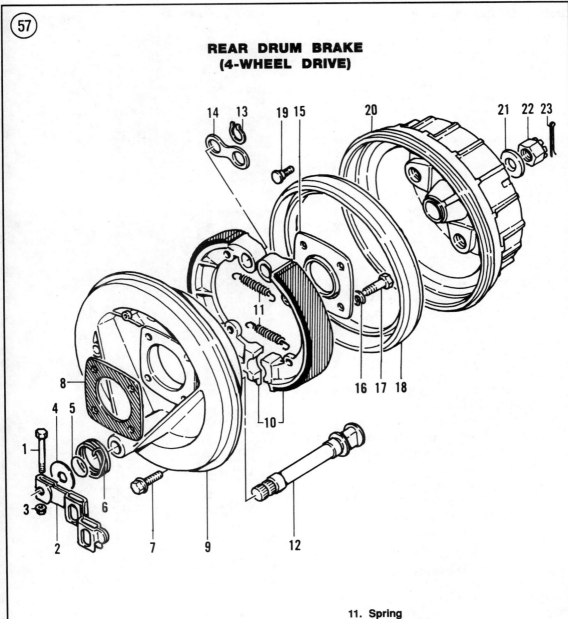

**REAR DRUM BRAKE
(4-WHEEL DRIVE)**

1. Bolt
2. Brake cam lever
3. Nut
4. Brake wear indicator plate
5. O-ring
6. Spring
7. Bolt
8. Gasket
9. Brake panel
10. Brake shoes
11. Spring
12. Brake cam
13. Circlip
14. Anchor pin holder
15. Position plate
16. Lockwasher
17. Bolt
18. Oil seal
19. Stud
20. Brake drum/rear hub
21. Washer
22. Nut
23. Cotter pin

13

Rear Brake Drum Inspection

1. Clean the brake drum in a detergent solution. Then allow to dry.

NOTE
Immediately discard the detergent solution and wash your hands.

2. Check the drum contact surface for scoring or other damage.

NOTE
If oil or grease is on the drum surface, clean it off with a clean rag soaked in lacquer thinner—do not use any solvent that may leave an oil residue.

3. Measure the brake drum inside diameter and check against the dimension in **Tables 1-3** for your model. Replace if measurement exceeds service limit.

4. Inspect the brake drum seal (**Figure 61**) for wear, damage, hardness or deterioration.

5. If the brake drum seal is excessively worn or damaged, replace it as follows:
   a. Support the brake drum and pry the brake drum seal out of the brake drum
   b. Clean the brake drum seal contact surface.
   c. Align the new seal with the brake drum, then slowly and squarely press the brake drum seal into the brake drum.
   d. After the seal has been installed correctly, uniformly pack the seal sealing lips (**Figure 62**) with a low-temperature grease. Do not over-grease the oil seal.

Rear Brake Shoe Replacement

Refer to **Figure 56** or **Figure 57** for this procedure.

1. Remove the rear brake drum as described in this section.

2. Measure the brake shoe lining thickness with a vernier caliper (**Figure 64**) and check against the dimension in **Tables 1-3** for your model. Replace if worn to the service limit. If replacement is necessary, continue with this procedure.

3. On 4-wheel drive models, perform the following:
   a. Disconnect the spring (**Figure 65**) from the anchor pin side of the brake panel.
   b. Remove the 2 anchor pin circlips (**Figure 65**).

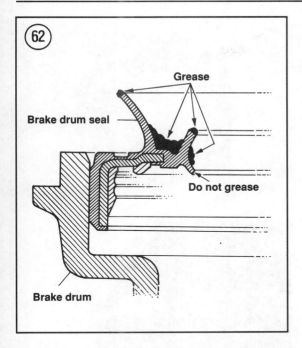

Grease

Brake drum seal

Do not grease

Brake drum

c. Remove the anchor pin holder (**Figure 65**).

4. Remove the brake shoes (**Figure 66**) from the rear brake panel by pulling up on the center of each shoe.

5. Replace the springs if weak or damaged.

6. Clean all old grease from the anchor pin(s) and brake camshaft.

7. Apply a light coat of grease to the anchor pin(s) and brake camshaft.

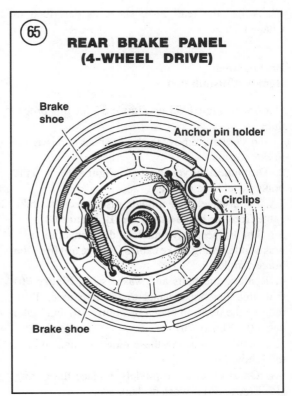

REAR BRAKE PANEL (4-WHEEL DRIVE)

Brake shoe

Anchor pin holder

Circlips

Brake shoe

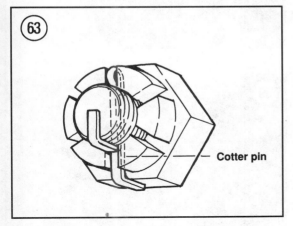

Cotter pin

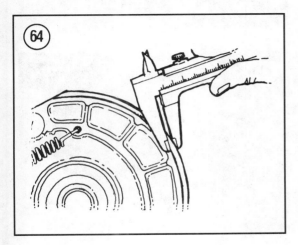

13

8. Fit the springs onto the brake shoes (**Figure 67**).

9. Wrap a clean rag around the brake shoes. Then spread the brake shoes and install them onto the brake panel. See **Figure 66**, typical.

10. On 4-wheel drive models, perform the following:

    a. Install the anchor pin holder (**Figure 65**).

    b. Install the 2 anchor pin circlips (**Figure 65**).

11. Install the rear brake drum as described in this chapter.

12. Adjust the rear brake shoes as described in Chapter Three.

Brake Panel
Removal/Installation

Refer to **Figure 56** or **Figure 57** for this procedure.

1. If necessary, remove the brake shoes as described in this section.

2. Disconnect the vent hose (A, **Figure 68**) from the brake panel hose nozzle.

3A. On 2-wheel drive models, disconnect the brake cable from the brake cam lever (B, **Figure 68**).

3B. On 4-wheel drive models, disconnect the rear brake and parking brake cables (**Figure 69**) from the brake cam lever.

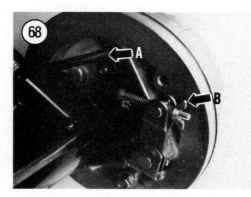

4. Remove the bolts and washers (A, **Figure 70**) that hold the brake panel to the rear axle. Then remove the position plate (B, **Figure 70**) and brake panel (C, **Figure 70**).

5. Install by reversing these removal steps, noting the following.

6A. On 2-wheel drive models, replace the O-ring (15, **Figure 56**) if worn or damaged.

6B. On 4-wheel drive models, replace the gasket (8, **Figure 57**) if torn or otherwise damaged.

7. Tighten the brake panel mounting bolts to the torque specifications for your model in **Tables 4-6**.

8. Install the brake shoes as described in this chapter.

Brake Cam Lever
Removal/Installation

Refer to **Figure 56** or **Figure 57** for this procedure.

1. Make punch marks on the brake cam and cam lever (**Figure 71**) so that they can be installed in the same position.

2A. On 2-wheel drive models, perform the following:

   a. Remove the brake cam lever nut and bolt and remove the lever (**Figure 72**).

   b. Remove the brake wear indicator plate and O-ring.

   c. Remove the brake cam from the brake panel.

2B. On 4-wheel drive models, perform the following:

   a. Remove the brake cam lever nut and bolt and remove the lever.

   b. Remove the brake wear indicator plate, O-ring and spring.

   c. Remove the brake cam from the brake panel.

3. Remove all old grease from the brake cam and cam hole in the brake panel.

4. Replace the brake cam if severely worn or damaged.

5. Replace the brake cam lever if severely worn or damaged.

6. Install by reversing these removal steps, noting the following.

7A. On 2-wheel drive models, apply grease to the brake cam.

7B. On 4-wheel drive models, fill the brake cam groove with grease.

8. On 4-wheel drive models, perform the following:

   a. Install the brake cam so that its triangle mark points toward the center of the brake panel as shown in **Figure 73**.

   b. Install the brake wear indicator plate so that its pointer points to the "USABLE RANGE" lower line (**Figure 74**).

9. Align the match marks when installing the brake cam lever onto the brake cam.

10. Adjust the rear brake as described in Chapter Three.

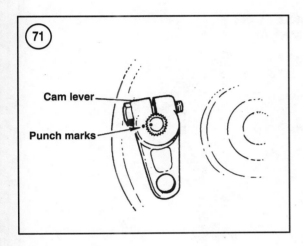

71

Cam lever

Punch marks

72

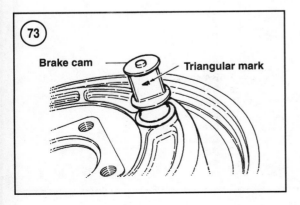

73

Brake cam — Triangular mark

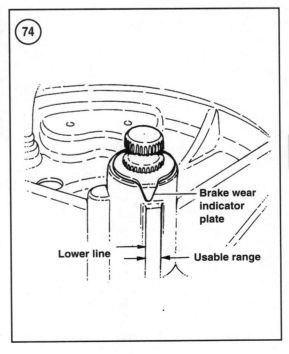

74

Brake wear indicator plate

Lower line — Usable range

13

BRAKE HOSE REPLACEMENT

The brake hoses should be replaced if they show signs of wear or damage. The front brake hoses and their fittings are identified as follows:

   a. 1986-1987 2-wheel drive: **Figure 75**.

   b. 1988-on 2-wheel drive: **Figure 76**.

   c. All-4-wheel drive: **Figure 77**.

1. Place a container under the brake line at the caliper. Remove the banjo bolt and sealing washers from the caliper or master cylinder.

2. On compression fittings, hold the brake hose with a wrench and loosen the bolt. Separate the hose from the bolt.

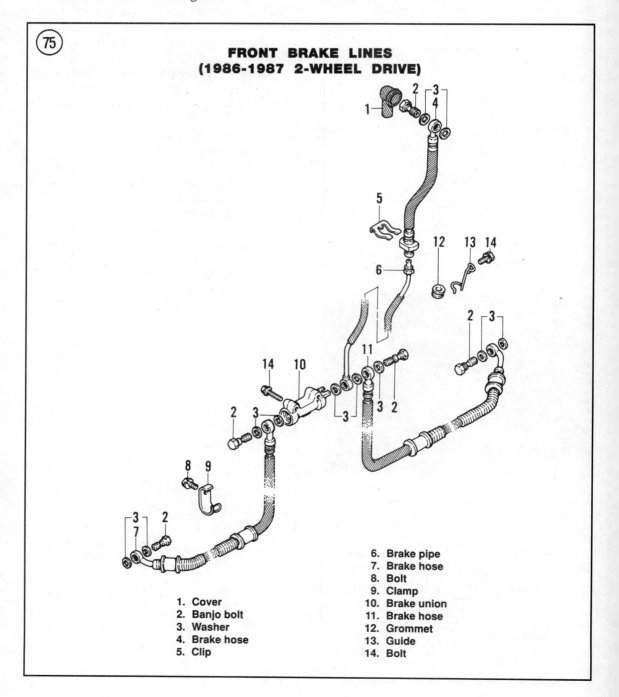

(75)

**FRONT BRAKE LINES
(1986-1987 2-WHEEL DRIVE)**

1. Cover
2. Banjo bolt
3. Washer
4. Brake hose
5. Clip
6. Brake pipe
7. Brake hose
8. Bolt
9. Clamp
10. Brake union
11. Brake hose
12. Grommet
13. Guide
14. Bolt

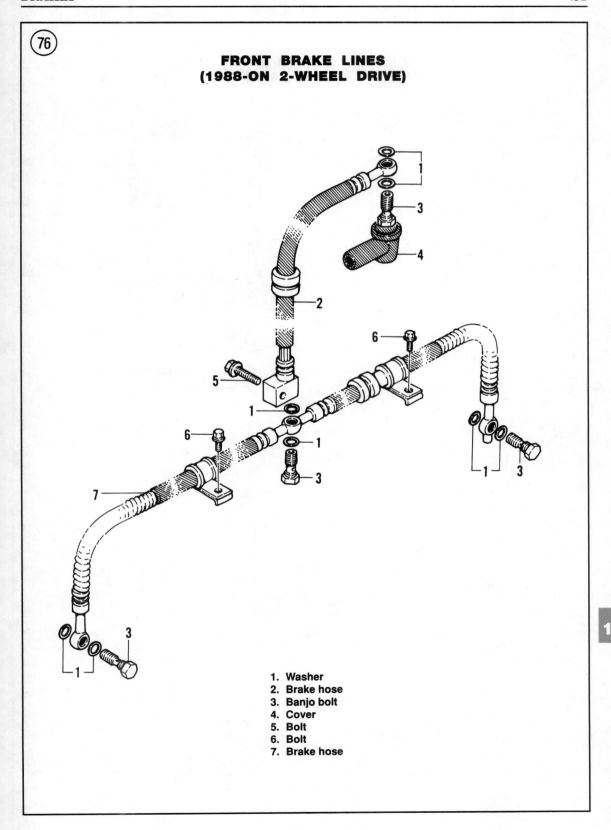

**FRONT BRAKE LINES
(1988-ON 2-WHEEL DRIVE)**

1. Washer
2. Brake hose
3. Banjo bolt
4. Cover
5. Bolt
6. Bolt
7. Brake hose

13

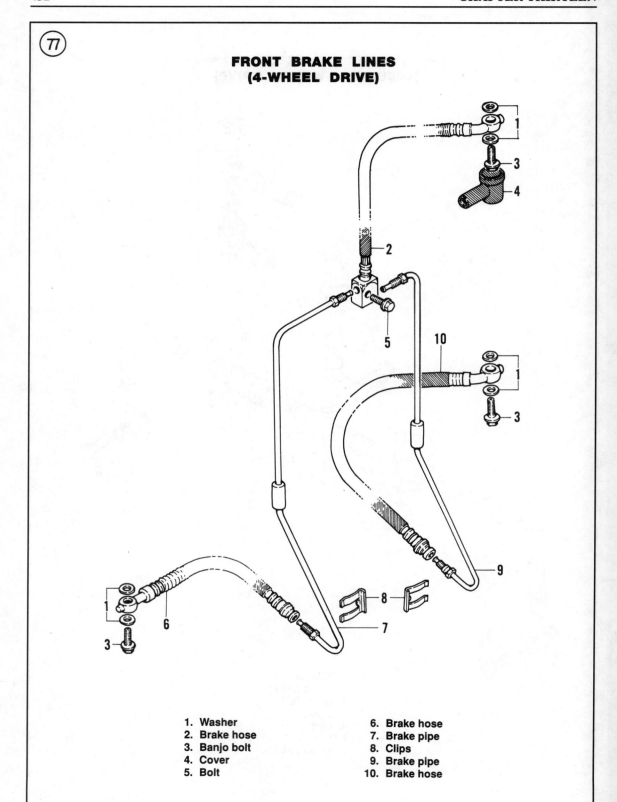

**FRONT BRAKE LINES
(4-WHEEL DRIVE)**

1. Washer
2. Brake hose
3. Banjo bolt
4. Cover
5. Bolt
6. Brake hose
7. Brake pipe
8. Clips
9. Brake pipe
10. Brake hose

3. Place the end of the brake hose in a clean container. Operate the front brake lever to drain the master cylinder and brake hose of all brake fluid. Dispose of this brake fluid—never reuse brake fluid.

4. Install a new brake hose in the reverse order of removal. Install new sealing washers and banjo bolts if necessary.

5. Tighten the banjo bolts to the torque specification for your model in **Tables 4-6**.

6. On compression fittings, thread the bolt onto the brake hose. Tighten the compression nut securely.

7. Refill the master cylinder with fresh brake fluid clearly marked DOT 3. Bleed the brake as described in this chapter.

WARNING
Do not ride the ATV until you are sure that the brakes are operating properly.

REAR BRAKE PEDAL/CABLES

The rear brake pedal/cables are identified as follows:
   a. 2-wheel drive: **Figure 78**.
   b. 4-wheel drive: **Figure 79**.
When servicing the brake cables or brake pedals, note the following:

1. Lubricate the brake cables as described in Chapter Three.

2. After replacing the brake cables, adjust the rear brake as described in Chapter Three.

3. Install new cotter pins during reassembly. Bend the cotter pin ends over to lock them.

4. Apply grease to the brake pedal pivot shaft prior to installing it.

5. When installing the brake pedal on 2-wheel drive models, note the following:
   a. Align the punch mark on the brake pedal with the punch mark on the brake shaft.
   b. Align the punch marks on the parking brake shafts.

WARNING
Do not ride the ATV until you are sure that the brakes are operating properly.

BRAKE BLEEDING

This procedure is necessary only if the brakes feel spongy, there is a leak in the hydraulic system, a component has been replaced or the brake fluid has been replaced.

NOTE
During this procedure, all the hose junctions in the brake system will be bled of air. It is important to check the fluid level in the master cylinder frequently. If the reservoir runs dry, air will enter the system which will require starting over.

1. Flip off the dust cap from the brake bleeder valve.

2. Connect a length of clear tubing to the bleeder valve on the wheel cylinder or caliper. See **Figure 80**, typical. Place the other end of the tube into a clean container. Fill the container with enough fresh brake fluid to keep the end submerged. The tube should be long enough so that a loop can be made higher than the bleeder valve to prevent air from being drawn into the caliper during bleeding.

CAUTION
Cover all parts which could become contaminated by the accidental spilling of brake fluid. Wash any spilled brake fluid from any surface immediately, as it will destroy the finish. Use soapy water and rinse completely.

3. Clean the top of the front master cylinder of all dirt and foreign matter. Remove the cap and diaphragm. Fill the reservoir to about 10 mm (3/8 in.) from the top. Insert the diaphragm to prevent the entry of dirt and moisture.

WARNING
Use brake fluid clearly marked DOT 3 only. Others may vaporize and cause brake failure. Always use the same brand name; do not intermix the brake fluids, as many brands are not compatible.

NOTE
During this procedure, it is important to check the reservoir fluid level periodically to make sure it does not run dry. If the reservoir should run dry, air will enter the system and you'll have to start over.

4. Hold the brake lever in the applied position and open the bleeder valve about 1/2 turn—do not release the brake lever while the bleeder valve is open.

13

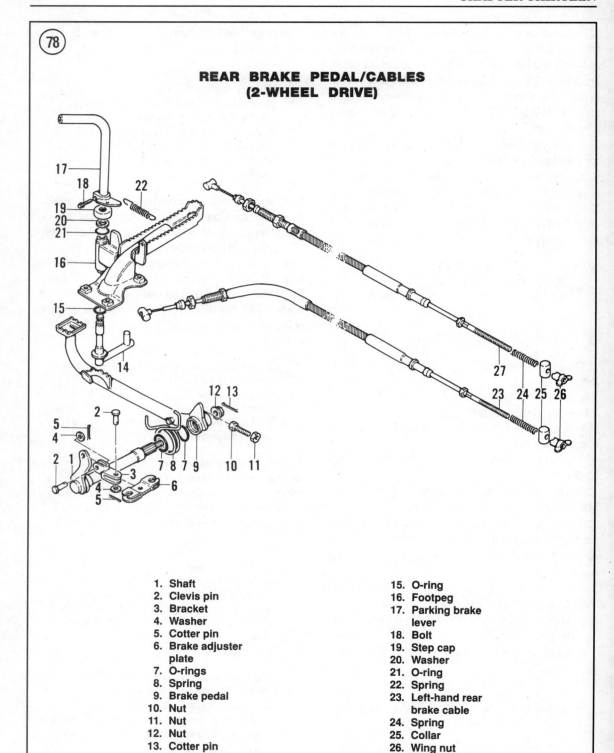

**REAR BRAKE PEDAL/CABLES
(2-WHEEL DRIVE)**

1. Shaft
2. Clevis pin
3. Bracket
4. Washer
5. Cotter pin
6. Brake adjuster
   plate
7. O-rings
8. Spring
9. Brake pedal
10. Nut
11. Nut
12. Nut
13. Cotter pin
14. Parking brake
   arm
15. O-ring
16. Footpeg
17. Parking brake
   lever
18. Bolt
19. Step cap
20. Washer
21. O-ring
22. Spring
23. Left-hand rear
   brake cable
24. Spring
25. Collar
26. Wing nut
27. Right-hand rear
   brake cable

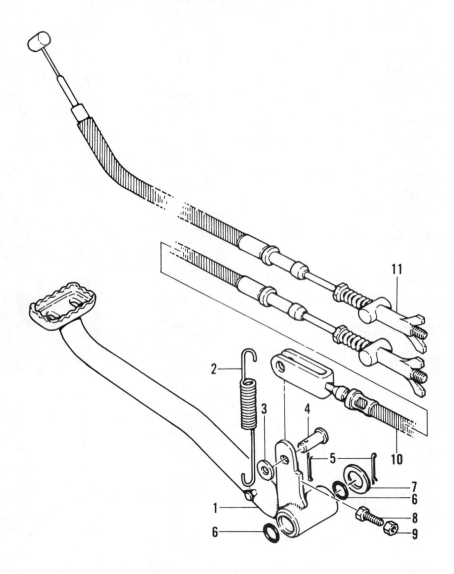

⑦⑨

REAR BRAKE PEDAL/CABLES
(4-WHEEL DRIVE)

1. Brake pedal
2. Spring
3. Washer
4. Clevis pin
5. Cotter pin
6. O-ring
7. Washer
8. Bolt
9. Nut
10. Rear foot
    brake cable
11. Parking brake
    cable

13

When you open the bleeder valve, you will feel the lever loosen a bit as it moves to the limit of its travel. At this point, tighten the bleeder screw, then release the brake lever.

NOTE
As the brake fluid enters the system, the level will drop in the master cylinder reservoir. Maintain the level at about 10 mm (3/8 in.) from the top of the reservoir to prevent air from being drawn into the system.

5. Repeat Step 4 until the system is bled. If you are replacing the fluid, continue until the fluid emerging from the hose is clean.

NOTE
If bleeding is difficult, it may be necessary to allow the fluid to stabilize for a few hours. Repeat the bleeding procedure when the tiny bubbles in the system settle out.

6. Remove the bleeder tube and install the bleeder valve dust cap.
7. If necessary, add fluid to correct the level in the master cylinder reservoir. It must be above the level line.
8. Install the cap and tighten the screws on the front master cylinder.

9. Test the feel of the brake lever. It should feel firm and should offer the same resistance each time it's operated. If it feels spongy, it is likely that air is still in the system and it must be bled again. When all air has been bled from the system and the brake fluid level is correct in the reservoir, double-check for leaks and tighten all fittings and connections.

WARNING
Before riding the vehicle, make certain that the brake is working correctly by operating the lever several times. Then make the test ride a slow one at first until you are sure the brakes are working correctly.

Table 1 BRAKE SPECIFICATIONS (1986-1987 2-WHEEL DRIVE)

	New mm (in.)	Service limit mm (in.)
Front and rear drum brakes		
Brake drum inside diameter	160.000-160.160 (6.299-6.305)	160.65 (6.325)
Brake shoe lining thickness	4.0 (0.157)	2.0 (0.079)
Rear brake camshaft diameter	16.957-16.984 (0.668-0.669)	16.83 (0.663)
Rear brake camshaft hole diameter	17.000-17.027 (0.669-0.670)	17.15 (0.675)

Table 2 BRAKE SPECIFICATIONS (1988-ON 2-WHEEL DRIVE)

	New mm (in.)	Service limit mm (in.)
Front disc brake		
Pad lining thickness	4.5 (0.177)	1.0 (0.039)
Disc thickness	3.3-3.7 (0.130-0.146)	3.0 (0.354)
Disc runout	0-0.2 (0-0.008)	0.3 (0.012)
Rear drum brake		
Brake drum inside diameter	160.000-160.160 (6.299-6.305)	160.65 (6.325)
Brake shoe lining thickness	4.0 (0.157)	2.0 (0.079)
Rear brake camshaft diameter	16.957-16.984 (0.668-0.669)	16.83 (0.663)
Rear brake camshaft hole diameter	17.000-17.027 (0.66-0.67)	17.15 (0.68)

Table 3 BRAKE SPECIFICATIONS (1989-ON 4-WHEEL DRIVE)

	New mm (in.)	Service limit mm (in.)
Front disc brake		
Pad lining thickness	4.5 (0.177)	1.0 (0.039)
Disc thickness	3.3-3.7 (0.130-0.146)	3.0 (0.354)
Disc runout	0-0.2 (0-0.008)	0.3 (0.012)
Rear drum brake		
Brake drum inside diameter	180.000-180.140 (7.086-7.092)	180.75 (7.116)
Brake shoe thickness	5.0 (0.197)	2.5 (0.098)

Table 4 BRAKE TIGHTENING TORQUES (1986-1987 2-WHEEL DRIVE)

	N·m	ft.-lb.
Brake panel mounting bolts		
Front	20	15
Rear	29	21
Brake hose banjo bolts	25	18
Brake pipe nipple	20	15
Brake pedal nut	29	21
Rear axle nut	145	107
Front hub nut	34	25
Front wheel cylinder mounting bolts	7.8	69 in.-lb.
Front brake shoe adjuster mounting bolts	7.8	69 in.-lb.
Master cylinder clamp bolts	11	97 in.-lb.
Wheel cylinder bolts	7.8	69 in.-lb.
Shoe adjuster bolts	7.8	69 in.-lb.
Brake lever pivot nut	5.9	52 in.-lb.

13

Table 5 BRAKE TIGHTENING TORQUES (1988-ON 2-WHEEL DRIVE)

	N·m	ft.-lb.
Brake hose banjo bolts	25	18
Caliper mounting bolts	25	18
Brake disc mounting screws	37	27
Rear drum drain bolts	29	21
(continued)		

Table 5 BRAKE TIGHTENING TORQUES (1988-ON 2-WHEEL DRIVE) (continued)

	N·m	ft.-lb.
Rear brake panel mounting bolts	29	21
Rear brake pedal mounting bolts	29	21
Rear axle nuts	145	107
Bleed valves	7.8	69 in.-lb.
Brake lever pivot bolt	5.9	52 in.-lb.
Brake lever pivot bolt locknut	5.9	52 in.-lb.
Front master cylinder clamp bolts	8.8	78 in.-lb.
Front brake fluid reservoir cap screws	1.0	9 in.-lb.

Table 6 BRAKE TIGHTENING TORQUE (1989-ON 4-WHEEL DRIVE)

	N·m	ft.-lb.
Brake hose banjo bolts	25	18
Caliper mounting bolts	25	18
Caliper pad pin Allen bolts	18	13
Brake disc mounting bolts	37	27
Brake pipe nipples	20	15
Rear brake panel mounting bolts	34	25
Rear axle nuts	145	107
Bleed valves	7.8	69 in.-lb.
Brake lever pivot bolt	5.9	52 in.-lb.
Brake lever pivot bolt locknut	5.9	52 in.-lb.
Front master cylinder clamp bolts	8.8	78 in.-lb.
Front brake fluid reservoir cap screws	1.0	9 in.-lb.

CHAPTER FOURTEEN

BODY

This chapter contains removal and installation procedures for body panels and luggage racks.

It is suggested that as soon as the part is removed from the vehicle all mounting hardware (i.e. small brackets, bolts, nuts, rubber bushings, metal collars, etc.) be reinstalled onto the removed part. Kawasaki makes frequent changes during the model year, so the part and the way it is attached to the frame may differ slightly from the one used in the service procedures in this chapter.

FRONT CARRIER

Removal/Installation

1. Park the vehicle on level ground and set the parking brake.

2. Remove the bolts securing the front carrier to the frame and front guard. See **Figure 1** (2-wheel drive) or A, **Figure 2** (4-wheel drive).

3. Remove the front carrier.

4. Install by reversing these removal steps.

FRONT GUARD

Removal/Installation

1. Park the vehicle on level ground and set the parking brake.
2. Remove the bolts securing the front guard to the frame and front carrier. See **Figure 3** (2-wheel drive) or B, **Figure 2** (4-wheel drive).
3. Remove the front guard.
4. Install by reversing these removal steps.

REAR CARRIER

Removal/Installation

1. Park the vehicle on level ground and set the parking brake.
2. Remove the bolts securing the rear carrier to the frame. See **Figure 4** (2-wheel drive) or **Figure 5** (4-wheel drive).
3. Remove the rear carrier.
4. Install by reversing these removal steps.

SEAT

Removal/Installation

1. Park the vehicle on level ground and set the parking brake.
2. Pull the seat lever up (**Figure 6**). Then lift the rear of the seat and slide it toward the rear of the vehicle.
3. Remove the seat.
4. Slide the seat hook (**Figure 7**) underneath the frame brace (**Figure 8**). Then push the seat down until it locks in place.
5. Check that the seat is firmly locked in place.

FUEL TANK COVER ASSEMBLY

Removal/Installation
(2-Wheel Drive)

Refer to **Figure 9** for this procedure.
1. Park the vehicle on level ground and set the parking brake.
2. Remove the seat as described in this chapter.

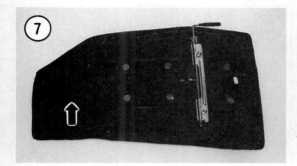

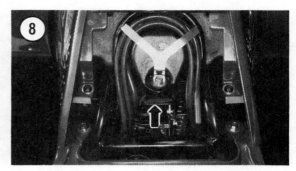

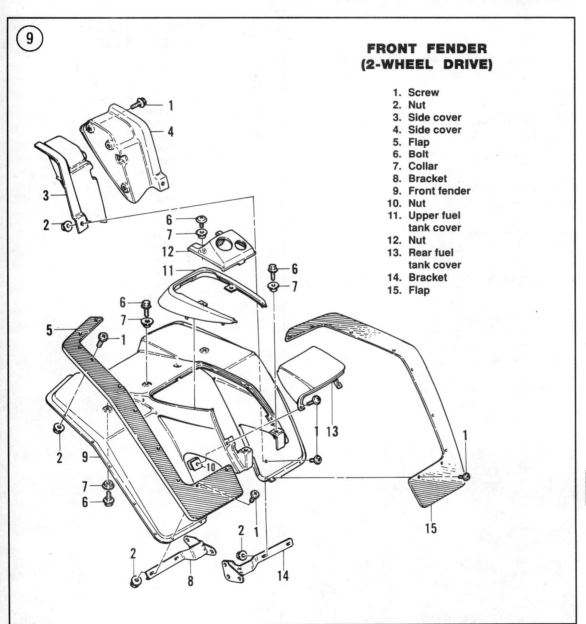

FRONT FENDER
(2-WHEEL DRIVE)

1. Screw
2. Nut
3. Side cover
4. Side cover
5. Flap
6. Bolt
7. Collar
8. Bracket
9. Front fender
10. Nut
11. Upper fuel
    tank cover
12. Nut
13. Rear fuel
    tank cover
14. Bracket
15. Flap

14

3. Remove the rear fuel tank cover screws and remove the cover (A, **Figure 10**).

> *WARNING*
> *Fuel vapors are present when removing the fuel tank cap. Because gasoline is extremely flammable, perform this procedure away from all open flames (including pilot lights) and sparks. Do not smoke or allow someone who is smoking in the work area as an explosion and fire may occur. Always work in a well-ventilated area. Wipe up any spills immediately.*

4. Remove the upper fuel tank cover screws. Then remove the fuel tank cap and remove the upper fuel tank cover (B, **Figure 10**). Reinstall the fuel tank cap immediately.

5. Remove the fuel tank side cover assembly (C, **Figure 10**).

6. Install by reversing these removal steps.

Removal/Installation (4-Wheel Drive)

Refer to **Figure 11** for this procedure.

1. Park the vehicle on level ground and set the parking brake.

2. Remove the seat as described in this chapter.

> *WARNING*
> *Fuel vapors are present when removing the fuel tank cap. Because gasoline is extremely flammable, perform this procedure away from all open flames (including pilot lights) and sparks. Do not smoke or allow someone who is smoking in the work area as an explosion and fire may occur. Always work in a well-*

FRONT FENDER (4-WHEEL DRIVE)

1. Front cover
2. Fuel tank cover
3. Screw
4. Collar
5. Damper
6. Screw
7. Flap
8. Front fender
9. Nut
10. Bolt
11. Nut
12. Nut
13. Bracket
14. Bracket
15. Bracket
16. Flap
17. Flap
18. Bracket

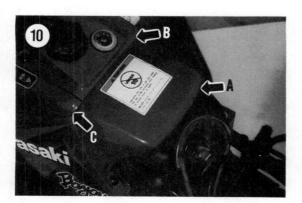

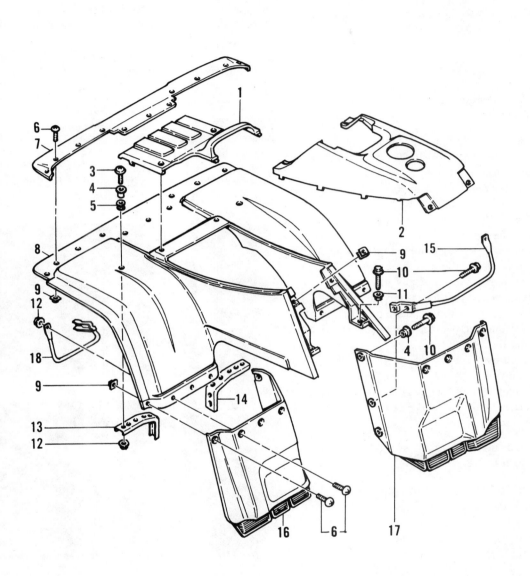

ventilated area. Wipe up any spills immediately.

3. Remove the fuel tank cover screws. Then remove the fuel tank cap and remove the fuel tank cover (**Figure 12**). Reinstall the fuel tank cap immediately.

4. Install by reversing these removal steps.

FRONT FENDER

Removal/Installation (2-Wheel Drive)

Refer to **Figure 9** for this procedure.

1. Park the vehicle on level ground and set the parking brake.

2. Remove the fuel tank covers as described in this chapter.

3. Remove the side cover mounting screws and remove the side covers.

4. Remove front fender mounting bolts and flanged collars at the rear of the front fender.

5. Remove the mud flap nuts and screws.

6. Remove the front fender mounting bolts.

7. Remove the 4 front fender mounting bolts (**Figure 13**) and remove the front fender and carrier assembly.

8. Install by reversing these removal steps, noting the following.

9. Tighten all bolts and nuts securely. Do not overtighten as the plastic fender may fracture.

Removal/Installation (4-Wheel Drive)

Refer to **Figure 11** for this procedure.

1. Park the vehicle on level ground and set the parking brake.

2. Remove the fuel tank cover as described in this chapter.

3. Remove the front carrier as described in this chapter.

4. Remove the front cover (**Figure 14**).

5. Remove the front fender mounting bolts and remove the front fender (**Figure 15**).

6. Install by reversing these removal steps, noting the following.

7. Tighten all bolts and nuts securely. Do not overtighten as the plastic fender may fracture.

REAR FENDER

Removal/Installation (2-Wheel Drive)

Refer to **Figure 16** or **Figure 17** for this procedure.

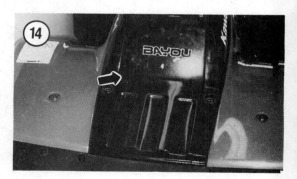

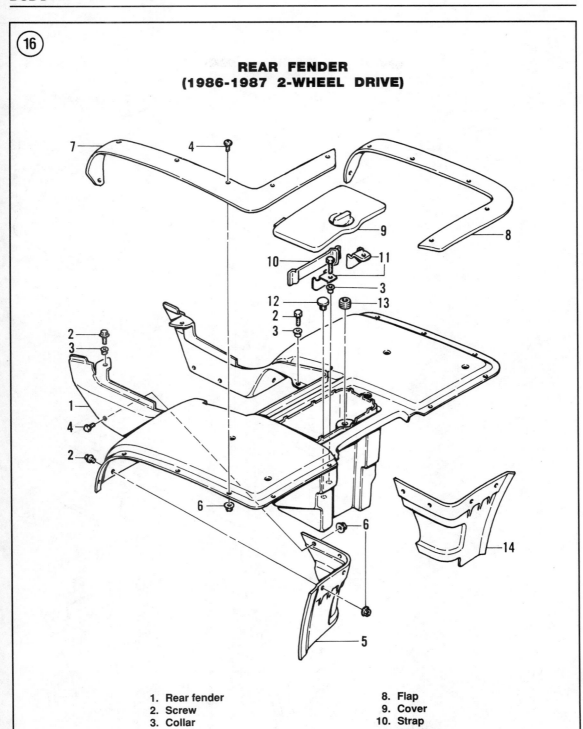

(16)

REAR FENDER
(1986-1987 2-WHEEL DRIVE)

1. Rear fender
2. Screw
3. Collar
4. Screw
5. Flap
6. Nut
7. Flap

8. Flap
9. Cover
10. Strap
11. Bracket
12. Screw
13. Damper
14. Flap

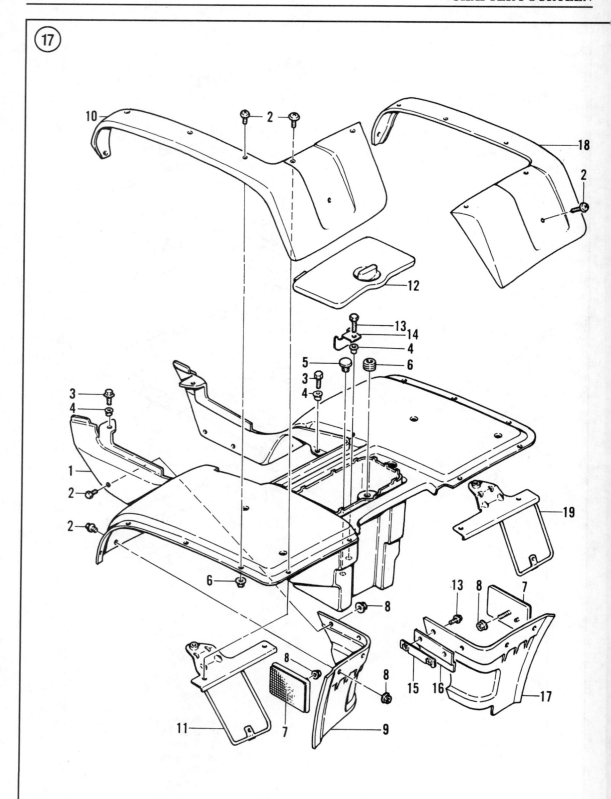

REAR FENDER
(1988-ON 2-WHEEL DRIVE)

1. Rear fender
2. Screw
3. Screw
4. Collar
5. Screw
6. Damper
7. Reflector
8. Nut
9. Flap
10. Flap
11. Bracket
12. Cover
13. Bolt
14. Bracket
15. Nut plate
16. Bracket
17. Flap
18. Flap
19. Bracket

1. Park the vehicle on level ground and set the parking brake.

2. Remove the seat as described in this chapter.

3. Remove the rear carrier (A, **Figure 18**) as described in this chapter.

4. Remove the storage cover.

5. Remove the rear fender mounting bolts and remove the rear fender (A, **Figure 18**).

6. Install by reversing these removal steps, noting the following.

7. Tighten all bolts and nuts securely. Do not overtighten as the plastic fender may fracture.

Removal/Installation
(4-Wheel Drive)

Refer to **Figure 19** for this procedure.

1. Park the vehicle on level ground and set the parking brake.

2. Remove the seat as described in this chapter.

3. Remove the rear carrier (A, **Figure 20**) as described in this chapter.

4. Remove the storage cover.

5. Remove the rear fender mounting bolts and remove the rear fender (B, **Figure 20**).

6. Install by reversing these removal steps, noting the following.

7. Tighten all bolts and nuts securely. Do not overtighten as this could cause the plastic fender to fracture.

14

⑲

REAR FENDER
(4-WHEEL DRIVE)

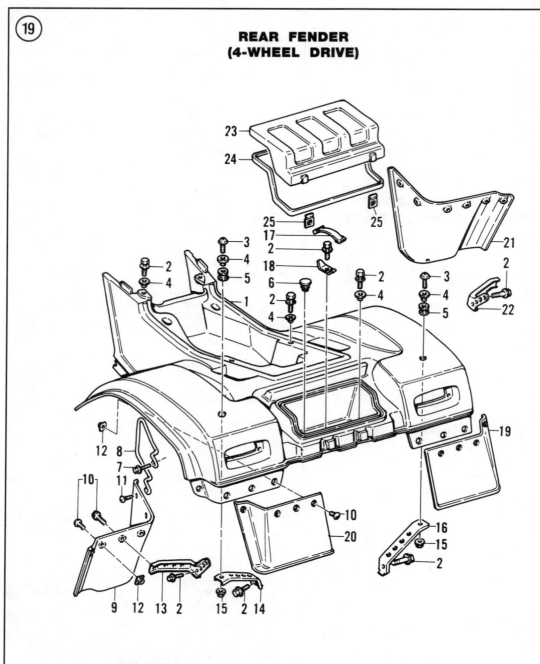

1. Rear fender
2. Bolt
3. Bolt
4. Collar
5. Damper
6. Screw
7. Bolt
8. Bracket
9. Flap
10. Bolts
11. Screw
12. Nut
13. Bracket
14. Bracket
15. Nut
16. Bracket
17. Strap
18. Bracket
19. Flap
20. Flap
21. Flap
22. Bracket
23. Cover
24. Seal
25. Nut plate

14

INDEX

15

15

KLF300 1986-1987 2-WHEEL DRIVE

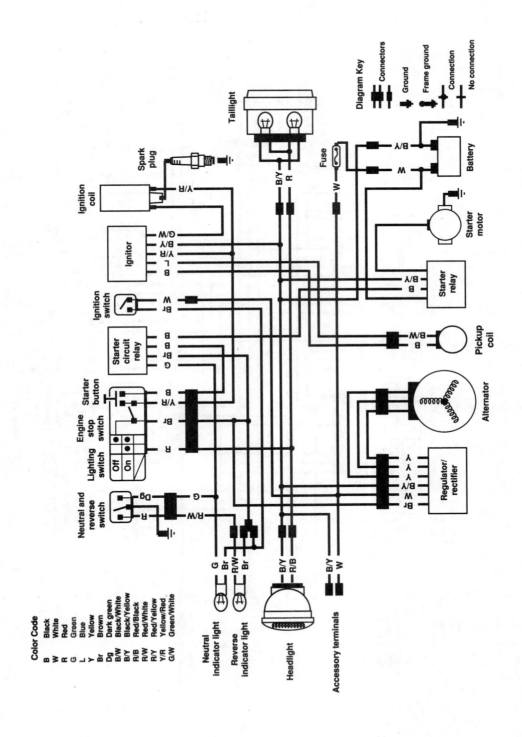

KLF300 1988-1994 2-WHEEL DRIVE

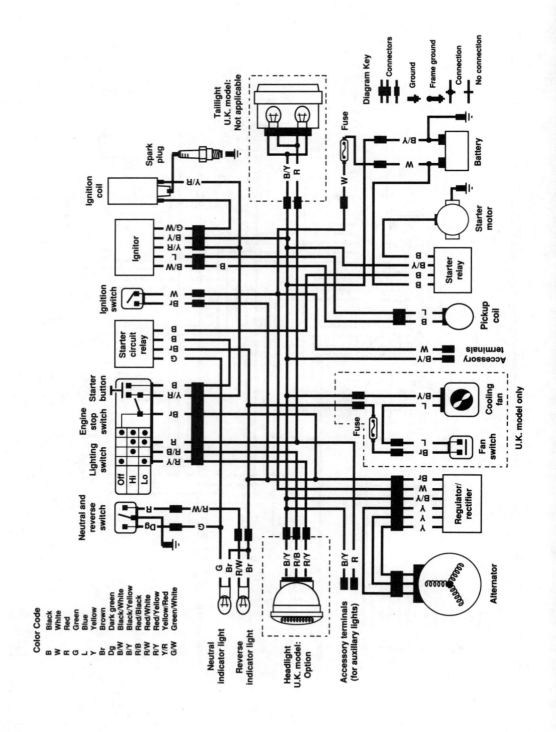

KLF300 (1988-1989 U.S. MODEL; 1989-1997 CANADA AND 1989-ON U.K. MODELS) 4-WHEEL DRIVE

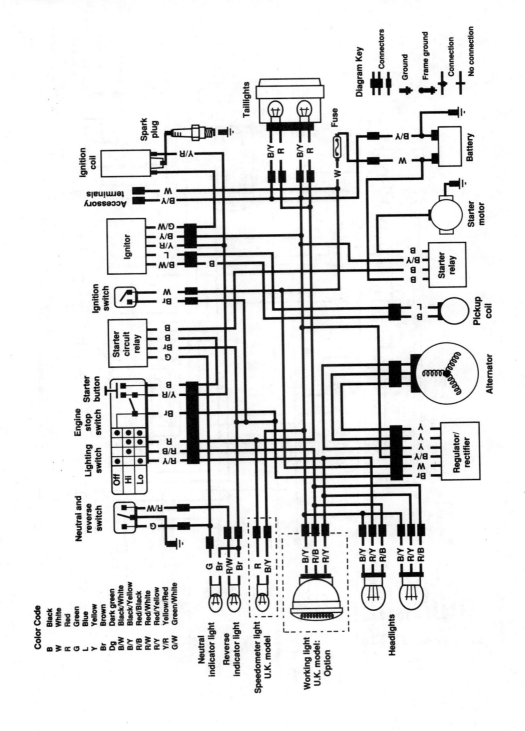

KLF300 1989-1997
(AUSTRALIAN MODEL) 4-WHEEL DRIVE

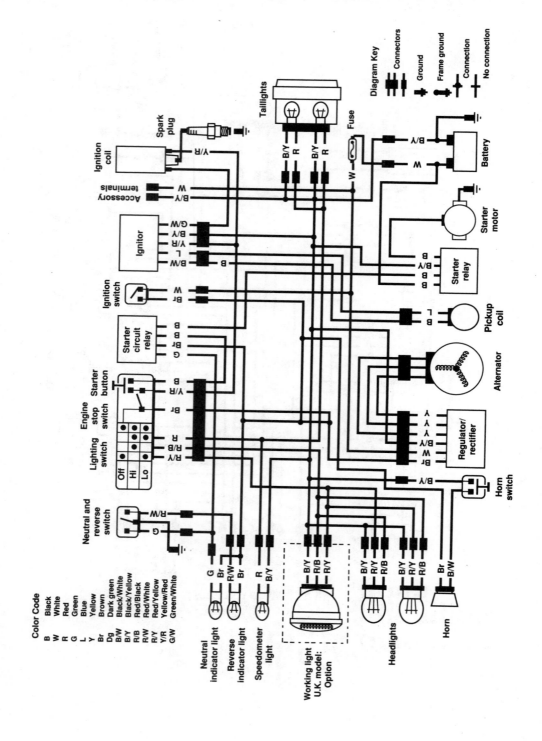

KLF300 1991-1997
(U.S. MODELS) 4-WHEEL DRIVE

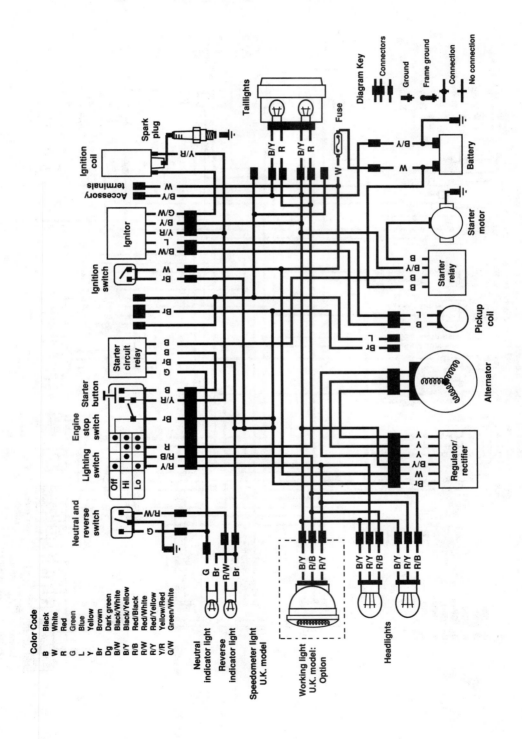

KLF300 1998
(U.S. AND CANADA MODELS) 4-WHEEL DRIVE

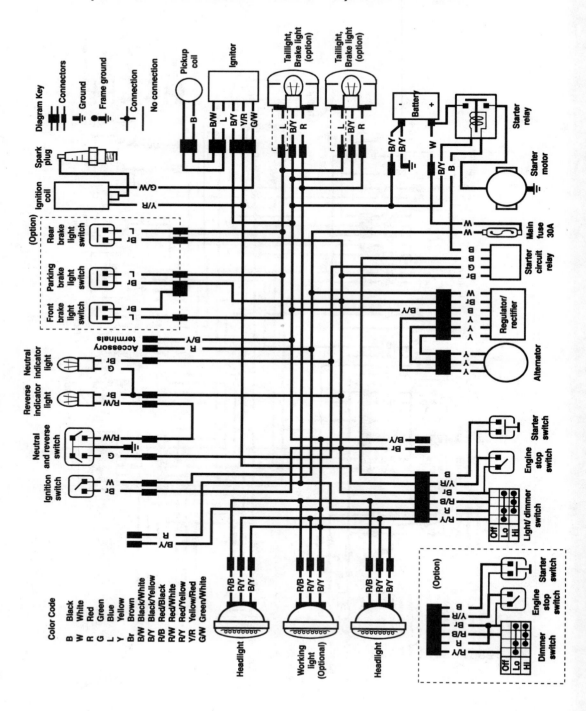

KLF300 1998
(AUSTRALIAN MODEL) 4-WHEEL DRIVE

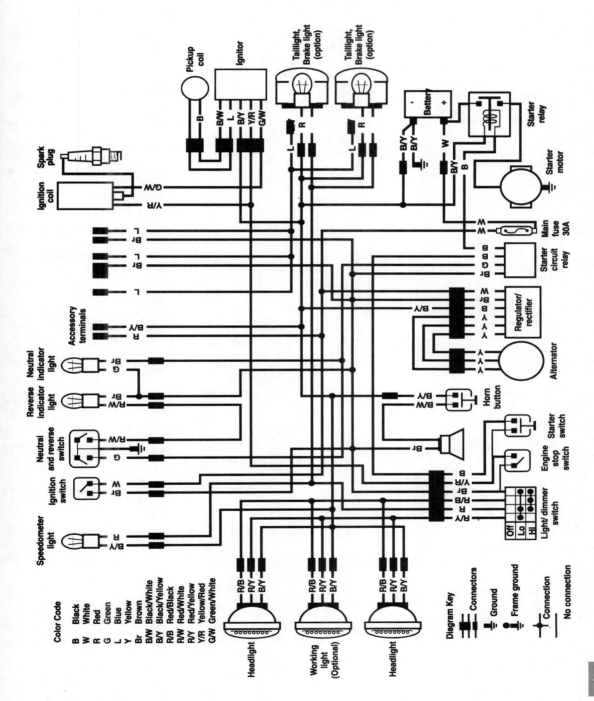

Color Code

B	Black
W	White
R	Red
G	Green
L	Blue
Y	Yellow
Br	Brown
B/W	Black/White
B/Y	Black/Yellow
R/B	Red/Black
R/W	Red/White
R/Y	Red/Yellow
Y/R	Yellow/Red
G/W	Green/White

Diagram Key

▮▮ Connectors
⏚ Ground
● Frame ground
┼ Connection
No connection

16

NOTES

NOTES

NOTES

NOTES

MAINTENANCE LOG

Service Performed   **Mileage Reading**

Service Performed					
Oil change (example)	2,836	5,782	8,601		